ISBN 978-1-330-58720-1
PIBN 10039648

For support please visit www.forgottenbooks.com

Similar Books Are Available from
www.forgottenbooks.com

RIGHTS

OF

SOVEREIGNS

AND

SUBJECTS.

Paolo Sarpi

By Father PAUL the *Venetian*, Author of
The History of the Council of Trent.

Translated from the *Italian*, and compared with
the *French*.

To which is prefix'd the

LIFE *of the* AUTHOR,

AND AN

Account of his Writings.

LONDON:

Printed for J. GRAVES in St. *James's-street*, C. KING
in *Westminster-Hall*, W. MEADOWS in *Cornhill*,
and J. HOOKE in *Fleetstreet*. MDCCXXII.

To the Right Honourable

Sir *PETER-KING* Kt.

Lord Chief Justice

OF THE

COMMON-PLEAS,

And One of His Majesty's

Moſt Honourable Privy-Council.

My Lord,

OOKS, according to the obſervation of the famous Lord *Verulam*, ought to have for their patrons Truth and Reason. Theſe are two

‡ 2   ſuch

DEDICATION.

such eftablifh'd qualities in the writings of *Father* PAUL the *Venetian*, that I may venture to affirm, no *Popifh* writer ever had a more favourable reception in the libraries of the moft diftinguifh'd Proteftants, whether for learning, virtue, or titles; infomuch that tho' the tranflators of that learned Frier's compofitions have, notwithftanding all their correctnefs been oblig'd to own how far they have fallen fhort of the dignity of his fublime originals, yet they have been honour'd with the patronage of fome of the moft illuftrious advocates for the reformation.

Being equally confcious, my LORD, of my own deficiency in this refpect, I prefumed to beg your Lordfhip to allow me to infcribe the following tranflation to your great name; and in the humbleft fenfe of
duty

DEDICATION.

duty and gratitude for your indulging me that honour, I take this opportunity of your Lordſhip's vacation from the more momentous affairs of ſtate, to ſubmit it to your kind protection and moſt favourable conſtruction.

The excellent author of it, tho' one of the brighteſt ornaments of the Church of *Rome*, was ſo much hated by the Pope and his Courtiers, that they not only traduc'd him as a heretic, but martyr'd him in effigie, and even employ'd cutthroats to take away his life; which made the good Father ſay more than once, *That thoſe who ſet them at work, would find him a more formidable adverſary after he was dead, than ever he was whilſt living*; a ſaying, my LORD, fully verify'd in the enſuing treatiſe.

I take

DEDICATION.

I take leave to observe to your Lordship, that Father PAUL having compos'd it to take off the panic of the *Venetians*, under the excommunication and interdict which was laid upon them by the Pope, intitled it, *The Comfort of the Mind in the good Conscience and Conduct of the Venetians, under the pretended Interdict of Pope* Paul V; but the author having a general view at the same time to fortify all christian Princes and States with such arguments against the usurpations of ambitious ecclesiastics, as are calculated for all meridians, protestant as well as popish, the title of *The Rights of Sovereigns and Subjects* was deem'd more expressive of its design, and more suitable for an *English* translation.

As daily experience shews how well your Lordship is vers'd in the

rights

rights both of *Sovereigns* and *Sub-jects*, so that profound knowledge you have difcover'd of the fcriptures and the fathers, as well as of the laws of the realm, when thofe *rights* have call'd for your defence, demonftrate that you have the abilities both of a lawyer and a divine. Father P A U L too made fuch a noble ftand under both thofe characters, for the liber-ties of his country, that his memory muft needs be grateful to your Lord-fhip upon that particular account, as well as for his vaft learning, wifdom, integrity, and moderation; virtues which are fo refplendent in your Lordfhip, that they cannot but na-turally incline you to have a more than ordinary efteem for all perfons adorn'd with thofe amiable qualities.

My L O R D, I beg pardon for ta-king up fo much of your time; but the

DEDICATION.

the entrance of the new year puts me
in mind that I am oblig'd by duty,
as I am sway'd by inclination, not to
conclude without wishing you the
happy enjoyment of this and many
more to come. Whether such a wish in
itself may be agreeable to your Lordship I know not; but if it be a fault,
'tis what every one is guilty of who
wishes well to his country. And of
this number I take leave to subscribe
my self,

> Your Lordship's
>
> Most devoted,
>
> Most obedient, and
>
> Most humble Servant,

THE
PREFACE.

THE *book, which is here preſented to the reader, was firſt publiſhed this year* at the Hague, *by* M. Scheurleer, *both in the* Italian *and* French *languages, and by him dedicated to* M. Maurice le Leu de Wilhem, *lord of* Waelwyck, *eldeſt preſident of the ſovereign Council, and of the feodal court of* Brabant, *at the* Hague ; *a perſonage of an illuſtrious family, of an eſtabliſhed character for his knowledge and love of the* Belles Lettres, *and of undoubted probity and candour.*

Theſe reaſons, added to the ſingular veneration which both this gentleman, and his honourable father always paid to the memory of Father Paul *and his writings, were what principally determined the bookſeller to make choice of ſo eminent a name to patronize, and protect his book, againſt the clamour that might naturally be expected from the* Romiſh *clergy, on ſeeing a book of this kind,*

a compoſed

composed by one of the greatest men of their communion, first published 100 years after the author's death, in a country which passes with the court of Rome for a land of heresy.

In order to remove all manner of doubts of the book's being authentic, M. Scheurleer the bookseller observes, that his learned patron was so thoroughly acquainted with the F A T H E R's stile, and way of writing, that he could not possibly be imposed upon in this respect ; and his French translator satisfies the world how he came by the original Italian manuscript, from which he printed it, and why it saw the light no sooner.

To take off the reader's wonder why a manuscript of such importance to all the sovereigns in christendom was suffer'd to lie so long dormant, the translator observes, that it was the author's own desire it should be confined to the archives of Venice, for the sole and proper use of the government under which he was born, whenever they should have occasion, as they had then, to withstand the usurpations and incroachments of the neighbouring court of Rome. And in confirmation of this, he takes notice of the Father's own words (page 3) where he says : I must own however, that as much as I desire to comfort all ranks alike, yet I don't think it proper that every thing I have to say on this head should be published, because the prince and the subject cannot help thinking differently on affairs of this kind —— For this reason I could wish that these few advices might be set apart,

like

like a prince's private treafury, for their fervice only who are at the head of affairs. Your
lordfhips can make a proper ufe and improve-,
ment of them in due time and place; but the
common people, like a man's taking phyfic in
a fit of the ague, would weaken their conftitution inftead of mending it.

*The moft illuftrious lords inquifitors of the ftate
of* Venice, *to whom* Father Paul *dedicated this
work in* 1606, *thought his requeft fo juft, and
his arguments for it fo rational, that they made
no fcruple to comply with it, and were content to
fight with his weapons againft all attacks that
were made upon their* Rights of Sovereignty,
*without letting either their friends or enemies
know from what armory they took them.*

The French *tranflator proceeds in the next
place to give fome account how* M. Scheurleer
*came to be mafter of fuch a fecret and valuable
copy. He does not make fo full a difcovery as
fome perhaps would expect, for fear, among
other reafons, of offending and prejudicing certain perfons, to whom he owns himfelf obliged
for it. Therefore he hopes he need fay no more,
than that a certain* (namelefs) Gentleman *brought
the copy of the Father's manufcript from* Venice,
*and put it into the bookfeller's hands, and that the
original ftill remains entire in the fenate's library,
to be confulted by thofe that may happen to have
any doubts concerning the genuinenefs of the copy.
However, there are thefe farther circumftances,
for the fatisfaction of fuch as are not acquainted*

with

with the Father's *ſtile,* viz. *that when the Sieur*
Scheurleer *was about to print the ſaid copy, he*
apply'd to ſome perſons of rank and learning, who
he thought might be capable of giving him ſome
light as to the authority of his copy; and that
when they had ſeen the title and the heads of
the chapters, and peruſed ſome of their contents,
they aſſur'd him that it was really a copy of Father Paul's *manuſcript, and that they wonder'd*
how he came by it, ſince they themſelves had ſeen
the original, and done all they could to get a copy
of it when they were upon the ſpot, but in vain;
ſo that after giving the work its due Encomia,
they conjured him to withhold it from the public no
longer.   The French *tranſlator adds, that juſt as*
this book came out of the preſs, he was well in-
form'd there was another copy of the ſame origi-
nal manuſcript in the library of a certain perſon,
illuſtrious by his birth, his poſts, and by his love for the
Belles Lettres. *He wiſhes he were at liberty to*
mention him, and other perſons, whoſe names alone
would be ſufficient to remove all doubt of its being
an authentic copy, but he ſays a world of reaſons
conſtrain him to ſilence. For the reſt, ſays he,
ſuch as have read him in any of thoſe different
languages into which his works have been tran-
ſlated, will know that this is Father Paul's *trea-*
tiſe from the beginning to the end.

What gave occaſion to the Father *to compoſe*
it was this.

Pope

Pope Paul V, *according to the character given of him in the* Lives of the Popes, *was so zealous, even before his advancement to the chair, for the ecclesiastical liberties and immunities, that he bore a mortal hatred to such as opposed the licentiousness of the clergy, and maintain'd the* Rights of Sovereigns *against their usurpations. No wonder therefore that he came to the chair with such an implacable grudge against the republic of* Venice, *which then made a nobler stand for the* Rights of Sovereignty *than all the other princes and states in the world.* This Pope *was scarce warm in his chair, but he sought to pick a quarrel with the most serene republic, accusing them of having invaded the authority of the Church and the holy See, on three Accounts.* 1. *By opposing the foundation of sacred places, and the exorbitant grants made to monasteries and other churches.* 2. *By submitting ecclesiastical estates to alienation by long leases:* And, 3. *By assuming a right to judge ecclesiastics in causes civil and criminal.*

The republic, in an answer to these complaints, shew'd that they were entirely groundless; which kind of resistance was enough to inflame the Pope's *choler, so that he issued out a formal excommunication, together with an interdict, against the doge and senate, which was dispatch'd* April 17, 1606, *and gave occasion to this treatise, at the End of which the reader will find the said bull inserted.* Father Paul *quickly perceived the*

consterconfternation with which the faid fentence had filled the minds not only of the honeft burghers, but alfo of fome noble perfonages who were at the helm of government; therefore he thought it his duty as a patriot, as a divine, and as a counfellor to the commonwealth, to diffipate that ground-lefs terror, by drawing an exact parallel between the pontifical authority and the refpective Rights of Sovereigns.

All the great lawyers and divines took up the cudgels; and, as Father Paul fays, an army of writers were got into the field before the month of Auguft.

Seignior Antonio Quirini, a fenator, was one of the firft that came out with a learned Dif-fertation on the Rights of the moft ferene Republic; and at the fame time our Father Paul publifhed a treatife entitled, Confiderations on the Cenfures of his Holinefs Paul V. againft the Republic of Venice. Then he was concerned with fix other eminent divines of Ve-nice, in compofing a Treatife on the Interdict, which at that time made fo great a noife. Two anonymous civilians joined iffue with thofe illuftrious writers, and publifhed a curious and learned Letter, addrefs'd to the Pope, in which they demonftrated the nullity of his brief of ex-communication, and the injuftice of his violent conduct. John Marfilli, a Neapolitan prieft, and doctor of divinity, entered the lifts alfo by the publication of an anonymous letter, entitled,

The

The PREFACE. vii

The Answer of a Doctor to a Letter from his Friend upon the Censures, &c. The famous cardinal Bellarmin, attacked him, but met with his match; for after he had answered the doctor's arguments with all the bitterness in his nature, the doctor repelled his sophisms, not by invectives, but by solid arguments, in an answer which he wrote, entitled, The Defence of John Marsilli's Answer to eight Propositions, &c. Then an extract was published of the famous Gerson's sentiments, touching the Validity of Excommunications, which seems to have been done by Father Paul; for, besides its being found in the catalogue of his works, he did not suffer cardinal Bellarmin to attack it in his usual stile with impunity, but vigorously undertook the defence of it, though always with moderation, and answered the propositions of that splenetic cardinal against the sentiments of Gerson, that famous oracle of the university of Paris, and of the Gallican Church. This answer is to be met with in the second tome of his works, and is entitled, An Apology against the Objections of Cardinal *Bellarmin.*

These were the principal tracts which were published on account of the said bull. There were a great many other small pieces which made little or no noise, and were distributed among the vulgar, to give ease to such consciences.

sciences as the conduct of certain monks, and especially the jesuits, had frightened almost into despair of salvation.

Whoever reads the pieces above mentioned, will find that this, now published for the first time in England, not only ncludes, but excells them all.

THE
LIFE
OF
FATHER *PAUL*.

THE chief materials for this great man's life are extracted from the account given of him by his constant friend and companion father Fulgentio, which has been printed and reprinted in Italian, and other foreign languages; but the only English translation we have of it, is that prefix'd by Sir H. Brent *to Father* Paul's History of the Council of Trent, the same word for word with that incorrect, unintelligible edition printed at London *in* 1651, which the person of quality himself that translated it owned to be obscure, by too closely persuing the literal sense of the Italian, and thereby confounding the idioms of both languages, which is a fault that the translator of this work has carefully avoided.

Ather *Paul* was born at *Venice* on the 14th of *August, anno* 1552. His father was *Francesco di Pietro Sarpi,* originally of the province of *Friuli,* who, tho' of a warlike temper, followed merchandize in that city,

and

and traded to the *Levant* ; but had fuch ill fuccefs, as reduced him to a low condition. His mother was *Ifabella Morelli* (of an honeft family in *Venice*) who, after her husband's death, put on a religious habit, was famous for her principles of religion, and extraordinary piety, and dy'd of the contagion in the year 1576.

She left only this fon and a daughter, who were both taken care of by their mother's brother, *Ambrofio Morelli*, a titular prieft of the collegiate convent of St. *Hermagora*, who taught grammar and rhetoric to feveral noblemen's children, afterwards able fenators ; and was fo fuccefsful with his nephew in particular, that he foon became a mighty proficient in, and mafter of the more folid arts and nobler ftudies of logic and philofophy.

He had what is very rarely known in one and the fame perfon, a great memory and a profound judgment, both which his uncle took care to apply, to their proper exercife. He manag'd his judgment, by keeping him to continual compofings with more ftrictnefs perhaps than was convenient for his childhood, and weak conftitution ; and he exercifed his memory, not only by forcing him to repeat many things by heart, but fome upon the very firft hearing. The fathers of the convent admired his uncommon thirft after learning, and reported wonderful things of his memory ; but he told them his uncle had never made him repèat more than thirty verfes out of *Virgil*, or any other claffic poet, at a time, after one curfory reading. He made fuch an unexpected progrefs in philofophy, and theology too, that his mafter confefs'd he had outran his abilities to teach him ; for he maintain'd arguments with fo much fubtilty of reafon, that his tutor was often forced to change his own opinion. He began alfo

in

in his childhood to learn the mathematics, together with the *Greek* and *Hebrew* tongues, from eminent mafters then at *Venice*.

By continual converfation and ftudy with them,
he became defirous to enter into the order of *Servi*,
or *Servants of the Virgin* Mary, a religious fociety
inftituted at *Florence* about the year 1232, and was
received into the Habit on the 24th of *November*
1566, when he was but 14 years of age; tho' his
mother and his uncle oppos'd it all they could, out
of a defire to make him a prieft of their convent.

Before he was of age, he was fingled out in a
public affembly of his fociety, that met ufually for
preaching and difputations, to anfwer and defend
a hundred and eighteen of the moft difficult propofitions in theology or philofophy, which he performed with wonderful fuccefs and applaufe, infomuch
that he was taken notice of by *William* then duke
of *Mantua*, a prince of profound skill in the fciences,
who requefted father *Paul's* fuperiors to let him eu-
ter into the fraternity of St. *Barnabas* of *Mantua*,
and honoured him with the title of his chaplain, at
the fame time that the bifhop of *Mantua* made him
lecturer of the cathedral, in which he read pofitive
divinity, cafes of confcience, and the facred canons,
and gave fuch extraordinary content, that even to this
day they have a common faying at *Mantua*, *non ve-
nera mai un fra Paolo*, we fhall never have another
frier *Paul*. He attained here to a greater perfection
in the *Hebrew* than he had done at *Venice*. His attendance at court, and upon the duke, made him
fee the neceffity of his underftanding hiftory, in
which he continued fuch a courfe of ftudy, and
made fuch a progrefs as can fcarce be parallel'd; for
his way was in this, as well as in all his other ftudies, when he encountered with any point of hif-

tory or learning, or any problem or theorem, he would perfue it without intermiffion, till, by confronting of authors, places, times and opinions, he had feen all that was to be feen on the fubject, and was fatisfy'd how far the knowledge of it might be carry'd. He was fo intent and indefatigable in his ftudies, that tho' he us'd to fpend eight hours a day in his clofet, yet upon a new thought he often rofe from table, and even from his bed at midnight; and his moft intimate friends obferved, that when he was come to years of maturity, he would fpend a whole day and night together upon a mathematical problem, or other fpeculation, without leaving it, till he could fay, *O, l'zo pur vinta; O, pui non ci voglio penfare.* I have overcome it; or I'll think no more on't. And yet this great man was fo modeft, that he would never write any thing for publication, unlefs the good of the publick extorted it from him.

His favourite companion at *Mantua* was *Camillo Olivo*, who had been fecretary to *Hercules* cardinal *de Gonfaga* of *Mantua*, who was legat in the council of *Trent*. From him the Father pick'd out the fecret of that famous council, and learnt moft of thofe particulars that are to be found in his celebrated hiftory of the faid council.

All men of learning that came to the duke's court loved to difcourfe with frier *Paul*; becaufe (tho' ftill young) they found him fo perfect in all the fciences, that as he treated of them feparately, each feem'd to be his mafter-piece. He had fuch a ready wit, that the duke would often come unexpected to the public difputations, and command him to argue on fome puzzling thefis, which perhaps he never thought on before. He had fuch a prodigious memory, that wherever he came, all the images, even

of

of the minuteſt things he ſaw, were too deeply im-
printed to be cancelled by new appearances; and
his friends would ſometimes ask him how it was
poſſible he could take notice of ſuch trifles.' He
read all books of note that came out, and could
remember the very page where he had obſerv'd any
thing, though of very little moment; but ſo modeſt
was he, that when any praiſed him for this noble
talent, he call'd it an imperfection and an excellent weakneſs, ſaying he took no greater care than
ordinary in reading, or his obſervations, but that his
great paſſibility and imperfection was the reaſon of
his retention, becauſe the object was not only moving in him, but every little relick and idea of it continued it.

He was ſo incomparably skilled in the mathematics, that whatſoever is extant of ancient or modern writers, who have treated on that ſubject, was
the leaſt part of what he knew; but he had a juſt
contempt for aſtrology.

He was the author of ſeveral mathematical inventions, but would fain have conceal'd it from the
world, particularly that called the two manners of
Pulſiligho, and the inſtrument for diſtinguiſhing the
variation of heat and cold; and when one of thoſe
perſpectives, call'd *Galilean* from the inventor, was
preſented to the government of *Venice*, and refer'd
to the Father's examination, he knew the uſe of it,
and the whole ſecret of its compoſition, before it
was permitted to be open'd, as *Galileo* himſelf
own'd. Nay, he made mathematical and aſtronomical inſtruments with his own hands, and, by giving
out models to artiſts, made the workmanſhip ſo eaſy and plain, that one would have thought he had
had both the heavens and earth in his head. He
found out the means to ſolve all the phænomena of

the *Copernican* fyftem with one only motion, ' but in vain inquired after workmen to make an inftrument for difcerning it; the want of which is matter of great lamentation to the curious.

His fame in religion made him to be fo much importuned by his friends and fuperiors, who wanted to make ufe of his labours in their profeffion, and his genius was fo averfe to a court life, that, with the duke of *Mantua*'s favour and approbation, he retired from his court.

Befide his skill in human literature, logic, philofophy, theology, and all the mathematics, he was perfectly well vers'd in the common law, underftood a great deal of the civil, was well acquainted with medicin, anatomy, botany and mineralogy, and had a fufficient underftanding of divers tongues, befide the *Latin*, *Greek*, *Hebrew*, and *Chaldean*; all which knowledge united in a perfon of riper years would have been very furprizing; but our Father had not yet exceeded 22, at which age he was confecrated prieft.

He went that year to *Milan*, whither he was fent for by cardinal *Borromeo* (afterwards fainted by the name of St. *Carlo*) who was then purging the churches and cloifters from ignorant and vicious confeffors. He made ufe of him, contrary to his inclination, to hear confeffions in the churches, had an uncommon efteem for him, and took great delight in his company.

It happened that before he left the dutchy of *Mantua*, he was profecuted by the inquifition there, for maintaining that the article of the trinity could not be deduced from the firft chapter of *Genefis*; but he excepted againft the judge, not only becaufe he was of the accufers party, but for his unacquaintednefs tedness with the *Hebrew* language; appealed to *Rome*, obtained a *Noli profequi*, without being once examin'd, and had the inquifitor feverely reprimanded for his ignorance.

Being called homewards by the affairs of his na tive country, and the inftances of his friends, all his feniors were ready to own him their fuperior; and having gone thro' the degrees appointed by the laws of his order, as ftudent, batchelor, and mafter (which is equivalent to the title of doctor of divinity) and having been admitted a member of the then moft famous college of *Padua* in 1578, he was next year with univerfal applaufe created provincial (which is the title they gave to the readers of divinity lectures) with the additional quality of regent. His judgment was fo unbiafs'd, that he would never receive the fmalleft bribe, nor admit of the leaft delay of juftice, and withal fo folid, that not one of the numerous decifions he made was thought fit to be repealed by any fuperior court. In his government he banifhed all factions and particularities, and none had ever any caufe to complain of him, except fome indifferent perfons that promifed themfelves more of his friendfhip than he gave them reafon to expect. He eftablifhed fuch excellent orders and cuftoms in his province at his firft entrance upon it, and fo dextroufly managed affairs, that thofe of the greateft intricacy and difficulty were brought for folution to him, as to the oracle of the republick, in confidence that he would foon loofe the knot, or that it would be vain for any body elfe to attempt it; and of all the numberlefs affairs that paffed thro' his hands, none were fo involv'd in difficulty, but his more than human wit found a way to the bottom of them.

He

He was ſcarce 27 years of age when he was made provincial of his order, a dignity never confer'd upon any ſo young before. In this year, *viz.* 1579, a general chapter of the whole order was held in *Parma,* when it was decreed that three of the moſt learned, pious and prudent men, ſhould be choſe out of the whole order of *Servi,* to make new conſtitutions for regulation thereof; and one of theſe was our frier *Paul,* who was but a youth, compared with the venerable and hoary hairs of the other two. Their chief buſineſs was to accommodate the forms of their judgments with the ſacred canons, as théy were reformed by* the council of *Trent*; but becauſe our Father had a more exquiſite knowledge of the canon and civil laws, and of conciliary determinations, they referred this particular entirely to him, and he alone accommodated the matter and form of judgments to the monaſtic ſtate, with ſo much conciſeneſs, clearneſs and ſolidity, that thoſe who were moſt converſant in matters of judicature, admir'd it as the performance of one that had ſpent his whole life in nothing but the ſtudy of the laws of his order.

When he had ended this charge of provincialſhip, and eaſed his ſhoulders of ſo great a burden, he had three years retirement, which he ſaid was the trueſt repoſe he ever enjoyed in his life. During this, hè gave himſelf totally to ſpeculations of natural things, proceeding at length to experimental operations, by tranſmuting and diſtilling all ſorts of metals; except gold; the poſſibility of which he always ridiculed. In ſhort, he was ſuch a maſter of the ſciences, as is hardly credible; for there.was no admir'd effect, no occult property, nothing either written or experimented, which he had not ſeen or examin'd; and he found out many ſecrets both in

art and nature, of which other perfons of the profeffion, to whom they were communicated, have
had the credit of being the firft inventors.

He fo well underftood the anatomy of the eye,
that the famous *Aquapendente* did not difdain to
quote his authority in his lectures and printed book
de vifu; the whole of which treatife, at leaft fo
much of it as contains the choiceft and neweft
fpeculations and experiments in optics, is afcribed
to Father *Paul*, according to the teftimonies of *Santorio*, and *Peter Affelmeau*, a *Frenchman*.

Aquapendente was however a very great man; and
when he mention'd the Father, he fpoke of him as
of the oracle of the age. And that good man *Affelineau* never talk'd of him without lifting up his
hands, and uttering words to this effect. *Oh, how
many things have I learnt of Father* Paul *in anatomy,
minerals and fimples! His is a pure foul, in which there
fhines candor, an excellency of nature, and an ignorance of
doing any thing but well.* In fhort, he was fuch a mafter of the feveral profeffions above-mention'd, that
he made inventions and difcoveries enough for an
entire volume.

But the fame of his capacity for government
forced him away from the fweet retirement, which
he had enjoy'd for three years, into a field of labour
and fatigue both of body and mind; for at a general chapter he was, by common confent, created
procurator or proctor general of the court, which
was the next dignity of his order to the general,
and conferred upon none in thofe days, but fuch as
were men of exquifite prudence and uncommon
learning; it being an office which required thofe
that bore it, to manage all difputes with the court
of *Rome* in matters relating to the order, to pray
before the Pope on particular days appointed for
that

that order, and to read public lectures upon wifdom, and maintain caufes in the pope's congregations.

In the three years that he dwelt in *Rome*, the Pope, finding by the incomparable prudence with which he treated of church affairs, that he had abilities and a difpofition for greater things, ordered him to be entered into feveral congregations, where there was occafion to difcourfe upon important and nice points of doctrine. At thefe meetings he firft got acquainted with father *Bellarmin*, who was afterwards a cardinal, and had a refpect for him as long as he liv'd. There it was he alfo fell in company with one of the ten companions of *Ignatius*, the founder of the Jefuits, whom he told very frankly, that if *Ignatius* was to return into the world, he would not know the fociety of Jesus, they were fo much altered. It is remarkable that our Father was in the good graces of cardinal *Santa Severina*, protector, a man of fuch an odd temper, that not a mortal upon earth had his good word; for if any body affented to what he ever faid, he call'd them poor fpirited flattering wretches; and if they did but oppofe or contradict him, then they were malapert and infolent. Pope *Sixtus* V. frequently employ'd him, not only in congregations, but other affairs; and one day, being in his pontifical litter, he called the Father to him, and difcours'd with him a good while in the ftreet, which was mightily taken notice of by the court: Every body talk'd how much he was in the Pope's favour, and fome prick'd him down immediately for a cardinal, which tho' he never defired, nor was, yet the bare report of it raifed him a world of envy, and, in the fequel, no little trouble. This Pope's fucceffor *Urban* VII. liked him fo well, that he thought he could not fee

him

him often enough. The Father having occasion to go to *Naples*, to sit president, as vicar general at the chapters, and to make the visitation, he grew acquainted with that famous wit *Gio. Battista Porta,* who makes very honourable mention of Father *Paul* in one of his printed works, and particularly of his specular perspective.

One of the first disturbances given to Father *Paul,* was thro' the means of *Gabriel Collason,* to whose counsel and directions he referred his friends when he first set out from *Venice,* and with whom he had joined formerly, in redressing the grievances which certain persons, abusing the power they were vested with, had tyrannically imposed upon the weaker part of the subjects. But this *Gabriel* prov'd afterwards such a lover of his own interest, that during the three years of the Father's absence from his country, he, by his extortion, had raised himself to absolute dominion, and feared nothing so much as the Father's return to *Venice,* who he was sure, from the constant experience he had of his uncorrupted integrity, would abhor his practices. To prevent the Father's return, he endeavoured to persuade him by his own letters, and those of his dear friends, that he was in a very fair way to great preferment at court, and that he had better stay at *Rome* to advance his fortune. But the Father in his letter testify'd his abhorrence of court favours, which he said were generally obtained by such vile methods, that he had much rather be without them: Mean time *Gabriel* sent the letter to cardinal *Santa Severina* the protector, whom he had corrupted in his favour; and when the Father returned home, after the three years of his office were expired, he found not only *Gabriel,* but the cardinal too his mortal enemy; and the latter being at the same time chief of the inquisition,

tho'

tho' he did not think fit to exert the authority of
that office againſt the Father, yet he ſought to give
him all the vexation poſſible, by putting his friends
into that court, and proceeding againſt them by methods ſo unuſual and baſe, that *Fulgentio*, who wrote
our Father's Life, forbears to mention many of
them, for fear of giving the world too great a ſcandal. One of them, which however he could not
help taking notice of, is this:

There was at *Venice* one frier *Julio*, a man of
an unblameable'life and converſation, who had for
many years been confeſſor and maſs-prieſt in the
convent of St. *Hermagora*. This good old man,
who had likewiſe been confeſſor to Father *Paul's*
mother, maintain'd him, till he was ſuperannuated,
in his cloathing, and the charge of his journies and
books (the monaſtery defraying his other expences.)
But ſo ſpiteful were our Father's enemies, that,
to ſhorten his poor, though ſatisfactory allowance,
they drew up deviliſh informations againſt the good
old frier, and got the patriarch *Priuli*, not only to
deprive him of the liberty of confeſſing, but to ba-
niſh him as far as *Bologna*; upon which Father *Paul*
was obliged, in meer love to the poor innocent
man, to take a journey to *Rome*, where he ſollici-
ted, and obtained his return to *Venice*.

Father *Paul* not only underſtood the canonical
laws and decrees, but when and why they were
made; and in the matter of benefices, which is a
ſubject ſo various and intricate, he knew all the
reaſons, controverted progreſſes, and alterations;
and beſides all this theory, he had ſeen the practice
of many congregations and tribunals, and their
precedents.

As to the knowledge of men, he scarce had his fellow; for 'tis in a manner incredible how far he could penetrate into their temper and behaviour, from being but once in their conversation, insomuch that those even of his own order raised a report, which has been since aggravated by his enemies, that he had a familiar spirit. This penetrating faculty gave him the happy means of treating with all sorts of persons to their satisfaction; for as a perfect musician judges of his instrument by the first touch, so by making men speak, he presently knew their ends, their interests, and resolutions, and what would be their answers; consequently, he was never at a loss for the most proper ones himself; so that of all who treated with him, from the highest to the lowest, seldom any left him without admiration.

He was as well versed in sacred and prophane history, as if his fancy had been the scene in which the parts were acted.

The particular proofs of his skill in the mechanics are enough for a volume, and to make the reader think he understood nothing else. He would talk of perspective, and other glasses, forty years after his exercising himself in that study, as readily as if he had just come from reading *Halazen*, *Vitellio*, or others of that profession.

When Father *Paul* was returned from *Rome* to his monastery, he constantly attended the divine offices, and what time he could spare from his public and private devotion, he spent in study, except when he had avocations to serve the republic with his counsels. About this time he wrote some essays in natural philosophy, physic, and the mathematics, which he review'd afterwards, and set to nought as childish performances; tho' master *Fulgentio* affirms,
that

that if men of learning had feen them, they would not have reckon'd them puerilities.

In 1587 there happened fuch a difpute betwixt Pope *Sixtus* V, and the Duke of *Tufcany*, about the election of a new general of the order of *Servi*, that the Pope order'd the Father to go to *Bologna*, where he ftaid fome months to fettle that affair; and in all controverted points his opinion was approved of, tho' the auditors themfelves ufed to be the arbitrators in matters of judicature.

When he returned to *Venice*, he was generally in the affemblies of the moft learned and noble perfonages of his own and foreign countries, and of the regular and fecular clergy, who met to difpute on various fubjects, with no other view but to find out truth. Here our Father argued upon all manner of fubjects without premeditation, and with fuch eafe that every one was furprized; yet afterwards, in his riper age, when he was put in mind of thofe exercifes, he would fmile at them as the performances of a fchool-boy.

The civil wars in *France* breaking out in his time, he was pleafed to hear fuch as could give account of them, was curious to know how the world went as long as he liv'd in it, and form'd fo good a judgment of what news he heard, that it made men wonder, and court his opinion as if he had been a prophet. He was always a man of few words, but thofe were pithy and fententious. He was acute, but not fcornful in his repartees, and with a dexterity, like *Socrates*, delighted to make difcoveries of others abilities, which he called *helping them to bring forth;* and this dexterity *Fulgentio* afcribes to his being fo vers'd in all forts of learning, that he was able to follow every one in his own element; for whatever

was

was the fubject he difcours'd on, fuch ftrangers as heard him, went away perfuaded that it was his chief profeffion and favourite ftudy. When he met with perfons eminent in any art or fcience, he had a happy modeft way of getting out of ·them what was poffible to be known, without difcovering the leaft impertinence or troublefome curiofity; but he 'was fondeft of converfing with travellers, himfelf having once had a great defire to vifit foreign coun‑ tries.

The Father, and his friends, had frequent meet‑ ings at *Padua*, at the houfe of *Vicenzo Pinelli,* which was the receptacle of the mufes, and an academy of all the virtues in his time. Signior *Pi‑ nelli* called him *il miracolo de quefto fecolo,* the wonder of his times; and being ask'd by *Ghetaldi,* one of the greateft men of *Ragufa,* in what profeffion? faid, in whatever you pleafe. *Ghetaldi* try'd his skill in the mathematics, and was fo aftonifh'd at his reafonings, that he faid he never believ'd it pof‑ fible for a man to know fo much in any one profef‑ fion, and defir'd not only to contract a ftrict friend‑ fhip, but to compare notes with him as long as he liv'd.

But now, fays *Fulgentio,* came the time when the purenefs of the gold was to be try'd by the touch‑ ftone; for it pleafed God to draw the Father out of his haven of reft into a tempeftuous fea of frefh troubles. '

ı Father *Paul* was a fecond time complain'd of· to the inquifition at *Rome* by Signior *Gabriel,* already mention'd, who pretended that he held a correfpon‑ dence with the *Jews.* And at the fame time he ftir'd up a nephew of his, called *Maeftro Santo,* to ac‑ cufe him to the inquifition at *Venice,* of having de‑ ny'd ny'd the affiftance of the holy fpirit; becaufe, when a chapter of his order waited for divine infpiration, the Father reply'd, it was fitter to operate by humane means. But the tribunals, both at *Rome* and *Venice*, having examined witneffes, thought the complaints fo unjuft, that they enter'd a *Noli profequi* upon both accufations, without giving Father *Paul* the trouble of putting in his anfwer. The court of *Rome* had a jealoufy all the while that the Father was an enemy to their greatnefs, but were at a lofs how to fix any charge againft him upon the fcore of religion.

There were fome who the rather fufpected the Father's integrity, becaufe he had been often complain'd of to the inquifition; but in anfwer to this, his friend *Fulgentio* made this pertinent remark, that *Ignatius*, afterwards canoniz'd for a faint, was put into the inquifition no lefs than nine times, and was cited and examined, tho' at laft acquitted; whereas our Father was complain'd of to the faid court but three times, and with fo little foundation, that he was not once cited or examined.

As to his communication with heretics, tho' not a tittle of it was prov'd, yet it made fuch an impreffion on Pope *Clement* VIII, that he bore him a grudge for it a long time after; infomuch that the Father being propofed to the bifhoprick of *Nerva*, the Pope, tho' he own'd him to be a man of learning and great abilities, added, that he deferv'd no preferment from the Church, for his dealings with heretics; a charge which had no manner of foundation, but the Father's general converfe with the many eminent men of all countries and profeffions, that came to *Venice* either upon bufinefs or meer curiofity, and who were fond of difcourfing with
one

one fo able as he was to give them fatisfaction in all the arts and fciences.

The Father was moreover obliged, not only by the terms of civility, but by ftrict canonical rules, not to fhun the company of any, but fuch as were nominally and individually condemned by the Church. Neverthelefs, when any *German, French-man,* or the like, vifited the Father, *Oltramontana* was the word, and they, immediately concluded them to be heretics.

By fuch gradations as thefe, divine providence began to inure the Father to the injurious calumnies of the court of *Rome;* and, in the progrefs of his life, for being a faithful fervant to his God, his Country, and the Church, his conftant piety and invincible patience were fufficiently try'd.

The domeftic troubles of the republic, which lafted many years with implacable heat on both fides, gave the Father fufficient occafion to fhew the wonderful command of his temper in all events, as well as his mildnefs in never giving or retaliating offences, and his fingular wifdom in making every thing in his power contribute towards a pacification; but his virtue was unfuccefsful, becaufe he neither pleafed thofe of his own fide, not even the General of his Order, nor yet the Cardinal Protector. And the hot heads of his own party term'd his ferenity of mind lukewarmnefs.

The Father was fo defirous to fee an end put to the divifions, that in 1597, he chofe for that very purpofe to go to *Rome,* notwithftanding what he had to fear from the Cardinal of *Sta Severina,* who was at that time head of the office of inquifition; but the Cardinal, contrary to his expectation, courted his friendfhip, and prevailed with him to be reconciled in like manner to *Gabriel,* which the Father

was

was the rather induced to, becaufe he knew that if he could but pleafe the Cardinal, all would be well.

Then he returned to *Venice,* where he liv'd quietly for fix years more, and ftudied moral philofophy. He wrote fuch notes on *Plato* and *Ariftotle,* as plainly fhew that he put them down either as memorandums, or elfe as materials for a future treatife ; but our author *Fulgentio* inclines to believe the firft, becaufe he always thought he fhould never live twelve months to an end. He alfo commented upon the fathers, fchool-men, and fciences, and upon fimples, minerals, and mechanics. Several very learned men fent to him for his opinion in the moft abftrufe parts of the fciences, and efpecially of the mathematics, and courted his judgment whenever they made any new difcoveries. He wrote many little tracts of moral philofophy, which he ufed to carry about with him, together with the fentences and documents of the moft ancient celebrated writers. *Fulgentio,* who faw three of them, fays they were as elaborate as *Plutarch's,* that the firft apply'd thofe aphorifms to the cure of the mind, which are prefcribed for the health of the body. That the fecond treated of the rife of our opinions, and their variation; and the third of atheifm, fhewing it to be repugnant to humane nature; and that they who acknowledge not a true deity, muft of neceffity feign to themfelves falfe ones. He made fuch a ftrict fcrutiny into his own heart, that he alfo wrote an examination of his defects, which were invifible to every eye but his own, as thofe, that liv'd intimately with him the laft twenty years of his life, do folemnly declare.

But all this was nothing, compar'd to his ftudy of the fcriptures, particularly of the New Teftament,

ment, which he read from the beginning to the end, without any expofitor, in the *Greek* and *Latin* Texts ; he read them fo often, that he had them all as it were by heart, and with fo much attention, that where he obferved any point for meditation, he drew a line ; and fo by reading them over and over, there was hardly a word but what was mark'd. He did the fame with his breviary, and recited the mafs fo readily, that in his latter days, when he could not fee but with fpectacles, he always celebrated that fervice without them.

During his fix years retirement, he was folicited to go to *Ferrara*, to attend the confecration of *Leonardo Mocenigo* Bifhop of *Caveda*, who wanted to be inftructed by him in the canonical and epifcopal profeffion. He had another call to *Rome*, to affift in the controverfy concerning the efficacy of divine grace. He was very much preffed to go thither, the rather becaufe he was fo well vers'd in the Fathers, that he had them at his fingers ends, efpecially St. *Auguftin*, who handles that doctrine more fully than all the reft. The bifhop of *Montepelofo*, who was one of the prelates appointed to examine that controverfy, fent letters after letters to him, to defire his prefence at *Rome*, and in them communicated his own thoughts upon the matter ; but the Father was refolv'd not to go, nor to open his mouth in the difpute ; and in all his papers there is nothing to be found, but certain anfwers of the faid bifhop to letters, which the Father had writ to him on that fubject, and which gain'd the prelate a great deal of honour. By thofe letters it appear'd that our Father was of St. *Thomas*'s opinion, agreeable to that of St. *Paul* and St. *Auguftin*, againft the ancient and modern Pelagians, and Semi-pelagians. All that is extant of his upon this point, is a little

Italian

Italian tract, which he wrote at the requeſt of a prince, wherein he clearly explains the whole ſtate of the myſterious controverſy.

The ſaid ſix years were not long expir'd, but *Gabriel*, the general of the order of *Servi*, dying, was ſucceeded by his aforeſaid nephew *Maeſtro Santo*, who had his uncle's ambitious views, tho' not his power. His uncle had charg'd him upon his death-bed, to attempt nothing of moment in his province without conſulting Father *Paul*; but the veneration always paid to this great man was ſuch an eye-ſore to him, that he deſpair'd of abſolute dominion till the ſaid mote was removed, which it ſeems he was reſolv'd on, *per fas & nefas*, tho' he never liv'd to accompliſh it.

I   To this end he reproached him, in a chapter of the order, that he had worn a hat, contrary to a form that had been publiſhed in the time of *Gregory* XIV; that he had worn pantables of the *French* faſhion, hollowed in the ſoles, by which he alledged he had forfeited his privilege of voting in the chapter, and that at the end of maſs he did not uſe to repeat the *Salve Regina*. But theſe things were no ſooner mentioned than they were exploded by the Vicar-General, the Provincial, and the whole Aſſembly, with the utmoſt indignation.

His pantables were indeed taken off by the judges order, and carry'd to the tribunal; which gave birth to a ſaying that is remembered to this day, *viz. Eſſer il Padre Paolo coſi incolpabile & integro, che fivio le ſue pianiſſe erano ſtate canonizate. Father Paul* was ſo blameleſs and pure, that his very pantables were canoniz'd. And as to his not reciting the *Salve Regina*, he had very good authority to omit it, becauſe it was contrary to the rites of the maſs, and, by a particular order of about thirty friers,

declar'd

declar'd to be derogatory from the univerſal order
of the Church.   It was obſerv'd that Father *Paul*
never ſpoke a word, or ſhew'd the leaſt concern at
ſuch unjuſt and trifling accuſations, but was as frank
with his accuſers as ever, and that *Maeſtro Santo* retir'd to *Rome*, where he ſpent 500 ducats of the
monaſtery's money in four months time, and then
went to *Candie*, where he turn'd merchant, but
prov'd a bankrupt.

   We come now to that glorious ſcene of the Father's Life, wherein he did ſuch ſignal ſervice to
his country.

   As ſoon as *Paul* V. came to the See of *Rome*,
he fell out with the Republic of *Venice*, declaring
ſome of their laws (which are mention'd in the
following treatiſe) to be contrary to the privileges
of the Church, unjuſt and void; while on the other
hand the Republic maintain'd that they were good
and juſt, and in no ſenſe repugnant to the lawful
liberties of the Church.

   The diſpute was carry'd on for a month by propoſitions and anſwers, and arguments on both ſides,
till about the beginning of the year 1606, which
the Court of *Rome* uſher'd in with monitories and
comminations of cenſure.

   The matter of diſpute being partly of theology
and partly of law, and the Senate of *Venice* reſol-
ving to chuſe a perſon that was both a divine and a
canoniſt, to aſſiſt their counſellors at law, conferr'd
this important poſt on Father *Paul*, who ſerv'd
them ſeventeen years, not only in that quality, but
as a counſellor of ſtate in all cauſes of the greateſt
moment; for thro' his hands paſt all matters of
peace and war, of their confines, their treaties, juriſdiction, tribute, &c.   And his ſervices were ſo
univerſal, faithful, and ſincere, that when their

b 3   counſellors

counsellors at law died, the Commonwealth was so
well serv'd by the Father alone, in all manner of
business, that they chose none to succeed in their
places, They did the Father an honour never granted before to any of their counsellors, *viz.* the admitting him to the inspection of all their records,
and those call'd the *Two Secrets*, which contain the
public laws of the State, the fundamental laws,
treaties of war and peace, truces and alliances,
and the like affairs of state; together with the
chief transactions in *Europe* for several centuries,
and the changes all over christendom, which are old
books writ in former ages, very hard to read, and
would have been the most valuable treasure in the
world, if part of them had not been twice con-
sum'd by fire. These the Father made himself so
acquainted with, that by the happy assistance of
his incomparable memory, he could turn in an in-
stant to any of the books or passages contain'd in
them; and he made such useful indexes to them,
with so many notes and registers, that the Senate
gave Father *Paul's* amanuensis an honourable salary
to add them to their records, which, in his time,
contain'd little less than 1000 treaties and acts of
councils, all bound up in volumes of parchment.

The Father, however, wanting an associate to
help him in the toil of collecting the allegations of
the Doctors of both laws, that he might have the
authorities he quoted always ready at hand, chose
for this purpose frier *Fulgentio* (to whom the world
is oblig'd for this account of his life.)   He was a
native of *Brescia*, whom (as he says himself) Father *Paul* had long favour'd with an intimate familiarity. When the Father sent for him, he was at
the university of *Bologna*, in the sixth year of his
reading lectures in divinity; but he left that, and

all

all hopes of preferment, together with his library and moveables, to follow the call of his beloved friend.

The controverſy betwixt the Pope and the Republic growing hotter every day than other, the Father, and the other counſellors, were conſtantly employ'd to find out the moſt effectual methods by which the Republic, ſaving the reſpect due to the See of *Rome*, might conduct themſelves ſo as to maintain their liberties and independent ſovereignty. Among other tracts, which the Father drew up on this ſubject, was the following, intitled *The Rights of Sovereigns*, and a ſmaller one of *Excommunication*, in which every thing eſſential to that cenſure was comprehended with the utmoſt brevity and clearneſs. This piece could never be found, after the moſt diligent ſearch, among the many and ineſtimable volumes of both Church and State tracts, which the Father wrote, a loſs not only lamented by his friend *Fulgentio*, but by all friends to true chriſtian liberty.

The Court of *Rome* having miſrepreſented the controverſy, and attack'd the validity of the *Venetian* marriages, and other ſacraments, by written libels fix'd up privately in the night-time at *Bergamo*, which was in the temporal domain of the *Venetians*, tho' under the ſpiritual juriſdiction of the Archbiſhop of *Milan*, it was thought neceſſary to publiſh a true ſtate of the caſe, which the Father was employ'd in night and day for four months together, with the aſſiſtance of his friend *Fulgentio*.

During this, he tranſlated into *Italian* a tract of excommunication, which had been written by the famous *Johannis Gerſon*, a *Pariſian* Doctor, and Chancellor of the *Sorbonne*. This tract the Father publiſhed, with a preface adapting it to the preſent
diſpute

difpute; which being attack'd by Cardinal *Bellar-min*, the Father was under a neceffity of defending both the book and the preface; which defence was printed, and is ftill extant, under the title of *The Apology of* Johannes Gerfon; in which the author has made a noble difcovery both of his learnihg and modefty.

Soon after this our Father wrote another folid pious treatife, intitled *Confiderationi fopre le Cenfure*, *i. e.* fome thoughts upon the cenfure; which was attack'd, among many others, by *Bovio* a *Carmelite* frier, whom Father *Paul* thought fit to anfwer by a treatife, intitled *Le Confirmationi*, or Confirmations, which came out under the name of *Fulgentio*, whom, as himfelf owns, the Father directed and affifted to compofe it. The Father alfo wrote that called *La aggiunta e fupplimento all' Hiftoria degli Ufcocchi*, *A Supplement to the Hiftory of the Ufcoques*; and another little tract *De Jure Afylou Petri Sarpi Juris*, which is the name the Father was known by abroad; and, by order of the Senate, he compofed a treatife of the immunity of confecrated places in the dominions of *Venice*, with the particular laws and treaties made with the Popes; and another long manufcript treating of the office of inquifition at *Venice*, which, tho' of particular ufe to that Republic, who kept it up a long time as a jewel, was neverthelefs publifh'd at laft, and proves of general ufe to mankind. About the fame time, a treatife of the interdict was compiled by him, and the fix other divines which were then employ'd by the Commonwealth to examine their difference with the Pope.

He took fo much pains to be inform'd of all the proceedings of the Council of *Trent* from minifters who were prefent at it, that 'tis not to be doubted

but

but he was the author of the celebrated hiſtory of that Council, which was divided into eight books, printed firſt in *Italian* at *London,* and afterwards tranſlated into all the moſt common languages of *Europe,* under the name of *Pietro Soave Polano,* the anagram of which is *Paolo Sarpio Veneto,* the chriſtian and firname of our Father.

He was about compoſing a treatiſe of the *Power of Princes,* to be divided into 206 chapters, which, *Fulgentio* ſays, bid fair to be one of the moſt important compoſitions in the world; but he does not tell us that he went any further in it than three chapters, and theſe he gave to the moſt illuſtrious lord *George Contai ini,* a man of fine wit and judgment, who could never be prevail'd on to part with them out of his hands; for he had ſuch an eſteem for the Father, that as he was almoſt ready to adore him while living, ſo no man (tho' others were obliged in gratitude to have done much more) was ſo zealous as he to honour him when dead; for he had his image graved in mother of pearl, caſt in braſs; and not content with this, intended, if he had liv'd, to have had it likewiſe done in marble.

The Father ſo nobly defended the cauſe of the Republic, that notwithſtanding his wonderful modeſty, he became the butt of all the poiſon'd arrows of ſlanderous libellers, never man being loaded with more heavy curſes or more impudent falſhoods; yet like a man never provok'd, he choſe to go on defending a good cauſe, rather than to anſwer a bad one by recrimination; for he kept all the laws of a true divine, and had always a due regard to the apoſtolic See, and to the pontifical dignity and authority.

On the other hand, there were not wanting thoſe, at that time, who took up the quill in vindication
both

both of the ferene Republic and the defenders of
her caufe ; but Father *Paul*, with his fix cóllegues,
did, by public command, examine in a canonical
way every thing that was committed to the prefs,
to the end that as little offence as poffible might be
given to the Court of *Rome* ; fo that many things
written on the fide of the Republic were never
fuffer'd to fee the light : And *Fulgentio* remembers
it, to the eternal honour of the Republic, that
they alfo deputed three of the greateft fenators
they had, for age, for merit, and for dignity,
whofe bufinefs was, after the divines had made their
report, to review every thing with the niceft cir-
cumfpection before it went to the prefs, that nothing
might be publifh'd which was either impertinent to
the caufe of the *Venetians*, or offenfive to the See of
Rome, whofe writers, on the other hand, kept no
manner of decorum, infomuch that *Fulgentio* himfelf could not forbear confeffing, that *it was notorious
to the whole world, that they fix'd an indelible fcandal
on the* Romifh *religion, by pufhing matters to that pafs, as
if felf-intereft and ambition were its governing principles.*

The Father was fo far from difputing the legal
immunities of the *Romifh* Church and Clergy, or
from advifing any thing prejudicial to the lawful
authority of the See of *Rome*, that 'tis well known
he always fpoke and wrote of the Popes, and their
See, with the greateft reverence ; and that with
wonderful wifdom and addrefs he often temper'd
that zeal and paffion, with which even the moft
moderate of the citizens were apt to be inflam'd
againft thofe that quarrell'd with their jurifdiction.
Yet for all this he had a citation to *Rome*, to give
an account of his writings, which he anfwer'd by a
manifefto, proving the nullity of the faid citation,
and that he was obliged not to go to *Rome*. Which
anfwer

anfwer was printed and publifhed in fpite of that court, (who did all they could to prevent it) and was never yet confuted. Neverthelefs he went to *Rome*, which was in the 55*th* year of his age ; but no lawful reafon was ever affigned to declare him obnoxious to the ecclefiaftical penalties or cenfures, and he drew up a writing, which was afterwards known to be prefented to the pope, wherein he collected the many heretical and tyrannical doctrines held by the champions of the papal fee. He like-wife offer'd to difpute with any one of his adver-faries, and to retract whatever he had afferted, as foon as caufe fhould be fhewn for his fo doing, if he might be allowed a place of fecuriry, and his enemies at that court would decline their en-fnaring way of citing him, as if he had been guilty of advancing propofitions that were heretical, fcan-dalous, erroneous, offenfive to godly ears, and the like.

During this it feems the Father, by order of the ftate of *Venice*, wrote a treatife fhewing with what devotion the fenate conducted themfelves amidft their continual provocations towards both the re-ligion and the pope of *Rome*, and with what wif-dom and clemency towards their own fubjects; which tract *Fulgentio* gives us to underftand was printed firft in *Italy*, and reprinted in *France* ; but he does not tell us its title.

The court of *Rome*, in the mean time, finding all other methods fail, try'd to corrupt the feven divines ; and what with promifes on the one hand, and threatnings on the other, they debauch'd two of them fo far, that, contrary to their confciences, they quite deferted the caufe of the republic. The pope gave a particular charge to his emiffaries, one of whom was general of the order of *Servi*, to

clofet

clofet both the friers *Paul* and *Fulgentio;* but they knew beforehand that Father *Paul* was proof againft all allurements or terrors, and therefore they durft not tamper with him; nor does it appear they were able to do any good with *Fulgentio.*

In the beginning of the year 1607, there was an accommodation betwixt the pope and the republic, which was mediated by the *French* king, and in which Father *Faul* could not but be included, the rather becaufe the pope faid that he had given his blelfing to all, and confented that what had pafs'd fhould be buried in oblivion.

The Father knowing the integrity of his own heart, thought he might fafely rely on the pope's promifes; but foon after the famous *Gafpar Schioppio* came from *Rome* to tell him that the pope ow'd him a deep grudge, which he would certainly feel one day or other with a vengeance, adding that the Father's life was in the pope's hands, who was refolved to have him brought alive from *Venice* to *Rome;* but that if the Father pleafed, he (*Schioppio*) would endeavour to make his peace for him. To this the Father anfwered, " that he had given the " pope no juft caufe of offence; that he was forry " he fhould be difpleafed with what defence he had " made: That as all counfellors of ftate are fuppofed " to be included in treaties with their fovereigns, " fo he, the Father, was individually comprehen- " ded in the accommodation; and that he could " not fuppofe fo great a prince would fo far violate " the public faith; but that as for any defign upon " his life, it would never break his reft: That " great princes, not fuch mean fubjects as he, were " expofed to affaffinations; but that if fuch a plot " was laid againft him, he was ready to fubmit to " the will of God; and that he was not fo great a
" ftranger

" ſtranger to human nature, as either to deſire life,
" or fear death, more than was neceſſary ; *adding,*
" that tho' he ſhould be carried alive to *Rome,* yet
" all the power of the pope would not be, ſtrong
" enough to make another man take away his life;
" but that in ſuch a caſe he was reſolved to be his
" own executioner. " For the reſt he thank'd *Schiop-*
pio for his good wiſhes ; but was ſo reſigned to the
will of God, and truſted ſo much in his innocency,
that he took no thought of his own ſafety , conſidering that his cauſe and intereſts were wholly, in-
ſeparable from thoſe of the republic.

Schioppio returning to *Rome,* reported that he had
found Father *Paul nec indoctum nec tumidum.*

It ſeems that *Schioppio* had good grounds for what
he ſaid, ſince it was not long after that the lords in-
quiſitors of the ſtate of *Venice,* to whom many ſecrets are uſually made known, gave him intimation
that a deſign was actually formed againſt his life,
and often warned him to be upon his guard; but
the Father, who was ſo good himſelf, that he did
not think it poſſible for any body to be ſo wicked,
ſeem'd to take no more care of himſelf than as if
the whole had been a dream, and always uſed to
ſay, that it was all one to him which way he
died; but that he was reſolved death ſhould never
ſurprize him unprepared

The Father thought, without doubt, that when
the heat of the controverſy was over, no man could
be ſo profligate as to entertain ſuch a helliſh deſign,
eſpecially after ſo ſolemn an accommodation; and
that all princes have learned men enough about
them to defend their actions without employing
cut-throats. But he found his miſtake to his own
coſt; for about ſix months after the accommodation,
it came to paſs that as the Father was returning
home

home to his convent, on the 1*st* of *October*, about three in the afternoon, he was affaulted by five affaffins, who with ftilletto's or daggers gave him two wounds in the neck, and another, which entering at the right ear, came out again betwixt his nofe and his right cheek. 'Tis remarkable that for above three months before, the Father was always attended, except that very evening, by his friend *Fulgentio*, and another ftout frier, befides the frier who was his fervant; but then it happen'd he had no body with him but his fervant, who was feiz'd and bound by one of the Ruffians, while another gave the Father his wounds. The affaffins left a dagger fticking in the Father's head, and thinking they had difpatch'd him, fled immediately to the water-fide, where a gondola lay ready to carry them to the houfe of the pope's nuncio, then refiding at *Venice*, and from thence they crofs'd over in a boat with ten oars well armed to the oppofite fhore; but the *Venetians* in the mean time hearing that they had fhelter firft from the nuncio, went in great numbers and furrounded his houfe, making fuch reproachful outcries that the nuncio was in great danger of his life; and the council of ten were obliged to fend him a ftrong guard to prevent worfe confequences. The chief conductor of the plot was *Ridolfa Poma*, once a reputable merchant at *Venice*; but failing, retired to *Naples*, and from thence to *Rome*, where he was well enough refpected, and efpecially by the cardinal *Borghefi*, who carry'd him to his uncle the pope, from whom he had a promife that two of his daughters, whom he had left at *Venice*, fhould be admitted into a nunnery there; and at the fame time this *Poma* furprized fome of his friends, by telling them, that e're long they would fee him in a gallant condition; and one might have

guefs'd

guefs'd by his letters that he thought of nothing lefs than a cardinal's cap. The reft of the gang were either exiles or vagabonds, except their fpy, who was a prieft that officiated in *Trinity* Church in *Venice*, who in the preceding *Lent* feafon ufed to go every morning to the convent of *Servi*, on pretence of being charmed with Father *Fulgentio*'s fermons; and conferr'd with him every day almoft about his foul and fcruples of confcience; from all which *Fulgentio* infers that this plot had been hatching many months before it came to light, and obferves very juftly how often religion is made a ftalking horfe to the greateft wickednefs.

It was faid that *Ridolfo Poma*, when he fet out with his accomplices for *Venice*, took up 1000 crowns at the chamber of *Ancona*; and that going to *Ravenna* after the fact, with news that Father *Paul* was killed, he was honourably welcomed, and had 1000 crowns more from the chamber of that city. There he got a coach and a guard of musketeers, with whom he travelled in a kind of triumph, being carefs'd in all places by the governors, till he came to *Ancona*, where the report being arrived before him, that Father *Paul* was not dead, tho' wounded, his glory was in fome meafure eclipfed; and proceeding with his confederates to *Rome*; they were promifed a penfion, but had none; and every one of them came to a miferable end, convinced of the truth of the maxim, that princes, tho' they love the treafon, hate the traytors.

The firft thing that Father *Paul* did, after being put to bed, and his wounds dreffed, was to prepare his foul for God; and next morning he received the communion with feveral of the Fathers, who could not refrain from tears, efpecially when he beg'd them to excufe him from talking much, becaufe

caufe of his wounds. He faid to the avogador, or advocate, who, according to the law of *Venice*, went to take his information, that he had no enemy that he knew of; that he forgave the affaffin, whoever he was, from the bottom of his foul, and therefore he often beg'd the high council that they would inquire no farther into the fact, than what might ferve to defend him better hereafter, if it fhould pleafe God to prolong his life. Thus he behav'd both as a true chriftian and a philofopher, by rooting out of his foul the feeds of revenge, that principle of favage juftice, which is fo deeply implanted in human nature.

When the general of his order, *Philip Aleffandrino*, heard of what had happen'd to the Father, he was for a while fpeechlefs. The Father defired only one chirurgeon to attend him; but almoft all the famous phyficians and chirurgeons in *Venice* were fent to take care of him, befides others from *Padua*; among whom was his old friend and admirer *Aquapendente*, who was ordered not to depart from the convent, till it fhould appear whether he was for life or death, which remained for a long time doubtful; for as he was, when at beft, little more than a moving skeleton, fo had he loft fuch a quantity of blood, that for above 20 days he could hardly ftir his hand.

The number of his phyficians, a mifery common to great perfons, added to his affliction; for fome were of opinion the wounds were given by a poifoned weapon, becaufe of the blacknefs of their orifice; fome thought that the inflammations proceeded from the treacle in the medicaments; and others were for making ufe of fcarification; fo that upon the whole he fuffered as much from his phyficians as from his wounds. He

endured

endured incredible torture, by the taking off his
plaisters, and dilating the orifices; and the bone of
his upper jaw being broken, occasion'd inflammations, which frequently threw him into Fevers till
it was healed; yet for all this, he behaved with his
usual piety and constancy, and was even merry
sometimes in the extremity of his pain; of which
Fulgentio gives us this singular instance, *viz.* That
once when his wounds were dressing, and no less than
a dozen physicians and chirurgeons attending him,
Aquapendente said, *the greatest wound was not yet cured;*
to which the Father reply'd immediately, *Ay, but
the world will have it that it was given STYLO RO-
MANÆ CURIÆ,* which set them all a laugh-
ing. And the same night being in bed, and told
that the dagger was in the room which the Ruffians
left sticking in his head, he desired to see it, and
feeling it with his fingers, said it was not filed. He
that pulled the dagger out of his wound would fain
have kept it as his due, but consented that it should
be preserved as a public memorial of the divine
goodness to the Father; and that therefore it should
be hung at the feet of a crucifix in the church of the
Servi; where it was accordingly placed with this
inscription, *DEI FILIO LIBERATORI.*

'Tis remarkable, that the Father seem'd very
much concern'd, for fear that the assassins, when apprehended, should confess something that might
give scandal to the world, and prejudice to religion.

'Tis farther observable, that the day after the
Father was wounded, hearing of the death of M.
de Maisse, it so much affected him, that he could not
forbear expressing himself on that occasion to *Peter
Asselineau* after this manner: *We have lost our dear
Friend M. de Maisse. This is a wound which admits no
remedy;*

remedy; but in this frail state we must expect either to be spectators, or a spectacle.

It is now high time to give an account how this villanous attempt upon the Father was resented by the most serene the Doge and Senate of *Venice*.

The Senate being assembled when the news came, immediately broke up in a mighty consternation, and the Council of Ten sitting at the same time, there was that evening as great a concourse of senators in the convent of *Servi*, as if they had intended to have held the senate there. They sent money to the monastery to defray the charge of his cure, deputed persons of note every day to visit him, commanded the physicians to report his condition to them from time to time, and rewarded Signior *Aquapendente* in particular with the honour of knighthood, and a rich chain and medals, for constantly attending his patient. At the same time every thing imaginable was done for the Father's future security. The murtherers, who were presently known, were subjected to the severest decree of banishment that the supreme Council ever pass'd for the worst of crimes; and proclamations were printed, with ample rewards for all such as should discover any future conspiracies form'd against the Father's life, and the same for killing or apprehending those who made the attempt. They also order'd an allowance, at the public charge, to maintain a guard for him, that should have the liberty of bearing arms of any kind, and appointed him a house at St. *Mark's*, where he might spend his days in security. But the Father resolving never to quit his monastic life, petition'd that he might be permitted to continue in his monastery, where he had liv'd so long, that he said it was become his natural element, and that he could not tell how to live

out of it. In this the government were pleas'd
to gratify him, only they caus'd some additions to
be made to his apartment, from whence, by a
small gallery and steps, he had the conveniency to
take boat; then passing through *Mercer's-street* he ar-
riv'd at St. *Mark's*; and returning the same way, as
he sometimes did by night, from the public service
to his monastery, he avoided the blind alleys in
which he was liable to be way-laid. And during
the remaining sixteen years of his life, he seldom or
never convers'd out of his chamber, except at
Church, in the Refectory, or other public places.

He spent the residue of his life in holy meditations, and in the most studious application to the
service of the State, or his neighbours; for in all
sorts of causes, even of the greatest difficulty,
as testaments, marriages, infeoffments, heredita-
ments, and arbitrations, they came to him for advice from all parts of the Republic; and he gave
mild and solid answers to all, and with as much
readiness as if he had been every man's advocate,
and as if he had never study'd any thing but
the point in question; for tho' his answers and
resolutions were surprizingly quick, yet they seem'd
to be the effect of mature deliberation, and not
capable of being render'd better. In ecclesiastic
controversies especially he was esteem'd an oracle,
insomuch that when universities and colleges were
consulted, if the Father was of a different opinion,
his had always the preference: And 'tis yet more
admirable, that in the various and intricate affairs
of benefices, and other kinds of ecclesiastical controversies which came before him, even the Court
of *Rome* could never find any thing in his judgmen s
worthy of censure; and *Fulgentio* defies all tht t
knew the Father, to prove that he ever err'd in his

decisions;

deciſions ; adding, that how hyperbolical ſoever it may ſeem to the reader, this, and even more than can poſſibly be expreſs'd, is fact.

' Tho' he took above ten times the pains that others of his faculty did,.who got good eſtates, yet he never took a fee or gratuity from any perſon whatſoever : What time he had to ſpare from the ſervice of God and the public, he apply'd to the mathematics, or employ'd it in reading the New Teſtament and moral philoſophy. Thus was his life compoſed of the active and the contemplative, always yielding to God what he *could*, and to his prince and country what he *ought*, and even more than he was oblig'd to by any law; beſides that of charity.

But from the firſt to the laſt he was revil'd by many, for no other reaſon than to ingratiate them-ſelves with the Court of *Rome*. For this end they gave out that he oppoſed the order of Prieſthood, that he always declaimed againſt eccleſiaſtical juriſ-diction, and exalted the power of ſecular Princes more than was neceſſary ; tho' the contrary will evi-dently appear from his following treatiſe of the *Rights of Sovereigns*, and that he was a perpetual advocate for the juriſdiction and liberty of the Church, that Church which his friend *Fulgentio* calls " the true canonical and legal Church ; not that " (ſays he) which is now uſurp'd and employ'd to " the ſubverſion of public government, and of reli-" gion itſelf; becauſe the Father always affirm'd that he was ſure nothing ſo much obſtructed the " progreſs of the (*Roman*) catholic religion, and " occaſion'd ſo deplorable a diviſion among its pro-" feſſors, as the extending the eccleſiaſtical liber-" ties into licenſe.

On the other hand the Father has not fpar'd, in many of his writings, to cenfure Princes for neglecting the prefervation of the jurifdiction and power granted them by God; and he blames their ignorant zeal, in fuffering fo great a part of their power to be ufurp'd, and thereby putting themfelves out of a capacity to rule the people committed to their charge, without altering the form of government; which negligence of princes, in this particular, *Fulgentio* himfelf afferts to have been pernicious to the Church of God and all the ecclefiaftical order.

Father *Paul*, far from fowing diffention in the Church, as his enemies objected, always bewail'd it as the true fource of all thofe mifchiefs which have brought into the Church the moft political worldly form of government that ever was, and which have interefted the clergy in things not only different from, but contrary to the minifterial inftitution of Chrift; and fuch as keep chriftendom in perpetual difcord. He held, that the divifions of his day among chriftians were irrevocable by any other means than the almighty hand of God; and that they proceeded not fo much from obftinacy in diverfity of opinions and contrariety of doctrine, as from the ftrife about jurifdiction, which afterwards degenerating, and growing into factions, put on the mask of religion.

Mean time this hatred againft Father *Paul* being daily nourifh'd, grew up into another plot againft his life, in the year 1609, which was laid and detected as follows. *Bernardo*, a frier of *Perugia*, having infinuated himfelf into the affection of Cardinal *Borghefe*, by fome fervices that he did him formerly, which were very acceptable to the common guft of youth, went afterwards to *Rome*, where he was made much of by the Cardinal, and fent *John Francefco*

Francefco, another *Perugian* frier, to the univerfity of *Padua*, on pretence of being a ftudent. From thence he us'd to go to the *Servites* College in *Venice*, where he contracted an acquaintance with frier *Anthony* of *Viterbo*, who was very familiar with Father *Paul*, and ferv'd him as a writer. The Father obferv'd a clofe correfpondence betwixt them, which he fufpected was not lawful; therefore he forbad *Francefco* to come thither again, and told his amanuenfis *Antonio*, that he muft not expect to enter his chambers, if he had any more to do with him. Neverthelefs they ftill carry'd on a private correfpondence, by letters fent to *Antonio* by a *Jew*, one of which being intercepted, when *Antonio* was not at home, and carry'd to the Father, gave a ftrong fufpicion that fome mifchief was a hatching; and it was foon after confirm'd, by a packet of letters dropt in the veftry, where they had had a meeting at break of day. The Sacriftan immediately carry'd the packet to Father *Fulgentio*, who found the letters in cyphers, and fuppos'd they contain'd fome bufinefs of no fmall importance, becaufe *Bernardo* had written to *Francefco*, to folicit *Antonio* to difpatch the Quadragefimale; fince that not only the 400 crowns were ready, and fhould be put into his hands, but that the 12000, and more too, were as ready and fure. In fome of them he faid, " That Signior *Padre*, and others, by whom
" were meant perfons not inferior to Cardinals, did
" all of 'em defire the Quadragefimale; that the
" Father-General of the *Servi* bid him not doubt
" of being canoniz'd; that Signior *Padre* had caufed
" all other fuitors to withdraw to give him au-
" dience:" With many fuch particulars. Which being made known to Father *Paul*, he prefently fmoak'd their defign, and immediately difmifs'd *An-*

tonio from his chamber and the convent, but defir'd *Fulgentio* to fay nothing at all of the matter, till it was poffible to come at the whole fecret of the contrivance. But *Fulgentio* carry'd the letters, without any more ado, to the inquifitors of the State; and telling how he came by them, *Francefco* and *Antonio* both were apprehended. It appear'd by the counter-cypher, that the Quadragefimale was the word, for the three methods by which they intended to take away his life: One was, that whereas the Father had a relaxation of the *SphinƐter ani*, and was oblig'd to keep that part fhav'd once a week, which he would admit no body to do but his fervant the frier *Antonio*; that therefore *Antonio* fhould take that opportunity to give him a mortal cut with his razor; but the frier defir'd to be excus'd from this, in a letter to *Rome*, wherein he affirm'd that the very fight of blood naturally made him fwoon.

The fecond was a defign of poifon, by which, faid they, 'tis poffible with one bean to catch two pidgeons, *viz.* Father *Paul* and his friend *Fulgentio*. But this, tho' better lik'd by *Antonio* than the former, was attended with fuch difficulties that it was not practicable.

The third, on which they rely'd moft, was, that frier *Antonio* fhould take the print of the keys of the Father's chamber in wax, in order to make falfe keys, thereby to introduce the murderers by night. But the whole was deteƐted and prevented in the manner above mention'd.

The Council of Ten being refolv'd to fearch to the bottom of it, fentenc'd father *Francis* to be hang'd, with this alternative, that if he made a full difcovery of the whole plot, and explain'd all the letters, that then he fhould only be punifh'd with a year's imprifonment, and after that, perpetual ba-

c 4   nifhment

nifhment from the *Venetian* dominions. And accordingly he chofe to make a full difcovery, even of more facts than were publickly known, the government having fuch a regard to religion, that they thought fit to conceal every thing that did not manifeftly tend to interrupt the execution of their mild juftice.

But fo good natur'd was Father *Paul*, that he often‧beg'd upon his knees, that for his own fake, who had done the Republic fuch eminent fervices, his enemies might not be made public fpectacles, to the difhonour of his religion, and was griev'd to the heart that his life fhould be the ruin of others; and 'twas believ'd that the alternative above-mention'd was chiefly owing to the Father's earneft intreaties.

Notwithftanding the treacherous attempts before mention'd were thus brought to light and juftice, yet the Father was advertis'd of other plots that were afterwards hatch'd againft him; one of which was a defign to take him alive, and tranfport him in a bark into another's dominions. But the caution us'd for his prefervation fruftrated all their defigns; befides that the confpirators finding the Pope's refentment againft him begin to cool, thought fuch a piece of fervice would be lefs acceptable than formerly.

·Among other warnings this was one : A young man came to *Venice* armed like a foldier, but in carriage and habit more like a frier, who would needs fpeak with Father *Paul*. But none being permitted to have accefs to him, except he was very well known, or introduc'd by fome particular friend, he addrefs'd himfelf to *Fulgentio*, telling him that he had fomething of the utmoft importance to fay to the Father, and that if he might but fpeak with him,

him, he would quit his arms, and submit to any re-
straint the Father should please to lay upon him.
But tho' he said he would advise him of something
that even concern'd his life, it was resolv'd that he
should not see the Father; upon which Father *Paul*
said, with some passion, that it was not so bad to
die a violent death, as to be under a necessity of living in continual fears, which proceed *ad infinitum*,
whereas mischiefs have their termination. The
young man finding it in vain to insist upon an au-
dience any longer, took his leave of *Fulgentio*, with
this expression, *Guardatevi da tradditori, &c.* " Have
" a care of traytors, for you have very great need.
" God preserve you, for you are honester friers
" than others would have you to be.

'Tis remarkable that Cardinal *Bellarmin*, tho'
they had attack'd one another in print, sent his
kind love to Father *Paul* once by a secular priest of
Rome, bidding him tell the Father that he had
great need to take care of himself; and another
time by one *Alberto Testini*, by whom he assur'd the
Father that he had as much affection for him as
ever, and at the same time acquainted him, " That
" one *Felice*, a frier, had composed a vile libel, un-
" der the title of *Father* Paul's *Life*, which he pre-
" sented to Pope *Paul* V, who desir'd his (the
" Cardinal's) opinion of it; and that he (the Car-
" dinal) said he knew Father *Paul* very well, and
" that his holiness might take his word for it, that
" the facts therein mention'd were so false and scan-
" dalous, that it would be a shame for any body
" to publish them." Now tho' Father *Paul* might
easily have ruin'd the injurious author of that infamous libel; yet such was his meekness and forbea-
rance, that as long as the Father liv'd, that author
kept his employments of honour; but the Father
was

was no fooner dead, than the populace reveng'd the injury he had done him, and forced the libeller to quit the dominions of *Venice*.

After this, the pope beginning to have an opinion of the Father's goodnefs and piety, feem'd to be pretty well reconciled to him, as fufficiently appears from this one inftance, *viz.* The bifhop of *Tine's* caufe, who was profecuted by the inquifition at *Venice*, being refer'd to Father *Paul*, he gave it fo much in favour of the bifhop, that inftead of being reproved, he obtain'd feveral privileges both for his church and perfon. This pleas'd the pope fo well, that he faid, " He had heard indeed " from many hands that the Father was a " great friend to juftice, and a man of extraordina- " ry prudence and fincerity ". On the other hand, the Father pray'd God to fend the pope a long life ; and he often faid to his friends by way of prophecy, that he believ'd pòpe *Paul* ow'd him no more ill will; but that when he died, his fucceffor would revive the old controverfy, becaufe it was only skin'd over, and would break out again; in which it appear'd that he was not at all deceiv'd.

The Father was neverthelefs in great repute with the moft eminent prelates at *Rome*, who, when they had occafion to fpeak of him, fhew'd that they thought him an honeft man, and a man of great learning. Cardinal *Bellarmin* however lamented in public that fo little account was made of fo confiderable a man, and faid that he wifh'd he could have been reconciled to the fervice of the holy fee, tho' (fays he) they had given him but a *dry flower to fmell on*; for he imagin'd the Father had reafon to be very angry with the court of *Rome*, becaufe pope *Clement* had refufed him two fmall bifhopricks, *viz.* *Melopotano*, and that of *Nona* in *Dalmatia*. The
cardinal

cardinal faid he always wifh'd that the Father would come and live at *Rome*, becaufe he knew him thoroughly, and what fervice he was able to have done the church.

The pope's nuncios *Zachia* and *Afcoli*, fpeaking to the *French* embaffador *Villers*, upbraided the Father with hypocrify; but the embaffador repell'd their venomous raillery by fully acquitting him of every circumftance attending fuch a crime; adding, that he had heard every body elfe extol him for his goodnefs and integrity. *Peter Affelineau*, who was phyfician to the embaffador, told the Father that the nuncios reprefented him as one of the vileft mifcreants in the world; at which the Father fmiled, and would fay fometimes, *it muft be fo, becaufe I am as different as 'tis poffible from their humour : And if they be the moft perfect and holy men, then of confequence I am the lewdeft and moft wretched perfon in the world.*

The Father, after a little merriment and facetious difcourfe, confidering how hard it is for a man to know himfelf, conjur'd an intimate friend of his to deal plainly with him, and to tell him his faults, particularly if he had any of the marks of a hypocrite mention'd in the gofpel.

Cardinal *Ubaldini*, the pope's nuncio at the court of *France*, always fcandalized the Father for his writings: But *Contarini*, who was embaffador there at the fame time from *Venice*, a man of great folidity and good nature, vindicated the Father's writings from the impiety and ignorance the nuncio had charg'd them with, took notice of the applaufe with which they had been receiv'd in all catholic ftates by the moft learned and pious profeffors of the fciences, and faid that he knew both by report and experience, that the Father's holy retired life and manners were both exemplary and unblameable. But

But the nuncio was pleas'd to reply, that what the embaſſador had ſaid, only confirm'd him the more in his opinion, that he was a profligate fellow, and a conſummate hypocrite. *Maffeo Barbarino,* another of the pope's nuncios in *France,* rav'd againſt him with ſo little decorum, that he ſaid he was worſe than *Luther* or *Calvin,* and that he deſerv'd to be aſſaſſinated ; for there the nuncio came to know that the Father correſponded by letters with ſome of thoſe noblemen who were counſellors of the parliament, and with the orthodox doctors of the *Sorbonne,* who defended the lawful ſecular power, and the liberties of the *Gallican* Church, againſt the uſurpations of *Rome.*

'Tis true enough that the Father did converſe with ſome of them, and particularly with the great *Caſaubon,* after it was known that he was turn'd catholic ; but all men were heretics with *Barbarino,* that had any correſpondence with Father *Paul ;* for they that knew not how to convict him of one criminal action, were ſo offended with his doctrine, rather than with the man, that they pretended to find imperfections in his fair ſoul, and to cenſure his very intentions, tho' they were only known to God, the *ſearcher of all hearts.* On the other hand, *Fulgentio* obſerves, that thoſe his enemies, being all minions of the court of *Rome,* did, to the great offence of God and ſcandal of the world, canonize all doctrines and opinions, that made for their grandeur, but cenſured all others, tho' never ſo catholic and orthodox, if they did not favour their exorbitant pretenſions.

Father *Paul* was ſo entirely devoted to the public ſervice next after God, that he was always reſolved no controverſies ſhould ariſe upon his account ; of which the following is a very good inſtance. When
Pope

Pope *Paul's* fucceffor, *Gregory* XV, enter'd on the pontificat, he infinuated to the embaffadors, who came from *Venice* to congratulate his election, that there would never be a perfect peace betwixt the Republic and the See apoftolic, but fuch a one as Father *Paul* fhould approve of. When the Father heard of it, tho' he was then in his declining age, yet rather than there fhould be another quarrel, he was refolved to retire not only from the fervice of the fenate, but even out of the ftate of *Venice:* And accordingly he made preparations for a voyage into the eaft countries, by the way of *Conftantinople*, being ready to encounter with any adverfity, rather than his country or his prince fhould be expofed to fuffering for his fake; tho' he very well knew that the fenate would rather have undertaken a war for him, than abandoned his protection. He often pleafed himfelf with the thoughts of enjoying that in his age which he had extremely defired in his youth, *viz.* the pleafure of travelling to fee thofe things with his eyes with which he was already fo well acquainted by the reading of geography and hiftory. Moreover, it look'd as if *Gregory's* fucceffor, Pope *Urban* VIII, was refolved to make the Father very uneafy in *Venice*; becaufe when he was only a nuncio in *France* in 1606, at which time he was created a cardinal, he exprefs'd an irreconcilable hatred of the Father, by fuch unchriftian and unmanly actions and forgeries, that, for reverence fake, *Fulgentio* paffes them over in filence, left the world fhould think that the petulancy of fpeaking and writing falfhood and flander (a thing bred in the bones, he fays, of our modern ecclefiaftics) was arrived at the utmoft height. But however things feem'd difpofed to make the Father's voyage neceffary; yet God and nature did not give him leave to under-
take

take it; for entring into the 69th year of his age, tho' his judgment and memory were as copious and perfect as ever, yet as he was in his ufual place, a withdrawing room of the fenate-houfe, a fudden chillnefs feiz'd him, together with a hoarfnefs, and a ftrange benummednefs. This is the firft time he 'was ever troubled with a catarrh, and it held him above three months accompany'd with an ague. Neverthelefs, he would not change his way of living, nor diminifh his labour, tho' he vifibly declin'd in 'his ftrength, and always faid he was never well after that fhock. But his indifpofition continuing, he betook himfelf entirely to devotion and meditation, and fatigued himfelf no more with reading or writing afterwards, than juft what his poft and the public fervice obliged him to. His meditation was generally before a crucifix and a death's head; and if any body happen'd to furprize him at it, he endeavour'd to conceal his devotion as much as poffible, and made as if he was contriving fome inftruments or figures in the mathematics; but it might well be imagined he had other contemplations more fuitable to his age and ill habit of body. He bore up as well as he could till the beginning of the winter 1622, and his entrance into the 71ft year of his age, when he decay'd apace, infomuch that his hands and feet grew as cold as a ftone, his face fell, his lips, efpecially the nether one, were black and blue, his eyes dull and hollow, nothing would keep him warm, and his appetite loath'd almoft every thing he took. Tho' he had his teeth left, yet 'twas troublefome for him to chew his meat, and he began to go very weak and double. His dreams were not confus'd as ufual, but diftinct, natural, fpeculative, and regular, which, he obferv'd to his friends, was a rifing of his foul by little and little from the bond

and

and commerce with his body. He was now very indifferent how the world went, which had been always his favourite inquiry ; and the only delight he had, when he awoke, was, after divine meditations, to think of his mathematical and aſtronomical figures ; and he would often ſay, ſmiling, how fertile have my brains been of invention ? And tho' his ſoul had all the indications of one ready to leave the body, yet he did not quit his poſt, telling his friends who advis'd him to be ſparing of his labour, That his duty was to ſerve, not to live, and that no man ſhould be afraid to die in his profeſſion. His friends uſed to blame him for his indiſcretion in ſtudying as hard in his declining age, as he did when he was younger and ſtronger, a reproof which pleaſed him, but did not reform him. He was ſo far now from concealing his illneſs, that he gave plain tokens that he fore-ſaw his approaching diſſolution, and ſpoke of it freely as a debt to nature, and as a long reſt after a weary journey. Beſides his devout ejaculations, which he often repeated with ſentences of ſcripture, he would moſt frequently ſay, *Nunc dimittis, Domine, ſervum tuum*; Lord, now let thy ſervant depart in peace. He uſed to ſay to his familiar friends, *Courage my maſters, we are almoſt at our journey's end* ; adding, in a facetious manner, that he could now be aſſured his death would be no miracle, ſince he had ſurvived *Baronius, Bellarmin, Colonna*, and the Pope himſelf, as well as many others, that had written for the court of *Rome*, tho' younger than he ; for which reaſon there would be no room for the raſh judgment that is too often pronounc'd, in their writings, upon whoever dies in diſgrace with that court, *viz.* That they died after a ſtrange manner, and were puniſhed ſome how or other by God himſelf, as if that juſt being, who

governs

governs the world, was always ready to execute their partial fentences, or as if thofe of their faction were not as liable to death as others.

When his friends went at *Chriftmas* to wifh him the ufual compliment of a happy new year, he faid with more than ordinary freedom and ferioufnefs, *This is the laft I fhall ever fee* ; for he began to be in a high fever. Tho' he had taken phyfic on the feaft of epiphany ; yet being fent for to the palace, he went without making any excufe, and returned much worfe, being not able for two days following either to eat or fleep. Neverthelefs, he could not keep his bed ; but rifing on *Sunday* morning, celebrated mafs, dined at the refectory, and, after taking a turn or two with one of his companions, went and lay down in his cloaths, according to cuftom, upon a cheft, with nothing over him but a coverlet.

He continued thus till the very day before he died, ftill rifing out of his bed, putting on his cloaths, and reading and writing as much as his ftrength would permit ; and when he could do no more, he threw himfelf upon the cheft, and made others read to him. On the *Monday* morning, having drefs'd himfelf, his hands and legs fo fail'd him, that he was not able to ftir them, and he had fuch a loathing to every thing, that nothing, except his refolution, made him take a cordial; but he had the fame ftrong judgment and memory as ever, and the fame ferenity of mind, comforting his vifitors, and intermixing fomething facetious in his difcourfe : But upon the *Saturday* he faid to thofe that were about him, I have made you merry as long as I was able, and now I can do fo no longer, you muft cheer me. He continued to admit all vifits, difcours'd of all matters as ufual, faid but little of his weaknefs, and that only to his phyfician, and fo

pafs'd

pafs'd his time, fitting upon a ftool, and hearing one read to him.

In all thefe his latter days he made a thorow enquiry into the ftate of his foul, with an entire refignation of it to God; and a heart as chearful as his body was afflicted, concealing his ficknefs fo much from thofe who were prefent, that they could fcarce difcover it but by his want of ftrength, and his loathing of food.

When his phyfician and cordial friend *Peter Affelineau* view'd his excrements, the Father put his finger to his mouth, as a caution to be filent, and then freely told him his condition; but defir'd him not to difcover it to Father *Fulgentio*, that it might not afflict him, becaufe he had endeavour'd to poffefs him with an opinion that he fhould have a long ficknefs, and that it might perhaps turn to a quartan ague.   He often faid in his life-time, that he hoped he fhould know when he was near his end, but that he would not fpeak of it to any of the convent, befides *Fulgentio*; becaufe it would only breed confufion, and make them neglect thofe duties which God would not have omitted; but he did not obferve this rule, and would not let his condition be known even to *Fulgentio*, any farther than it manifefted itfelf.   It muft not be forgot, that on *Thurfday* morning he defir'd the prior of the Convent to recommend him to the prayers of the Fathers, and that he would bring him the holy facrament; adding, that he had liv'd in the poverty of the religion, without any thing of his own; and that as whatfoever was in his chambers was granted him for his ufe, fo it was now, as it had been always, at the free difpofal of his fuperiors; and he gave him the key of a cupboard, wherein was the remainder of what the republic had beftow'd upon

d

him;

him, nothing being lock'd up but what was in that cupboard, and one more, in which were the writings that concern'd the public. He again put on his cloaths as ufual, and fpent all that morning in hearing his friend *Fulgentio,* or frier *Marco* his amanuenfis, read *Pfalms,* or fome paffages of the Evangelifts, particularly of our Saviour's fufferings, making them ftop whenever he enter'd into any devout meditation. He often try'd to kneel ; but tho' the fpirit was willing, the flefh was too weak. As foon as mafs was ended, the fathers of the monaftery being call'd together by a little bell, went in proceffion, with torches in their hands, and the prior at their head carrying the holy facrament, which he received with fuch marks of piety, as drew tears from all that ftood about him, and convinced them that he was well prepar'd to die.

He was always unwilling to let any body watch with him in the night, faying it only ferv'd for pomp, and to incommode others, and that it did himfelf more harm than good to fee them lofe their reft.

He was fo ftrict an obferver of the rites of the Church, that notwithftanding the many new ones which were introduc'd in the ten preceding popedoms, he readily comply'd with all of them, tho' he did not heartily approve of them ; faying, that things of cuftom had their remedies, but that innovations were never without incurable mifchiefs : He was always, not from fuperftition, but a habit to fet a good example, a very ftrict obferver of *Lent,* infomuch that on *Friday,* the morning before he dy'd, he would not eat broth, or any thing that was not proper for the day ; and it was fo hard to perfwade him to have any but *Lent*-fare for his dinner,

ner, that he ask'd his cook whether he ufed to make
his friends break fafting days.

The night before he dy'd, when he was almoft
fpent for want of reftoratives, tho' he had then three
companions who fate up with him, he only took of
fuch neceffaries as lay ready at hand, and was heard
to fay nothing diftinctly, except now and then *Oh Dio!*

Saturday, Jan. 14, 1623, the laft of his life, was
the only day he fpent in his bed during his ficknefs;
and tho' his body was extremely weak, yet his mind
remain'd in its full ftrength, infomuch that the Doge
and Senate fending for our *Fulgentio,* to know how
he did, and being anfwer'd that he was ftill the
fame Father *Paul,* in his judgment and memory,
that he had been for feventeen years paft, they en-
joyn'd him to confult the Father upon three very
important articles of ftate, to which the Father
caus'd diftinct anfwers to be written by his amanuenfis; and the Senate having read them that very
night, conformed to his opinion in every point.

The Father ftill received vifits, and when night
came, he caufed St. *John's* account of our Saviour's
paffion to be read to him, and fpoke of his own
mifery, and of his entire truft in the blood of
Chrift, often comforting himfelf with thefe words,
*Quem propofuit Deus mediatorem per fidem in fanguine
fuo.* He faintly repeated feveral paffages out of St.
Paul, lamented that he had nothing to prefent
God with on his part, but fin and mifery, and defir'd to throw himfelf into the abyfs of divine
mercy; a declaration which came from him with
fo much fubmiffion, and yet fo much alacrity, that
it drew tears from all that were prefent.

He was again vifited by the phyficians, who
fhewing a reluctance to leave him without fome
fpark of hope, *Fulgentio* faid, the Father was not a

man

man to be flatter'd, and therefore he defir'd them
to be plain with him ; which the dying Father feem-
ing to affent to by a fort of fmile, one of the doctors then told him, that his pulfe fhew'd he would
be a dead man in a few hours : To which the Father, with a gladfome countenance, made anfwer,
Sia lodato Iddio, mi piace cio ch' a lui piace, &c. bleffed
be God, whatfoever pleafeth him pleafeth me : With
his help we fhall perform this laft action. Then
the phyfician recommending fome cordials to him,
the Father interrupted him, faying, *let's have no more
of thefe fooleries,* and defir'd they would refolve him
of two doubts ; firft, whether he might abfolutely
depend upon the goodnefs of what they gave him,
becaufe as often as he put it to his mouth he loath'd
it. But as he was going to mention the fecond,
his breath left him, fo that he could not fpeak,
and the phyficians finding by his pulfe that his vital
fpirits were departing, they order'd him a little
Mufcadine, at the taking of which he faid, *Quefta
vefta mi pare cofa violenta.* This feems to me a violent thing.

About fix at night, not long before he expired, he rub'd his tongue with a fmall inftrument,
which he had us'd for that purpofe a great while,
and without a groan, or any other token of grief
utter'd feveral memorable words from time to time
repeating devout paffages of fcripture, and crying
out, *Horfum andiamo ove Dio chiama.* Away, let u
be gone whither God calls us. The ftanders by
feeing his fpeech begin to faulter, and his pulfe going off, beg'd him to take a little reft, at which h
only fmil'd, and pafs'd his remaining time in fuc
low whifpers, that he could hardly be underftood
except in fome fentences of fcripture, and onc
when he faid, *Andiamo S. Marco che tardi,* i. e. let u

go

go to St. *Mark*'s before 'tis too late, which is the only thing he fpoke in all his ficknefs without connection. When the clock ftruck eight he counted it, and bid his fervant give him what his phyfician had order'd, but he could take very little of it; and finding himfelf expiring, he call'd *Fulgentio* to him, and being willing to be embrac'd and kifs'd by him, he bid him take his leave and depart, with thefe words, which *Fulgentio* fays he could never forget, *Hor fum non reflate, &c.* Now ftay no longer to behold me in this ftate, it will not be needful; therefore go to your reft, and I will go to God from whence we came.

Fulgentio indeed parted from him, but it was only to fetch the friers to pray with him, to whom tho' he could not fpeak, yet he convinced them that he had his underftanding faculty till it departed with his foul. His laft words, which were hardly intelligible, tho' often repeated, were *Efto perpetua*; from which *Fulgentio* infers, that at the fame time that he recommended his foul fo fervently to God, he did not forget to pray for the perpetual welfare of the moft ferene Republic. With thefe words in his mouth his fpeech went off; and then putting his arms acrofs, and fixing his eyes a while upon a crucifix which was before him, together with a natural death's head, he fhut them, and fo breath'd out his fpirit into the hands of God.

This calm departure of his pious foul to eternity was teftified to the Senate by a public writing, fubfcrib'd and fworn to by all the reverend Fathers of the college of *Servi* that were prefent, in order to defeat the impudent lies which went abroad, that he dy'd howling and crying out, with apparitions of black dogs, and the like; and that his cell was difturb'd with unufual, horrid noifes. But as *Ful-*

d 3

gentio very well obferves, 'tis ftrange fuch apparitions and noifes could be feen and heard fo far as *Rome*, when he is fure they never were by thofe that lived in the next chambers to his. The truth is, that the Father dy'd with fo wonderful a character for integrity and piety, that 'twas generally faid, if he had been in the favour of the court of *Rome*, and ferv'd its interefts, he would have been canoniz'd for a faint.

His death was fuch good news to *Rome*, that the then Pope could not help fpeaking of it *as the handy work of God to take him out of the world,* as if it had been a miracle for a man to die at the age of feventy one.

His corps being open'd, there appear'd the faireft conformity in all the parts of it that could be defir'd, except the heart, which was exceeding fmall, and feem'd as it were deferted. His ftomach was fo far from being foul, that it had nothing at all in it. His face had fo good and fmiling a colour, that fome thought it look'd more venerable and beautiful than when he was living. He was bury'd at the public expence, and attended to his grave by a vaft number of great perfons of all forts ; yet his funeral was no more grand than what fuited his private condition, except in the univerfal grief of the public. *Fulgentio* adds, that his coffin being open'd nine months after, he was found ftill entire, and his face frefh-colour'd.

When he was living he was thought very like his mother *Ifabella*, efpecially in the eyes, and face, which was of a fair complexion, with the moft humble and gentle countenance. His head, in the hinder part and upward, was round and well proportion'd, his forehead very large, and declining a little from the middle part toward the left temple,

There

There appear'd a great vein down the middle of
the forehead to the beginning of his nofe, which
was often full and empty, and when full it look'd as
big as a finger, but when empty it left a channel big
enough to lay the little finger in. His eye-brows
were well arch'd, his eyes large, quick, and black,
and he had an excellent fharp fight till he was fifty-
five. His nofe was large and long, but very ftraight.
He had a very thin beard, and in fome places his
chin was bald, but not in the leaft unfightly. His
face was rather flefhy than otherwife, his colour
pleafing, and when he was in health, it was white
and red, with a little yellownefs that did not mif-
become him; yet his afpect was altogether grave,
tho' pleafant. His lips, efpecially the nether one,
had a fmiling fweetnefs. His hands were fair and
long; and his fingers, which were alfo very long,
feem'd to turn backward. He was commonly extream cold in his hands and feet, for which he had
not found a better remedy than warm irons, which
he always carry'd wrapt up in balls. His head,
compar'd to his body, was very large, for he was
hardly any thing but skin and bones. He was a
ftranger to all the pleafures of the palate; and confidering with how little food he nourifh'd himfelf,
'twas a wonder how he liv'd.

His carriage, even when a youth, was a plain
earneft of his future deportment, when he .cor-
rected by virtue fuch of his natural inclinations as
were more imperfect, and raifed the better fort to
a great degree of perfection. He was, for the moft
part, retir'd, always thoughtful, but rather melancholy than ferious, and was of few words with
thofe of his own age, without caring even for the
moft moderate and healthful exercifes, which children are fo naturally fond of, infomuch that 'twas a

common faying among the novices, *We are all for.
trifles and pamphlets, but Frier* Paul *is for books.* He
was the fame all his life long, and he ufed to fay that
he could never underftand the delight of a gamefter,
except it were in gratifying his avarice.

While he was yet a youth, he was refpected by
all men for his modefty, piety, and all the other
virtues both chriftian and moral.   He never fwore
fo much as by his faith, fpoke no unhandfome word,
nor did an indecent action ; and fuch an influence
had his prefence over the behaviour of others, that
whenever the young *Servite* friers faw the Father approaching, they put on countenances as grave and
ferious as if he had been an officer of the black
rod ; fo that it became a proverb among the fraternity, whenever they faw the Father at hand, *E qua
fpofa, la mutiamo propoftio, i. e.* Here comes the bride,
let us call a new caufe.   Yet for all this he was fo
pleafing and humble to all men, that not one could
fay the Father ever gave him a harfh word, or an
angry look, except when they interrupted him in
the public bufinefs.

His abftinence was fo great, that he lived, for
moft part, upon bread and fruit, eating very little
flefh till he was paft fifty-five, complaining that it
made him fick, and fubject to great pains in the head.
Many days he drank not at all, and when he was
thirfty he us'd to go to the well and take but one
draught, which made him fo coftive, that he commonly ftaid three days, and fometimes a week, before he had a ftool, and when he had, it was painful
to him, becaufe he was always troubled with the
piles, attended with a *procidentia* of the *rectum*, and
an *hepatic* flux that continued to his old age.   In the
mean time he began to confult phyficians, tho' he
underftood phyfic fo well, that he chofe rather to

discourse

difcourfe them on their art, than to make ufe of their receipts. His friends however often advifed him to drink wine; but fo hard was it for him to alter his refolution, when he had form'd a judgment, that he could never be brought to tafte it, except it was at the communion, till after the 30th year of his age; nor then, without much ado to perfwade him; and in the 41 remaining years of his life, he would drink no wine but white, becaufe of its refemblance to the colour of water; and he faid before he dy'd, that one of the things he repented of, was that he had been perfwaded to drink wine. His fenfes were the moft acute and lively that any man had. His tafte was fo quick, that he difcern'd a relifh in things that to others were infipid, and nicely diftinguifh'd the feveral Ingredients of fuch as were compounded.

As for his natural affections none knew how to command themfelves better. As he would gratify his palate with no food which he thought hurtful, fo he did not fcruple the taking of any phyfic he thought would do him good.

He always reckon'd every day his laft, and faid that he never remember'd himfelf fo young that he could hope to fee another year; and, as is generally the temper of people who think they are not long liv'd, his acquaintance obferv'd that he never appear'd active or refolute, but cold and indifferent to all actions of importance, till the importunities of his friends, and the embroil'd ftate of his country, put him upon thofe glorious fervices which he afterwards performed, as counfellor of ftate to the moft ferene Republic.

Tho' (as has been faid) he was naturally ferious and melancholy, yet he was neither fevere nor morofe, but fo compaffionate, that he would do injury

to

to no body, nor permit another, if it was in his power to prevent it; and fo tender was he, even to the creatures appointed by God for the fupport of life, that in his latter days, except in the greateft neceffity, he would rather have fafted than kill'd any of them with his own hand, and feem'd to exprefs a compaffionate difpleafure at the mention of the many living creatures he had formerly anatomized. Tho' he had the ftricteft regard to juftice in his writings or converfation, yet he was more inclined to mercy than feverity.

The Father, to his dying day, would never have more than one garment at a time, nor any ornament nor moveables in his chamber, but a portable quadrant of CHRIST in the garden, a crucifix with a natural death's head at the foot, and three hourglaffes. He never carry'd more money than what would fuffice for one day's expence. He had no books but thofe he was daily fupply'd with from his great friends, which he had fo treafured up in his memory, that no prince in the world had a library equal to it. He divided his time in this manner: After his private devotions, which he always began before fun-rifing, he fpent the morning in ftudy, till the hour of common fervice, on which he was a conftant attendant; and the afternoon he employed in operations of his own hand, tranfmutations, fublimations, and the like, or in bufinefs of the ftate, and converfation with men of letters.

Tho' he feemed to rely on divine providence as entirely as if he thought fecond caufes not to be regarded, yet he never omitted the proper means, where fuch fecond caufes were likely to produce their effects.

As to his infirmities of body, he try'd many remedies for the *Procidentia* of the *Rectum*; and when

he

he was about 55 years of age, he contrived an inſtrument with which he bore it up to the laſt day of
his life, without being cumberſome to him, or giving the leaſt pain, as many others in the ſame caſe
experienced, to whom he imparted his invention;
for ſo friendly and generous was his natural temper,
that he was always ready to communicate to every
one according to their neceſſity. His hepatic flux
indeed was not cur'd till it had ſpent its courſe;
but the retention of his urine troubled him not after
fifty-five, till he was ſeventy years old.

Tho' ſeveral gentlemen and friers, whom he edu-
cated, were compleat maſters of the mathematics,
and of both natural and moral philoſophy; yet to
read lectures upon *Ariſtotle, Plato,* St. *Thomas, Scoto,*
or *Gratian,* was ſo contrary to his genius, that he
thought it a pedantic method, tending rather to ſupply perſons with ſophiſtical wit, than to increaſe
knowledge or improve the mind, and to make men
ſtiff in their opinions, than ſincerely inquiſitive after
the truth.

The Father was of ſo very mild a diſpoſition,
that whenever he was conſulted about any heinous
offences committed againſt the ſtate, he ſoften'd the
vindictive juſtice of the ſenators, as much as the
caſe would bear. In ſhort, he always ſtrove to incline them to acts of clemency, never omitting his
endeavours to reſtrain the violence of fiery ſpirits,
yet humbly ſubmitting all to the wiſdom and prudence of the government. And even in his own, as
well as other writings deſign'd for the preſs, he was
ſo careful to ſtrike out every thing which might be
offenſive, that defalcation took up more of his time
than addition. He was ſo far from revenge, as has
been already ſeen, that how unjuſt and intolerable
ſoever his wrongs were, the moſt he was heard to

say,

fay, by way of refentment, was, without altering
the ferenity of his countenance, *Videat Dominus & re-
quirat* ; and he would even extenuate the injuries
done him as much as poffible, by faying that thofe
who did them knew no better, or were oblig'd to it
by intereft.

He was fo generous by nature, that when he was
at the loweft ebb of fortune he never deny'd his
friends what was in his power to grant them.   But
tho' the Republic allow'd him a handfome falary
from the firft time he enter'd into their fervice, he
made no more ufe of it than was confiftent with the
povery of his order.   Neverthelefs, after he had
been way-laid and ftabb'd by the aflaffins, he found
it neceffary, for his own defence, to accept of the
whole provifion made for him by the public, that
he might be able to exercife fuch acts of benevolence
and liberality to the convent, as might intereft them
in his prefervation.   For this end he took two friers
into his fervice, one to look after him, and the other
to write for him.   To Frier *Marco,* who was his
writer, he gave 600 ducats as a prefent, befides 50
per annum ; and to the other, who was Frier *Mar-
nio,* he gave 300 in bank to put forth 10 *per cent.* becaufe he might have fubfiftence, and 40 *per annum*
afterwards.   He alfo thought it convenient to be liberal to thofe who manag'd the bread and wine, and
to fome cooks he gave no lefs than 60 ducats in one
year.   He was alfo very liberal to the convent upon
other occafions, infomuch that to one man alone,
who only defir'd to *borrow* fo much, he *gave* above
2000 ducats ; for his manner of lending was always
with this generous condition, that except he demanded it, the debtor fhould never offer to repay
him.   And here we cannot but admire the happy
choice of his motto, which we find round his effigies ;

gies; for it was his common saying, *Imitiamo Dio e la natura,* i. e. let us imitate God and nature; since whatever they give they never expect again; and let us avoid the vulgar error of those, who think that to lend is to lose, or else put a friend to the blush, by requiring security.

The Father was so far proof against the attacks of ambition and vain glory, that, besides the many instances given of it in the course of his life, this was his constant advice, *Si spiritus dominantis super te ascenderit, locum tuum ne deseras,* i. e. if the spirit of bearing rule strive to get the mastery over thee, be sure to stand thy ground. And he used to say moreover, that he who walks upon stilts, or sits in a high place, does not lessen his labour, but goes in greater danger

He was so modest, that he let his friends have the honour of publishing many of his ingenious discoveries and compositions, and never set his name to what he printed himself. In short, he was so little fond of perpetuating his memory, by any means whatsoever, that he would not so much as sit for his picture; so that tho' many effigies of him go abroad for originals, yet they are all but copies of one said to be in the gallery of a great king, which was taken by stratagem, for he would not give his consent, tho' he was courted to it by kings and great princes; and especially by the most illustrious and excellent senator lord *Dominico Molini,* his very good friend, and one whom the Father highly valu'd for his exquisite knowledge of ancient and modern history, and of the state of all the princes and governments in *Europe.* This noble senator had provided an eminent painter to take the Father's picture, and promised he should not sit at it above an hour, but could not obtain leave, tho' he got his confident

Fulgentio

Fulgentio to fecond his requeft; infomuch that being flatly deny'd, after he had kept the painter a fortnight in expectation, he was fo much out of humor with the Father, that they did not fpeak to each other for fome months after, tho' there paffed very few days in feventeen years before, in which they did not fpend fome hours together.

His learning had render'd him fo famous in all parts of *Europe*, that all perfons of quality who came to *Venice* were fond not only to fee him, but, as is the cuftom in thofe parts, to enter in their books his remarkable fayings. He had letters from the famous *Gillot, del Ifle, Lefchaffier, Salmafio, Richer, Bouiel, Cafaubon, Thuanus*, and other learned men in *France.* He had alfo the honour of letters from many princes, and of vifits from their fons; and there was one great prince in particular, who fending his fon into *Italy*, charg'd him to vifit *Orbis terrarum ocellum*, meaning the Father. And when the *Dutch* embaffador *Arfens* faw the Father crofs the anti-chamber, as he was waiting for the fenate's anfwer to his commiffion, he faid to one of the fenators in his company, that having now feen the moft eminent man in the world, he could not think much of the fatigue and expence of his journey, tho' the *Venetians* fhould not grant his demands. *Fulgentio* adds moreover, that two crown'd heads invited him, by their embaffadors, to enter into their fervice; but the Father, with terms of the greateft acknowledgment, defir'd to be excus'd from quitting the fervice of the government under which he was born.

In 1622, the year before the Father dy'd, the Prince of *Conde* coming to *Venice*, defir'd by all means to difcourfe Father *Paul*, who not caring to be feen by him, the Prince fo befieged him in his monaftery, that the Father often fhut himfelf up in

his

his cell without his dinner. The Prince, who knew he was within all the while, complain'd, with some uneasiness, that it was harder to get a sight of Father *Paul* than of the Pope himself. But a *Venetian* gentleman who accompany'd the Prince, giving him to understand, that the Father, as a counsellor of state to the Republic, could not answer to converse with foreign princes, or their ministers, without licence from the Senate, the Prince not only got a permission, but a command for the Father to see him. The Father obey'd with reluctance, because he rightly suspected that the Prince wanted him to resolve not only his own questions, but those started by the curiosity of others. However, the Father prevail'd that their meeting might not be in the monastery, but in some public place, where others might be witnesses of the conversation, which was in substance as follows :

The Prince, who was a man of extraordinary sense and learning, wanted to know the Father's opinion of the protestants in *France*, whom he was pleas'd to represent as dangerous to the government. But the Father seeing him condemn the men, without touching on the least point of their doctrine, artfully diverted him, by putting him in mind of the wisdom and valour of the old Princes of *Conde*, his father and grandfather, of which the Prince quickly understood the meaning, and so that subject was wav'd.

Then the Prince ask'd his opinion about the difference of superiority between the Pope and Councils; but the Father got clear of this question also, by putting him in mind of the *Sorbonne*, and how much they were alter'd for the worse since the admittance of the Jesuits into *France*.

The

The Prince propos'd another queſtion; what he thought of the liberties of the *Gallican* Church? But the Father paſs'd it over in general terms, ſaying that the Parliaments of *France*, and the *Sorbonne* itſelf, had maintain'd theſe liberties as the natural rights of all Churches, and that they have been better defended in *France* from uſurpations than any where elſe.

The Prince put a fourth queſtion to the Father; about the lawfulneſs of being aſſiſted in war by thoſe who differ from us in religion: To which the Father ſaid no more, than that Pópe *Julius* II made uſe of the *Turks* at *Bologna*, and *Paul* IV of the *Griſons* at *Rome*, calling them angels ſent from God to defend him, at the ſame time that he thought them heretics. They diſcourſed largely of the ex-communication of Princes, and particularly whe-ther Princes, tho' excommunicate, have not the ſame right as ever, by the laws of God and nature, to the allegiance and obedience of their ſubjects; or whether they ought tamely to ſit ſtill, and leave not only their crowns and ſcepters, but their lives, to the mercy of unnatural rebels and ſeditious incen-diaries. The Father's opinion upon this ſubject is learnedly and fully ſhewn in the enſuing treatiſe.

The Prince alſo ask'd him who wrote the *Hiſtory of the Council of* Trent. To which the Father anſwer'd, that it was ſtrange his highneſs did not know, after he had reported to the *Venetian* embaſſador, at the *French* court, that the author of it was Frier *Paul!* And the Father only thought fit to add, that it was very well known at *Rome*.

The diſpute betwixt the Republic of *Venice* and the Court of *Rome*, which was purely temporal, about juriſdiction, *Fulgentio* obſerves, was, by the advocates of the *Romiſh* See, artfully ſuggeſted to be altogether ſpiritual and religious; and he adds,

that

that they affirm'd, both from the pulpit and the prefs, that thofe brave Senators, who maintain'd the caufe of the Republic, had a defign to make *Venice* a proteftant ftate. He fays further, that they particularly inveigh'd againft Father *Paul*, as one who had not only ftirr'd up the proteftants to publifh books againft the Church of *Rome*, but had infinuated to the noble *Venetians*, that there was a neceffity of altering their religion, or the Popes would enflave all *Italy*. " But if ever there was a
" falfhood in the world, fays *Fulgentio*, this was
" one ; for tho' the Father had as much charity as
" any man for chriftians of differing opinions, he
" always taught and inculcated, that every chrif-
" tian, and much more princes, ought, for the fake
" of confcience and good government, to endeavour
" the prefervation of the *Roman* catholic religion :
" That God had conftituted princes as his lieute-
" nants, in all chriftian ftates, to be its protectors
" and nurfing fathers : That they were bound to
" blefs God continually, for placing them in the ca-
" tholic and apoftolic Church of *Rome* ; and that to
" abandon it would be the worft misfortune that
" could befall them : That whatever might be the
" abufes in the *Romifh* Church, they were only to be
" imputed to the members of it ; that therefore no
" man ought to be wavering in that faith, and that
" the catholic princes efpecially fhould not fuffer an
" alteration of the religion fo much as to be men-
" tion'd. He attributed the great diverfity of reli-
" gious orders and fects to the grofs neglect of
" princes, who, for their own intereft or grandeur,
" fuffered defigning men to impofe continually on
" the people, under colour of devotion, without
" confidering that every innovation gains fome
" credit among the vulgar, who are always fondeft
e " of

" of fuperftition ; that religion is moulded by it to
" fuch form as fhall beft anfwer the ends of thofe
" who manage it ; and that time and cuftom tranf-
" mit it to pofterity with the ftamp of authority."
Here *Fulgentio* touches on the Father's opinion of
Popes, Canons, and the rights of Princes; but thefe
articles are fo fully treated of, under particular
chapters, in the enfuing difcourfe, that 'tis needlefs to mention them in this place.

Fulgentio tells us, that for all this the court óf
Rome proceeded fo far, as to brand the Father for a
man of no religion. But is it poffible, fays he, that
fo fpotlefs a life as the Father led fhould be chargeable with atheifm and impiety, or that any argument fhould be drawn for fo monftrous an accufation
from the Father's great learning, confidering that the
holy fcriptures impute atheifm to ignorance, and
the uncontroll'd affections of the mind!

At the fame time that *Fulgentio* celebrates the
Father for his great piety and devotion, he defies
any man to tax him with favouring fuperftition,
either in his words or actions.

He takes particular notice, that when the Father
was advanced in years, he not only converfed with
the fenators of his own age, but with the young
nobility, to whom he was a treafury of records and
hiftory.   One of them, Signior *Marco Ernifano*, was
fo dear to him, that notwithftanding the Father's
great and important employments, he had accefs to
him whenever he came ; and if the Father was very
bufy, he always took the liberty to defire him to
retire, and he comply'd without taking it amifs.
Father *Paul* blefs'd God that he had met with one
man that fpoke to him without a mask, for Sign or
Marco let him fully into the characters of all perfons,
and the ftate of all affairs at *Venice* ; and, when the
                                              Father

Father was in his declining age, modeſtly rallied him for perſuing his ſtudies with more intenſeneſs than was ſuitable to his years.

Father *Paul* was ſo ſubjeɔ to fevers, that every little accident threw him into long and violent ones, in which he obſerv'd a regimen very different from the common praɔice; for he would not alter his ordinary diet, nor keep his bed, but roſe to read, write, ſtudy, and perform all his uſual funɔions; ſo that no body could tell when he was ſick, but by his aſpeɔ. If a raging fit came upon him in the day-time, he would lay himſelf along in his cloaths upon a cheſt or a table, but ſeldom in his bed. He appointed his own hours for eating; and when he took phyſic it was of his own preſcription, not com- pounded, but ſimple, as caſſia, manna, or the like. He publickly declared it as his opinion, that the common praɔice of phyſicians in preſcribing, and of patients in taking ſo many purgations and other recipes, only ſerv'd to protraɔ recoveries; and that to confine people, eſpecially thoſe in years, to their beds, and make them ſo ſuddenly abandon their uſual diet and exerciſes, naturally tended to weaken them. This was the Father's conſtant method of governing himſelf, till he was ſixty-one years of age, when he was ſeiz'd with a violent fever, that held him eighteen days together, in the hot month of *July*, during which he had no appetite for either meat or drink, but loath'd all that came near him; ſo that he was forc'd to take the advice of doɔors, which *Fulgentio* ſays was the firſt time that he knew him reſign himſelf to phyſicians. The public having appointed them to attend him, he had many viſits from them, but often complain'd of his being oblig'd to alter his uſual method, and to take others opinions of himſelf before his own. The phy-

ſicians,

ficians, and particularly his old friend *Santorio*, told him he was a dying man; but the Father rightly guefs'd he fhould not die that bout, and rallied his friend *Fulgentio* for being fo much concern'd at what *Santorio* had faid. *Santorio* going afterwards to fee him, and feel his pulfe, the Father ask'd him why he would go to flatter him, after he had already declar'd him a dead man; and when *Santorio* prefcrib'd afles milk againft his drinefs, he merrily thank'd him for his advice, faying, that he thought a man of above fixty years of age, as he then was, too old to be a fofter-brother to the young afs of whofe milk he prefcrib'd him a part. *Fulgentio* adds, that he was thus merry and facetious in all his ficknefles; and that tho' he was above fixty, before he fubmitted himfelf to phyficians, yet in the latter years of his life he chofe to truft to the skill of thofe of the faculty, rather than to his own.

The Father was not a little to be admir'd for fuch a happy union of virtues, as are rarely to be met with in one and the fame perfon. For both in his converfation and writings he was learned and humble, and wife and courteous. Tho' retir'd, he was active; ferious, and pleafant; fharp, but inoffenfive; his ftyle being both concife and plain, fweet and manly. *Fulgentio*, who faw the notes he left behind him upon humane nature, thinks that no philofopher ever div'd fo far into that knowledge as he did. He ufed, neverthelefs, to blufh when he heard himfelf prais'd for any of his excellent parts, and he avoided a very polite learned gentleman of his acquaintance, for no other reafon but becaufe he always faluted him with the title of *Illuftriffimo Padre*; and he defir'd *Fulgentio* to tell him how much he diflik'd fuch compliments; but the gentleman faid, to whom

whom then can that title be due, if not to that angel of heaven? and whenever he enquired after the Father's health, he ufed this or the like expreffion, how does that angel of paradife?

The Father, however, was not without his Foibles, being at firft, like moft other men of profound learning, fomewhat rigid, untractable, and hard to pleafe, as at length himfelf own'd, when told of it; but he fo combated thofe defects, that he intirely conquer'd them, and, as has been already fhewn, became no lefs affable, mild, and obfequious, than he was religious, wife, and learned. He was indeed to the laft as flow in his refolutions, as he was quick in his fpeculations; but this *Fulgentio* imputed to his extraordinary knowledge of hiftory, and to his affiduous obfervation of examples and events, which, fays he, naturally makes wife men cautious and diffident of their own notions and opinions.

Fulgentio, before he clofes his dear friend's illuftrious character, juftly obferves how impoffible it is, efpecially in ariftocracies, to find a body fo united for the good of the public, in which there are not fome who will hate, threaten, and perfecute thofe who thwart their interefts, affections, and defigns, be the oppofition ever fo juft and neceffary: And here he laments the unhappy fate of Father *Paul,* who, by his conftant poftponing all private views to the public honour and juftice, gain'd the ill-will of feveral great families in the fenate, which fome of them could not diffemble even while he was living. But his death was fo lamented by others of the chief fenators, that when they vifited his cell, which very many did upon that occafion, they were pleas'd to obferve the religious

e 3 poverty

poverty of it, and faid it was a paradife where a good angel dwelt.*

Fulgentio was one of the firft that went about to honour the Father's memory by fome monument, and would very probably have done it, if the convent of *Servi* had not hinder'd him, by refolving to make it a public act. But the Senate of *Venice* decided the difpute, by decreeing that there fhould be a monument and an infcription, at the charge of the State, which, fays *Fulgentio*, is like to be the more magnificent and durable, becaufe as yet there is nothing done in it. † But tho' he has been now dead very near a century, yet he ftill lives, and ever will live, in his own and the works of other great men of all nations, who were his contemporaries and admirers, with whofe character of him we fhall conclude his life, after giving the following catalogue of the learned and ufeful tracts he left behind him, calculated not only for the fervice of the *Venetians*, but for the whole republic of learning, and the common caufe of chriftianity throughout

---

* *Morery*, in his *Hiftorical Dictionary*, fays, the people ufed to pray at the Father's grave, as fuppofing him a faint in heaven, till Pope *Urban* VIII. forbad it.

† The late Bifhop *Burnet*, who was at *Venice* in 1685, fays that he vifited the convent of *Servi*, and was furprized to find Father *Paul* not fo much efteemed there as elfewhere. But Mr. *Miffon*, who likewife vifited this convent in 1688, fays that he found the friers to have a great veneration for the Father's memory, and that they faid, though they knew not where his body lay, they did not doubt but God would difcover it in due time. Mr. *Miffon* adds, that he faw and took a draught of that dagger the Father fo juftly call'd *Stylum Romanum*, which, till 1709, when he heard it was remov'd, was to be feen at the foot of the crucifix, which is upon the Altar of St. *Magdalen*, near the tomb of *Thomas Lipomanus*, almoft over-againft that of the Doge *Andrew Vendramieno*.

out *Europe.* They are, befides many anonymous
pieces of feveral kinds,

1. *Hiftory of the Council of* Trent.*
2. *Treatife of the Eye.* Under the name of *Aquapendente.*
3. *Treatife of Excommunication.*
4. Another on the fame fubject, with his defence
of *Johannes Gerfon* againft cardinal *Bellarmin.*
5. *Confiderations upon the Cenfure.*
6. *Le Confirmationi,* being a defence of the confiderations, under the name of *Fulgentio,* againft frier
Bovio.
7. *Supplement to the hiftory of the* Ufcoques.
8. *De jure afylou Petri Sarpi Juris* (the name he was
known by abroad.)
9. *Treatife of the Inquifition at* Venice.
10. *Hiftory of the* Venetians *during the Interdict.*
    The two laft tranflated into *Latin* by Dr.
    Bedell, afterwards bifhop of *Kilmore.*
    The latter was printed in 1626 by the
    Bucks at *Cambridge.* It was alfo tranf-
          e 4   lated

---

* The *Venetians* defiring Father *Paul* to write an anfwer to
a book that was publifhed during the quarrel with *Rome,* intitled *Scrutinio del la Liberta Veneta,* or an inquiry into the
Venetian liberties ; the Father told them he had an anfwer
ready, and delivered them the hiftory of this Council, which
he defign'd to have intitled *Concilia Tridentina Evifcerata* ; but
being apprifed of the danger of it by his friends, he alter'd
his mind. It came firft into the world by the means of
Mark Antbony de Dominis archbifhop of *Spaleto,* who being
exafperated by the court of *Rome,* got it printed at *London*
in 1619. *Bedell,* who tranflated part of it, fays it was divided
into eight tomes. We find it was tranflated twice into *French,*
once by *Deodati,* and another time by M. *Amelot de la Houfay,*
but both thofe tranflations are reckon'd faulty. There is an
abridgment of this hiftory done by M. *Jurieu.*

lated into *English* the fame year by Dr.
Potter, and printed by *Bill* the King's
Printer.

11. *Rights of Sovereigns*, &c. firft printed in *Italian*
and *French* in *Holland*, in 1721.

12. *Hiftory of the* Valteline.

13. *Maxims of the Government of* Venice.

14. *Tract of matters beneficiary.*

15. •Two others upon the *Dominion of the* Adriatic Sea.

Out of the many great teftimonies that might be
collected, we have made choice of thefe that follow,
which not only fupport the mighty character *Fulgentio* has given the Father, but contain fome particulars which he feems to have been unacquainted
with.

I. *Mark Anthony de Dominis*, ARCHBISHOP OF
SPALATO, *who deferting the Church of* Rome *came
over to* England, *and was by King* James I. *made Dean
of* Windfor.] This was the Perfon, who, as was
before obferv'd, had the chief hand in publifhing
the firft edition of the Father's *Hiftory of the Council
of* Trent; and he infcrib'd it to his majefty, with
the following eulogium on its great author, the fame
which Mr. *Bedell* quotes in his dedication of the
Father's *Treatife of the Interdict* to King *Charles* I.

" He was a man of great learning, judgment,
" and integrity, and of a moft even difpofition;
" one who moft fincerely endeavour'd to compofe
" ecclefiaftical difcord, and who, notwithftanding
" the difadvantages of a cramp'd education, made
" it manifeft that he fram'd his life by the rule of
" a good confcience, and not by the prejudices of
" the world around him. He heard with uneafi-
" nefs any indecent reflections on the Church of
" *Rome*, and yet he fhow'd an earneft diffent from
" thofe

" thofe who regarded its abufes and corruptions
" as facred inftitutions. He was moreover a fteady
" adherent to, and conftant follower of the truth,
" and thought it his duty to receive and embrace
" it wherever he found it.

II. Sir HENRY WOTTON, whom King *James* I.
fent three times embaffador to the ftate of *Venice.*]
This Gentleman having been well acquainted with
the Father, and lived hard by his monaftery, gave a
very good account of him to his friends here, which
is tranfmitted to us in his remains, called *Relliquiæ*
Wottonianæ, printed by Meffieurs *Tooke* and *Sawbridge*
in 1685. The firft thing we fhall take notice of, is
a letter which Sir *Henry* fent to King *Charles* I. in
1627, recommending *William Bedell,* who had been
his firft chaplain at *Venice,* to the vacant poft of provoft of the college of *Dublin,* which he accordingly obtain'd and enjoy'd, till he was advanc'd to the
bifhoprick of *Kilmore.* Sir *Henry* thought he could
not give his favorite a greater encomium, than to
let his Majefty know how much he was efteem'd by
the great Father *Paul.* Therefore, fays he, " this
" is the man whom *Padre Paolo* took, I may fay,
" into his very foul, with whom he communicated
" the inwardeft thoughts of his heart, and from
" whom he profeffed to have receiv'd more know-
" ledge in all divinity, both fcholaftical and pofi-
" tive, than from any that he had ever practifed in
" his days; of which all the paffages were well
" known to the king your father, *&c.*

The fecond is a letter dated *January* 17, 1637.
which Sir *Henry* fent, with the Father's picture inclofed, to the provoft and regius profeffor of divinity in *Cambridge.* In it are thefe words:
" I make bold to fend you, for a new year's gift,
" a certain memorial, not altogether unworthy of
" fome

" fome entertainment under your roof; namely, a
" true picture of *Padre Paolo* the *Servita*, which was
" firft taken by a painter whom I fent unto him
" from my houfe then neighbouring his monaftery.
" I have newly added thereunto a title of mine own
" conception, *Concilii Tridentini Evifcerator* ; and had
" fent the frame withal, if it were portable, which
" is but of plain deal, colour'd black like the habit
" of his order. You have a luminous parlour — In
" that room I befeech you to allow it a favourable
" place for my fake: And if any fhall ask, as in the
" table of *Cebes*, τινός έςι τὸ δ ἄγαλμα, I am defirous
" to characterize a little unto you fuch part of his
" nature, cuftoms, and abilities, as I had occafion
" to know by fight or by inquiry.
" He was one of the humbleft things that could
" be feen within the bound of humanity ; the very
" pattern of that precept, *Quanto doctior tanto fub-
" miffior*, and enough alone to demonftrate, that
" knowledge well digefted *non inflat* : Excellent in
" pofitive, excellent in fcholaftical and polemical
" divinity : A rare mathematician, even in the moft
" abftrufe parts thereof, as in algebra and the
" theoriques ; and yet withal fo expert in the hifto-
" ry of plants, as if he had never perufed any book
" but nature. Laftly, a great canonift, which was
" the title of his ordinary fervice with the ftate:
" And certainly, in the time of the Pope's inter-
" dict, they had their principal light from him.
" When he was either reading or writing alone, his
" manner was to fit fenc'd with a caftle of paper
" about his chair, and over head ; for he was of
" our lord of St. *Alban's* opinion, *that all air is pre-
" datory*; and efpecially hurtful when the fpirits are
" moft employ'd. You will find a fcar in his face,
" that was from a *Roman* affaffinate, that would
" have

" have kill'd him as he was turned to a Wall near
" to his convent; and if there were not a greater
" providence about us, it might often have been eafily
" done, efpecially upon fuch a weak and wearyifh
" body. He was of a quiet and fettled temper,
" which made him prompt in his counfels and
" anfwers; and the fame in confultation which
" *Themiftocles* was in action, Ἀυτοσχεδιάζειν-ἱκανότατος,
" as will appear unto you in a paffage between him
" and the Prince of *Conde*. [*Here Sir* Henry *confirms*
" *the dialogue that* Fulgentio *relates between the Father*
" *and that Prince.*] Then he gives an account, that
" when the Archbifhop of *Spalato* above-mention'd
" return'd, upon fome difcontent, from *England* to
" *Rome*, where he renounc'd the Proteftant religion,
" cardinal *Ludovifio*, nephew to Pope *Gregory* XV,
" went to welcome him into the lap of the Church,
" and told him that the Pope expected he fhould re-
" cant fome books he had publifh'd whilft he ftood
" in revolt; but that as to *The Hiftory of the Council*
" *of* Trent, tho' the archbifhop had an epiftle be-
" fore the original edition, the Pope would not prefs
" him to difown it; *Becaufe*, faid the cardinal, *we*
" *know well enough that Frier* Paul *is the author of that*
" *brat*. But Sir *Henry* fays, that, to his knowledge,
" no fuch recantation was ever printed, whether be-
" caufe he dy'd foon after, or whether the court of
" *Rome* thought, upon farther confideration, that
" things extorted with fear carry no credit, even
" by the Prætor's edict. Neverthelefs, other hifto-
" ries of that time tell us that he dy'd in prifon,
" and that after his death his corpfe and writings
" were burnt for herefy in *Flora's-field*. Sir *Henry*
concludes his remarkable letter as follows. " Thus
" —I have taken pleafure to remember that man
" whom God appointed and furnifh'd for a proper
" inftru-

" inftrument to anatomife that pack of reverend
" cheaters, among whom (I fpeak of the greater
" part, *exceptis fanioribus*) religion was fhuffled like a
" pair of cards, and the dice fo many years were
" fet upon us.

Dr. *Ifaac Walton*, who wrote Sir *Henry's* life, takes
notice, " That the conteft betwixt the Pope and
" the Republic was the occafion of Father *Paul's*
" knowledge of and intereft with King *James*; and
" that for his fake he compiled *The Hiftory of the*
" *Council of* Trent, which, as faft as it was written,
" was fent in feveral fheets in letters, by Sir *Henry*
" *Wotton*, Mr. *Bedell, &c.* to King *James* and the
" Archbifhop of *Canterbury*, and publifhed here both
" in *Englifh* and *Latin*." The Doctor remarks farther,
" That the report of the *Venetians* being inclined to
" turn proteftant, obtained the more credit, be-
" caufe Sir *Henry Wotton* was often in conference
" with the Senate, and his chaplain *Bedell* more
often with Father *Paul*.

III. Sir I s a a c W a k e, *who was King* James's *Minifter at the Court of the Duke of* Savoy.] In the
Cabala, which was printed at *London* in 1654, there
is a letter from Sir *Ifaac*, dated from *Turin* in *October*
1619, and directed to the then fecretary of ftate;
in which he has thefe very words: " Signior *Donato*,
" who was the *Venetian* embaffador, hath not been
" wanting to ruin, as far as he could, *Padre Paolo*
" and *Fulgentio*, two perfons in *Venice* that have
" done his Majefty very long and faithful Service,
" as by an inclofed paper your honour may fee,
" which is an abftract of a letter written from *Ful-
" gentio*. N. B. *We don't find this abftract in the*
Collection.

IV. *Dr.*

IV. *Dr.* BURNET, *the late bishop of* Sarum.] In his Life of Dr *William Bedell,* bishop of *Kilmore,* he gives this Character of Father *Paul.*

" He was equally eminent for vast learning and
" most confummate prudence, and was at once one
" of the greateft divines and of the wifeft men of his
" age. But to commend the celebrated hiftorian of
" the Council of *Trent,* is a thing fo needlefs that I
" may well ftop. Yet it muft needs raife the cha-
" racter of *Bedell* much, that an *Italian,* who befides
" the caution that is natural to the country, and
" the prudence that obliged one in his circumftances
" to a more than ordinary diftruft of all the world,
" was tied up by the ftrictnefs of that government
" to a very great refervednefs with all people, yet
" took *Bedell* into his very foul, *&c. repeating Sir*
Henry Wotton's *character of him in his aforefaid
letter recommendatory to King* Charles.

The bifhop fays, " That the Father affifted
" *Bedell* in acquiring the *Italian* Tongue, in which
" he became a perfect mafter ; and that in requital
" he drew a Grammar of the *Englifh* tongue for
" the Father's ufe; and he alfo tranflated the
" *Englifh* Common-Prayer Book into *Italian,* which
" Father *Paul,* and the feven divines, who, during
" the interdict, were commanded by the fenate
" both to preach and write againft the Pope's au-
" thority, liked fo well, that they refolved to have
" made it their pattern, in cafe the difference be-
" tween the Pope and them had produced the effect
" which they hoped and long'd for. The intimacy
" between them grew fo great and fo public, that
" when Father *Paul* was wounded by thofe affaffins
" that were fet on by the court of *Rome* to deftroy
" fo redoubted an enemy, upon the failing of which
" attempt a guard was fet on him by the fenate,
" that

" that knew how to value and preferve fo great a
" treafure, and much precaution was ufed before
" any were admitted to come to him, *Bedell* was ex-
" cepted out of their rules, and had free accefs to
" him at all times. They had many and long dif-
" courfes concerning religion. He found Father *Paul*
" had read over the *Greek* New Teftament with fo
" much exactnefs, that (as *Fulgentio* tells us in his
" life) *he had mark'd every word of it :* And when
" *Bedell* fuggefted to him critical explications of
" fome paflages which he had not underftood be-
" fore, he received them with tranfports of one
" that leap'd for joy, and that valu'd the difcove-
" ries of divine truth beyond all other things.

The bifhop takes notice of a book printed by
Thomas Maria Caraffa a Jefuit, containing feveral
hundred thefes of philofophy and divinity, and by
him dedicated to the Pope, with fuch an impudent
and extravagant infcription, as no true chriftians
could read without aftonifhment, it being infcribed
To P A U L V. *the* · V I C E - G O D, *the moft invincible
Monarch of the Chriftian Commonwealth, and the moft
zealous Afferter of the Papal Omnipotency.* But the Bifhop fays, " That *Bedell* obferving the numeral let-
" ters of the firft words, *Paulo* V. V I C E - D E O,
" being put together, made exactly *666,* the number
" of the beaft in the *Revelations,* he communica-
" ted this to Father *Paul* and the feven divines,
" who carry'd it to the Doge and Senate ; and that
" it was entertained almoft as if it had come from
" heaven ; and it was publickly preached in all
" their territories, that here was a certain evidence
" that the Pope was Anti-chrift.

The Bifhop obferves, " That at laft the breach
" between the Pope and the Republic was brought
" fo near a crifis, that it was expected a total fe-
" paration,

" paration, not only from the Court, but the
" Church of *Rome,* was like to follow upon it ; and
" that it was forwarded by Father *Paul* and the
" seven divines with so much zeal, as well as pru-
" dence, that Father *Paul* and the seven divines
" pressed Mr. *Bedell* to move the embassador, who
" was his patron Sir *Henry Wotton,* to present King
" *James*'s premonition to all Christian Princes and
" states, which was then put in *Latin,* to the Se-
" nate, and that they were confident it would pro-
" duce a great effect ; but the embassador could not
" be prevailed on to do it, tho' Father *Paul,* with
" the seven divines, and many others, were weary
" of the corruptions of their worship, and groaning
" for a reformation. But when the reconciliation
" with *Rome* was concluded, Father *Paul* was out
" of all hopes of ever bringing things back to so
" promising a conjuncture ; upon which he wished
" he could have left *Venice,* and come over to *Eng-*
" *land* with Mr. *Bedell*; but he was so esteem'd by
" the Senate for his great wisdom, that he was con-
" sulted by them as an oracle, and trusted with
" their most important secrets; so that he saw it
" was impossible for him to obtain his conge ; and
" therefore he made a shift to comply, as far as
" he could, with the established way of their wor-
" ship; but he had in many things particular me-
" thods, by which he rather quieted than satisfied
" his conscience. In saying of mass he passed over
" many parts of the canon ; and in particular those
" prayers in which that sacrifice was offered up to
" the honour of saints. He never pray'd to saints,
" nor joyn'd in those parts of the offices that went
" against his conscience ; and as in private confes-
" sions and discourses he took people off from those
" abuses, and gave them right notions of the puri-
" ty

" ty of the chriftian religion; fo he hoped he
" was fowing feeds that might be fruitful in an-
" other age; and thus he believed he might live
" innocent in a Church that he thought defiled.
" And when one preffed him hard in this matter,
" and objected that he ftill held communion with
" an idolatrous Church, and gave it credit by ad-
" hering outwardly to it, by which means others,
" who depended much on his example, would be
" likewife encourag'd to continue in it; all the
" anfwer he made was, that God had not given
" him the fpirit: of *Luther.* He expreffed great
. " tendernefs and concern for *Bedell* when he par-
" ted with him; and faid that both he and many
" others would have gone over with him, if
" it had been in their power; but that he might
" never be forgot by him, he gave him his picture,
" with a *Hebrew* Bible without points, and a little
" *Hebrew* Pfalter, in which he wrote fome fentences
" expreffing his efteem and friendfhip for him; and
" with thefe he gave him the invaluable manufcript
" of *The Hiftory of the Council of* Trent, together with
" the Hiftories of the *Interdict* and the *Inquifition;* be-
" fides other papers of great importance, which
" were afterwards loft; for in Mr. *Bedell's* letter to
" Dr. *Ward,* he mentions a collection of letters that
" were fent him weekly from *Rome,* during the con-
" tefts between the Jefuits and Dominicans, concer-
" ning the efficacy of grace, of which Father *Paul*
" fent him the originals, but would not allow him
" to print them.

V. *M.* J U R I E U, *the famous* French *divine, who
abridg'd Father* Paul's Hiftory of the Council of
*Trent; and wrote, befides other folid difcourfes, thofe called
the* Paftoral Letters.] In his twenty-firft letter he fays,
" The Father knew the corruption of the *Roman*
" Church,

" Church, at leaſt, as well as *Luther*, made no ſe-
" cret of it, and no eminent proteſtant paſſed by
" *Venice* to whom he did not diſcover himſelf con-
" cerning it. They often repreſented to him, how
" obliged he was in conſcience to break with a
" Church, the impurity and idolatry whereof he
" ſo well underſtood; but he had a thouſand rea-
" ſons to offer in his own behalf, ſaying ſometimes
" that he ſeparated the good from the bad, ſome-
" times that he was of uſe to a thouſand perſons
" who lay hid, and had good ſentiments. And at
" laſt, when preſſed hard, he would own that God
" had not given to him the heart and ſpirit of *Lu-*
" *ther*. Upon the whole, ſays M. *Jurieu*, 'tis cer-
" tain that if Father *Paul* had been of the temper
" and ſpirit of *Luther*, *Venice* had been at this day
" what *Geneva* is; and if *Luther*, *Zuinglius*, and
" *Calvin*, had been of the temper and ſpirit of Fa-
" ther *Paul*, all *Europe* had been yet what *Venice* is
" to this day.

VI. Sir THOMAS POPE BLOUNT *Bart.* in his
Cenſura celebriorum Authorum, quotes ſome authorities to prove that Father *Paul* was the firſt that diſcovered the circulation of the blood; but this being a matter too important to be taken intirely upon the credit of thoſe authorities, and Father *Paul*
wanting not the acceſſion of any honour that does
not really belong to him, an *Engliſh* chirurgeon has
been conſulted upon this ſubject, who is celebrated
for one of the moſt accurate, and indefatigable
inquirers of this age into ancient and modern
hiſtory, eſpecially that of phyſic and chirurgery,
and who was not long ago, for his ſervices to the
faculty in that reſpect, admitted a fellow of the
royal ſociety. The Perſon here meant is Mr. *William*

Beckett,

Beckett, who has juſt publiſhed that curious diſſertation concerning the *Touching for the Cure of the King's
Evil,* in two letters to Dr. *Steigertahl* phyſician to
his Majeſty, and Sir *Hans Sloan* Bart.   This gentleman, whoſe opinion commands no ſmall deference,
ſeems to give the merit of the diſcovery of this
noble ſecret to our learned countryman Dr. *William
Harvey,* who was chief phyſician to King *James* and
King *Charles* I. and profeſſor of mathematics and
chirurgery in the *College of Phyſicians* in *London.*
However, we will firſt give Sir *Thomas Pope Blount's*
teſtimonies, together with *Fulgentio's* account of this
matter in favour of Father *Paul;* and then bring
Mr. *Beckett's* teſtimony in favour of Dr. *Harvey;* ſubmitting both to the judgment of the curious.   Sir
Thomas's teſtimonies are theſe.

   Johannes Leonicenus, who ſays, tome 1. of
Nouvelles de la Republique des Lettres, " That Father
" *Paul* diſcovered the circulation of the blood and
" the valves of the veins, but that he did not care
" to publiſh it for fear of bringing a ſtorm upon
" him, becauſe he was ſo much ſuſpected before,
" that his very ſtarting of this new hypotheſis was
" enough to have confirmed him for a heretic in
" countries of the inquiſition.   Therefore he di-
" vulged his ſecret to no body but *Aquapendente,*
" and the *Engliſh* embaſſador.   The former was ex-
" ceeding cautious how he reveal'd it, and ſtaid till
" the Father was dead before he put the book,
" which he had compos'd touching the valves of
" the veins, into the hands of the Republic of
" *Venice;* and foraſmuch as even the leaſt novelties
" make a mighty noiſe in that country, the book
" was conceal'd in the library of St. *Marks.* But
" *Leonicenus* obſerves, that as *Aquapendente* made no
" ſcruple however to reveal the ſecret to a very cu-
                                          " rious

" rious young gentleman, Mr. *Harvey,* who ftudied
" under him at *Padua;* and as Father *Paul* had al-
" fo imparted it to the *Englifh* embaffador, thofe
" two *Englifh* men returning home, and finding
" themfelves in a free country, publifhed the hypo-
" thefis, and having confirmed it by experiments,
" had all the honour of it.

Carolus Fracaffatus, in his prefatory epiftle to
Malpighius, fays that a certain *Italian* found out the
circulation of the blood before *Harvey;* and *John
Walæus,* in his epiftle to *Bartholinus* à phyfician of
eminence in *Sweden,* brings Father *Paul* upon the
ftage as the firft difcoverer of that noble fecret.

Dan. Geo. Morhof fays alfo, that the Father difcovered the circulation before *Harvey,* and takes notice that the *Englifh* were angry with *Bartholinus*
that he fhould go about to rob their doctor of the
glory of the invention. This *Morhof* adds that the
Father, whom he calls the *Phœnix of his Age,* wrote
to *Ifaac Cafaubon* in *England,* to make intereft for him
with the King, if the ill ftate of affairs fhould o-
blige him to leave *Venice.*

Fulgentio's account of this matter is as follows:
" The difcovery of the valves of the veins was
" firft ftarted by *Aquapendente* at a public anatomy;
" but there are ftill living many eminent and lear-
" ned phyficians, among whom are *Santorio* and
" *Peter Affelineau* a *Frenchman,* who know that it
" was no fpeculation or invention of *Aquapendente,*
" but of Father *Paul's;* who, confidering the gra-
" vity and weight of the blood, conceived a no-
" tion that it could not ftay in the veins, except
" there were fome bunch to hold it in, fome folds
" or fhuttings, at the opening and clofing of which
" there was given a paffage and neceffary *equilibrium*
" to life. And upon his own natural judgment he

" apply'd

" it; but on the contrary, his inquiries difcovered
" the certainty of *Harvey*'s demonftrations; and, as
" *Plempius* in his writings afterwards acknowledges,
" he was by this means refuted and exploded him-
" felf. When this would not do, *Walæus* trumps up
" the ftory of Father *Paul*; but not bringing any
" authority to juftify from whence he had it, and
" he being a declared enemy to *Harvey* and his doc-
" trine, any one may readily judge what credit is
" to be given to it. Another perfon, who attemp-
" ted to rob *Harvey* of the honour of this difcovery,
" was *Thomas Bartholine*, who pretends to affirm
" that *Veflingius* had communicated to him, as a
" fecret never to be reveal'd to any third perfon,
" that the circulation of the blood was the inven-
" tion of Father *Paul* the *Servite*, who had written
" a book of it, which was in the cuftody of *Fulgen-*
" *tio* at *Venice*. But to prove that this whifpered
" ftory was a mere forgery, we are to obferve, that
" this *Fulgentio*, who wrote the life of Father *Paul*,
" and who has taken care to attribute to him all
" the fubtile fpeculations and natural fecrets he
" was mafter of, fays not one word about his ha-
" ving difcovered the circulation of the blood, or
" that he had in his hands any fuch manufcript as
" *Bartholine* has talk'd of, the mention of which he
" would never have fuffer'd to have efcap'd him,
" feeing it would have added fo much to the glory
" of Father *Paul*, to whom he has done fo much
" honour. Befides this, it's very plain from *Ful-*
" *gentio*'s account of Father *Paul*'s difcovery of the
" valves in the veins, that he did not know the
" true ufe of them; and from his mentioning the
" flux and reflux of blood in the fame veffel, he
" was ftill much farther from having any juft idea
" of the blood's circulation. So that we fhall ftill
" find

" find that Dr. *Harvey* was the man, who, by the
help of an admirable fagacity, affifted by a vaft
" number of anatomical diffections, and an affidu-
" ous application to thefe affairs for many years to-
" gether, did at laft arrive at the invidious felicity
" of. this great difcovery.

'Tis confeffed, that the teftimonies we have quoted, relating to the circulation of the blood, would
have been fitteft for a treatife of anatomy; but we
hope that none will think it an unneceffary digreffion, fince thereby a fact is fettled, which has been
much controverted by fome foreigners, who envied
our learned countryman, Dr. *Harvey,* the honour of
fo noble a difcovery.

There is óne teftimony more from Sir *Thomas
Pope Blount,* relating to the Father's character in general, and with that we fhall conclude. It is that of
Johannes Baptifta Porta, a *Neapolitan,* who flourifhed
about the end of the 16th century. He fays, *lib* 7.
Magiæ naturalis : " We knew Father *Paul* at *Venice,*
" and, far from being afhamed, value ourfelves for
" what we learned from a man, than whom we
" have not yet feen one more learned or acute ; and
" who was, in fhort, not only the ornament and
" glory of *Venice* or *Italy,* but of the whole world.

Many other teftimonies of Father *Paul's* great
piety, wifdom, learning, and virtues, might be collected, if it were neceffary, from the writings of
King *James,* Bifhop *Cofin,* Bifhop *Barlow,* Dr. *Cra-
kenthorp, Ifaac Cafaubon, Jof. Scaliger, Hugo Grotius,
John Gerlard Viffius, Nich. Rigaltius, Edm. Richerius,
Dominicus Baudius,* and even Cardinal *Bellarmin* ; but
'tis hoped thefe already given will be thought fufficient.

Mr.

Mr. *Brown,* Rector of *Sandridge* in *Kent,* who tranſlated Father *Paul's Letters,* ſays, in his Preface, that King *James* had a reſpect for the Father, and would fain have had him over here, as he had *Iſaac Caſaubon,* and other eminent men. The reverend tranſlator promiſed the world alſo, many years ago, to give a new tranſlation of the Father's life, and to compare it with *Fulgentio's* manuſcript copy of it, which Sir *Roger Twiſden,* by means of his Brother, who was very intimate with the ſaid frier, procured from *Venice.* But as neither Mr. *Brown,* nor any body elſe, has yet printed any other *Engliſh* tranſlation of *Fulgentio,* beſides that obſcure one we mention'd in the Introduction, 'tis hoped that ours will meet with a favourable reception ; not only for its own ſake, but alſo for the noble teſtimonies we have added in favour of the Father's character, which will certainly be of much more weight than the malicious and ſcurrilous aſperſions caſt upon Father *Paul* by the Jeſuit *Maimbourg* in his *Hiſtory of Lutheraniſm,* or by Cardinal *Pallavicini* in his *Counter-hiſtory of the Council of* Trent.

THE
RIGHTS
OF
SOVEREIGNS.

OF the many infirmities to which mankind is liable, there are few more dangerous, or more difficult to be cured, than the diftempers of the mind. Phyfic abounds with fimples and remedies, either for correcting a peccant humor, or for renewing our whole conftitution; but the afflictions of the mind are not fo eafy to be remov'd; nay, not at all, but by the entire change of forrow into joy. External remedies fignify nothing to a troubled mind, and nothing is capable to expel the chagrin which frets it, but the voluntary furrender of the mind to comfort when 'tis offered. I myfelf,

most

moft illuftrious Noblemen, tho' convinced of
the indivifibility of the foul, by that unity of actions I have always obferved in my own, which
has hitherto profeffed the moft conftant refpect
and ftricteft fubmiffion to your Government,
do neverthelefs feel the effects of that forrow,
which I perceive in perfons who command, as
well as thofe who obey; for I will be bold to
fay it, I fee you all in fome fort of concern
at the pretended *Interdict* which 'tis imagin'd
you are now under. Indeed, upon fome occafions, you affect to feem wholly unconcern'd,
and to carry it off with an air of courage;
but is not this rather the language of your lips
than of your hearts? Really, for my own
part, when I confider the great piety of this
republic, I am not furpriz'd to fee the whole
body alarm'd, at the threats and curfings of
thofe who pretend to be the fole judges, guar-
dians, and defenders of the faith of *Jefus
Chrift*, who induftrioufly give out that princes
have nothing to do with fuch affairs, as at prefent concern us; and when told that *David*
was both a King and Pfalmift at one time, think
to ward off the objection, by faying, that was
purely owing to the divine grace, which made
him a man after God's own heart, and not in
the leaft to nature.

Be this as it will, I now propofe to examin
the matter to the bottom, to anatomize it, to
ftrip it of its artful difguife, and expofe it
naked to the whole world; for as *Seneca* faid
very

very juftly, *Take off but the mask of Death, and it lofes all its deformity.* I therefore perfwade myfelf, that not only thofe who difcover fo much fagacity and prudence at the helm of affairs, but even the common people will throw off all that filly fear, that panic fort of terror, and be convinced, that by depending on their own innocence, they will not fail both of comfort and encouragement, from the teftimony of a good confcience.

I muft own, however, that as much as I defire to comfort all ranks alike, yet I don't think it proper to publifh every thing that I have to fay on this head, becaufe the prince and the fubject cannot help thinking differently on affairs of this kind. God has eftablifh'd fuch a difference betwixt one foul and another, that tho' it be not effential to them, 'tis, neverthelefs, fo real, that it has been often a queftion, whether all men are of the fame fpecies. Knowledge, like wine, exhilarates great men, but intoxicates little ones, in proportion to the quantity they take of it. Nothing is fweeter and more tempting, than to excel others in knowledge, and nothing more difficult than to conceal or difguife fo noble a talent. For this reafon I could wifh that thefe few advices might be fet apart, as the prince's private treafury, for their fervice only who are at the head of affairs; your lordfhips can make a proper ufe and improvement of them, in due time and place; but the com-

mon

mon people, like a man who takes phyſic in
a fit of the ague, would weaken their conſti-
tution inſtead of mending it : If it be good
for the commonalty to be kept in ignorance
of ſtate affairs, 'tis abſolutely neceſſary they
ſhould be as ignorant of matters of faith ; becauſe hidden myſteries are always treated
with more regard than things that are familiar. 'Tis enough for the people to be able
to read their deſtiny in the countenance of
their prince ; and as the happineſs of the ſoul
conſiſts in the beatific viſion, ſo the vulgar
may pleaſe themſelves with obſerving the ſe-
renity of their Governors countenances, and
note from thence that the affairs of ſtate go
well, becauſe *tribulatio & anguſtia in omnem
animam operantis malum*; *i. e.* tribulation and
anguiſh are upon every ſoul that worketh evil.
A watch, tho' it contains ſeveral wheels, has
its various motions from but one ; I ſhall
therefore ſucceed in my deſign, if I reſtore
the ſovereign to himſelf, becauſe at the ſame
time I ſhall reſtore tranquility to my fellow
ſubjects, which is the greateſt ſervice I can poſſibly do for my country.

All chriſtians are oblig'd to obey the Pope
——States are nothing elſe but a mixture of
a great number of chriſtians——There is but
one weight in God's balance——The Church
is only a body compos'd of as many members
as there are perſons who have receiv'd baptiſm
——A perſon excommunicated is a rotten
member,

member, feparated from the body and unity of the Church, for fear it fhould corrupt the other found members——There is no other catholic Church by which there is an entrance to paradife, but St. *Peter's*.   The excommunicated perfon is like ufelefs lumber in a fhip, which is thrown over-board left it fhould fink the reft of the cargo.

All thefe thoughts are like fo many court maxims, true in one fenfe, but fome are fo rafh as to borrow arguments from them, for fcattering terror among the people ; and from hence proceeds that panic fright with which fo many poor fouls are terrify'd.   We will now oppofe them with certain propofitions, which, when fet in their natural light, and difengaged from all artful turns, may give great hints to thofe who would weigh this matter as it ought. Therefore let us examin,

1. Whether the Pope and the Church have a power to excommunicate?

2. What perfons are fubject to excommunication, and for what caufes fhould recourfe be had to it?

3. Whether an appeal may be lodg'd againft excommunication ?

4. Whether the Council or the Pope is fuperior ?

5. Whether a lawful prince may be deprived of his dominions by virtue of excommunication ?

6. Whether

6. Whether a perfon who difturbs what is call'd ecclefiaftical libeity juftly incurs excommunication ?

7. What that liberty is, and whether 'tis confined to the Church, or extended to all her people ?

8. Whether the poffeffion of temporalities, which belong to the Church,- is of divine right ?

9. Whether a free republic can be deprived of its dominions by virtue of excommunication ?

10. Whether a fecular prince has a lawful light to appropriate the tenths of the clergy, and an independent authority to ordain what is ufeful to the ftate, with refpect to ecclefiaftical perfons and eftates ?

11. Whether a fecular prince has, of himfelf, a right to judge ecclefiaftical criminals ?

12. Whether the Pope is infallible?

We will be fo complaifant to our adverfaries, as to allow them all we can in the examination of fo many nice points, and we will grant them even more than they defire, protefting that we only take up the pen for the fake of truth, and that we have no other view than to give peace to confciences, and even to theirs, who have fo much at heart the intereft of the court of *Rome,* if it be poffible for fuch to acquiefce with equity.   I fhall not here

here ufe any of thofe arguments which favour
of the monk, but exprefs myfelf in as general
and familiar terms as poffible, knowing that
the monfter ignorance is often conceal'd in the
labyrinth of hard words; fo that like a pi-
lot who is tofs'd about by contrary winds in
the ocean, without any other guide than the
compafs, whofe needle always points to the
north, I fhall render to every one his due,
and fhall only aim to bring back mens fouls to
the harbor of peace, which they have loft;
and if after all this, they exclaim againft me as
wicked, becaufe I tell the truth, I fhall fay of
my adverfaries, in my own defence, what is
faid of fome phyficians, that, for their own
intereft, they would have people rather fick
than well.

C H A P. I.

Whether the Pope and the Church have a power to excommunicate?

WE treat of this queftion, not becaufe
we doubt of it, but for the fake of
order and diftinction. Being under the power
of the gofpel, we think it our duty to obey
thofe who are jealous of the privilege *that* has
given them of commanding others: *Quodcun-
que ligaveris fuper terram, erit ligatum & in cœlis,*
i. e. " Whatfoever ye fhall bind on earth, fhall
" be bound alfo in heaven." 'Tis true, that

fome

some pretend this passage ought not to be understood of excommunication, which, say they, is not a bond, but the cutting off a member; yet the best catholic authors have generally explain'd that text in favour of excommunication; and this was also the opinion of the ancient Church, in those times when such as were promoted to ecclesiastical dignities had no patrimony but the glory of God, and very often the torments of martyrdom. In this sense too we heartily subscribe it. So that here is the legal authority of excommunication recognized, in the first place, in the Pope, and in all who shall be invested with the pontifical dignity, according to that maxim, *Quod Petro dicitur, omnibus dicitur, i. e.* What is said to *Peter*, is said to all. They derive this power from the gospel itself; and the other ecclesiastic judges, who are not Popes, derive it, as some say, from them, by a sort of delegation. But I shall not enter into an enquiry, whether the said authority is communicable, according to the good pleasure of men.

Let us now examin what excommunication is.

It must be own'd, in the first place, that excommunication is not sin, but the punishment of sin; consequently, excommunication takes place only when there is sin, and such sin moreover, as is committed after excommunication threatned. It may, perhaps, be inferred from hence, that the enormity of sin

must

muſt therefore be the cauſe of that threatning; but this is ſo far from being true, that 'tis univerſally allowed, that there is an infinite number of very enormous ſins, which are not ſubject to excommunication. And from hence it may be concluded, that excommunication depends on the pleaſure of the eccleſiaſtic judge, who fulminates it when and how he pleaſes.

Excommunication is an eccleſiaſtical puniſhment, by which the prelate ſeparates a perſon from the body of the Church, by depriving him of all the ſpiritual benefits, which the ſaid Church diſpenſes to believers; and this he does, left that rotten corrupt member ſhould infect the ſound members of the myſtical body. The benefits which the Church diſpenſes to believers are innumerable; for not to mention the infinite merits of *Jeſus Chriſt,* of the holy virgin and the ſaints, which cannot be deny'd, all the good works of ſurviving believers become the common ſtock of all the faithful, as brethren regenerated by baptiſm: Thus the riches of the greateſt ſaints go towards the relief of the vileſt ſinners, *Particeps ego ſum omnium timentium te & cuſtodientium mandata tua,* i. e. I am a partaker with all that fear thee and keep thy commandments. In like manner excommunication is an act derogatory from the contract made by a chriſtian at baptiſm, as to his part and portion of ſo many ſpiritual benefits; and 'tis the ſame with a perſon excommunicated, as it is with a ſon diſinherited

herited for having offended his father, and
who, on that account, is, in some sort, cut
off from the number of his brethren.

- Besides, there are two sorts of excommunication, the *major* and the *minor*. The *major*
excommunication is that which is fulminated
immediately against the criminal. The *minor*
excommunication, that under which a person
falls, for associating or conversing with a person already excommunicated. Custom has
established the terms *major* and *minor*; tho' I
think the meaning of them might be better ex-
pressed by the words *principal* and *accessary.*
In short, if we consider the fatal consequences
of both the *major* and *minor*, one can discern
no difference betwixt them, since those who
are punished with either the one or the other,
are alike deprived of the spiritual benefits of
the Church, and cut off from her body, with
this distinction only, that whoever suffers the
major excommunication, not only feels the
pain of it in his own person, but wherever he
is known, his very presence is enough to hinder the functions of other believers; insomuch
that if a person excommunicated enter pub-
licly into a Church, the divine offices must
be stopt and deferred, which is really more
than what is done at the approach of one
possessed with a devil. There is, moreover,
this difference, *viz.* that the former cannot be
absolved, if he does not first of all purge
away his contumacy, an obligation which the
latter

latter is not ty'd up to, becaufe he is not a criminal. In like manner the punifhment of excommunication is fuch, as renders the perfon unworthy to partake of the facraments; infomuch, that tho' he fhould be confeffed and abfolved by the prieft from his fins, the abfolution would fignify nothing, till he be alfo abfolved from the excommunication. Well may it therefore be faid, that the Church, by fulminating excommunication, ufes fuch feverity, that fhe feems to have forgot that chriftian compaffion which fhe commonly fhews at other times. Indeed, the Church prays for all finners, even for thofe that are out of her pale, as well *Jews* as *Pagans,* but never makes mention of excommunicated perfons in her prayers, as if fhe had quite fuppreffed all defires of their falvation, while they live under excommunication; and tho' fhe prays for heretics and fchifmatics, who have incurred excommunication, fhe does not pray for them as excommunicated perfons. Having firft eftablifhed the authority of excommunication, I thought fit to note all the preceding diftinctions, in order to fhew its real importance, which will lead us, in the next place, to find out who are the perfons on whom it may be inflicted, and for what reafons.

CHAP.

CHAP. II.

What perſons are liable to excommuni-
- cation, and what are the cauſes for
- which recourſe ſhould be had to it.

WHAT we have already mention'd,
may ſuffice to ſhew the nature and
quality of excommunication, which is ſo ſe-
vere, that if baptiſm did not imprint an indelible character in the ſoul, it were able to turn
a chriſtian into a very infidel ; for this puniſhment is ſo rigid, that there is no body of common ſenſe, tho' perfectly ignorant of the deciſions of theology and of canon law, but
would infer from it, that the crime, againſt
which recourſe is had to ſo terrible a ſentence,
muſt of neceſſity be enormous, deſperate, and
even remedileſs. We ſee that diſeaſes of the
body are treated quite otherwiſe, for if any
member of it happen to be gangreen'd, or ulce-
rated, firſt 'tis dreſſed, the putrifying humours
of it are expelled, then corroſives are applied ;
and if theſe don't do, recourſe is even had to
cauſtics ; but at laſt, when 'tis come to an extremity, and a cure is deſpair'd of, then, and
not till then, the inſtrument is brought to cut
it off, leſt the infection ſhould reach ſome
other part of the body. The member, indeed, thus cut off, is no more to be dreſs'd,
becauſe then it can never be cur'd ; but by
this

this means, the other members, which might have partaken of the infection, are happily preferved. From hence we conclude, that the effect of excommunication, is not only the fpiritual damnation of the perfon excommunicated, but the evident danger of expofing others to the fame punifhment, and rendring them unfortunate companions in the fame damnation.

It muft be confeffed, that were we, with a truly chriftian charity, to feek for a fin fo enormous, as to deferve fuch a punifhment, one fhould hardly find it, in the confcience even of *Judas*, confidered not only as having betray'd his mafter, but alfo as entertaining the heretical opinion that his wickednefs was greater than the power of *Chrift*. As to *Peter's* denying his lord, *Thomas's* incredulity, and the flight of the other apoftles, they not only repented, but found favour with *Jefus*. If we defcend to particulars, this heinous crime cannot be adultery, nor fornication, nor murder, nor theft, for all thefe fins, how great foever, find both pardon and abfolution. I will go yet farther, and fuppofe a man, who entertains erroneous opinions about the myfteries of religion, and believes what he lifts, without obedience either to the Gofpel, or the Church, or to the common precepts; fuch a man, were he even one of the moft obftinate heretics that ever liv'd, may not, for all this,

‡ be

be excommunicated, unless he discover his sentiments by some external signs; for if the ulcers of his soul do not break outwardly, he is not subject to excommunication. These are also the sentiments of the court of *Rome*.

Nevertheless, we hear every day, that one prelate has excommunicated a person who found something that was lost, because he did not carry it back to the loser; that another has excommunicated a person, who, when summoned before the spiritual-court to pay some rent, did not discharge it, tho' perhaps he was insolvent.

Let us now hear the opinion of the famous Council of *Trent*, which appear'd for the papal authority, like the *Ignis fatuus*, in the midst of a violent tempest, and which established several prerogatives by law, that were only derived from custom. This Council, in one of its canons, recommends the great circumspection that ought to be observ'd in the use of excommunication, condemning those who recur to it immediately, for such trifles as above; tho', upon the whole, it does not absolutely forbid such conduct, but only confines it to the authority of the bishops, whereas it extended before to all the inferior prelates. This canon has one thing in it very remarkable; every magistrate, it says, shall be held guilty, if he offer to molest the bishop in publishing excommunication, or commands him to revoke

voke it, tho' it fhould be evident that the
fame is unjuft, both in its caufe .and confequence, for want even of obferving the conditions prefcribed by the canon. From hence
it follows, that rather than the ecclefiaftic jurifdiction fhould be molefted, things muft be
left in confufion ; and that there is lefs harm in
punifhing an innocent perfon, contrary to all
right and reafon, and depriving him of the facraments, than in difturbing the peace of the
prelate. I leave it to perfons of good fenfe,
to make their own judgment of fuch a decifion. But this is not all yet, which that canon
fays ; it adds, that if an excommunicated perfon live a year under excommunication, he
fhall be deem'd as a heretic ; and, by confequence, be obnoxious to the inquifition. It
follows therefore, that if a perfon under excommunication for not paying a debt, be not
in a condition to pay it within a year, he deferves as much to be burnt, as the moft obftinate heretic. When our lord *Jefus Chrift*
warned St. *Peter* of the ftrong temptation
which the devil was preparing for him, I don't
find that he talk'd of excommunication. *Satan
hath defired you to winnow you as wheat, but I
have prayed for thee that thy faith fail not ; therefore when thou art converted, ftrengthen thy
brethren.* So that if the apoftles, and after
them the believers, had denied the faith of
Chrift, it was *Peter's* duty not to excommuni-

cate them; but, *when converted,* to *ſtrengthen*
his brethren.

When *Simon* the magician tryed, in St. *Peter's*
preſence, to ſeduce the primitive chriſtians, by
his diabolical miracles, *Peter* deferred puniſhing him for whole years; but when he ſet up
for a god, by lifting himſelf, up into the air,
and had by time acquired great credit among
the people, *Paul* ſolicited *Peter*, more than
once, to temporize with him no longer, becauſe the ſcandal too viſibly increaſed; and at
length *Peter* reſolved to curſe him, and compell'd the devil to caſt him down headlong.

If in after times the ecclefiaſtical diſcipline
introduced the uſe of excommunication in
caſes of the laſt importance (for I am not willing to reject the Church's authority in this matter, becauſe I have already owned it) certainly the enormity of the crime muſt have been
proportioned to the rigour of the puniſhment.
'Tis enough for me to demonſtrate that this
ſentence may be ſometimes unjuſt, and that,
by conſequence, 'tis no article of faith, to hold
that every excommunicated perſon is deprived
of the grace of God; juſtice is abſolutely neceſſary in excommunication, becauſe *Chriſt*
cannot favour injuſtice: Now, beſides other
faults in the excommunication, 'tis ſufficient to
make it unjuſt, if it exceeds the enormity of
the crime; becauſe, while it only depends on
the opinion of men, 'tis ſubject to the errors of
their underſtandings; and the caſe is the ſame,

at

at leaſt, with excommunication, as it is with all the other ſentences of judges, which, if they exceed the deſert of the criminal, ought to be amended, if not annulled.

They make a diſtinction at the court of *Rome* betwixt one excommunication and another. They call the one excommunication *a jure,* and the other excommunication *ab homine.* The former is univerſally decreed by a canon of the Church againſt all who commit a certain crime; the latter is only decreed by a ſpecial judge againſt a crime already committed or intended. Of theſe two, that called excommunication *a jure* ſeems the moſt grave and important, becauſe it muſt be ſuppoſed, that there has been more care and exactneſs obſerved in the eſtabliſhment of a law, which is to ſerve as a rule in the government of a people, and, perhaps, of the whole world, than a ſentence paſſed by a ſingle judge of one juriſdiction only, and in a caſe ſometimes unknown to him; neverthelefs, the very ſame canon of the Church declares, that excommunication *a jure* may be abſolved by every ordinary confeſſor; but that excommunication *ab homine* can only be abſolved by him who pronounced the excommunicatory ſentence, or by a ſuperior judge : Therefore it would not, perhaps, be uncharitable, to advance that excommunications of this ſort were introduced, rather to aggrandize the prelate, than to reform the ſinner, and contribute to his

C   ſalvation.

salvation. It has been already aſſerted, that excommunication ought to have ſome deadly ſin for its object; yet if any one is unable to pay a debt, he is excommunicated, tho' he has not abſolutely ſinned. This excommunication therefore is not valid; 'tis poſſible for him who pronounces it to be miſtaken; if the firſt may be deceived, ſo may the ſecond and third in like manner, according to St. *Paul,* who ſays that every prieſt is encompaſſed about with frailties.

In the catalogue of excommunications, drawn up by the court of *Rome,* there is one againſt him who diſcovers, either by converſation, or by other evident proof, that any one holds an heretical opinion, and does not inform againſt him to the inquiſition. This is the ſame thing for example, as if any common perſon in * this city (which is impoſſible) ſhould hear a ſenator talk heretically; or if in any other country, a courtier ſhould make the ſame obſervation, either in the king's brother, or in any of the princes of the blood, tho' neither the burgher nor the courtier would be willing to accuſe perſons of ſuch diſtinction, either for fear or reſpect ſake; yet their ſilence ſhall be a crime bad enough to ſubject them to ſeparation from the reſt of the faithful, and to deprivation from the ſacraments. I leave the public to judge whether ſuch an opinion is

* *Venice.*

is allowable. The confequences of this canon extend yet farther; for it being abfolute and without exception, in impofing the obligation on perfons to be informers, if, in obedience to the canon, the criminal is accufed without proofs, either becaufe there are no witneffes, when the herefy of the perfon accufed is difcovered, or becaufe, if there be any, they are loth to fwear it; it follows, that the accufer fhall be punifhed by the court as a flanderer; and if they have a mind to make ufe of *Lex Talionis* upon his account, he fhall be expofed to the fame punifhment as the heretic would have incurred, befides what he has to fear from the hatred and revenge of the perfon accufed.

If there are fo many things to be done for avoiding excommunication, and if confciences are to be reduced to fuch a rigorous conftraint, what becomes of thofe words of *Jefus Chrift, my yoke is eafy, and my burden is light?* When this divine faviour recommends brotherly correction, he prefcribes the manner of it, *inter te & ipfum folum; between thee and him alone;* and that it be done with love; and it were even neceffary for fuch a one to ask pardon of him whom he has corrected, or is going to correct, that he may not incur the blame of a peevifh hypocrite.

The court of *Rome* diftinguifhes alfo between excommunication *latæ fententiæ,* and the excommunication which *attendit declarationem,*

tionem, which laft is ufed in cafes of greater importance than the former, and is paffed immediately after the commiffion of the crime. Upon this we fhall confider, firft, how many exceptions the fuppofed criminal might urge, in refpect either of the crime committed, or the contumacy incurred ; they are thefe, ignorance, violence, refpect, inability, the fear to which a fickle mind is fubject, and many others of this nature; neverthelefs, without any comfort, he is already excommunicated; and, by this means, deprived of the liberty of felf-defence, tho' it be of divine right. Was God under a neceffity to call either *Adam,* or *Cain,* in order to be informed by themfelves of the crime they had committed? Neverthelefs, before he condemned them, he brought them into his prefence.

There is a particular cafe of confcience decided by the aforefaid council, which imports, that if a penitent defiring confeffion for a fin of fenfuality, or any other whatfoever, fufpects that the father confeffor will be able to difcover the female with whom he committed that fin, he ought to omit fome circumftances, in order to puzzle his confeffor, and prevent him from gueffing at the accomplice of his fin. This is a charitable precaution, the end of which is to hinder fcandal; but how may fuch wife conduct be reconciled with obedience to the abovemention'd canon, which threatens a perfon with excommunication, that does not

inform

inform againſt a heretic, who undoubtedly is the cauſe of much greater ſcandal than a ſin committed thro' frailty ?

I infer therefore, from the premiſes, that 'tis certain there is an excommunicatory power in the Church ; and that excommunication does of itſelf deprive the excommunicated perſon from the benefit of the ſacraments ; but that it cannot have its effect without being juſt ; that to be ſo, the puniſhment which it inflicts muſt not be greater than the crime ; and finally, that the criminal be left without excuſe. Beſides, the judge who fulminates it being liable to be miſtaken, 'tis impoſſible for excommunication abſolutely to deprive a ſoul of the grace of *Jeſus Chriſt*, who is truth itſelf, and cannot err. What is here ſaid relates only to a private perſon, who has incurred excommunication. Now if all theſe reaſons plainly ſhew the neceſſity of obſerving the conditions abovemention'd, for excommunicating a private perſon, and for rendring the excommunication fulminated againſt him valid, how much rather ought thoſe very conditions, if not many others, to be obſerved in the excommunication of a ſovereign, conſidering that princes have infinite allowances made them, which private perſons cannot poſſibly have ? inaſmuch as the crimes of the former are more reſtrained, and, by conſequence, leſs expoſed to that ſhock, beſides the regard that ought to be had to the ſcandal, which is much

greater

greater in the excommunication of a fovereign than in that of a private perfon.

Let us really confider a little, how great inconveniencies would arife from thence to fociety. When the people find their prince, as it were, feparated from the myftical body of *Chrift*, and hated by the Church as much as the plague; would they continue in fubjection to his laws, whom they look upon as a rebel againft the precepts of the vicar of *Jefus Chrift?* The obligation of obedience to a prince, is not a law of civil fociety, but founded upon religion, and the exprefs command of God himfelf. And, indeed, the founders of any religion, be it ever fo filly and extravagant, always made it their bufinefs to convince the people, that the laws they gave them, derived their origin from a principle above humane nature, being perfwaded in their own breafts, that the confent of the people alone was not fufficient for the fetting up a prince over them; becaufe that after they had given fuch their confent, nothing could hinder them from revoking it, whenever they found it their intereft to do it. They alfo thought arms and guards too weak to oblige them not to withdraw fuch their confent; becaufe that which contains, is always fuppofed ftronger than that which is contained; as a town is ftronger than the garrifon within it; therefore, in order to render fovereign majefty more refpected, they thought it neceffary to make it dependent on the

the divine will; fo that he who difobeys his prince becomes a rebel againft God himfelf, and his very confcience tells him he is criminal, and deferves eternal punifhment. It appears that the ancients, who were ftupid enough to be led away by mere delufions, received this notion from their legiflators, who had fome faint glimmerings of religion. *Cofingas being defirous to found that fovereignty, to which he afpired in *Thrace*, upon the laws, raifed very high ladders towards heaven, and mounting them, feigned that he went thither to receive the orders of the deity, for making laws and eftablifhing his authority. *Numa* made the *Romans* believe that he converfed familiarly with the goddefs *Egeria*. The impofter *Mahomet* boafted that *Gabriel* the archangel was at his elbow when he compofed his Alchoran; and in the true law, we find that *Mofes* kept the tables of the law, written with God's own finger, forty days upon the mountain.

From hence it comes to pafs, that when a people are fuffered to part with the refpect
.G 4   which

---

* *Polyænus*, from whom father *Paul* took this ftory, relates it quite otherwife, *Chap.* 22. *Book* 7. of his Stratagems. He fays, that this *Cofingas*, Prince of the *Cerrhenians*, and a prieft of *Juno*, obferving that his fubjects were rebellious, in order to bring them to a fenfe of their duty, caufed a great number of ladders to be ty'd one to the other, giving out that he intended to go up to heaven, to complain to *Juno* of their difobedience, and beg her to punifh them: Upon which the ftupid *Thracians*, fearing he would make his words good, returned to their duty.

which religion infpires, they immediately become a gang of affaffins.   It was to render the

Samuel, when the *Jews* requir'd a king, to
anoint one of the fons of *Kifh* the *Benjamite* (a
cuftom ftill ufed in *France* at coronations.)
Thus kings derive the refpect they challenge,
even from that which is paid to the divinity.
If therefore excommunication declares them
deprived of that divine protection, what mur-
murs, what diforders, may we not expect
among the people, who will be apt to think,
that by difobeying the prince, they do not act
againft the mind and will of God, and that
their difobedience is warranted by that of the
prince, who is excommunicated only for refufing to obey the Church?
   All this proves clearly what diforder and
fcandal the excommunication of a fovereign is
attended with; therefore chriftians are obliged in charity, to convince the Pope how cautious he ought to be in fulminating it, and
how fearful of imitating the ignorant quack,
who ufed fire and fword in the cure of all diftempers, indifferently; for thereby the remedy becomes worfe than the difeafe. 'Tis
true, that Sovereigns are equally oblig'd, for
their own part, not only to guard againft fuch
crimes as deferve this punifhment, but to take
care to give the people fuch a good opinion of
them, that if ever a prelate fhould proceed to
extremity with them, for any trifling and ima-
ginary

ginary crime, their subjects may not from thence take occasion to turn rebels.

Besides, it must be observ'd, that excommunication being the sentence of a judge, this sentence cannot be pronounced by a person who has no jurisdiction over the person try'd, and no cognizance of the matter in question, who would, by so doing, make himself ridiculous. From this principle it naturally follows, that (waving the nature of the crime for the present) excommunication, to be valid, ought to be pronounced by a prelate, whose authority extends over the sovereign so far, as amounts to a power of judging him; and that moreover the case upon which he pronounces ought to be within his cognizance.

As for the common prelates, the bishops, if they abide by the maxims of the court of *Rome*, which will have all bishops to be not only in dependence, but subjection to the Pope, they must own, that all the authority they have being subordinate, cannot extend over a secular authority, which owns no subordination, and holds the sovereignty as a patrimony and inheritance.

Tho' a bishop be invested with the priesthood and pontifical authority, he is, nevertheless, subject to a secular prince, either by birth, or by his place of residence, for the Church can neither usurp nor diminish the secular powers; *non eripit mortalia qui regna dat cælestia;* it does not take away earthly kingdoms,

doms, tho' it gives heavenly ones. There-fore the prelate, as a perfon fubordinate, has no right to judge a perfon, or body of per-fons, who are neither fubordinate nor depen-dent; fo that whenever fuch Judgment hap-pens to be abfolutely neceffary, it muft be re-fer'd to a fuperior judge, one who ftands in the fame parity of independency as the prince who is to be judged. But enough of this has been now faid, and let the bifhops be as much bigotted as they will to thofe maxims of the court of *Rome*, which would perfwade them they have this authority over princes, furely they will never fuffer themfelves to be fo far blinded, as to come to this extremity, fince they themfelves would have reafon to fear the fame fate.

If all the arguments hitherto alledg'd, are not fufficient to convince bifhops of their obli-gation to pay this refpect to free and indepen-dent princes, we will add one more from a certain canon of the Church. But the reader muft not think to find an exprefs canon, for eftablifhing fuch a diminution of the epifcopal authority, fince an acknowledgment of this nature, made voluntarily, is hardly ever ufed in the facrament of penance; but what we mean, is a confequence which follows from the faid canon. The Council of *Trent* de-clares, that the bifhops, not only in their pri-vate authority, but even as delegates of the apoftolical See, have a right to prefide over, vifit,

vifit, and govern hofpitals, mounts of piety, and other places of devotion, lay fraternities, and lay fchools, to oblige the agents and governors thereof to give them an account of their management of their revenues; and, in a word, to do all other things that appertain to abfolute and defpotic jurifdiction. But the council excepts fuch holy places and fchools, as are under the immediate protection of the emperor or king, with whofe government the bifhops cannot meddle without their leave. From hence then we may infer, by neceffary confequence, *a pari*, or even *a majore*, how great refpect the bifhops are obliged to pay to the perfon of the emperor or king, if they ought to be thus refpectful to things which are only under their protection.

If it be afferted, that tho' a bifhop cannot excommunicate a fovereign prince, he has, however, a power to excommunicate inferior magiftrates, we fhall prove this alfo to be a very grofs miftake, not with regard to rank, of which we have now treated at large, but with regard to merit. For all magiftrates are fubordinate to their prince, from whom they not only receive the authority of commanding, but alfo the bounds to which they may venture to extend it. So that if the magiftrate be guilty of a mifdemeanor, and deferve excommunication, he muft not for this caufe be excommunicated, but recourfe fhould be had to the prince, by whom he was conftituted,

ted, to the end that he himfelf may redrefs what the magiftrate has done amifs. For as long as any other remedy may be try'd, 'tis not good to make ufe of excommunication, which is the laft remedy, or rather extremity, and the end of all remedies whatfoever. Add to this, that whoever, without having recourfe to the prince, immediately excommunicates the magiftrate, is guilty of a crying injuftice, by punifhing him who has committed no crime; for the magiftrate often acts, not of his own accord, but by commiffion, as the prince's minifter. Thus, let the fentence of a judge be ever fo unjuft, the executioner is not in the leaft refponfible for it, either in *foro judicii,* or in *foro confcientiæ,* becaufe the judge does every thing by other hands, according to that rule, *qui per alium facit, per fe ipfum facere videtur, i. e.* what a man does by another, is deem'd his own act and deed.

From all this we have ftrong reafon to conclude, that if an ordinary prelate excommunicate an independent prince, or an inferior magiftrate, without previous application to the prince on whom he depends, for obtaining a remedy of the diforder charg'd upon fuch magiftrate, the prince fhall be at his liberty to difregard the faid excommunication, as being unjuft, and, perhaps, worfe than the crime, againft which it is fulminated, according to that fentence, *fæpe majus eft peccatum judicii, quam illius peccati de quo fuerit judicium, i. e.*

There

There is often greater fin in the fentence, than in the crime on which it is paffed. In this cafe the prince may alfo ufe what means he thinks neceffary, for preventing any diforder that may enfue, having the law of nature to authorize fuch his Conduct, which teaches us to endeavour by all methods poffible to extinguifh the fire of one's own houfe, without ftaying for the affiftance of our neighbour, becaufe, as is often the cafe, the houfe may tumble down while he is confulting and paufing what to do. The example of *Jefus Chrift* himfelf is our warrant for this conduct, who, when the *Pharifees* were offended at his curing a man, that had a palfey, on the fabbath-day, reprimanded them, and convinc'd them that they were in the wrong, by asking them, if their afs fhould fall into a pit, whether they would fcruple to take it out on the fabbath-day ? Was not this, furely, to teach us, that we ought to do good at all times, without delay ?

We proceed next to treat of the excommunication fulminated by the Pope himfelf againft a fovereign prince, or a body which confifts of feveral perfons conftituting a free and independent principality. We have already acknowledg'd the Pope's lawful authority to excommunicate a prince, be he ever fo free, and his fovereignty abfolutely independent ; and we hoped, at the beginning of this treatife, to re-eftablifh a peace with the

court

court of *Rome*, provided they would acquiesce with equity; and we flatter ourselves we shall succeed, by the help of a single distinction, which may serve as a compass to guide us in this ocean.

Let us first examin wherein a secular prince ought to be subject to the Pope, for by this means we shall easily penetrate as far as the cause of his jurisdiction, and the obligation that princes are under to obey him; for to derive a general subjection from a special obligation, is an argument drawn, as they call it, *de minori ad majus,* which is a method of argument used only by sophists, and which can never conclude affirmatively: For this reason true logicians place arguments of this nature in the list of puzzling and deceitful ones, because they have, indeed, an appearance of proof, but without any foundation.

I don't believe I shall be charg'd with an error, if I lay it down for a principle, that the Popes of these later times have no greater authority than the antient Popes, and *St. Peter* himself. Tho' *Paul* V. fills *St. Peter*'s See, I don't mean that he has therefore grace and sanctity from him who wrought miracles with his shadow, but that being advanc'd into his chair, his authority is granted him by the blind obedience of the faithful, as we have already own'd: But if it be infer'd from thence, that every Christian Prince is obliged to obey the Pope implicitly, then we must distinguish, and

and grant, that he is obliged to obey him in things which are under his cognizance as Pope, *viz.* in doctrine, opinions, in the administration of the sacraments, and in whatever has been commanded by the Apostles, by *Peter*, and all the Popes that have sate in his chair, without temporal dominion; for then their ordinances were meerly ecclesiastical, and without any mixture of worldly interest: because they were poor in spirit, resembling the poverty of *Jesus Christ*, but rich in heavenly treasures. If the Pope explain the doubtful sense of some articles of the catholick faith, all Princes are obliged to receive that explanation as good, and to conform their own *
sentiments, and those of their subjects to it: And the Pope may say upon this occasion, *visum est spiritui sancto & nobis*; it hath seemed good to the Holy Ghost and us. If in such a case the Prince delays his belief too long, if his negligence be the reason why his subjects don't adopt the Pope's decision: And if, after admonition, he does not submit to it, he

---

* This, and what follows must be understood of such States where there are no laws to limit the Pope's decisive or legislative authority, in point of doctrine, opinion, &c. for this sentiment of Father *Paul* being perfectly *ultramontane*, will not hold as to countries where no bull or constitution of the Pope can be received till it has been first examined by the Bishops, who in these matters are altogether as competent judges as the Pope, either with him, or without him.

he deserves to have excommunication fulminated againft him ; becaufe he endangers not
only his own foul, but thofe of his fubjeds,
by difobeying the decrees of the common Father in the functions of his paternal authority.
When it was added to the Creed, that the
Holy Ghoft proceeded from the Father and the
Son, though the *Greek* Church has refufed to
admit of that addition ever fince, yet becaufe
it does not appertain to laymen, even invefted
with fovereign and regal dignity, to meddle
with the difcuffion of matters of faith, all catholics were obliged to fubmit their belief
to that decree. When the antient ufage of
communicating to the laity in both fpecies
was changed, and they only receiv'd the communion in the fpecies of bread, tho' the *Greeks*
do at this day obferve the antient ufage at
certain times and places ; neverthelefs the king
of *France* was obliged to fubmit to this innovation.   And if, at prefent, as the *German*
nation propofed in the council of *Trent*, the
antient ufage was renewed, every Prince
would be obliged blindly to fubmit to it,
whether they thought the alteration good or
not § †, becaufe the Pope's mouth is the oracle
of faith.   If

---

† In all Father *Paul's* arguments, between thefe two
marks § §, he continually attributes to the Pope what
he fays neverthelefs of the Church in general, which is
true in the fenfe wherein he expreffes it, but not in the
fenfe of his application.

If any opinions are introduced into a ftate contrary to thofe of the *Roman* Church, from whom would the fovereign of that ftate be oblig'd to demand the decifion thereof, but from that very Church? For otherwife he could not regulate his own belief, nor that of his fubjeds, upon fuch article; and how extravagant foever the decifion might feem to him, he would be oblig'd to adopt it, inafmuch as the decifion of fuch doubts is not under the cognizance of the fecular power; for inftance, 'tis decided, that a prieft, who, at his ordination, receives immediately from *Chrift* the power of abfolving fins, may, neverthelefs, be hinder'd *jure pofitivo* (by pofitive law) from abfolving them; fo that if he then gave abfolution, the fame would be null and void. The diftindion introduced by the Court of *Rome*, between the power of order and the power of jurifdidion, does not feem to me to have been eftablifh'd by *Jefus Chrift*, when he ordained his difciples priefts of a flock where there was no jurisdidion to exercife. Neverthelefs, this diftindion muft be adhered to from the obligation all are under to obey the Church in matters of opinion, and to believe whatever fhe believes to be true, becaufe the Church is the proper judge of all fuch points. Every prince is fubjed to the holy fee in this cafe, and in this fenfe the ecclefiaftical monarchy may be called univerfal; fo that if a fovereign become difobedient on this account,

D   he

he deferves to be feparated from the body of the Church, for fear left his bad example fhould infect the found members, and to be marked, as Cain was, in the forehead, that being known and abhorred by all men, they may fhun his company, and not hear what he might fuggeft from his evil confcience. §

Having fhewn that the Pope's authority flows immediately from *Chrift*, let us now examin how far it may extend, and for what end *Jefus Chrift* gave it to him, becaufe the extenfivenefs of the obedience, which princes and all Chriftians ought to pay him, fhould be regulated according to the extent of the faid authority ; fince to give him greater bounds than *Jefus Chrift* has fet him, would be no lefs than ufurpation, as well as a criminal prefumption, in pretending to exprefs what the gofpel does not exprefs, it being as much as to fay that the gofpel wants words for its matter. Now in all the New Teftament there are but two paffages where *Jefus Chrift* fpeaks of St. *Peter's* authority. The firft expreffes the reward of that apoftle's zeal and faith, who was the firft that owned the divinity of *Jefus Chrift*. *But whom fay ye that I am ?* Peter *anfwer'd, Thou art* Chrift *the fon of the living God.* Jefus *anfwer'd, Bleffed art thou,* Simon, *the fon of* Jonas, *for flefh and blood hath not revealed this to thee, but my father which is in heaven. And I alfo fay unto thee that thou art* Peter, *and upon this rock I will build*

build my Church, and I will give unto' thee the
of heaven ; and whatsoever
thou   *earth, shall be bound in hea-*
ven,   *er thou shalt loose on earth,*
shall   That was the time
when *Peter* was defign'd for a Prieft, but not
eftablifh'd. The fecond time was after the
refurrection, when *Jefus* put this Queftion
to *Peter*, *Loveft thou me?* And *Peter* anfwer'd, *Lord, Thou knoweft that I love thee.*
Then *Jefus* replied to him, *Feed my Sheep.*
And thefe were the words by which *Jefus*
Chrift eftablifh'd his priefthood. When he
promifed it to him, he gave him the power
of *binding* and *loofing* ; and when he put him
in poffeffion of it, he charged him to feed
men. Now this flock is fed two ways; with
facraments, and with doctrine. If in the exercife of the priefthood, and paftoral care of
feeding the fheep of *Chrift*, by adminiftring
the Sacraments to them, and teaching them,
any one fhould ftart up, pretending to explain the doctrin, and abufing the nourifhment of the facraments, the Pope is concerned to make ufe of his power of *binding*
and *loofing*, by excommunicating him for his
rafhnefs, and cutting him off from the body of
the faithful. Neverthelefs, it muft be remember'd all this while, that we are treating of the
eftablifhment of the Church, when *Jefus Chrift*
pronounc'd the Words *bind* and *loofe* ; and
that by confequence the ufe of the power of

bindirg

binding always ought to have for its object the *eſtabliſhment* of the Church, and not her deſtruction. In like manner *Jeſus Chriſt* did not pronounce the words, *feed my ſheep*, till he had asked *Peter* ſeveral times, *whether he loved him?* becauſe, without love, yea, without redoubled love, it was impoſſible to feed his flock; therefore *St. Peter's* immediate authority was altogether ſpiritual, his power conſiſting in the liberty of *binding* and *looſing* ſouls, *ſed in ædificatione eccleſiæ caritate conjuncta.*

The faith and obligation of chriſtians upon this article extends thus far, and no farther: And if the Pope pretends from this prerogative to derive an univerſal authority of commanding princes, and under colour of diſtributing to chriſtians the nouriſhment of ſacraments and of doctrine, to oblige princes to give his holineſs an account of their actions, and upon their refuſal to do it, to proceed againſt them with the utmoſt rigor, as if they were apoſtates from the chriſtian faith, this is to challenge a power not expreſſed in the goſpel, nor commanded by *Chriſt*, but is a mere invention of the ſtate, which aims at the command of the whole univerſe for worldly intereſt. This can never be denied till a new goſpel be found out, any more than what we ſaid above, *viz.* That the authority of the Popes in our days cannot be greater than that of St. *Peter*, and the other apoſtles and Popes of the primitive Church. Read the New Teſtament ftament over and over, you will find no place where *Jefus Chrift* fettled his difciples in any domain or temporal intereft; fo far from it, that he bids them not trouble their heads about what they fhall eat or put on, but to expect all from the good providence of their heavenly father, who knew how to cloath them better than *Solomon*; for he who gives cloathing and nourifhment to the plants and fowls of the air, will not abandon the faithful.

Jefus Chrift himfelf abhorred fovereignty, and being ask'd one day, whether he were a king? anfwer'd, That he was a king indeed; but his kingdom was not of this world. And forefeeing by his divine prefcience that the people who follow'd him, and had experienc'd his great power by his miraculous multiplication of the loaves, had a defign to carry him away, and make him a king by foice, did he not fly and abfcond to avoid thofe vain honours? But the Pope, *Jefus Chrift*'s vicar, is fo far from imitating the example of this divine minifter, that he arrogates to himfelf the power of making kings and princes when he pleafes, wherein he has fometimes fucceeded; witnefs what happen'd not long ago in *Ireland*, and afterwards in *Tufcany*. Now, fince it has been fhown that *Jefus Chrift* has not given him this authority, no prince is oblig'd to obey him upon that account; and if any body is excommunicated for refufing to own *Ireland* for a

kingdom,

kingdom, or *Tuscany* for a great dutchy, this excommunication would be void, becaufe 'tis not the Pope's bufinefs to beftow fecular dignities, to which the Pope himfelf is fubject in his own perfon, and to which he was formerly fubject in the exercife of the papal miniftration.

We fay it again, that the Pope is fet up to form, feed, and inftruct the flock. On this account every one ought to obey him ; and whoever fails in this point, the Pope may excommunicate and curfe him ; but the Pope cannot make one fingle body of laws, compofed of articles of faith and the canon laws, becaufe the latter are blended with an infinite variety of human interefts, which do not oblige to fubmiffion.

Mahomet was very cunning, when in the compofition of his Alcoran he added the civil laws of political government, that all his fubjects might think themfelves equally oblig'd to obferve the articles of their creed, and the laws of their prince. The Court of *Rome,* rather than copy after *Mahomet,* ought to be contented with the honour of fuch as own their obligation to obey the Pope, in matters of faith alone. Tho' there were fovereigns, who, out of a godly principle, thought fit to ftrip themfelves of their treafure and dominions for enriching the Church with them; the Popes have not on this account acquired any greater authority than when they had only a ftone

feat

feat and a wooden crofier. Thofe princes had no intention to fet up one who fhould be their lord and mafter, to exchange their freedom for flavery, and to be forced to g ve an account of their actions in temporal affairs, as muft have been the cafe, if they had been oblig'd to obey all the canon laws and innovations introduced by the Council of *Trent*, which, to fay the very truth, did in this refpect put in their fickle into other men's corn.

A reflection occurs to me juft now, which I cannot pafs over in filence, *viz*. That excommunication is generally threatned for the tranfgreffion of fome pofitive law, and very rarely, if ever, for difobedience to the divine laws. Princes have their authority from God, and are accountable to none but him for the government of their people. The Pope cannot pretend to be God's vicar in this refpect; in the firft place, becaufe it is not written; fecondly, becaufe princes were before Popes; from whence it follows that it muft be proved not by tradition, but by the Gofpel itfelf, that God is the author of fuch derogation from the fecular authority, in favour of the Pope. But this is what can never be demonftrated, and reafon itfelf is fufficient to convince us of it, for the care which the Pope would be obliged to take of temporal affairs would fwallow up his concern for fpirituals, and 'tis impoffible to ferve God and the world at the fame time. Tho' the Pope by any accident

D 4 fhould

should be deprived of his dominions and treasure, and reduced to that poverty which was the appanage of the primitive pontiffs, the princes would undoubtedly be obliged to obey him nevertheless as Pope, and in the same quality he has a right to command them, and they to obey him, now he is encompass'd with splendor and grandeur; so that if they refuse to obey him as such, he may excommunicate them with reason, and the punishment would be proportionable to the crime; for the crime being spiritual, the punishment inflicted by a spiritual judge, would be purely spiritual in like manner, and by consequence valid and effectual. But the Pope must take heed how he extends this right to other matters, because, if he go beyond the bounds of his authority, he would cease to act in quality of Pope, and princes being no longer subject to him, would not be obliged to obey him.

If there be any who call this distinction fantastical, and refuse to admit of a truth so universally receiv'd, *viz.* That the Pope may be consider'd in different qualities, let it be remember'd that I aver the same of legates, vice-legates, and of the governors of towns in the land of the Church, who, if they condemn a criminal to death, or loss of member, act irregularly as priests, be their sentence ever so just; nor can they demand satisfaction, or reparation, for any injury done, even to their own persons, unless they first protest before

fore the fecular judge, that their demand is *citra pœnam fanguinis.* Yet thofe fame prelates condemn criminals to death every day, and perhaps with more feverity than other governors, having no other plea to palliate their canonical irregularity, but the diftinction that they exercife this charge, and pronounce this judgment, not as Priefts, but as princes, and the minifters of a prince. 'Tis not therefore a contradiction, according to them, to confider the pope one while as pontiff and chief prieft, in the functions of the priefthood, and another while as a temporal prince, who is taken up with fecular interefts and maxims of ftate. Neverthelefs, it would be ridiculous in the Pope, confider'd even as a temporal prince, to affert that he has any more authority over other princes than one neighbour has over another ; which imports no fuperiority, and by confequence no right to command. But this has been fufficiently handled already.

CHAP.

CHAP. III.

Whether excommunicated perfons may appeal.

WE have fully prov'd that excommunication is a fentence pronounc'd againft a criminal for fome fuppos'd crime. Now cuftom and reafon tell us, that appeals againft all fentences are lawful, becaufe all judges are liable to be deceived by falfe and plaufible arguments. 'Tis therefore lawful to appeal from excommunication to a fuperior judge, otherwife chriftian obedience, inftead of being an eafy yoke, and a light burden, would be worfe than *Babylonifh* captivity. Thus if fentence comes from the tribunal of a bifhop, an appeal may be brought to the archbifhop ; if from an archbifhop, to a primate; if from a primate, to a patriarch; if from a patriarch, to an apoftolical nuncio; and if from a nuncio, to a provincial fynod, according to the cuftom of every province: And finally, appeals may be made from all provincial or patriarchal fentences to the Pope.

Indeed this cuftom of appealing to the Pope from a patriarchal fentence is a novelty in the Church, which was unknown in the primitive times. In the age that fucceeded next to the Apoftles, the whole chriftian world was divided

vided into four patriarchates. That of *Rome*, by dignity and prerogative, was the firſt; that of *Antioch* the ſecond, that of *Alexandria* the third, and that of *Conſtantinople* the fourth. Many years after, when chriſtianity was eſtabliſh'd in the parts about *Jeruſalem*, that city was alſo erected into a patriarchate, and added to the other four; ſo that all chriſtendom was then divided among thoſe five patriarchs, who had each certain kingdoms and provinces aſſigned them, that they might have the overſight of the inferior prelates in thoſe dominions, as biſhops, archbiſhops, and primates; ſo that all appeals in any part of chriſtendom, when brought before the patriarch of the Country, had their final deciſion without further appeal: The chief of all the patriarchs, in point of precedency, was that of *Rome*, and he received this prerogative from St. *Peter*, who exerciſed his juriſdiction, and kept his reſidence there a long time; but before St. *Peter* went to *Rome*, he founded the ſee of *Antioch*, from whence it happen'd, that that which was the firſt in the order of the patriarchates, became the ſecond by St. *Peter*'s departure, whoſe chair at *Antioch* is kept holy to this day. But tho' the patriarch of *Rome* is firſt in preheminence, he is not the firſt in authority, but only ſo in point of order, in the ſame ſenſe with the preſident, or chief of an aſſembly, who is one that is honour'd with the chief place among his collegues, tho' they are

equal

equal to him in authority. Thofe patriarchs fucceeded the four evangelifts, who had the fame equal meafure of authority, tho' not of grace ; for two of thofe evangelifts had the marks of an apoftolick character, but without any preheminence over the others.

This fuperiority of the fee of *Rome* was unknown in ancient times, of which there needs no other proof, than what paffed at the election of bifhops and archbifhops in all the eftates of chriftendom. When a city wanted a bifhop, both the laity and the clergy, or the clergy alone, according to the cuftom of the town, elected him ; and when, in procefs of time, difputes arofe about thofe elections, recourfe was prefently had to the patriarch, in whofe jurifdiction fuch city lay. When the election was ended, the prelate elect was prefented to the patriarch, who confecrated him, and gave him the bifhop's pall. In the firft Council, which was held by St. *Peter* and the other apoftles in *Jerufalem*, the elders of the people were prefent, to give their opinion about the decree which was defign'd for abolifhing circumcifion. And the laity affifted in all the Councils for a long time after. Then canonical punifhments were inftituted *ad corrigendos fratres* ; and afterwards the laity neglecting their attendance in thofe affemblies, ftations were decreed, and indulgences granted for thofe who fhould repair to the faid affemblies, wherein all things relating to the state

ftate of chriftianity were determined. The
laity continued alfo, a long while after this,
to give their votes at the election of prelates
and Popes; for *Celeftin* II. who was advanc'd
to the holy fee in 1143, was the firft who was
chofen Pope folely by the cardinals; and this
gave the court of *Rome* a handle to obtain
two great prerogatives, *viz.* the exclufion of
the laity, and the delegation of the cardinals
alone, who, at their inftitution, had no other
title than curates of the chief Parifhes of
Rome, and were therefore much inferior to
bifhops. But to return to our fubject:

A fentence of excommunication is in its
own nature fubject to an appeal, not only to
the end that the perfon who is injured may
obtain relief, but alfo, becaufe it would be
tyranny to fubject the perfon accufed to the
opinion of a fingle judge, who would thereby be in a condition to opprefs him at difcretion. Upon this account, fovereign princes
are wont to make no difference betwixt civil and criminal judges; and being perfuaded
that there is no judgment which is not fuf-
ceptible of a more ferious examination, and
a more exact difcuffion, they therefore do not
pafs fentence themfelves, to the end that the
perfon condemn'd may have the liberty of
recourfe from one judge to another. Thus,
if a fovereign prince himfelf fhould pafs
fentence, and not permit an appeal, he would
do the parties an injury; and it would feem

as

as an injury done to himſelf, if he admitted of a judge to over-rule his deciſions. He who was condemn'd by *Cæſar*, appeal'd to *Cæſar* himſelf when his anger was over ; and even now, when there is a neceſſity for the inter-vention of the Pope's judgment in a caſe of importance, he gets the fulleſt information poſſible ; and tho' he is ſatisfy'd in his own conſcience of the merits of the cauſe, yet, for all this, he does not pronounce ſentence, but deputes judges to do it, that he may not be expos'd to the common law of appeals from his judgment ; and it generally follows, that ſentence is pronounc'd in favour of the complainant, becauſe, by naming ſuch depu-tation, he does in effect declare that he ad-mits of the complaint.

As to the ordinary prelates, there is no doubt but as ſuch a one owns a ſuperior, he is oblig'd to admit of appeals from his ſentences ; the diſpute therefore only relates to the ſentences of the Pope, who acknow-ledges no ſuperior ; and this point depends on the queſtion, whether the Pope or a Coun-cil is ſuperior ? If we admit the ſuperiority of a Council, all doubts concerning this mat-ter would vaniſh ; but ſince the champions for the court of *Rome* will not acknowledge this ſuperiority, the difficulty remains entire. Be-ſides, tho' they ſhould admit of the ſuperi-ority of a Council, they would hardly grant them the liberty of receiving appeals, by pre-

pretending that this tribunal does not always subsist, that it would be unneceffary trouble to call a Council for a particular affair; and moreover, that when affembled, it would not only pronounce judgment on the affair for which it was called, but would hear all who thought themfelves injured by the Pope; which as we fay, would be falling out of the frying-pan into the fire, and terribly expofe the authority of the holy fee. Therefore we may not expect to have a general Council call'd by the Pope's order for many ages: No, the Court, of *Rome* too well remembers how dear they have paid for thofe in time paft. If I don't miftake, befides the two Vows of obedience and chaftity, which all priefts make at their ordination, a third vow is required of him who is raifed to the papal dignity, *viz.* That he abjure general Councils, or promife never to call one in any cafe whatfoever. If, in order to diffipate the Pope's dread of a Council, it were propofed (which is perhaps impoffible) fo to circumfcribe the authority of the Council when affembled, that it fhall not meddle with any other affair befides that for which it is fummoned, then it would be objected, that the prelates of many dominions would not care to attend them, as not thinking themfelves oblig'd to undergo fuch fatigues for the fake of a particular prince; from whence this inconveniency would arife, that many of the prelates would be for reaffem-
bling

bling fuch a Council at pleafure.   Be this as it
will, I am inclin'd to think, that if a Council
was affembled under fuch conditions, all
kingdoms would heartily concur; for it would
be univerfal; and the common intereft of all
provinces, were it once eftablifh'd, 'that the
Pope would admit of appeals to a Council, in
all cafes where people fhould think themfelves injur'd by the court of *Rome*, and that
he would authorife the validity thereof by his
own confent.   But I muft own this is only a
chimerical fpeculation, and what is never like
to come to pafs; there being not the leaft appearance that the Pope will ever confent willingly to the calling of a Council for any caufe
whatfoever, no not for the fake of all chriftendom, and much lefs for that of a fingle potentate. 'Tis poffible, neverthelefs, that the court
of *Rome* refufes to admit fuch appeals, becaufe
of the impoffibility there is of obtaining a final judgment, and not becaufe they think they
have a right to refufe them, and that their fentences are not fubject to reviews of the like
nature.   For by allowing of fuch appeal to a
tribunal that does not really fubfift, the appeal
alone will have the force of a fentence, according to the maxim, *Appellatio fingit non ju-
dicatum.*   Therefore, from the very moment
that any one appeals from a fentence of the
Pope to a future Council, the fentence, and
all that follows thereupon, remains in fufpence
till a definitive judgment, which cannot be
obtain'd

obtain'd while there is no judge ; so that the
bare appeal is sufficient to annul the former
sentence. Undoubtedly 'tis to avoid these inconveniencies that the court of *Rome* rejects
the superiority of councils, tho' they are superior in their own nature, and the Popes are
convinc'd of it in their own consciences. Therefore their disowning of it is a poisonous remedy, for it is making an article of faith contrary to all manner of reason, merely for a-
voiding a political inconvenience.

'Tis in vain to think of engaging the court
of *Rome* to admit of appeals of this kind, by
telling them, that an appeal makes no more
account of a sentence than if it had never been
pass'd, and suspends all the effects of it, and
that an excommunicated person, who appeals,
is not sensible of any prejudice from excommunication while his appeal subsists ; but that
those appeals ought to have a certain time fix'd,
after which sentence may be fulminated, if
no final judgment intervene, because 'tis then
suppos'd to be the appellant's own fault if the
process is not ended, especially in the present
case ; for the canons of the Church are express
to this purpose, allowing but two years, at
most, to dispatch all ecclesiastical process. No,
I say, the court of *Rome* would not suffer
themselves to be taken by this specious bait.
They know full well that this limitation of
time can only be to the disadvantage of the

E   ap-

appellant, when he is permitted to obtain such final Judgment, and that as soon as it becomes impossible for him to obtain it, because the tribunal, to which he hath recourse, doth not always subsist, he is consequently no longer subject to the prescription of time: Such is the condition of a pupil, till he is able himself to take care of his own Interests. Therefore the court of *Rome* sees plain enough, that, by admitting of appeals, one of these two things would certainly be the consequence, either that its sentences must continue in suspence till a judge was constituted, or that for want of the ordinary judge, the Pope would be oblig'd to appoint one on purpose for this particular affair ; but with this condition, that it should be by consent of the parties concurring in the choice of the judges. For otherwise, if the persons chosen were suspected by either of the parties, the other could not be compell'd to appear before a tribunal thus establish'd, contrary to the laws of natural right. For avoiding all the confusion and perplexity, in which the bare acknowledgment of the superiority of a Council would involve the pontifical authority, the court of *Rome*, who foresaw all the prejudicial consequences of it at a great distance, cuts the knot at once, and absolutely denies the said superiority, a remedy which I confess is violent, but absolutely necessary to answer their views.

We

We will now make a general Inquiry into the Equity of this article, and then proceed to the particular decifion of another queftion.

There are only two pretences for rejecting an appeal from a fentence, *viz.* the infallibility of the judge•who paffes it, or elfe his fuperiority. If his infallibility be pretended, it may be faid to be a reafon both natural and juft at the fame time ; but if his fuperiority be pretended, which confifts in his owning no other judge above himfelf, 'tis a reafon of ftate, which only refpects the chief judge. As to the former, 'tis certain that if the law could have fuppofed fuch infallibility in a judge, it would never have allow'd of appeals, that may be aptly compar'd to Medicine, which is defign'd for the recovery and health of the conftitution, and on that account ought to be acceptable ; but if it be confider'd abftractedly, as the means only, 'tis impoffible not to hate it, becaufe of the diforders into which it throws the patient, who would never take phyfick if he was fure of recovering his health by any other method. Appeals confider'd in themfelves, and in their end, are good, becaufe they ferve to repair the mifchief, and divert the prejudice attending the falfe judgment of a former judge : But otherwife they are odious, in that they tend to prolong law fuits, and to elude the authority of a former judge ; now the law having not the leaft hopes that equity

would

would be inseparable from all sentences passed in the first, instance, thought it indispensably necessary to constitute a superior judge, tho' it plainly foresaw it would be a means for a litigious person to indulge his passion ; so that finding itself between two extremes, either of authorizing an unjust sentence, or of feeding the passions of such who seek to spin out causes to a great length ; it chose rather to permit the latter, as the least of those evils : Besides, by the admitting of appeals, there was no certainty of avoiding the injustice of a sentence, since the judge being deceiv'd in the first instance, it might happen that the superior judge might also be mistaken in approving and confirming his sentence. For we can expect no less from human weakness, nothing but the spirit of God being capable to enlighten the understanding. Proceed we now to the other Question.

The court of *Rome* rejects all appeals from a sentence of the Pope, for this reason, that the Pope being infallible, cannot err in passing such sentence. If it can be proved that the Pope possesses this extraordinary prerogative, which raises him above human infirmities, so liable to error, without doubt the holy father is very much in the right not to suffer his decisions to be subjected to a scrutiny, since the law cannot grant the same privilege to the ordinary judges. But of what use is infallibility

ty in this caſe, ſince we have demonſtrated in CHAP. II. that excommunication, to be valid in *foro conſcientiæ*, muſt have ſome deadly ſin for its object? Now every one knows that this aggravation of ſin can only be diſtinguiſh'd in confeſſion, becauſe, tho' an action be never ſo evil, it cannot be ſinful, if, among other circumſtances, it is not voluntary; ſo that the Pope may happen to excommunicate a perſon who may ſeem to have incurr'd excommunication, tho' indeed, and in *foro conſcientiæ*, he has not deſerv'd it; or one, who, tho' he may have deſerv'd it, is capable of offering ſo many exceptions as would make it appear he has not incurr'd it. Perhaps the court of *Rome* may approve of my opinion,. with reſpect to excommunications decreed before the act done; becauſe indeed the Pope, who pronounces excommunication, cannot foreſee what exceptions the criminal may produce; but they will not admit of any plea againſt excommunication fulminated after neceſſary admonition, becauſe if the criminal had any thing to offer by way of exception, he had time to produce it to the judge, before he was excommunicated; but having not done it, he manifeſts his contumacy, and proves himſelf guilty; which, ſay they, is a ſin bad enough to authorize excommunication. That's their opinion. To which I anſwer; It may, and commonly does happen, that the perſon accus'd being persuaded his condemnation is inevitable, does not produce his exceptions, because 'tis certain he had better be condemn'd for contumacy, than after he has been heard, since then he reserves to himself a right of producing them *ex integro* before the judge to whom he appeals, and who is the proper judge, because he had no concern in the former sentence, and is not acted by any interest; but it rarely falls out that the Pope gives admonition before his excommunications, even when it has happen'd to be in his own causes, as when he complains of the violation of his jurisdiction, or of any hurt done to the ecclesiastical livings, or when he claims any fiefs or lordships escheated, and the like. In cases of this nature, if the person summon'd obey, he runs the risk of losing all his rights entirely, and if, after having sent his reasons to this tribunal, he is condemn'd tho' absent, what might he not fear were he to appear there in person? To avoid this double inconveniency, persons are oblig'd to let sentence of outlawry pass against them for non-appearance, reserving to themselves an appeal to a competent judge *in integro & sine prejudicio*. Is it not visible that this refusal to appear in the first instance is neither obstinacy nor rebellion? 'Tis absolute necessity, therefore no sin, and by consequence no valid cause of excommunication; and if the same be fulminated, 'tis unjust, and serves at best only to discover the iniquity of the judge, who suffers him-

himfelf to be carry'd away by his own private intereft. We conclude therefore that the court of *Rome* has no ground to reject appeals on account of the judge's *infallibility.*

Since the faid court, which hates to difpute or argue, but aims at nothing lefs than abfolute defpotic power, refufes to hearken to all the reafons that may be alledg'd againft fuch pretended infallibility, and lays fo much ftrefs on the words of our Saviour, and the prerogative he granted St. *Peter,* as to make the Pope's infallibility an article of faith, it will be neceffary to have recourfe to the fcriptures, which we propofe to do in a future chapter, wherein we will try the force of this infallibility by the true meaning of thofe facred writings; for the prefent I think it fufficient to obferve, that if the Pope were infallible, he would confequently be happy in this life, I mean happy with celeftial beatitude; for I am not fo rafh as to attack his worldly beatitude, nor his ordinary title, and much lefs his temporal felicity; I mean, therefore, fuch a beatitude as St. *Peter* enjoy'd, when Jefus Chrift faid to him, *bleffed art thou* Simon, *fon of* Jonas; for, being predeftinated to glory, he was affur'd of recovering himfelf from his lapfes by repentance. But I can hardly think the Pope is fo abfolutely confirm'd in grace as the Angels were after the fall of *Lucifer,* and St. *Paul* after his converfion; for if the Popes had this precious privi-

E 4   lege

lege, Pope * *Marcellin* would not have facrific'd
to idols for fear of death. 'Tis true, he own'd
his crime, confefs'd his guilt, and intreated the
Council to inflict fuch punifhment on him as
he deferv'd; upon which the Council only put
it home to his own confcience, and he became
fo good a penitent, that he afterwards obtain'd
the crown of martyrdom. His fanctity was
the fruit of his repentance, not the fign of his
innocence. Now, if a Pope may err fo far as
to fall into idolatry, his pretended infallibility
cannot be made an article of faith, and I don't
believe

----

* *Marcellinus*, the 30th bifhop of *Rome*, including St. *Peter*, fucceeded *Caius*, at a time when the Church began to reft
from perfecution; but the emperor *Dioclefian* being acted by
the perfecuting fpirit of his predeceffors, *Marcellinus*, for
fear of being put to death, did not fcruple to offer facrifice to
Jupiter, *Hercules* and *Saturn*, in the temple of *Vefta*. Some
time after his fhameful apoftacy, a great number of priefts
and believers affembling at *Sinueffa*, near *Rome*, *Marcellinus*
was call'd to an account for his conduct, when he own'd his
fault, and defir'd punifhment, upon which, 'tis faid the members of that affembly anfwer'd, *prima fedes a nemine judicatur ;
tu reus, tu judex ; ex ore tuo juftificaberis, ex ore tuo condem-
naberis*, i. e. no body judges the chief See; thou art both
criminal and judge; out of thy own mouth thou fhalt be juftify'd, out of thy own mouth fhalt thou be condemn'd. 'Tis
added, that the fcandal of his action touched him fo to the
quick, that he went before the judges, boldly confefs'd Jefus
Chrift in their prefence, and wafhed his guilt in his own blood,
by fuffering martyrdom at the end of the 8th year of his pontificate. Some authors, great fticklers for the Pope's infallibility, treat this hiftory as fabulous, but tradition has preferv'd
it fo carefully in the office of the Church, that it cannot be
queftion'd, without giving the lie to an infinite number of
Facts receiv'd on the fame authority.

believe the champions of the court of *Rome*
can be fo fenfelefs as to require it. Indeed,
when one puts the queftion to them, whether
the Pope is liable to err or not ? They fay, error in opinion muft be diftinguifh'd from error
in practice; that as to practice, the Pope is no
more than other frail men; and may therefore
be either faved or damned; but that as to opinion in matters relating to the government of
the Church, he is infallible by virtue of the
dignity granted by *Jefus Chrift* to *Peter*, and
in his Perfon to all his fucceffors. But to this
it may be anfwer'd, that all the actions of men,
whether good or bad, have one and the fame
juft or unjuft intention for their principle; befides, man commits no crimes, how enormous
foever, but with hopes of finding his account
in them. With this view the revengeful perfon fatisfies his revenge, the covetous perfon
heaps up wealth; and fo of others, *fallimur ratione boni.* From hence it may be concluded,
that whofoever is capable of finning, is capable of having an evil thought; for the will
being blind, fubmits tamely to the dictates of
the heart. St. *Auguftin* fays, *beatitudinis caufa
faciunt omnes homines quidquid boni vel mali faciunt.* But we will refer the examination of
this infallibility to the XIIth Chapter, and will
own it with the above diftinction, tho' there
are many who pretend it died with St. *Peter*,
and that it was a perfonal privilege, in no
wife attached to his dignity; but as I faid before,

fore, I chuſe rather to be laviſh in my obedience, than to rob the Pope of that juſt duty
and reſpect we are obliged to pay him.

It follows from what has been already ſaid,
that the ſentences of all judges whatſoever
are ſubject to appeals; that excommunication
is a ſentence the moſt liable to it perhaps of all
others, for want of the proofs requiſite to eſtabliſh the juſtice of it. The bare appearance
of proof is ſufficient to vindicate the equity of
other ſentences, whereas excommunication
ought to be founded on a certain knowledge
of the perſon's criminal intention; which is a
circumſtance that can be known only to God.
It follows alſo from the premiſſes, that the
Pope is not infallible in all things, one Pope
having been guilty of Idolatry; and that an
appeal entirely ſuſpends the effects of a ſentence, till definitive judgment is paſs'd upon
the cauſe; ſo that an excommunicated perſon
who appeals, is, during that interval, no ways
affected by the excommunication. As to the
court of *Rome*'s refuſal to admit of an appeal,
becauſe the Pope, by whom ſentence is pronounc'd, has no ſuperior that can amend his
judgment: I anſwer, that's only a reaſon of
ſtate, dictated by ſelf-intereſt, which rather
than admit of a ſuperiority in any other, would
oblige the pretended criminal to acquieſce in
the firſt ſentence, tho' it were pronounc'd by
the judge in *cauſa propria*; but this ſingle circumſtance is ſufficient warrant for an appeal;
and

and I fain would know of thofe gentlemen,
whether every prince, whofe authority is independent, ought to acknowledge a fuperior
in temporals. If they anfwer in the affirmative, who does not fee that it deftroys the fuppofition of fuch princes being free, independent, and not feudatory? If they fay no, then
fuch prince ought not to fuffer an appeal when
any of his fubjects put in a plea againft him on
account of taxes, damages, or freehold; yet
we fee free princes every day, whether kings
or emperors, permitting their fubjects to bring
their caufes into the court of exchequer, not
only in the firft inftance, but alfo in the nature
of an appeal; and if the ordinary judge of
appeals be not in the way, they name one
ad hominem, to the end that the perfon, who
thinks himfelf injur'd, may have an opportunity
to offer all his reafons againft the demands of
the attornies of the exchequer court. Now
does this permiffion in any wife diminifh the
prince's fuperior authority? does it injure his
honour? Or rather on the contrary, does he
not difplay his equity, in ftooping fo low to
his fubject, as to give him the liberty of pleading boldly againft himfelf? therefore the zea-
lots for the court of *Rome* muft acknowledge,
that the Pope would not lofe an ace of his fuperiority, but rather manifeft his honefty, by
admitting of appeals, and appointing certain
judges to examine the equity of his fentences;
whereas by refufing appeals, it would feem
that

that he is afraid to ftand the teft of them, left they fhould difcover the injuftice of his conduct, or elfe rob him of his pretende'd prerogatives. But we will now proceed to another article.

***

C H A P. IV.

Whether a Council, or the Pope, is fuperior ?

FOR the clearer underftanding of this queftion, 'tis neceffary firft of all to define what a Council is ; for when the effence of a thing is known, 'tis eafy to difcover its real virtue. There are three forts o Councils. 1. *Diocefan* ; which is compos'd o a bifhop and his clergy. 2. *Provincial,* confifting of a metropolitan, archbifhop, primate or patriarch, and his Suffragans. 3. *General,* where the Pope appears in his own perfon, or by his legates, and all the archbifhops, bifhops, primates and patriarchs of chriftendom, befides all the prelates, who by privilege or cuftom have a vote in general Councils ; for the bifhops are allow'd their votes by law, the regular abbats by cuftom, and the generals of the orders by privilege. To thefe three fome add a national Council ; but this is not mention'd tion'd in the lift of legal Councils; becaufe, were they to be admitted, a king, or other fecular prince, might affemble them at pleafure, * which would involve him in the fcandal of a fchifmatic. Neverthelefs, if the Pope fhould permit a nation to affemble in Council, this affembly would be legal, as well as whatever it fhould decide ; but then fuch Council, and the canons which it might decree, would be only calculated for the faid nation, and not for the reft of chriftendom. To leave this long digreffion, and return to our fubject: I fay then, that a *Diocefan* Council, or Synod, may be fummon'd

---

* Father *Paul* here falls in with the opinion of the court of *Rome*, that the Pope alone has a right of calling Councils, and feems to have forgot that this pretended right is a manifeft ufurpation, which has been a long while contefted with the Popes by the emperors, who have the fole right of calling thofe facred affemblies ; witnefs the firft Councils, which, by the confeffion of all faithful hiftorians, were fummon'd by circular letters from the emperors. But they did not prefide therein any more than the Pope, who had his feat in common with the other prelates ; the holy gofpels being placed upon a throne, to reprefent the Holy Ghoft, the head of the church. In after times, the emperors had fo much authority in the Councils, that they not only called them without the Pope's advice, and fent circular letters to the bifhops, fignifying what routs they fhould take, and where they fhould find carriages and provifions at the emperor's charge, *Eufeb. hift. lib.* 10. *cap.* 5. but alfo took cognizance of the things tranf-acted there, prefcribed fuch and fuch points for their decifion, and reprimanded the Councils, tho' the bifhop of *Rome* was prefent, when they found them fall into the leaft caballing or diforder, *Socrates, lib.* 2. *cap.* 39 & 40. *Idem, lib.* 4. *cap.* 34. Befides, in thofe early Councils every thing was refolved upon, not in the name of the Pope, nor of the emperor, but in the name of the facred affembly.

,mon'd by the bifhop, and alfo that he is oblig'd to affemble one every two Years, to
remedy *fmall* abufes that may creep in among
his *Diocefans* ; I fay *fmall* abufes; for if they
be of fome importance, he would be oblig'd
to have recourfe to the metropolitan, who in
this cafe ought to affemble a provincial Council for remedy of fuch abufes; but in cafes of
the utmoft importance, recourfe muft be had
to the Pope himfelf. A provincial fynod may
be fummon'd by the metropolitan, archbifhop,
primate or patriarch ; but its decrees are only
intended for their refpective provinces. Indeed, in cafes where feveral provinces have
been concern'd, the feveral metropolitans of
fuch provinces have heretofore united towards
forming a Council ; but this is now difufed,
recourfe being had, in fuch cafes, directly to
the holy See. Notwithftanding, as many metropolitans as pleas'd might lawfully hold a
Council at this day, and their decrees would
be binding to the refpective provinces for which
they are concern'd.

An affembly of this kind might well pafs
for a national Council, when all the metropolitans of a nation are met together. But as
this would be impoffible, except for an affair
of the laft importance, fo the Pope's decifion
would be abfolutely neceffary. Befides, for
as much as fuch an affembly could not be held
without the prince's confent, it would feem
to carry in it a contempt of all recourfe to the
Pope,

Pope, and be attended with the imputation of fchifm.

It muft likewife be noted, that all the infe-rior Councils, as the court of *Rome* calls them, are only capable of remedying thofe diforders which are committed againft pofitive law, and that when difputes arife concerning matters of faith, or divine right, there is an abfolute neceffity of recurring to a univerfal Council, or elfe demanding a decree from the Pope. The reafon is plain, becaufe it may happen that in matters of Church difcipline one province may fpy a fault in another, and concur with it for a remedy; but as to opinions and articles of faith, all catholics ought to have the fame be-lief, and to affent to the truth of whatfoever is propos'd to them with that character.

Therefore a general Council, affembled by the Pope's authority, is the fame thing with refpect to the whole chriftian world, as the *States General* to the *United Provinces,* the parliament to *England,* the cortes to *Spain,* the diet of the empire to *Germany,* and the gene-ral diet to *Poland*; in a word, 'tis the very quintefcence of chriftianity; fo that whatever is determin'd in fuch an affembly may be re-garded as the fenfe of the univerfal Church. The Pope fummons this affembly, not only be-caufe he is the firft in dignity and authority in the chriftian republic, but alfo to the end that it may not be fummon'd without due exami-nation of the caufes for which it is defir'd, it
being

being not reasonable that pastors sh'ould leave
their flocks for trifling matters, or only for private views, which would never want the specious name of the public good, if every one
was at liberty to call a Council. Be this ever
so true, 'tis no less certain, that when 'tis necessary for the good of the Church to assemble
a Council, and the Pope neglects to do it, or
refuses it, if requir'd, the cardinals may lawfully call one, as they have pretended to do at
other times. And where they are wanting in
this point, the bishops have the same right,
being equally concern'd to watch over the
Lord's heritage ; and finally, if the Pope,
cardinals and bishops are all asleep, it is the
business of the * secular princes to call one,
viz. the emperors, as advocates of the Church,
and kings and sovereign princes, as they are
distinguish'd members of the body of the
Church, and constituted by God's grace, as
well as the prelates and Popes, to take care of
Christ's flock. Therefore we find in the catalogue

---

* Father *Paul* continues in his *ultramontane* prejudices,
since it appears even by the inscription of the Council of
Sirmium, which he quotes a little after, that the emperor
alone order'd the assembly ; and if he had but vouchsafed to
read the inscription of former Councils, he would have there
found the same thing. , In fine, the history of *France* would
have furnish'd him with instances of several national Councils assembled by the authority of her kings, who for all that
were never reckon'd heretics, *Greg. de Tours hist. Hincmar Con-
cil, Gall.* Therefore he should have said, that things are as
he says they are now, not thro' any right of the court of
Rome, but thro' custom, establish'd by its usurpations.

logue of orthodox Councils, *Anno Domini* 352, *fuit concilium Sardinense, a Sardignâ dictum, congregatum præcepto Constantini imperatoris pro Atanasio.* And again, *A. D.* 353, *fuit Sirmiense sub Julio Papa & Constantino Imperatore, quod paulo post Constantinus in Firmio jussit congregari. Vni fratres regulas tradiderunt fidei ortodoxæ contra Arium.* And afterwards, *A. D.* 650, *fuit Toletanum nonum provinciale, Imperatore & Papâ jubentibus, quod a correctione præfatorum est inchoanda synodus, & ab eisdem tertia pars danda est ecclesiis.*

I said above, that a national Council, call'd by the authority of a prince, might be reckon'd schismatical, whereas here I aver that a secular prince has a right to call a Council in certain cases. Whatever this may seem, yet 'tis no contradiction; for a national Council may be liable to that suspicion which a general Council cannot, to the summoning whereof all christian princes concur; now such a Council being summon'd by the concurrence of all christian princes, and passing for the universal body of christendom, it could not be chargeable with schism. I was very willing to be the more explicit upon this head, that critics might have no manner of handle to censure my propositions.

Therefore the champions of the court of *Rome* are basely mistaken, when they infer, from the Pope's having a right to call a Council, that he is consequently superior to a Council;

F

cil; for when a Council is called by any other, he who calls it may challenge the fame fuperiority, which furely they would not be willing to acknowledge in any princes, nor even in any prelate; confequently the right of calling thofe affemblies is no mark of fuperiority. The Council of *Chalcedon* declares, that every Council held without the concurrence of the Pope's legates is invalid; which I think a reafonable decree, becaufe a Council ought not to be held without the Pope's confent; yet this does not conclude any thing for the Pope's fuperiority; for, does it follow from the neceffary intervention of fuch and fuch perfons in a fenate, that thofe perfons are fuperior to the faid fenate? On the contrary, that canon of *Chalcedon* formally eftablifhes the fuperiority of a Council, becaufe itfelf declares the reafons that are capable of rendring it invalid; for otherwife, if the Pope fhould think fit to renew a Council by reafon of his legates not being prefent in it, there had been no need of that decree, and a bull from the Pope would have been fufficient to declare fuch Council null and void. We likewife read of feveral provincial Councils, which having been confirm'd by the Pope, their canons and decrees have thereby acquired the fame virtue as if they had been decifions of the holy See; but this is no better argument than the former for the fuperiority of the Pope over an univerfal Council, becaufe a provincial Council is as

much

much inferior to a general one, as a province to the whole world. We might alſo men-tion the Council of *Trent*, which was general, and confirm'd by the Pope. Now it muſt be obſerv'd that theſe confirmations are of two ſorts. One, which may be call'd confirmation in the proper ſenſe of the word, and without which, all eſtabliſhments are of no validity; but this was not that ſort of confirmation which the Pope gave to the Council of *Trent*, as we ſhall ſhew hereafter. The other ſort may be call'd an atteſtation, or a declaration of the reality of any decree, that it was thus deliver'd in writing, and thus determin'd in Council. This was that confirmation which the Pope gave to the Council of *Trent*; but from hence there is no more room to infer the Pope's ſuperiority over a Council, than to ſay, ſuch or ſuch a biſhop, or other ordinary, is ſuperior to the Pope, becauſe a bull granted by his holineſs was atteſted or ſubſcribed by that biſhop or ordinary. Will any body ſay that the biſhop's name at the bottom is a confirmation of the Pope's bull? Does it amount to any thing more, at beſt, than an atteſtation to remove all doubts of its being authentic? But to make this matter ſtill plainer, the Council of *Trent*, in the fourth Seſſion, regulated the canon of the books in the Old and New Teſtament. Dare any be ſo bold as to ſay the Council thereby confirm'd the goſpel?

Methinks

Methinks I hear fome warm ftickler for the court of *Rome* running down my diftinction, and demanding, with an air of confidence, why is all this wafte of words thrown away to prove what fort of confirmation the *Pope* gave to the Council of *Trent*, when the thing is fo exprefly demonftrated in the hiftory of that Council? Well then, let us turn to the decree of that Council, which actually enjoins the legates to demand confirmation of their decrees and decifions in thefe terms: *Illuftriffimi Domini ac Reverendiffimi Patres, placetne vobis ad laudem Dei omnipotentis, ut huic facræ fynodo finis imponatur, & omnium & fingulorum, quæ tam fub fælic. record. Paulo III. & Julio III. quam fub fanctiffimo noftro Pio IV. Romanis pontificibus, in ea decreta & definita funt, confirmatio, nomine fanctæ hujus fynodi per apoftolicæ fedis legatos & præfidentes, a beatiffimo Romano pontifice petatur? Refponderunt, placet.

The cardinals *Moron* and *Simonette* demanded the fame confirmation in the terms following: *Beatiffime pater, in decreto fuper fine Concilii æ umenici Tridentini, pridie nonas Decembris præteriti publicato, ftatutum fuit, ut per fanctitatis*

---

* This ceremony was obferv'd at the clofe of the 25th and laft Seffion of the Council. See *The Hiftory of the Council of Trent, by our Author Father* Paul. And what is there faid of this pretended confirmation from page 788, to the end, of the third edition in quarto.

titatis vestræ legatos peteretur nomine dicti Con-
cilii a sanctitate vestra confirmatio omnium &
singulorum in eo definitorum. 'Quapropter nos
cardinales volentes exequi, humiliter petimus no-
mine dicti Concilii a sanctitate vestra confir-
mationem omnium & singulorum in ipso definito-
rum. Quibus auditis, petitioni vestræ, nomine
Concilii, consentientes, quæ definita sunt de car-
dinalium consilio, & assensu, autoritate apostolica
confirmamus. And in the bull : *Cum autem ipsa*
sancta synodus, pro sua erga sedem apostolicam
reverentia, antiquorum Conciliorum vestigiis inhæ-
rens, decretorum suorum omnium confirmationem
a nobis petierit, nos & omnia confirmamus, &c.

I doubt not but when those two cardinals
returned to *Rome,* they chose to express themselves in this manner, on purpose to tickle the
vanity of that court ; and I own, had I been
in their place, I should have done the same,
otherwise I am persuaded the printer would
not have been suffer'd to publish my speech,
which could not be sincere without being dis-
agreeable. The terms of the bull of confirmation cannot be drawn into a precedent, since it
cannot be denied that those who dictated it
were both judges and party ; for which there
need no other proofs than the words *antiquo-*
rum Conciliorum vestigiis inhærens. Indeed the
term *generalium* is not added, which is the
point in dispute ; for as to provincial Councils,
I have already shewn they are out of the question ; and I am surpriz'd that a court, which

has

has fo many fagacious minifters that thoroughly underftand its interefts, fhould be guilty of
fuch a grofs omiffion as the word *generalium*.
But 'tis a proof that they thought they had not
good grounds to ufe it ; for I am perfuaded if
they had, they would never have forgot it.

The court of *Rome* thinks the Pope's fuperiority authoriz'd in a fpecial manner by the
terms of the faid decree of Council ; but to
confute this, one need only reflect upon the
manner how the faid decree was formed. To
this end it muft be remember'd that all the
prelates being quite tired out with the long
duration of that Council, with the expence
they were there obliged to, and with the lofs
of fo much time, without improving it to the
advantage of chriftendom in general, all their
decrees being formed after the model of the
maxims of *Rome* ; they watch'd with impa-
tience for the moment of their feparation, that
they might return home and reft from their fatigues. In fhort, the whole world waited to
fee an end put to this Council, and even the
princes, who were not there in perfon, long'd
as heartily for their feparation, as they did at
firft for their meeting. The emperor himfelf,
who preffed more than any body for their affembling, that he might have the means to
crufh thofe heretics who began to grow formidable in his dominions, or at leaft to oblige
them to be filent, till the controverted points
were decided, finding by fad experience, that
what

what would have been a healing remedy at other times, did only inflame the wound, heartily confented to their feparation. Mean time, if the princes had not thus defir'd it, the Pope would never have put an end to this Council, tho' 'tis very certain he fecretly wifh'd for it more than any body, to free himfelf from the greateft danger, to which the papal authority had been expos'd for many ages : And *Zachary Delfino,* a *Venetian* nobleman, who was his nuncio at *Vienna,* obtained a cardinal's cap for perfuading the emperor *Ferdinand* to confent to its diffolution. Now the Council was diffolv'd, and declar'd at an end by the following propofition to the fathers, *placetne vobis ut huic facræ fynodo finis imponatur ?* And without ftaying for an anfwer to that, they added in the fame breath, *& petatur confirmatio omnium, &c.* To which the fathers anfwer'd, *placet.* When one confiders the difpofition the fathers were then in, as has been before remark'd, who can doubt but this word *placet* was pronounc'd fo quickly, only becaufe it was the word intended to put an end to that tedious Council, and that the fathers gave little or no regard to the confirmation which they were required to intreat of the holy father ? Nor can it be doubted that thefe two propofitions were clofely coupled together, artfully to eftablifh the dependency of the Council, and the fuperiority of the holy See ? But who does not perceive that in a matter of fuch importance as the eftablifhing

blifhing

blishing the Pope's authority by the decision of a Council, it was necessary, without delaying, or confounding it with the Council's last words, to make a special decree for that purpose, after mature deliberation? But it was much to be question'd whether they would have had the desir'd Success, so that the shortest way was to have recourse to artifice; but an artifice so gross and staring, as shews it to be wilful neglect. Having said enough on this head, we proceed to examine the validity of this confirmation.

A general Council being, as I have already said, an assembly of all christendom, does not exclude the secular princes, who are many times present; not indeed to vote in articles of faith, which are things not within the jurisdiction of the secular power; but to give the Council their protection and advice. And at this day, when their interests will not permit them to be absent from their dominions, they send their embassadors, and the Pope does not forget in the bull of convocation to invite and exhort them to go thither in person. The Popes themselves have many times been personally present in Council, and now they send their legates; so that the presence of the Popes, either immediately in their own persons, or mediately by their substitutes and vicegerents, or representatives, is necessary to render the Council valid, according to the afore-cited decree of that of *Chalcedon,* which declares every Council

cil null that is pretended to be general, without the prefence of the Pope's legates. Then what a vain, whimfical piece of formality is it, to defire of the Pope at *Rome*, the confirmation of what has been decreed by himfelf, or with his own concurrence, at *Trent*? Is it not plain, that if the decrees made at *Trent*, with his approbation and advice, tho' abfent, were good, juft, agreeable to fcripture and tradition, it were needlefs to revife them at *Rome*, and that this was done with a view only to raife the Pope's fuperiority, and not to examine or confirm any thing already examin'd by himfelf, and corroborated by the votes and prefence of others? Moreover, is it not demonftrable that nothing was offer'd to the confideration of that Council, but what was propos'd by the Pope's legates? fo that nothing was brought upon the ftage but what the court of *Rome* had a mind to: Which cuftom, tho' not obferv'd in the primitive Councils, was a check to thofe who had a defign to encroach upon the Pope's prerogative In the firft feffion, under *Pius* IV. a decree was propos'd by the holy father, that the Council fhould make fuch decifions only, touching the chriftian faith, as might be thought neceflary; and this decree was paffed as well as all the others that were propos'd. The prelates and princes faw indeed, when 'twas too late, that the *ablatives, proponentibus legatis*, was a fure fign of their flavery, and they complain'd of it to the Pope;

but

but he brought himſelf off without much difficulty, by pretending he had not time to examine either the *gender* or the *caſe.* And this
was the conduct obſerv'd during the whole
Council, in which nothing was propos'd but
from the Pope by his legates. To what purpoſe then was this confirmation deſir'd ?

Here follows a piece of hiſtory worthy of
remark. The court of *Rome* apprehending
that the Council might hereafter be told, by
way of reproach, in a full aſſembly, that they
were not free, took care that another decree
ſhould be propos'd in the 24th ſeſſion, declaring that by the terms, *proponentibus legatis*, it
was not their intention to change the methods
of treating uſually obſerv'd in general Councils. On the other hand, the court of *Rome*
being, to the laſt degree, jealous of the Pope's
privileges and authority, took great care to
have it declar'd in one of the canons paſs'd in
the 25th ſeſſion, that in all things eſtabliſh'd
by the ſaid Council, touching reformation and
eccleſiaſtic diſcipline, a ſalvo is intended for the
Pope's authority. But can any thing be more
ſuperfluous ? for in other decrees, either
this authority is attack'd, or it is not. If it
be particularly attack'd, this general exception
cannot help it ; and if it be not, the ſaid exception is needleſs. In the ſame ſeſſion it was
declar'd, that if any embaſſadors ſhould give
place to others in this Council, the princes,
their maſters, ſhould not thereby ſuffer at all in
their

their rights. But is not this too a mere complement from his holinefs; fince, if the remedy was good, it were needlefs to have fo
long difputed the punctilioes of honour?

I beg pardon of the courteous reader for
bringing the Council of *Trent* fo often upon
the ftage. For I look upon it as an argument
ad hominem, a thoufand times more conclufive
than a hundred general arguments, fince none
can be ftronger than thofe taken from the canons even of this Council, which pioufly defended the rights of the holy See; and yet
with all this they could not pleafe the court of
Rome, unlefs the Pope's fanction were added
to their proceedings. We fhall in the next
place examine the nullity of this confirmation;
and when that is prov'd, it will be eafy to
eftablifh the fuperiority of a Council over the
Pope, and confequently decide the queftion
which is the main fubject of this chapter.

If the confirmation of a decree ought to be
receiv'd at the fame time with the decree it
felf, one cannot fuppofe the infallibility of
judgment, becaufe that would need no confirmation, according to the maxim, *fruftra fit
per plura quod poteft fieri per pauciora.* Mean
time this infallibility is plainly fuppos'd, becaufe in every feffion of the Council of *Trent*
there is this expreffion, *fancta fynodus in fpiritu
fancto legitime congregata,* i. e. *the facred fynod
lawfully affembled in the Holy Ghoft.* Now, how
is it poffible for a decree to be falfe or erroneous,

neous, which is inspir'd by the holy Ghost? There is no variableness in God, but in the Pope there may, for 'tis a mark of imperfection. If therefore God in his mercy inspires a Council, he will not alter his purpose, whatever may happen, because the Lord is not subject to accidents, and changeth not. Now, who, that has heard *Jesus Christ* say, *wheresoever two or three shall be gathered together in my name, I will be in the midst of them*, can doubt of this invisible direction of God? After so positive a promise, ought a Council, the assembly of all christendom, to be fearful of erring, and can they want confirmation? If, notwithstanding this promise of Christ, it be asserted that the Pope's presence is necessary in a Council, 'tis not because he has any authority there, but purely to fulfil the conditions laid down by *Jesus Christ*, in these words, *in my name*; which signify that the assembly have the service of *Christ's* Church for their moving cause, and final object. The same conclusion may be drawn from the terms of applause given to the said Council, *viz. sancta œcumenica synodus Tridentina, ejus fidem confiteamur, ejus decreta servemus*; i.e. *let us confess the faith, and observe the decrees of the sacred general Council of* Trent. To which the prelates answer'd, *semper confiteamur, semper servemus, item omnes ita credimus, omnes idipsum sentimus, omnes consentientes & amplectantes subscribimus : Hæc est fides beati Petri, & apostolorum ; hæc est fides patrum,*
                                                              hæc

hæc est fides ortodoxorum, ita credimus & senti-
mus ; i. e. this is the faith of *blessed* Peter,
and the apostles, of the fathers, and the orthodox,
we unanimously believe, embrace, and subscribe
it, and will all confess and keep it. After such
a confession as this, the question is, whether,
if the Pope had refused his confirmation, the
christians would not have been oblig'd to believe the decisions of that Council ? If it be
said no, the consequence is plain, that the
Council told a lie, in saying it was the faith of
St. *Peter*, and the apostles. If it be answer'd
in the affirmative, then the Pope's confirmation
was not at all necessary

Perhaps the court of *Rome* will reply to this,
that confirmation only extends to the decrees
of a positive law, and not to those matters of
faith which are already declar'd to be the faith
of St. *Peter* ; and that therefore every Council, which undertakes to limit the authority of
the court of *Rome*, cannot avoid falling into
an absurd temerity, since it will always lie in
the breast of that court, either to confirm, or
reject its decisions upon this so nice an affair.
But what will those gentlemen say to a decree
passed in the 6th session of the same Council,
under *Julius* III. whereby the continuation of
the Council was suspended for reasons therein
mention'd ? And then 'tis added, *interea tamen*
sancta synodus exhortatur omnes principes chri-
stianos, & omnes prælatos, ut observent, & re-
spective observare faciant in suis regnis, omnia
& sin-

& singula, quæ per hoc sacrum œcumenicum Concilium fuerunt hactenus statuta & decreta ; i. e. the holy synod exhorts all christian princes and prelates, that they observe, and cause to be observ'd, in their respective dominions, all and singular the statutes and decrees hitherto passed by this sacred general Council. But had the Council been of opinion that its decrees could not be valid, without being confirm'd by the Pope, it would have been extravagant rashnefs in them to recommend the observation thereof before they had desir'd such confirmation. And in the last session, the following words were register'd a little before the passing of that decree which requires the Pope's confirmation. *Supereſt nunc ut omnes principes, quod facit in domino, maneant ad operam suam ita præſtandam, ut quæ ab ea decreta sunt ab hæreticis depravari aut violari non permittant, sed ab his & omnibus devote recipiantur & fideliter obferventur quod si in his recipiendis aliqua difficultas oriatur (quod non credit) quæ declarationem aut definitionem poſtulat, præter alia remedia in hoc Concilio inſtituta, confidit sancta synodus sanctiſſimum Romanum pontificem curaturum, ut vel evocatio ex iis præsertim provinciis, unde difficultas orta fuerit, iis, quod eodem negotio tractando videbitur expedire, vel etiam Concilii generalis celebratione, si neceſſariam judicaverit, vel commodiore quacumq; ratione ei viſum*

sum fuerit, provinciarum necessitatibus pro Dei gloria & ecclesiæ tranquilitate consulatur.

Now let every conscientious person determine whether it may be lawfully inferr'd from these words, that the Council thereby own'd the dependency of its decrees on the Pope ; or rather, if they are not as it were a delegation of authority to the Pope, to concern himself in dubious cases relating to the decrees establish'd by the said Council.

And in the 25th Session, C H A P. II. concerning reformation, there are these words : *Præcipit sancta synodus patriarchis & omnibus aliis, ut in synodo provinciali post finem hujus Concilii habenda, omnia palam recipiant, necnon veram obedientiam Romano pontifici spondeant & profiteantur.* Which imports a command of the synod to the patriarchs, *&c.* to pay true obedience to the Pope. Now, if the Council were inferior to the Pope, I should think it senseless and ridiculous to recommend them to that obedience. Lastly, towards the conclusion of the same chapter, the Council having prescrib'd the form of regulating the catholic universities, adds, *the Pope shall take care that the universities, which are immediately under his protection and visitation, be visited and reform'd by his delegates,* &c. I make two remarks upon these words : 1. That the Council saw very plainly, that if they had not made this exception touching the *universities subject to the Pope,* he would have thought himself authoriz'd al-

so

fo to vifit and reform the others above-mention'd, elfe the exception would be needlefs.
2. That this conduct of the Council, in pre-
fcribing to the Pope what he has to do, clearly
fhews that they did not own him for a fuperior. What pafs'd in the 23d feffion on the
queftion concerning the chalice, proves the
truth of this ; for the Council refers the decifion of it to the Pope, in thefe terms, *decrevit*
integrum negotium ad fanctiffimum dominum no-
ftrum effe referendum ; which formal delegation
is a proof that the Council does not depend on
the Pope; for the inferior does not delegate to
the fuperior, becaufe the latter has a natural
right of judging, whereas it belongs to the
former only by way of reference : To conclude, in the laft feffion 'tis faid that fome
prelates were deputed, by order of Council, to
form an index of prohibited books, and examine the catechifm, miffal, and *Roman* breviary, and to make a report thereof to the Council, which was to form a decree thereupon :
* [and the Council being not able to give their
judgment of all in a trice, becaufe of their
number, referr'd the whole to the judgment
of the Pope.] This feems to me a plain
decla-

---

* What is inferted betwixt the two crochets, is not
exprefs'd in the *Italian*, but 'twas taken from the hiftory
of the Council, and 'twas thought neceffary to place it here at
length, becaufe the confequence, which the author draws
from that refolution of the Council, is founded upon the laft
words, *referred the whole to the judgment of the Pope.*

declaration, that the Council meant rather to *give* authority *to*, than *receive* it *from* the Pope, and that they only regarded him as their vicar, *or* suffragan, whofe power was under their regulation. Tell me not of *Pius* IVth's bull of confirmation, in which are thefe words: *Nobis adeo Concilii libertati faventibus, ut etiam de rebus fedi apoftolicæ proprie refervatis, liberum ipfi Concilio arbitrium per literas ad legatos noftros fcriptas ultro permiferimus ;* i. e. *we have fuch a regard to the freedom of the Council, that, of our own accord, we have, by letters written to our legates, permitted them to judge arbitrarily, even of things properly referv'd to the apoftolical See.* But this liberty is all mere delufion, ·if (·as is pretended) 'tis abfolutely neceffary to defire the Pope's confirmation of what is concluded ; for if he has a power to grant it, he has the fame power to refufe it ; which at once deftroys this pretended freedom. I chofe to fingle out all thefe remarks from the Council of *Trent*, becaufe, as that Council was moft partially zealous for the papal authority, I thought it would the better anfwer our end, *viz.* to eftablifh the authority of a Council over the Pope.

In the catalogue of lawful Councils there is this note, *Anno Domini 466, Romanum tertium provinciale fub Hilario Papa à quinquaginta epifcopis congregatum potiffimum ftatuentibus, ut canones Niceni Concilii & apoftolicæ*

G

fedis

ſedis conſtituantur; i. e. *it was chiefly ordain'd by fifty biſhops, aſſembled in the third provincial Council at* Rome *, under Pope* Hilary*, A. D.* 466, *that the canons of the* Nicene *Council, and the apoſtolical See, ſhould be obſerv'd.* So that here is a ſingle provincial Council commanding obedience to the decrees of another Council, and of the holy See. Another aſſembled at *Worms,* under Pope *Leo* III. and the emperor *Charles* the Great, exprèſly orders, that no perſon be excommunicated for a trivial fault, that the miniſters of God be ſober, and the table of the biſhops frugal. Another general Council, aſſembled at *Vienna* in 1311, approved the decrees of Pope *Clement* V. call'd *Clement's* conſtitutions. But we'll go back ſtill higher, not forgetting the principle I before laid down, that the Pope has undoubtedly, at this day, no more authority than St. *Peter* had. Now the firſt general Council, which was held at *Jeruſalem* by St. *Peter* himſelf, by the apoſtles and other diſciples of the primitive Church, proves it to have been the opinion of thoſe times, that a decree, made by all together, had more force than if made by St. *Peter* alone. The queſtion debated in this Council was, whether circumciſion was neceſſary any longer? *Peter* ſays, *Men and brethren, you know, how that a good while ago God made choice among us, that the gentiles by my mouth ſhould hear the word of the goſpel and believe. And God, who know-*

eth the hearts, bare them witnefs, giving them the Holy Ghoft, even' as he did unto us. Hitherto *Peter* acknowledges that God had given all baptiz'd believers as great a portion of his grace and fpirit as to himfelf. After him, *Barnabas* and *Paul* fpoke of the miracles which God had wrought among the gentiles; and then *James* fays, *Men and brethren, hearken unto me : Simon hath declar'd how God at the firft did vifit the gentiles, to take out of them a people for his name.* After which he goes on thus : *Wherefore my fentence is, that we trouble not them which from among the gentiles are turn'd to God, but that we write unto them that they abftain from pollutions of idols, and from fornication,* &c. *Then it pleas'd the apoftles and elders, with the whole Church, to fend chofen men out of their own company to* Antioch, *with* Paul *and* Barnabas; *namely,* Judas, *firnamed* Barfabas, *and* Silas, *chief men among the brethren: And they wrote letters by them after this manner. The apoftles, and elders, and brethren,* &c. ------ *We have therefore fent* Judas *and* Silas, *who fhall alfo tell you the fame things by word of mouth ; for it feemed good to the Holy Ghoft and to us, to lay upon you no greater burden than thefe neceffary things : That ye abftain from meats offer'd to idols, and from blood, and from things ftrangled, and from fornication : From which, if you keep your felves, ye fhall do well. Fare ye well.* 'Tis palpable from all the tranfactions of this Council, that St. *Peter* did not

pretend

pretend to the leaft fuperiority over thofe who compos'd it, that they regarded him only as their colleague, and even embrac'd the opinion of St. *James*, who, after he had made the decree himfelf, put an end to the Council, in the name of the Holy Ghoft. In another part ˚of the *Acts of the Apoftles*, we find thefe words : *When the apoftles, who were at* Jerufalem, *heard that* Samaria *had receiv'd the word of God, they fent unto them* Peter *and* John. Is it not evident from this circumftance that *Peter* valued himfelf upon obeying the apoftolical college, inftead of pretending to any fuperiority over them ? For the college fends *Peter*, and he forthwith obey'd. From that time to this I can't find any augmentation of authority ever granted to the holy See, except by tradition. When the Pharifees reproach'd *Chrift*, that his difciples *tranfgreffed the tradition of the elders, becaufe they did eat with unwaſhed hands, laying afide the commandments of God,* he tells them, that they (the Pharifees) *who were fo zealous for the tradition of the elders, did thereby tranfgrefs the commandment of God.*

It may indeed be faid with too much juftice, that 'tis the conftant fate of the high priefts to be captivated by this˚ paffionate thirft after worldly grandeur, tho' there's no crime in the whole gofpel againft which *Jefus Chrift* has exprefs'd more refentment. St. *John* the evangelift tells us, in his 8th chapter, that *Chrift*, in a long difcourfe which he had one
day

day with the chief prieſt, (and we don't find throughout the whole goſpel that *Chriſt* ever expreſs'd himſelf with more warmth) gave him theſe hard words: *If I ſay the truth, why do ye not believe me? ------ He that is of God, heareth God's word ; ye therefore hear it not, becauſe ye are not of God.* He adds afterwards, *It is my father that honoureth me, whom ye ſay that he is your God, yet ye have not known him ; but I know him ; and if I ſhould ſay I know him not, I ſhould be a liar like unto you.* Theſe reproaches of being not of God, of knowing not God, and of being liars, did not move them a jot ; but when he attacks the antiquity of their origin, by ſaying, *before Abraham was, I am,* they took up ſtones to caſt at him. No wonder therefore to find this ambition of worldly honour lurking, even at this day, in the chief Prieſts, ſince they have it as by inheritance from the ſynagogue. But to return to the authority of a Council.

We don't find that *Jeſus Chriſt,* when he conferr'd the prieſthood on his diſciples, gave them any authority different from that of *Peter.* When he inſtituted the ſacrament of the euchariſt, after he had ſupped with them, he ſaid to them all, *take, eat, and as often as ye do this, do it in remembrance of me.* So that he conferred on them all equal authority of conſecration. And when he was riſen again, he gave them equal power of binding and looſing. He breathed on them, and ſaid unto

them,

them, *Receive the Holy Ghost. Whosoever sins
ye remit, they are remitted unto them; and whose-
soever sins ye retain, they are retained.* So that
Peter in these *two* functions, 'or rather *three*,
had not the least superiority over the rest, and
those words afford ho manner of foundation
for the distinction made by the court of *Rome*,
betwixt the power of order, and that of jurifdiction. Consequently, the bishops being the
successors of the apostles, as the Council of
Trent declares; and the Pope, the successor of
St. *Peter*; it follows, that in the exercise of
their episcopal authority, they depend no more
upon the Pope than the apostles did on St. *Peter*; but when united together, they have an
absolute superiority over him, as has been
shown in the two preceding pages. But the
Romanists object, that the keys were promis'd
to St. *Peter* alone. *I will give thee the keys of
the kingdom of Heaven.* I allow it; but since
they take it for granted that the power of binding and loosing is exercised by the *power of the
keys,* they must yield me this point; that the
said promise is not singular, because the power
that flows from it is exercised by many. St. *Peter*, at another time, who was subject, as well
as all mankind, to the frailty of human nature, which is apt to demand large rewards for
the least service done to God, took the liberty to say, *behold we have forsaken all and follow'd thee, what shall we have?* It cannot be
deny'd there was a deal of presumption in this

demand;

demand ; for what reward could he think he had deferved, for leaving a paltry fishing boat, and a ragged net ?

This ambition of preheminence discover'd it self in the disciples, even in the presence of *Jesus Christ. There arose a strife among them, which of them should seem to be the greatest ; but* Jesus *said unto them, let the greatest among you be as the least, and the chiefest as he that serveth.* If our Saviour had approv'd of a superiority in a proper sense, was not that a fit opportunity to have declar'd it ?

If a Council be not superior to the Pope, to whom should the Church of God apply, when ever there should be more Popes than one, as happen'd at the time of the Council of *Constance,* when no less than three assum'd that name; one of whom was *Gregory* XII. a *Venetian.* As to the other two, one pretended to excommunicate the other, who denying his competitor's authority, excommunicated him in his turn. Now what was the consequence of all this ? Why the flock of Christ did not know their true pastor. But 'tis impossible that God, who in his goodness has provided remedies for the body, should forget to make the same provision for the Soul, as they do in effect declare, who deny the superiority of a Council.

I intend not, by this, to deny the primacy of St. *Peter,* and by consequence that of the Pope. I own this primacy, but I can never al-

low

low that ufurpation of authority which St. *Pe-*
ter never had, and which by confequence is not
attainable at this day by the Pope; for tho' he
was the head, or chief of the apoftolical college, he was not therefore fuperior to the others.
There would be a contradiction in fuppofing a
fuperiority among colleagues. But having fully difcuffed this queftion, I fhall now conclude this chapter, hoping I have fufficiently
prov'd that a Council is fuperior to all ecclefiaftical dignities.

C H A P. V.

Whether a lawful prince may be de-
priv d of his dominions by reafon of
excommunication ?

IN fome foregoing chapters we have fufficiently fhewn the rigor of the punifhment
of excommunication, that it extends fo far as to
render a chriftian incapable of fharing the benefit of *Chrift's* redemption. We have likewife
demonftrated that a punifhment fo terrible is
due to none but thofe who are guilty of the
moft enormous crimes; yet the defenders of
the papal authority don't think this chaftife-
ment fevere enough, and therefore they add,
that every prince under excommunication may
fome-

fometimes be depriv'd of his dominions, and
that the next poffeffor needs no other title to
them than executioner of the Pope's fentence: I fay *fometimes*, becaufe excommunication does not always carry with it this two-
fold punifhment, but only when certain circumftances of the crime engage the Pope to
add this claufe to it. Thofe even who are not
acquainted with modern hiftory, and have only ftudy'd the canons of the Church, will think
this claufe ftrange and abfurd; for thofe very
canons, which feem to have been made purely
for eftablifhing the rights of the Pope, mention not a word about it; but it muft appear
ftill much more extravagant to thofe who have
any knowledge of antiquity, efpecially if they
compare the carriage of modern princes towards the holy See, with the infults that were
put upon it by the princes of ancient times. Indeed we read that fome were excommunicated, but never that they were depriv'd of
their dominions, or fo much as reprimanded,
tho' they had extremely injur'd the holy father.

In the time of the Emperor *Juftinian*,
Pope *Vigil* was cited before the judges, and
went to *Conftantinople*; where, at the folici-
tation of the Emprefs *Theodofia*, who favour'd
the *Arians*, he was laid in irons; yet the emperor was not excommunicated for that infult,
neither then nor after. Another time, when
Gilfulfus, Duke of *Benevent*, carry'd an army
into

into *Campagna di Roma*, deftroying all the country with fire and fword, Pope *John* fent to tell him, that if he would avoid the divine vengeance, he muft decamp immediately. This was only a charitable admonition, but fo effectual, however, that the duke obey'd; for admonitions are commands, when accompany'd with the fanctity of the prelate who gives them. On the other hand, if one confiders the lamentable condition of the king of *Navarre*, who was turn'd out of his dominions by the king of *Spain*, one cannot but ftand aftonifh'd at the feverity of the punifhment, compar'd with the lightnefs of the crime. This unhappy prince made an alliance; it feems, with *Lewis* XII. king of *France*, whom Pope *Julius* II. had excommunicated, and confequently incurr'd only the *minor* excommunication; yet, tho' he had committed no crime, the catholic king, who was a zealous executioner of the Pope's fentences, immediately feiz'd his dominions. Many things might be faid upon this fubject, but now we will examine it as matter of law; for as to the fact, the *Romanifts* are fo far from denying it, that they feem to boaft of it, without ftaying to confider what crime deferves fuch a punifhment. We proceed now to inquire whether the Pope has the power of decreeing it againft any fovereign? And to make this inquiry with the greater exactnefs, the queftion muft not be reftrain'd to the Pope only, but extended in
general

general to all the bifhops; for according to the maxims of the court of *Rome*, all bifhops have a right to excommunicate Princes, tho' we have no inftance of the fact in our times; and tho' indeed it ought not to be, becaufe a fubordinate power has no right to cenfure a power which is abfolute and independent. This is fo conftant a maxim, that if the *Romanifts* will affert this right in the bifhops, they muft of courfe own them to be independent; and if they aver on the other hand, that they are dependent and fubordinate to the Pope, they muft difown their pretended authority, and not fuffer them to extend it over free princes; but to gain their point, they deny our inference, and affert that a king or emperor ought to be fubject to the meaneft bifhop, as long as he lives in his Diocefe.

But I defire them to anfwer me this queftion, whether they would approve of a bifhop of *Spain*, who, conducting himfelf according to their maxims, fo advantageous for the ecclefiaftical authority, fhould excommunicate a king of *Spain*, for reafons which he might think very juft, and deliver up his dominions to another? If they fay no, I would ask them the reafon, whether it is for want of authority in the faid prelate, or becaufe they think the punifhment too fevere? If the former, let them fhew me thofe different degrees of excommunicatory power in the gofpel. For my part, I find no text there upon this fubject,

but

but that addrefs'd to St. *Peter, you fhall bind and loofe;* and that in another place, directed to all the Apoftles, *ye fhall remit and retain,* which are terms fo near the fenfe of the former in a fpiritual language, that they may be call'd fynonymous. If the terms of the text were duly confider'd, when *Jefus Chrift* fpeaks to St. *Peter,* he addreffes him in the fingular number and future tenfe, *I will build----- fhall be bound and loofed;* but when he fpeaks to St. *Peter* and all the apoftles together, he ufes the prefent tenfe : *Receive ye the Holy Ghoft; whofefoever fins ye remit, they are remitted; and whofefoever fins ye retain, they are retained.* Moreover, 'tis to be obferv'd that *Jefus Chrift* fays this to *Peter* before his paffion, when he could not be the paftor of a flock not yet redeemed, and when it was not yet expedient to give the power of binding and loofing, becaufe the knots which bound up mankind in chains were as yet too tight, before *Adam's* fin was repaired; but when *Jefus* fpeaks to the apoftles, the redemption had been wrought by our Saviour's death and refurrection. From hence I infer that the authority of the apoftles was at leaft equal, if not fuperior to that of St. *Peter,* and that the bifhops have confequently the fame in their functions as above.

If the court of *Rome* condemns fuch conduct of the *Spanifh* prelate, as being too fevere, it fairly implies that there may be a fault in excommunications of this nature; and in the

the inflicting of thofe punifhments; confequently 'tis lawful for all perfons to examine
them whether they are faulty or not? Therefore 'tis not an article of faith to be believ'd
implicitly. They will fay, perhaps, that they
fhould not blame this act of the bifhop, for either of thofe reafons, but only for its tendency to involve chriftendom in confufion, by authorizing princes to invade the territories of
their neighbours. And I infer further, that
when excommunication is to be fulminated,
regard fhould be had to the intereft of the
public, and to reafons of ftate, for avoiding
univerfal fcandal; which is a maxim we laid
down before.

But, if upon the whole, they fhould fay
they would approve the conduct of a bifhop
that fulminates excommunication with this
referve, that the motive of it feems to him to
be juft, they muft pardon me for frankly owning that I cannot believe them, becaufe this
would be acknowledging that every bifhop is
a Pope in his Diocefe; an opinion by them de-
tefted as much as that which fets a bifhop upon a level with the Pope, to whom they
afcribe greater authority than to a bifhop, tho'
they can produce no text to fupport it.

This monarchical authority of the Pope has
caufed me to make a reflection, which I think
very true and juft, *viz.* that all other things of
this world, whether created or generated, lofe
their vigor and force in procefs of time; but
the

the Pope's authority is fo far from lofing, that it always gains ; and, which is very miraculous, is more vigorous in its old age 'than its youth. If we caft our Eyes on the productions of nature, and the ordinary generation of things, we find them declining with age, and deftitute of their former vigor. Men do not live fo many months now, as heretofore they did years. The brute creatures are not fo capable of fatigue as formerly. The fruits of the earth have not the fame favour, fweetnefs and fub ftance, and are more dangerous to the confti tution.' Then as to bodies politie ; thofe, which were once fam'd for their wifdom and power, are become weak and fupine ; and the fubjects, who formerly burned with zeal and duty to their fovereigns, upon all occafions, are now become cold and indifferent : The arts and fciences have fuffer'd the fame diminution ; where is there now an *Apelles*, a *Phidias*, and a *Policletus* ? Our age has no *Ariftotle*, *Plato*, nor *Socrates* in the fchools, nor no *Achilles*, *Alexander*, and *Hannibal* in the field. The *Turkifh* empire is a farther proof of this viciffitude ; this empire, founded upon the flavery of the people, and their blind obedience to the fovereign ; which they think honourable in this life, and meritorious in the next ; how is it fallen from its ancient fplendor ! The *Mahometans*, who now fee thro' all the whimfies of the *Alcoran*, and find how contrary its laws are generally to the prefervation and advantages

ges of fociety, have not that faith which their anceſtors had in *Mahomet*. Theſe decays are all natural, and there's nothing in this world in which they are not viſible. In my opinion this ſingle argument might have convinc'd *Ariſtole* that the world would have an end; which he ſo abſolutely deny'd, becauſe, ſaid he, expe-rience taught him, that corruption is the cauſe of generation; ſo that he thought it impoſſible for the world to ceaſe, conſidering the daily reſurrection of individuals.

On the other hand, in an eccleſiaſtic monar-chy we find, that, excepting holineſs, which does not increaſe; and reſpect, which dimi-niſhes from time to time, authority augments every day. But this increaſe is owing purely to a refined piece of ſecret policy, by means whereof the Popes have artfully worked them-ſelves into ſecular affairs, and eſpecially when a ſtate finds it ſelf under an obligation to change its ſovereign. Then, if the Pope's help is im-plored, tho' the affair is purely civil and inde-pendent of the eccleſiaſtical juriſdiction, he does not loſe a moment, but flies to the af-ſiſtance of the ſovereign who deſires it, as a ſure way to gain him over to the intereſts of the holy ſee, and to make him a defender of its authority. Thus when *Pepin* depriv'd *Ghil-peric* III. King of *France*, of his crown and dignity, on pretence that he was a weak ſlug-giſh prince, Pope *Zachary* confirmed his elec-tion in 750. So when *Charlemain*, King of
France,

France, ſeiz'd the imperial crown, excluding *Conſtantin*, the ſon of *Irenæus*, Pope *Leo* crowned him in St. *Peter's* Church at *Rome*. In like manner, when the empire was divided betwixt him and *Nicephorus*, the Pope gave his approbation. Theſe, and many other accidents of this kind, are what the Popes improve to juſtify their titles, and to make it believ'd that they can do every thing as well as he from whom they pretend to hold their power. By this method alſo, the Popes have engag'd *England* more than once to become tributary to the holy See, by paying it an annual tribute of a hundred marks of gold, which was called St. *Peter's* Pence. And this the *Engliſh* government conſented to, for warding off a blow then threatned by the *French*, who had too great a reſpect for the Church to invade a fief of the holy See. To this very cauſe muſt be aſcrib'd the advancement of ſome rich aſpiring princes to the dignity of king, great duke, &c. who thinking their former titles too mean, have recourſe to the Pope; and if they do but engage to make ſome ſmall acknowledgment to the holy See, they need no more to obtain their wiſhes. The court of *Rome* has ſlip'd no opportunity to put in practice a method ſo effectual for augmenting the Pope's authority; and as it thereby makes princes defenders of that authority, which the holy See claims to it ſelf in ſecular matters, ſo in ſpirituals he has ſecured the monks of all orders whatſoever to

his

his own intereſt, by exempting them from the juriſdiction of the biſhops.

This was the courſe which the See of *Rome* took to make itſelf neceſſary. Yet the ancient ſovereigns, and thoſe who had no need of the Pope's protection to eſtabliſh or aggrandize their authority, could not bear thoſe uſurpations, Indeed they became familiar by time, which brings all things to maturity, and by the Pope's cunning improvement of the neceſſities of princes, who before had oppos'd their authority, or by the ſpeedy aſſiſtance of others, whoſe towering hopes of greatneſs call'd for ſuch a ſupport. But for a Pope to pretend to take away a prince's hereditary dominions, under colour of ſome ſlight diſobedience, is what princes ought never to ſuffer; becauſe the injury of turning a prince out of his property, is much greater than the courteſy of granting it to him who deſires it ; for a title granted, tho' perhaps irregularly, does not immediately offend another; and if it ſhould, that's all ; but a prince cannot be depriv'd of his dominions without being injur'd; ſo that if the firſt action may paſs for a favour, tho' againſt law, certainly the ſecond is a very great injury.

All the diſſentions which have been, and are ſtill in the Church, have their ſource from the new cuſtoms and pretenſions of the court of *home*, who would fain ſet humane tradition upon an equal foot with the goſpel of

H   *Jeſus*

Jefus Chrift, becaufe 'tis on fuch tradition that they found the many prerogatives of the Pope, which were entirely unknown in the pureft times of antiquity. From hence comes that diverfity in opinion between thofe who are for hearkening to tradition, and others who are for confulting only the facred text, as the fountain of revealed truth, becaufe infpir'd by God, and who fet by tradition as a mere human production; for which they are branded with the odious character of heretics and fchifmatics. But the cafe would be quite otherwife, if the Pope would tread in the fteps of St. *Peter* and the other apoftles, and primitive fathers, who were infpir'd by God with a holy zeal for his glory, in comparifon whereof they accounted all this world's honour, and even life itfelf, as lefs than nothing. If the Pope, I fay, would imitate their conduct, I don't know one chriftian that would not be afham'd to deny him all poffible reverence, and the moft entire obedience, I mean, to his pofitive laws; for as to the articles of faith which are conformable to the fcriptures, whoever prefumes to call them in queftion, muft be heretics in my efteem, as I have already protefted more than once.

Now, the claufe which is fometimes added to excommunication, *viz.* that a prince excommunicated fhall be depriv'd of his dominions, as a punifhment for his offence, that they fhall devolve to the next poffeffor, and
that

that his fubjects are thenceforth abfolv'd from
their oath of fidelity, and from all obligation
of obedience to their former fovereign, was
never *practifed,* did I fay? no not fo much as
ever *mention'd* in the primitive times. *Lycur-
gus,* when tax'd with an omiffion in the com-
piling of his laws; becaufe he had prefcrib'd
no punifhment for a parricide, anfwer'd that
he did not think it poffible for fo horrid a
crime to enter into the heart of man, becaufe
nothing was more contrary to human nature:
Therefore, I fay, 'tis utterly needlefs to rake
into antiquity for a proof whether the Pope
may, or may not, make ufe of this claufe,
fince 'tis an innovation of but a hundred and
fifty years ftanding. Confequently, if the
moft holy Popes of antiquity did not inflict
fuch punifhment for the moft flagrant crimes
that ever were committed by princes in rebellion againft the See of *Rome,* it muft be infer'd as their belief, either that they had no
authority for it, or that it was unjuft. I know
fome will object, that thofe Popes were neg-
ligent, and did not confider they had
that power; but this is a notion I can never
come into, becaufe many of them demonftrated, both by their practice and doctrine,
that they were enlightened by the divine fpirit.
Proceed we now to examine the nature of that
claufe.

'Tis an augmentation of fpiritual punifhment with that which is corporal. But is it

not

not abfurd to make the leaft comparifon betwixt the damnation of the foul, and the
fufferings of the body; the former being confider'd as infinite, and the latter by their own
nature limited and temporary? This made our
Lord *Chrift* fay, *What fhall it profit a man, tho'*
he fhould win the whole world, if he lofe his foul?
What need then is there for adding the lofs of
temporal goods to excommunication, which
of itfelf deprives a man of everlafting glory,
by denying him the facraments, which are the
means and pledges thereof? Is not this actually adding finite to infinite, which addition
cannot make it more infinite than it was before? Is it not as much as to fay that the firft
punifhment is infufficient; becaufe, if it were
fufficient, the addition would be needlefs and
unjuft, and would rather diminifh than add to
the weight of excommunication? The common law fays, that a judge may not condemn
a criminal to corporal punifhment, and to' pay
a fine for one and the fame fact. If the criminal (fays the law) be guilty of fuch crimes as
deferve fevere punifhment, 'the punifhment
fhall be proportion'd to the guilt. If it be a
petty crime, and the judge thinks fit to punifh
him *ab extra*, that is to fay, by a fine, he may
not lay corporal punifhment on him at the
fame time, becaufe to fubject the criminal
both to corporal and pecuniary punifhment at
once, would be punifhing him two ways at a
time. Now when one mean is fufficient for an
end,

end, 'tis in no wife expedient to make ufe of
two ; but if the crime be fo heinous as to deferve the fevereft punifhment, *viz.* death, it is
ftill more unjuft to add pecuniary punifhment to
it; becaufe death makes fatisfaction for the
greateft crime in nature, and the law of God
teaches, *that he who is put to death is juftified
from his fin.* 'Tis true, indeed, that fometimes
the judges join pecuniary and corporal punifhments together; but 'tis only when the corporal
punifhment is unufual, and lighter than what the
law prefcribes for fuch crime ; fo that I affert,
that when the punifhment is capital, the criminal ought not to be fined.

Therefore, upon due examination of the
matter, it will appear that the Pope cannot
condemn an excommunicated perfon to the
lofs of worldly goods ; which may be as fitly
compar'd to a fine, as excommunication, which
is the death of the foul, to the lofs of life.
Confequently, when the Pope acts otherwife,
it muft be allow'd that he either fets common
law at defiance, or that excommunication is
not really fo terrible a punifhment as is given
out. Tell me not that the Pope is above the
law, and by confequence not oblig'd to obferve fuch forms ; for the law is founded
not only on the civil power, but alfo on the
law of nature, to which all mankind is fubject, and which no perfon can refift ; becaufe,
according to the order of fecond caufes, the
law of nature fupplies the place of the divine

H 3   law.

law. Besides, whoever compliments a judge so far as to own him bound by no rule, gives him full range to make what criminals he thinks fit, and to punish the innocent at discretion. But our Lord *Christ*, to avoid such an imputation, says, *I came not to break the Law, but to fullfil it.* For my own part, I cannot help comparing this complication of punishment to a candle lighted at noon-day, which rather exposes the folly of the person that kindles it, than adds to the light of the sun. But now to argue *de minore ad majus.* When a prelate, or the Pope himself, excommunicates a private person, they never add the clause of confiscation or loss of goods; why then is that clause inserted against a prince, to whom greater respect is due than to a private person? Let it not be said that the crimes of a private person, and a prince, are not weighed in the same balance; for I should have recourse immediately to this certain axiom, that God has but one balance for the crimes of all mankind; for as the apostle says, *with God there is no respect of persons, whether bond or free.*

It may be objected perhaps, that when the civil power banishes a person, it commonly adds the confiscation of estate. This I own; for banishment is only an accidental punishment, which consists merely in a person's deprivation from the society of his fellow-citizens, and may render that person more happy abroad, than if he staid at home. This made *Aristides*
say

fay in his exile, *perieramus nifi periuffemus.*
Now the law punifhes a man in his eftate,
when it cannot come at his body, by reafon of
his abfence; but 'tis not fo in the prefent cafe.
The Pope has already condemn'd the criminal
to the moft rigorous punifhment, in depriving
him of the facraments, and driving him from
the Church; which, accoiding to the court of
Rome, carries along with it the death of the
foul. Therefore 'tis not requifite to add the
confifcation of eftate to that fentence, becaufe
the death of the foul is more than fufficient fatisfaction for the groffeft crimes. Let it never
be faid that an excommunicated perfon is as
one condemn'd, who has loft the relifh of all
comfort in this life, and may therefore be lawfully depriv'd of his dominions. This argument deftroys itfelf; for we know by faith,
that all the damned do not feel the extremeft
degree of punifhment; there being greater
and leffer degrees of torment in hell, as there
are different degrees of glory in heaven; from
whence it follows by parity of reafon, that the
extremity of punifhment ought not to be inflicted, in this world, for a fin which is an act of
the foul, fince they are not all equally punifh'd
for fuch fins in the world to come.

But the Pope's conduct would need no better warrant than a demonftration that he has receiv'd worldly power from *Chrift;* who, if he
confer'd it on *Peter* and the other apoftles,
certainly did not give it them to make no

ufe

afe of it. 'Tis plain then, that if the courtiers of the *Roman* See could produce only one word out of the holy fcriptures, to authorize this important claim, it were enough; but fince nothing like it can be found throughout the whole Bible, let them not pretend to urge it with this plea, that becaufe *Chrift* gave power to *Peter.* to govern his Church; and becaufe, for the well governing of it, 'tis neceffary to cut off the rotten members; therefore when a prince is excommuhicated, it were better he fhould ceafe to be a prince, be ftrip'd of all he has, and reduc'd as near as poffible to no-thing, that his punifhment may be a terror to others. This argument is exactly of a fize with a very trite maxim at *Kome,* that a here-tic ought either to be converted, or burnt. 'Tis not only a very fallacious and inconclufive way of reafoning, but injurious to mercy, that moft glorious attribute of God, hinders re-pentance, and makes the prophet a liar, by whom God declares, *In the day that a wicked man returneth from his wickednefs, all his ini-quities will I not remember.* The judgments of God are vaftly different from thofe of men; but always for the better: For example, if a delinquent confeffeth his crimes to men, he expofeth himfelf to condemnation; but if he confeffeth them to God, he obtaineth forgive-nefs. Thus, faith he, *My ways are not as your ways.*

There

There are innumerable fouls in heaven that were once the vileft of finners, but were afterwards juftify'd, and now excel thofe in glory who always preferv'd their innocence. *There is greater joy in heaven over one finner that repenteth, than over ninety and nine juft perfons that need no repentance.* If therefore repentance gives fuch a luftre to the foul, as renders it more beautiful than it was before its fall, why then, to apply it to the prefent cafe, may not a prince, depriv'd of his dominions for a fpiritual crime, which can only be repair'd by the contrition of the foul; why, I fay, fhould not fuch prince be reftor'd to his former, if not greater fplendor, when he repents, returns to his duty, and defires to be readmitted to favour? Tell me not of his having fpiritual grace alone; for I would fain know why he may not, together with that grace, have reftitution alfo of his temporalities taken from him by reafon of his offence, fince his converfion renders him the better man for having offended.

Pope *Gregory* the Great fhewed this to be his real fentiment, when, like a true penitent, he cry'd out, *It is good for me, O Lord, that I have finned.* When God chaftized *Job*, that eminent pattern of patience, as foon as he found himfelf reduc'd to the fevereft extremity, he was fo outragious as to curfe the very day of his birth, and to tax God with cruelty and injuftice; but afterwards, when he came

to

to himſelf, he beg'd pardon, obtain'd favour, and the Lord gave him twice as much as he had before. The Pope affects to imitate God in the ſeverity of puniſhment, but not in pardoning or reſtoring the offender, and only does it by halves; for when once the dominions of an excommunicated prince are become the poſſeſſion of another, the Pope, with all his authority, cannot make him reſtore them; becauſe, if the Pope's decree be juſt, the poſſeſſor always thinks himſelf ſufficiently authoriz'd to keep them as his lawful property. That which involv'd *Judas* in a ſtate of damnation, was his deſpair of ever obtaining reſtoring grace for his former crime. So the depriving a prince of all poſſibility of being reeſtabliſh'd, is the way to make him deſpair of ever being reſtor'd to favour. If the Pope pretend, in his excuſe, that ſuch prince ought to be very ſpeedy in his obedience, if he would avoid double puniſhment: I anſwer, that *Chriſt* did not act after this manner; for he promiſes to repair the loſs ſuffer'd by ſin, at all times, without limitation. And if the Pope replies, that he alſo makes all the reſtitution, in his power, to ſuch excommunicated prince, by reſtoring him the pledges of divine favour: I anſwer again, that the holy father is in the wrong to be the occaſion of ſuch loſſes as he cannot repair; for if he would imitate God, he ought to know that repentance not only wipes out all the evil of ſin, but alſo renders
the

the finner a better man in the fight of God than he was before he had finned.

But now, under favour, we will examine both the good and the evil that attend fuch excommunications as deprive a prince of his dominions. The benefit which arifes from hence is twofold, according to them; for firft, fay they, the crime for which fuch punifhment is inflicted, being fuppos'd to be very heinous, the more fevere the punifhment is, the more it will be proportion'd to the crime. Secondly, if the prince fhould continue obftinate in his crime, fuch fevere punifhment will ferve as a continual fpur to urge him on to confefs his fault and repent. Thus the *Ninevites*, who were drown'd in their fins, did not repent till they were threatned with an univerfal conflagration. They add further, it ferves for a warning to others to abftain from the like crimes, left they fall under the fame punifhment; *Oderunt peccare mali formidine pœnæ.* The wicked are deter'd from fin by the fear of punifhment. Thus far thefe gentlemen. But for my part, I find that what they here call good, is attended with very great evil; and like a drop of neat wine mixt in a glafs of poifon, which lofes its goodnefs, and becomes homogeneous with the poifon itfelf. For as to the firft argument, it will eafily be demolifh'd by the following reflection, *viz.* that excommunication being a fpiritual punifhment inflicted on the foul of a finner, 'tis undoubtedly

ly the greateſt of all puniſhments, ſince 'tis
a cutting off from the body of the Church,
and therefore it cannot be augmented; whereas the adding corporal puniſhment to it, ſuppo-
ſes that excommunication is not ſo efficacious
as is given out; becauſe the joining of two
puniſhments together, the one ſpiritual, and
the other temporal, is a fair confeſſion that the
ſpiritual is not ſufficient; for a remedy, that
will do of itſelf, is never compounded with an
auxiliary.

As to the other advantage, which, ſay they,
flows from this two-fold puniſhment, *viz.*
that it ſpurs the criminal to repentance; I refer them to their own argument; from whence
it muſt be infer'd, that ſuch converſion is not
the effect of puniſhment already inflicted, but
of more which is threatned : For example,
the *Ninevites*, when threatned, repented; but
the people of *Pentapolis*, when puniſh'd, died
without remedy; ſo *Pharaoh*, the more
plagues *Moſes* brought upon his land, the
more he harden'd his heart. Would to God
that the Popes had been more cautious and deliberate in excommunications of this nature;
they would have been ſtill ſovereign Pontiffs,
whereas they are now no more than biſhops,
and ſuch biſhops too that are deſpiſed and abhorred as antichriſts. The truth is, that after
all they have advanc'd, where one excommunicated perſon has been converted, there are
ten who have puſh'd their diſobedience to
apoſtacy;

apoſtacy; ſuch is the condition of the damned, who belch out the moſt horrid blaſphemies; having no greater torments to fear, nor pardon to expect; and ſuch is the corruption of our nature, that we are prone to render evil for evil.

When the Pope excommunicates a prince, and deprives him of his dominions, he cannot make his condition worſe, for he deprives him of ſpiritual and temporal life both together. To be ſure then, ſuch prince, if he were able, would deſtroy the Pope and papacy with all his heart; nay, would do worſe, if worſe could be. When *Luther* was excommunicated, he had only preach'd againſt indulgences; but after his excommunication, he publiſh'd above a hundred propoſitions againſt the *Roman* Catholic faith, and the Pope's authority. When *Henry* VIII. was' excommunicated for the divorce of *Catharine* of *Arragon*, he and all his kingdoms apoſtatiz'd from the Church, and became the ſharpeſt perſecutors of the papacy, to which they had, till then, been devout tributaries. Let no one therefore boaſt of the good effects of excommunication, becauſe the ſucceſs of the juſteſt puniſhment depends entirely upon the good diſpoſition of the perſon corrected.

How many canonical puniſhments are now out of uſe, becauſe the pious zeal of the people, who even courted martyrdom, is cool'd in the ſame proportion as the perſonal ſanctity

of

of the Popes is diminifh'd ? And it will be juft fo with excommunication, when once it is attended with the deprivation of dominions. Who knows what may be the dreadful confequences of fuch a claufe? What defolations and plunderings? How many maffacres of the innocent? How many rapes and burnings? What rapine and violence? If fuch are the means, what will the end be? It will be in vain to pretend that fuch dominions are tranffer'd into the hands of a prince more pious and obedient. *We muft not do evil, that good may come on it.* But this is not all yet; who knows what difturbances may happen in the recovery of fuch loft dominions? It cannot be expected that fuch an undertaking, as the feizing a prince's dominions, will always be attended with the fame eafy fuccefs, as when the king of *Navarre* was depriv'd of his dominions. For at that time the very novelty of the attempt frightned that unhappy prince's fubjects, who, rather than be put under the curfe, fubmitted to the ufurper without refiftance. But now people's eyes are open'd, and perfons of the meaneft rank can difpute, and prove, that the Pope has exceeded his authority; and that if chriftians are oblig'd to obey the Pope in matters of faith, they are equally oblig'd to fpend their lives in defence of their prince and country. In fhort, if man was fo wife as to forefee contingencies, I cannot but think, that if a Pope forefaw the misfortunes

*

which

which fuch conduct would occafion, tho' in his
confcience he thought he had the jufteft reafon
for it in the world, he would tremble with
horror, as the elect will in the laft day of
judgment at their neighbour's condemnation,
tho' they are fecure of being fav'd themfelves.

Thefe are the reafons produc'd to juftify the
conduct of the court of *Rome,* in point of excommunication, becaufe there's no paffage in
the gofpel on which it can be clearly eftablifhed ; and tho' fomething like it may be
found there, it muft be underftood in a reftrain'd fenfe ; for the gofpel fays, *If thine eye
offend thee, pluck it out.* But where's the man
that obeys this command in the letter ? Or
where's the Pope, who, tho' as liable to vice
as other men, plucks out his eyes or his ears,
that are commonly the inlets of fin ? Surely
then there is much lefs reafon to do a thing
which has no manner of precedent ; for *in odi-
ofis non eft ampliandum.* When *Chrift* gave
commiffion to the difciples to go and convert
the Gentiles, he told them exprefly, that
whereever the people did not receive nor hear
them, they fhould depart thence, and fhake
off the very duft from their feet, as a teftimony that they would have nothing more to do
with them : So when he prefcrib'd them the
rules of brotherly correction, he told them it
ought to be done with modes and forms, and
that if a perfon did not amend after admonition, they fhould account him as a heathen
and

and a publican. In short, I never could find that our Saviour inflicted any temporal punishment on the most obstinate sinner. But the Popes have acted far differently. History tells us, that *Pius* V. who was a Pope of a holy life and conversation, threatned the emperor *Matthias* to depose him, as having forfeited the imperial government, if he did not revoke a certain decree which he had passed against the ecclesiastical liberties. But here are two things to be consider'd, First, that he threatned him; and that was all; now such a menace is better than putting it in execution. Secondly, that tho' he had depriv'd that emperor of his dignity, he would, by so doing, have only exercised an act of temporal authority, which the Popes have over the emperor, tho' not *de jure,* yet at least *de facto & de confuetudine,* and by consent of the party; for 'tis owing to the Popes that the empire, which passed from the east to the west, and first into *France,* is at this day fix'd in *Germany;* and 'tis no less owing to the indulgence of the Popes, that the imperial government, which was at first elective, became afterwards successive. From hence it follows, that they have as much right to depose him, as any private man can have to make void a grant for the ingratitude of the person to whom he gave it. But to take away the dominions of a free prince, who derives his power immediately from God alone, without being oblig'd to the least favour from
the

the Pope, for his establishment, is crying injustice. .: Therefore let the See of *Rome* be contented with the power of excommunication, which is great enough in conscience, and let them keep as much as possible within the bounds of the ecclesiastical monarchy, which is purely spiritual, without being so vain as to imagine that a christian prince, tho' disobedient, may, for the edification of the Church, be lawfully depriv'd of his dominions; for St. *Peter* himself, whom the Popes ought to propose for their pattern, says, *Honour the king. Servants be subject to your masters with all fear; not only to the good and courteous, but also to the froward. For this is thank-worthy,* &c.

If St. *Peter*, who prescrib'd this submission to the secular power, had, in his conscience, thought it lawful to treat temporal princes, in any case, with so much severity, surely he would not have been silent in a point of such importance as this. Mean time he is so far from approving it, that he recommends the observation of a precept the very reverse to it, I mean, absolute submission. From hence I conclude, that since *Peter* did not believe such conduct equitable in itself, or even consistent with the papal function, it ought not to be introduc'd by the means of human tradition; which, as I have said already, has been the source of numerous disputes, and given birth to their opinion, who accuse the Pope of assuming

I

suming

suming more authority than St. *Peter.* Having said enough on this point, we difmifs it.

CHAP. VI.

Whether excommunication is juftly incur'd by infringing ecclefiaftical liberty?

FOR the better folution of this queftion, 'tis neceffary to diftinguifh that ecclefiaftical liberty is violated fometimes by private perfons, and fometimes by fovereigns: If by a prince, it may affect either the perfons of ecclefiaftics, or their eftates; the former, by hindring them in the exercife of their functions, or when they concern themfelves not as ecclefiaftics, but as private perfons, in affairs out of the jurifdiction of ecclefiaftics; the latter, by cutting off the clergy's tenths, and the like grievances. I thought this reflection very neceffary for deciding feveral queftions, which will occur hereafter, and cannot be difcuffed afunder, becaufe of the relation they have to one another.

When an injury is done by a private perfon to ecclefiaftical liberty, in refpect either to eftates or perfons, the prelate may with juftice proceed againft him, even to fentence of excom-

communication; if, after he has twice admo-
nifh'd him, the criminal obftinately perfifts in
the violation of fuch liberty, or offers no excufe, efpecially when the injury is important
and notorious ; I fay, if the injury be important and notorious ; becaufe, tho' it be manifeft, and yet trifling, the prelate ought to remember the decree of the Council of *Worms*,
formerly mention'd ; which orders, *that no perfon fhall be excommunicated for a trivial caufe :*
I add, that the bifhop may lawfully inflict
this punifhment for the injury done, as well
to the eftates as perfons of the clergy, becaufe
private men are oblig'd to refpect both alike.
If a perfon is convicted of a defign upon the
life of an ecclefiaftic, he incurs excommunication *ipfo facto,* without previous admonition ; which is not neceffary in this cafe, every one being fufficiently forewarn'd in law not
to attempt the life of a clergyman ; fo that
whoever ftrikes a clergyman, is as much excommunicated as if fentence were actually paffed againft him, and publifh'd. Neverthelefs,
I muft not forget to take notice, that cafes of
felf-defence ought always to be excepted ; for
if it be decided that a prieft, who, going to
celebrate mafs, kills a man in his own defence, *cum moderamine inculpatæ tutelæ,* is not
only exempt from the breach of the canon
againft homicide, but from the very imputation of fin ; fo that he may approach the altar
with unwafh'd hands, and legally celebrate

mafs ;

mafs; and all this becaufe felf-defence is authoriz'd by a law. of nature, not made, but
implanted in our very beings, and. from which
no other law can derogate; we have the fame
reafon to make this exception at another time
in favour of the laity, who, being not fo ftrictly oblig'd as the clergy to fubmit to the canons, are more at liberty to obey this law of
nature.

It ought alfo to be confider'd, in regard to
the conduct of a private perfon, who violates
the ecclefiaftical liberties with relation to
eftates, that if his attempt be barely injurious,
he deferves the ecclefiaftic cenfures; but with
this precaution before-mention'd, that fuch cenfures be preceded with two admonitions.
Now if the criminal, after the faid admonitions, offers no plea in excufe for his conduct,
and actually perfifts in his attempt, it ought
certainly to be deem'd injurious; but on the
other hand, if he protefts againft the admonition, pretending to have acted *jure proprio*, and
by virtue of fome title, be it what it will,
then the ecclefiaftics, whom it concerns, fhall
not fummon fuch laymen before the ecclefiaftical court, but before the fecular tribunal,
which fhall judge of the validity of the pretended title; for 'tis a rule in law, that the
plaintiff or profecutor bring his action in that
court to which the defendant belongs. Thus
for example; if a *Venetian* has any demand
upon a citizen of *Bergamo*, he muft bring his
action

action againſt him at *Bergamo*, and not cite him to appear at *Venice*. If indeed ſo much time is ſpent in proving the title as renders the ſuit tedious, then excommunication may be publiſh'd ; but if it be publiſh'd before ſuch proteſtation, all the conſequences of it ought to be ſuſpended ; for the delinquent cannot be deem'd contumacious while his injury does not appear ; and if not contumacious, he cannot be ſubject to excommunication. 'Tis needleſs to dwell longer upon theſe conſiderations, which are not ſo much as controvertible, if the juriſdiction of the judge, which uſes to be diſputed, be not refus'd, or call'd in queſtion.

If a ſovereign prince breaks in upon eccleſiaſtical liberty, we have already obſerv'd, that diſtinction ough to be made between eſtates and perſons ; if a ſeizure be made of eſtates, there ſhould be another diſtinction between the tenths and other eccleſiaſtical eſtates. Every thing relating to the tenths ſhall be refer'd to its proper head, and the power of a prince to ſeize them, ſhall be the ſubject of the tenth chapter. Therefore, if a prince lay hands, not upon the tenths, but other eſtate of the clergy, and ſeize it for the good of the publick ; for inſtance, if he make uſe of the Church-lands for building a wall, making ditches about a city, or trenches for the paſſage of a river, or canal, or any thing elſe for the publick good and ſafety ; tho' ſuch

ſove-

sovereign refuse, after the Pope's admonition, to restore those lands, whatever censure he may deserve in other cases, he incurs none in this, because it falls under the law of necessary defence, which, I have already shewn, is excepted out of this question.   But if a sovereign prince usurp the estates of the clergy, with no other view but to fill his own coffers, to furnish him diversion, to pamper his luxury, or to maintain the splendor and vain pomp of his court; notwithstanding all that has been said to prove that the authority of the Pope over princes is purely spiritual, and consequently that they are accountable to God's tribunal only for their crimes; yet, for all this, I say, that such prince deserves excommunication, because the power given to the Pope by *Christ* himself to feed the christian flock, includes in it an obligation to defend the ecclesiastics in the peaceable enjoyment of their temporal maintenance, that they may be the better prepar'd to perform the offices of the priesthood, and to distribute that bread, which is the chief and truly celestial nourishment.

It cannot be deny'd that the use the prince makes of the estate of the clergy which he seizes, may either diminish, or augment the nature of his crime.   We read that *Herod*, king of the *Jews*, sent some of his confidents to the tombs of *David* and *Solomon*, to carry away the sacred treasures, which were there reposited; and a sudden flash of fire came

out

out of the tomb and confum'd them. But king *Hyrcanus*, who, fome time after, took three hundred talents out of thofe tombs, to buy a Peace from the king of *Egypt*, came to no harm, nor thofe whom he fent with that commiffion. God was pleas'd to make it appear by this variety of fuccefs, that the end and defign which a perfon propofes is always more to be regarded than the action itfelf, becaufe the former renders the latter either good or evil. Very pertinent to this purpofe, I remember a laudable action of Pope *John* IV. whofe Memory I therefore revere. This Pope made no fcruple to ftrip all the Churches of *Rome* of their moft precious ornaments, for redeeming a number of chriftian flaves from the infidels, remembring from the *Revelations*, that thofe animated ftones were the truly precious ftones, which were to go towards the building of the heavenly *Jerufalem*. A prince may be faid to make an attempt againft ecclefiaftical liberty, with refpect to perfons, when he molefts the Clergy, either in the exercife of their functions, or in actions which they do, not as priefts, but as ordinary perfons. If a prince difturbs a clergyman in his prieftly character or functions, he deferves excommunication (provided two admonitions be given in the firft place) for 'tis faid, *Touch not my anointed*: Now, by the word *anointed*, all thofe are underftood who are anointed, or confecrated by divine ordination. But this point deferves

parti-

particular regard, and the nicest examination, in order to avoid mistakes on either side.

A prince neither can, nor ought to concern himself with the functions of the priesthood, which is an office above the secular power; neither is it his business to introduce new rites, or new modes of performing the offices of a priest, this being a point..reserv'd to the Pope and Church alone. But if, for just reasons, a prince commands the priests to perform their functions in the ordinary way, this cannot be called an infringement of ecclesiastical liberty, but rather an encouragement and protection of it; and no man in his right senses could reckon it criminal in a governor, or other secular magistrate, much less a prince, to bid his chaplain, when he celebrates mass, do it in the common way.

If a prince infringes the liberty of ecclesiastics, for actions which they do, not as priests, but as laymen, he is undoubtedly so far from incurring excommunication, that he is not in the least blameable; for tho' the prelate is not subject to the secular power in his quality of priest, yet when he commits any worldly, civil, or secular action, he is forthwith suppos'd to act as a layman, and consequently responsible to that prince who is lord of all that are born within his dominions. All ecclesiastics are oblig'd to obey the common laws of their country, and the prohibitions which the prince thinks fit to issue for the well-governing of his domi-

dominions. ₁For inſtance, if a prince forbid his ſubjects from trading in ſalt, or prohibit all commerce, or intercourſe, with the dominions of a neighbouring prince, it would be ridiculous for eccleſiaſtics to plead the privilege of their order for an exemption from theſe obliga♦ tions. A prince would have but the ſhadow of power, if he muſt be oblig'd to the prelates approbation, before he can make a decree that ₁includes the clergy as well as his other ſubjects. · The prince demands to be obey'd on this occaſion, not·by the order of prieſthood, but by the perſons therewith inveſted. It might be here expected, ·perhaps;· that· 1.ſhould.ex♦ amine whether, when₁ eccleſiaſtics are puniſhable for ſecular actions, their lay ſovereign has a right to judge them ? But 1 refer this inqui♦ ry to its proper head, *viz.* the XIth Propoſition. But obſerve, by the way, that·I ſpeak of ſecular actions ·only ; for if· an eccleſiaſtic renders himſelf criminal in adminiſtring the ſa♦ craments, or ·in· his other,]ſacred functions, ·he would· be accountable to none ·but· an₁eccleſi♦ aſtic judge, who is alone₁ capable and authoriz'd to take cognizance of his fault. · ·⸱ ·

⸱ Another remark is very neceſſary in. this place, *viz.* ₁that all₁ this authority here aſcrib'd to ſecular princes, over the eccleſiaſtics, muſt be₁ underſtood only of .princes who are inveſted with the royal or ſupreme dignity ; for if he be of an inferior rank, if he be only a feudatory prince, ·his authority will not be near ſo fo extenfive; for fuch hold their fovereignty not *jure proprio*, but *jure adventitio*, and are as the reprefentatives of another fuperior prince; and in this refpect, having their hands ty'd up from making new laws and orders, they muft be content with thofe that were in force, either when the government was confign'd to them, or at the time of their acceffion. But if it happens that by the change of the times, or unexpected accidents, fuch fubordinate princes think fit to make new laws, or to derogate from old ones, they are oblig'd to have the confent of the lord of the fief, or fome other perfon or Council, from whom they receiv'd their inveftiture; fo that if, on fuch occafions, they themfelves violate ecclefiaftical liberty, they well deferve to be cenfur'd, becaufe they want the privilege of fovereign authority to protect them.   Some perhaps will accufe this diftinction of fulfome flattery towards thofe who enjoy that privilege, and as an infult on thofe who are depriv'd of it; but let fuch remember that my authority for this is the Council of *Trent*, where, in more places than one, there are exceptions in favour of an emperor, a king, and all that are invefted with fovereignty, whereas there is not one in favour of inferior princes, who have only the title of petty fovereigns.

Befides the violation of ecclefiaftical liberty, which a fecular prince may commit, with refpect spect either to persons or estates, he may likewise violate the privilege or immunity of consecrated places. Indeed a great respect ought to be paid to those places, as they belong in a special manner to God; and they are not subject to the distinction we made use of with regard to his ministers, whose actions are sometimes holy, and at other times profane. For those places are always sacred, be they profaned never so often. We read of *Asylums* in all ages and countries. Under the old law, cities of refuge were constituted by divine appointment in every tribe, where criminals might shelter themselves from the pursuit of justice. The capitol was vested with the same privilege in old *Rome*, and the pagans thought they honour'd their *Jupiter* by giving him the title of *Capitolinus*. In the succeeding ages, those who fled only to some statue of their prince, enjoy'd the like privileges. In the history of *Alexander* the Great, we read of an order that prince gave to *Megabizes*, that if he could apprehend a certain notorious criminal, he should bring him to exemplary justice, but with a caution not to hurt him, if he had taken sanctuary in an *Asylum*. And while *England* was in the *Roman* Catholic Church, the history of those times makes mention of the famous sanctuary at *Westminster*, which, according to tradition, was the residence of angels. In short, consecrated places have always enjoy'd this franchise, and a prince who refolutely goes about to violate it, deferves all the ecclefiaftical cenfures, and becomes highly guilty before God's tribunal, who has always fhewn himfelf a jealous guardian of the immunities of fuch places. Among the cafes of confcience, this is one, that the minuteft robbery committed in the Church is heinous facrilege ; and every private perfon who violates the freedom of a confecrated place, on any pretence, be it never-fo-flight, not only falls under the ecclefiaftical cenfures, but is accountable for the crime to the fecular tribunal, and ought to fuffer punifhment. Yet for all this, it muft be obferv'd that this propofition, relating to the immunity of places confecrated, is not fo univerfal, but that 'tis many times fubject to exception. The canon law mentions twelve cafes, in which perfons are not oblig'd to regard fuch immunity. Thefe cafes include fuch enormous and heinous crimes, for which chriftian charity cannot poffibly grant a fafeguard to mifcreants, that are unworthy of human fociety. This exception is founded upon a fuppofition, that it would be a greater fin againft God to fuffer enormous crimes to go unpunifh'd, than to violate the immunity of fuch places ; for the faid act is not accounted a criminal violation, when 'tis done to obviate a greater crime. So a furgeon, who takes away the life of a man by cutting off a limb, is not liable to be punifh'd as a murderer, becaufe he propos'd to cure him

him by that operation, and not to kill him.
Since then the *Partizans*, even of the court of
Rome, do allow, that there are cafes which do
not oblige to the obfervance of ecclefiaftical
immunity, I will venture to affirm, that befides thofe twelve cafes, a fecular prince may
fet himfelf above the laws in numberlefs
other cafes, of equal importance, not provided for by the law ; for there are more cafes
than laws ; and let a legiflator be never fo
exact, 'tis impoffible but that an infinite number of other accidents will efcape his exactnefs ; for all thefe different cafes are fo numerous, that a man may as well number the
grains of fand on the fea-fhore, as pretend to
reckon them. Therefore, if a prince, in a
cafe that is altogether new, but important,
fhall neglect the obfervation of this immunity, he is not liable to excommunication,
tho' another perfon fhould think the cafe to be
of no importance ; for, provided a man's intention be good, 'tis not abfolutely neceffary
for his opinion to be right, and a prince's good
intention will excufe him from any crime, and
by confequence from the punifhment of excommunication, which can never be fulminated againft him for violating a confecrated
place, in taking out a criminal, in order to punifh him for a crime which he accounts heinous ; for no body knows the principle of a
man's own actions better than himfelf, and it
may eafily happen that a ftranger may think
light

light of a crime, which the perſons concern'd, and preſent, may reckon very conſiderable. But note, that in this caſe ·the prince alone, and not the ordinary magiſtrate, ᴄis the proper judge of the nature of the crime, 'and the importance of the caſe, unleſs, after better conſideration, he thinks fit, in reſpect to the Church, to act otherwiſe, even when he finds it neceſſary to lay 'that reſpect aſide. But enough of this ſubject.

C H A P   VII.

What eccleſiaſtical freedom is ? whether it includes only the concerns of the Church, or all eccleſiaſtical perſons ?

THE great reſpect we owe to our parents, is the rule of that, which all Chriſtians ought to bear to the Church. This precept of the decalogue enjoyning filial duty, has been religiouſly obſerv'd even by the idolaters, who, tho' they never ſaw the glorious beams of divine reaſon, have learnt from nature itſelf how much they are oblig'd to obey and honour their parents ; and no body can give a greater indication of a brutiſh nature, than to know this to be a duty, and ‚at the ſame time forget to

pay

pay it. Now, I fay, that the obligation of
refpect to the Church, may be deduc'd as *a
minori ad majus*, from our duty of obedience
to parents ; for, if we confider what the
Church is, we muft acknowledge her to be a
very affectionate mother, who nurfes us, brings
us up, and gives us nourifhment fuitable to our
weaknefs, and our natural ignorance of the.
divine myfteries. 'Tis by her affiftance that
the mind of man is foitify'd in the knowledge
of God, and of the duty of believers, in the
ufe of the facraments, and in the obtaining of
grace and glory. From thefe great benefits
may be judg'd the importance of fuch a requital, efpecially when compar'd with the merit
of human actions; in regard to which, 'tis a.
treafure of inexhauftible riches, therefore the
obligation of refpect to the Church ought, ·
with great reafon, to be plac'd at the head of
the duties of believers. Whoever afpires to
the glorious name of a true chriftian, whether
he be a fubject, or a fovereign, ought to practife this duty, which is fo light a burden, that
no dignity whatfoever can exempt a man from
bearing it. The traces of this refpect may be
found in, the grofs darknefs of barbarous nations, which are obferv'd to pay the greateft reverence to perfons and things facred ; the
two fpecies that conftitute a Church. Thefe
few reflections may feem fufficient to decide
the prefent queftion ; for if it be allow'd that
the Church confifts of places and perfons, it
apparently

apparently follows, that whoever violates either the one or the other, is guilty of injuring ecclesiastical freedom; which includes things, as well as persons, that are deem'd ecclesiastical. The knowledge which results only from such general topics, is that which is most pleasing to the court of *Rome*, who would confine our understanding to the single operation of conception, without permitting it to examine and distinguish between the different sorts of obligations, and the various ways of discharging them. Nevertheless; we shall continue as we began, by recurring to the distinction, by which, as by the pole star, we shall steer our course, not doubting but it will safely guide us to the port of true knowledge.

. To prevent all manner of dispute, I lay it down for a principle, that whoever violates ecclesiastical liberty, whether in things or persons, belonging to the Church, deserves excommunication; for by such behaviour he acts in contradiction to the character of a christian, which obliges him to respect both the one and the other.. I add, moreover, that this proposition takes in both the condition of a subject, and the high dignity of a prince; for the supremacy of the latter does not at all excuse, but rather adds to his obligation to protect the Church, in proportion to the abundant advantages with which God has been pleas'd to furnish him. Let these few words serve for the text, and we will now proceed to the commentary.　　　　　　　. First,

Firſt, let us inquire wherein the concerns of the Church conſiſt. If I advance that the Church had its birth at the death of our Saviour, I believe no body will dare to contradict me. It aroſe like the bright moon at the ſetting of the ſun of grace, to chaſe away the darkneſs of our minds ; but the ſoul of man is not able to contemplate its ſplendor, nor his weak eyes to behold its dazzling rays, which light us in our ſlippery paſſage thro' this world, leſt, by taking a falſe ſtep, we ſlide into the bottomleſs pit of hell. The Church being born at that ſeaſonable criſis, became the tender nurſe of believers, and was ſupply'd by *Chriſt*, from that very moment, with the milk of the ſacraments, whoſe virtues flow'd from our Redeemer's wounds. Then it was the Church had its beginning ; and in order to promote the converſion of Jews and Gentiles with ſuccefs, by mollifying the hard hearts of the former, and diſpelling the darkneſs of the latter, *Chriſt* gave the Church apoſtles for her coadjutors, who were diſpers'd over all parts of the world, to ſow the ſeed of the word of God, which was follow'd with a wonderful harveſt, for the field was water'd with the blood of the divine huſbandman.

Such were then the concerns of the Church, being, as it were, the firſt bloſſom of this tender plant, which yielded ſuch a fragrant ſmell, as was ſufficient to revive the ſouls of thoſe who were at the very gates of death. Now, I ſay, the concerns of the Church, as they

K   were

were then, were the true concerns of the
Church ; for it has been never brighter, never
more pure than then, when being juſt ſprink-
led all over with the blood of *Chriſt*, and aſſiſted by the virgin, the diſciples and martyrs,
it obtain'd grace from heaven in abundance :
Then the Church had no other care nor view
but to make known the divinity of *Chriſt*, the
neceſſity and conſummation of the redemption, and to adminiſter the ſacraments to thoſe,
who obey'd the goſpel, in that purity in which
they were inſtituted by *Chriſt*; ſo that the
Church then apply'd itſelf chiefly to theſe two
things, the propagation of the faith, and the
comfort of believers. Nor do I think that
this will be diſputed even by the creatures of
the holy See. Therefore every other concern,
with reſpect to the Church, is altogether foreign, if not ſpurious.

If therefore a prince, or private man, hinders the propagation of the faith, and the increaſe of believers, the one, as well as the
other, deſerves the ſevereſt puniſhment ; ſince
by ſuppreſſing faith in *Chriſt*, they carry their
wickedneſs to the higheſt pitch. The propagation of the faith is ſo much the duty of all chriſtians, that whoever would be ſuch in practice,
as well as in profeſſion, ought not to be afraid
of death, but to loſe the laſt drop of their
blood, rather than commit a ſingle action contrary to the faith. For *Chriſt* tells us, *Whoſo-
ever doth not own my name before men, I will
not own him before my father.*

If

If it be prov'd that a private perſon oppoſes the propagation of the faith, he ought, to be not only excommunicated, but alſo corporally puniſh'd as a heretic, it being a contradiction to ſuppoſe that a perſon, who is found and orthodox in his private opinion, would hinder another from embracing the faith.

As to princes guilty of this crime, whoſe high rank exempts them from corporal puniſhment, they ought, however, to be anathematiz'd and branded in the forehead, as perjurors, and deſerters from the body of chriſtians. But to ſay the truth, this, which is the firſt and principal concern of the Church, is very ſeldom attack'd, and has not yet fallen under the cenſure of excommunication ; for the Popes have never fail'd to recommend the propagation of chriſtianity with zeal, in order to engage princes to carry the faith to infidels, at the point of the ſword, it being not enough to ſend it by the tongues of the preachers. But all ſuch undertakings generally come to nought, and ſerve, at the moſt, to uſher in a bull from the Pope. Thus ſome princes play the ſame game. They not only profeſs their obedience, but the moſt flaming zeal for thoſe catholic expeditions. They offer their arms, their ſoldiers, and even their lives ; but they only bluſter with words, while their guns and trumpets are ſilent ; ſo that the ſincerity of ſo many fine promiſes is never brought to the touchſtone. Conſequently, all our reflections on this main concern of the Church are altoge

ther

ther superfluous. For princes are well enough pleas'd with fair promises, because, in truth, they pay the same coin to others in the like case; it being out of fashion, in our days, to merit saintship by martyrdom.

As to the protection due to the faithful, we will adjourn the inquiry for the present, in order to consider the pretensions of the court of *Rome*, who would make us believe, that all the actions of the Pope tend either to command what ought to be done, or to decide whether the actions of others are consistent with the rule of protecting the faithful.

The interest of the court of *Rome* very much resembles leaven, the least quantity of which, in a measure of flour, immediately causes it to ferment, swell and increase. 'Tis the same with the Pope's universal power. The faithful are the last persons 'on whom he bestows ecclesiastical livings; nevertheless, this consequence is undoubtedly drawn from it, that every thing which the Pope does is in pursuance of that prerogative.

To make due provision, say they, for the clergy, all the faithful must be taught to respect and observe the ecclesiastical liberties, and not to meddle, by any means, in things relating to their estates, persons, and places, on pain of being punish'd. Nay, as if this were not enough, they go farther, and, without considering the absurdity of making circumstantials greater than the principal, assert, that in all cases where ecclesiastical estates, persons, and

and places, are admitted to be of the leaft concern, the acceffary claim ought to fuperfede the principal. To give an example with refpect to 'eftates. If a layman, fay they, be in poffeffion of a piece of land, and the Church, or clergy, put in a claim to any part of it, the caufe ought to be try'd in the bifhop's court, and the civil courts muft be filent, and not offer to fupport the reafons, which the layman is capable of giving, to defend his right of fucceffion, or feoffment in truft ; and if a lay judge prefumes to interfere in the caufe, he deferves, according to them, to be cenfur'd, as having violated ecclefiaftical liberty. To give another Example, with refpect to perfons. If a clergyman makes an attempt upon the life, or honour, of a layman, as too often happens, they infift that the complaint be laid before the ordinary of the place, and that the injur'd layman acquiefce in his decifion ; and if he fhould find fault with it, they would not fail to exclaim againft it as a breach of ecclefiaftical liberty. If, for the fake of peace and good order, a prince fhould think fit to forbid the carrying of arms, and a clergyman fhould, notwithftanding, appear arm'd in public, he would plead his innocence of the crime of difobedience, and that if he were guilty, none but his bifhop had a right to try him. If thefe ecclefiaftics do not obferve the common laws, either in buying or felling, if they pretend to be not oblig'd by the commands of the prince, and to be exempt from taxes and gabels, and

from

from being convened before lay-tribunals, on refusing to pay their debts, who will presume to say their pretensions are groundless, or refuse to own them, since they immediately trump up the common outcry of an infringement of the ecclesiastical liberties?

We will now give an instance, with respect to ecclesiastical places. Notwithstanding the regard which pious princes shew every day for Churches, a respect from which they never recede but in cases of the utmost necessity; yet the court of *Rome* would have all convents, and prelates houses to be sanctuaries for the greatest villains. Thus they are for building those places on the top of *Olympus*, above the thunder of justice, and the orders of their sovereign, be they ever so advantageous to the public; for, according to their maxims, nothing in society is preferable to the respect which they claim for ecclesiastical liberty; so that if it should happen that a bastion could not be erected, for defence of a town, against an enemy, without violating that liberty, it were better to leave the town expos'd to the rage of the enemy, than to violate that liberty. Nay, they go farther, and say that all laymen, who are employ'd in a prelate's house, ought to be exempt from lay-jurisdiction. If a layman injures a clergyman, they pretend it belongs only to the clergy to be judges of it, and that if a man, or woman, are accus'd of adultery, according to their laws, they, the the clergy, only ought to try them, and to
judge

judge of them *active* and *passive*. · If an hospital, a school, or mount of piety, be erected, they will have them to be immediately subject to the bishop. In short, where the Church is concern'd for no more than a brass farthing, they immediately recur to ecclesiastical liberty, and say the prince has nothing to do in the matter. Now, after what has been said, I think I had reason to compare the interest of the clergy to leaven, a little of which leaveneth a whole lump of dough. This exorbitant interest is a colour for forming an ecclesiastical state within every civil state, when, upon any turn, the clergy will be ready to cry out of the infringement of their liberties. Let those, who have shoulders broad enough for such a burden, carry it.

i I, for my own part, do assert, according to the distinction I before laid down, that if a private person, or even a prince, injure the Church, either in preventing the propagation of the faith, or in pretending to regulate the doctrine of *Christ*, in the dispensation of the sacraments, which are the ordinary nourishment of believers, whereby the soul is fortify'd in the true faith, and in the practice of good works; I say, whosoever does this, violates ecclesiastical liberty, in attacking the real interest of the Church, and consequently deserves her censure: And the said punishment would then be adequate to the offence; for 'tis not just that he, who, instead of serving the Church, does her all the injury in his

power,

power, fhould enjoy the benefits of the Church, which are purely fpiritual; and 'tis no more than what right and reafon require to cut off and feparate fuch perfon from the body of the Church, who difcovers himfelf to be a rotten member, and capable of infecting the reft. In the year 728, when the emperor *Leo* was prevail'd on by the fuggeftions of an apo-ftate, to break to pieces all the facred images in the fquare of *Conftantinople,* Pope *Gregory* III. held a Council of *Italian* bifhops in the *Vatican,* who made decrees for eftablifhing the veneration due to images, and put that emperor under excommunication. I might here alfo mention the edict call'd the *Interim* of *Charles* V. who, for the fatisfaction of thofe who diffent-ed from the catholics, drew up fuch a regu-lation of the controverted articles, as pleas'd neither of the parties, and both anathematiz'd him; but the *Romanifts* made leaft noife, be-caufe they had a fingular refpect for him. I add, that the fame cenfure is juftly applicable to any one who difturbs an ecclefiaftic in the exercife of his functions: Thus, when the em-peror *Frederic* fet himfelf up for a judge to de-cide the fchifm between Pope *Alexander* III. and *Victor* the Anti-Pope, and *Alexander,* for many reafons, refus'd to appear before the emperor's tribunal; yet that prince, in *Alexander's* abfence, gave fentence in fa-vour of the Anti-Pope, and forbid *Alexander* to perform the pontifical functions; and what was the confequence? why truly, *Alex-*

Alexander excommunicated the emperor; who, being frightned, fled, for the fecurity of his perfon, to the city of *Venice*, and, imploring the affiftance of the republic, they took arms, and reftor'd him to his dignity; after which, he made his peace with the Church, and the *Venetians* had all the honour of it. For what relates to the injuries of ecclefiaftical perfons, I find in the hiftory of Councils, which *Clovis*, king of *France*, wrote to the Council of *Orleans*, that he and his would be obedient to the commands of the church and the Pope, particularly in not forcing the clergy to lift in his troops. All fuch violations of perfonal liberty deferve excommunication as juftly as violating the interefts of the Church; for the freedom of her minifters, in the exercife of their functions, is one of her principal concerns. But the general pretence of the court of *Rome*, that all perfons and eftates, which are in any wife whatfoever depending on the Church, are therefore exempt from lay-jurifdiction, and that to touch them would be a violation of ecclefiaftical liberty, tho' they are included in the diftinction we eftablifh'd above, is what a man muft have the ftomach of an oftrich to digeft. Surely one would imagine they had forgot what they fo often boaft of, *viz.* that this ecclefiaftical liberty, which takes in both eftates and perfons, owes its origin to the emperor *Conftantin* the Great, in the time of Pope *St. Sylvefter*; from whence it appears to be a favour granted by the fecular power,

for

for the greater honour of the Church; so that
'tis the highest ingratitude to retort, what was
only owing to the courtesy of princes, against
their liberty. I do not mean by this, that I
would have ecclesiastical liberty violated upon
all occasions, much less in matters relating to
the true interests of the Church, sacred places, or ecclesiasticks in the exercise of their
functions. But to pretend, that a prince is not
a sovereign of his ecclesiastical subjects, is to
abridge him of that authority which he derives immediately from God, nature, and the
law of nations. Note, I intend only a free
prince, who owns no superior authority in his
government.

I find by the 20th chapter of the 25th session of the Council of *Trent*, that they spoke
of princes with greater respect than the court
of *Rome* have ever done on these occasions.
This chapter, which was compos'd purely for
defence of the ecclesiastical liberties, is some-
what long, but begins thus: *Cupiens sancta
synodus, ecclesiasticam disciplinam a quibuscunq;
impedimentis conservari, seculares principes ad-
monendos esse censuit, jus suum ecclesiæ restitui, sed
& subditos suos ad debitam erga clerum reveren-
tiam revocaturos, nec permissuros ut officiales aut
inferiores magistratus ecclesiæ & personarum ecclesiasticarum immunitatem violent: decrevit itaq;
sacros canones in favorem ecclesiasticarum personarum libertatis ecclesiæ contra violatores esse ob-
servandos ; prætered admonet imperatorem, reges,
respublicas, principes, ne ab ullis baronibus, do-
micellis,*

*nicellis, rectoribus lædi patiantur, sed severe in
eos qui libertatem, immunitatem, atque juris-
dictionem impediunt, animadvertant, imitantes
anteriores optimos religiosissimos principes, qui res
ecclesiæ suæ imprimis authoritate ac munificentia
duxerunt, nedum ab aliorum injuria vindicarunt.*
i. e. The sacred synod being desirous that the
ecclesiastical discipline should be secur'd from all
impediments whatsoever, thought it convenient
for secular princes to be admonish'd to restore the
church to her rights, and to remind their subjects
of the reverence due to the clergy, and not to permit the officials, or inferior magistrates, to violate the freedom of the Church and ecclesiastical
persons. Therefore the said Council decreed several sacred canons, to be observ'd, in favour of
such persons, against the violaters of the liberty
of the Church. Moreover, the Council admo-
nishes the emperor, kings, republics and princes,
not to suffer the clergy to be injur'd by any lords of
manors, rectors, or the like, but severely to ani-
madvert upon such as violate their liberties, immunities, and jurisdiction, in imitation of those
most religious princes, their ancestors, who defended the interests of the Church from the injury
of others, as well as promoted the same by their
authority and bounty.

I think the zeal of the Council for ecclesiastical liberty appears very plain in this canon, by
their exhorting the secular princes to defend it,
in imitation of the princes that liv'd in the primitive ages of christianity, who, at the same
time

time that they made it their business to enlarge the pale of the church, thought it equally their duty to defend her from injury But I don't perceive that the excommunication of princes is so much as pretended throughout, the whole history of that council ; so far from, it, that if any differences happen, relating to the violation of ecclesiastical liberty, it refers the decision thereof to princes ; and instead of treating them as criminals, as the court of *Rome* sometimes does, calls them the protectors of that liberty.

Above all the different kinds of ecclesiastical liberty, the court of *Rome* is most jealous of the violation of these three, *viz.* persons, estates, and sacred places ; tho', in truth, they have not the last much at heart, being far more ready to forgive transgressors for an injury done to places, than to persons and estates:

As far as I can see, we have now sufficiently examin'd all that relates to the subject of ecclesiastical liberty, and shew'd, that the worst the laity can do, in prejudice of ecclesiastical liberty, is, 1. The hindring the propagation of the faith, and the meddling with the administration of the sacraments, and doctrines essential to salvation. 2. Molesting ecclesiastical persons in their ministerial functions. 3. Seizing the estates of ecclesiastics for the conveniency, or pleasure of the prince.

And

And laftly, The offering contempt to facred places, when the fame may be avoided.

I believe there is no chriftian prince but would value himfelf for not taking thofe fteps, that might involve him in the guilt of the things which I have condemn'd ; and if he acts other-wife, I own I am of opinion that he deferves the cenfures of the Church. We will now take to pieces all the other pretenfions of the court of *Rome*; who-finding it impoffible to eftablifh an univerfal monarchy in temporals, would, at leaft, curtail the authority of fecular- princes, as far as lies in their power.

CHAP. VIII.

Whether the poffeffion of temporalities, belonging to the Church, is not of divine right ?

I Am perfuaded, that by the propofing of this queftion, I may be faid, once in my life, to have given into the meaning of the court of *Rome.* Others perhaps will think it wrong ftated ; but that court, inftead of be-ing of their opinion, will think it a neceffary difpute, becaufe it gives them a handle for determining it by a pofitive decree. But fince it is no difficult matter to refolve a queftion, whofe

whose very foundation is dubious, I fear, tho'
we might seem perfectly agreed at the first, it
will not hold long; and that we shall clash a-
gain as soon as the question is decided in the
negative.

The court of *Rome* being concern'd to procure all possible sanction to the Church's possession of temporalities, has, for some time
past, labour'd to persuade mankind that such
possession is of divine right ; but 'tis so far from
being true, that whoever should offer to maintain it, would expose himself for a mere *ig-
noramus*, by calling in question a matter which
has been clearly determin'd long ago. It being, however, necessary, in some measure, to
suit ones self to the temper of a patient, in
order to compass the chief end, the recovery
of his health ; we will, therefore, for once,
allow it to be a disputable point, that we may
have the opportunity of deciding it in such a
manner, that it shall not be, so much as question'd hereafter ; otherwise 'tis well known
the court of *Rome* will always think themselves at liberty to improve their pretensions
on this score. We will examine the question
both as to law and fact.

Whoever is willing to be guided in this
matter by the Scriptures, will there find that
the children of *Israel* were divided into twelve
tribes. God promis'd this people, in the person of *Abraham*, that happy country, which
was afterwards call'd *The Land of Promise*,

according to the promise which God made to *Abraham.* After *Joshua* had made himself master of it, 'twas divided. Now all the people fought to conquer it, yet 'twas divided among eleven of the tribes only ; that of *Levi*, consisting of all the priests and ministers of the temple, being excluded, which the sacred scriptures express in these terms ; *The lord hath given no inheritance to the tribe of Levi, because the Lord God of Israel is their inheritance, as he hath said unto them.* From whence God would give us to understand, that those who are dedicated to the service of his altar, ought, without embarassing themselves with possessions, to depend on providence alone for their maintenance, and to stick entirely to the work of the ministry ; and that the laity should take pains to supply the necessities of the clergy, because they stand continually as a wall of separation betwixt the sins of the people and the wrath of God. *I sought a man to stand as a hedge between me and the earth, that I might not destroy it.* King *Hezekiah*, who well understood the will of God, knowing it was impossible for the mind of man, while embarass'd with the management of temporal affairs, to be duly intent upon the functions of the priesthood, took away their estates ; but to reward them with interest, commanded the laity, at the same time, to pay the clergy the tithes of all they had. For it was but reasonable, that while the one were wholly employ'd

ploy'd in the service of God, instructing the
people in the law, and praying for their sins,
the others should reward them with the sweat
of their brows, not only in furnishing them
with their daily bread, but also in giving them
every tenth year the entire harvest of their
lands for their maintenance. This cannot be
reckon'd poverty, but rather wealth without
inheritance, - profit without pains. *He that
serveth at the altar, ought to live by the altar, as
having nothing, and possessing all things.* If the
tribe of *Levi* had been admitted to a share with
the other tribes, they would have had but one
twelfth part of the land ; whereas, by being
excluded, they had a right to a tenth part. In
a word, by this means the clergy render'd the
most frightful monster in the world agreeable,
a monster which was worse than all others,
inasmuch as the sight of other monsters was a
satisfaction of curiosity ; but this has been abhorred and avoided at all times and places.
The reader will perceive, by this description,
that I mean *Poverty, of all monsters the most
monstrous. Inter monstra monstrosior egestas.*
The laity think it a scandal, but the clergy
their honour; and he comes nearest the character of a true clergyman, according to them,
who is in the state of the greatest poverty ; for
things are always the more valuable, the near-
er they come up to their original production
or institution, otherwise we cannot but esteem
them degenerated, and as fruits out of season,
which

which have the fame colour indeed as others, but not fo good a tafte.

In the law of grace, *Jefus Chrift* fpeaks ftill more plainly, *Take no thought of what ye fhall eat, or wherewith ye fhall be cloathed, for your heavenly father knoweth what ye have need of. Care not then for the morrow ; but feek ye firft the kingdom of God, and all thefe things fhall be miniftred unto you.* And in another place, *Bear no bag, neither fcrip, nor fhoes.* Again, he ask'd the difciples, *When I fent you without bag and fcrip, lacked ye any thing ?* This is the very effence of the priefthood, to lay afide earthly affections, and to throw off the things of this world, in order to have a greater portion in heaven. While the Church was poor, it was fear'd, reverenc'd, and, in a word, always affifted by the holy fpirit, which far exceeded all human force. In the very fame manner, the *Ifraelites,* while they were in the defert, without poffeffions, without water, or even pafture, found the almighty power of God ready to fupply their wants, by raining down *manna* upon their camp, and fending them water out of the rock ; but as foon as ever they had pafs'd *Jordan,* and faw themfelves mafters of *the land of promife* ; where they reap'd without the labour of fowing, Providence feem'd fufpended as to them, or, at leaft, more conceal'd ; for no more *manna* came down from heaven, nor did rivers gufh any more out of the rocks by the touch of a rod. *I am*

L *a jea-*

a jealous God, faith the lord.   Whoever trufts folely to human induftry, does in fome meafure fet limits to God's power and providence. A beggar intreating St. *Peter*, one day, to give him but a penny by way of alms; he faid, *Silver and gold have I none ; but fuch as I have, that I give unto thee* ; that is to fay, he blefs'd him in the name of God.

In the primitive age of the Church, a perfon could not be admitted, into the number of apoftles, without firft felling all his poffeffions ; for riches ftick like glue to the wings of the foul, and hinder it from mounting aloft ; and they are like a ftone, which hangs as a dead weight to the body, and drags it upon the ground, when it has a defire to afcend heavenward. The *Greek* Church, which was always poor, has fuffer'd far lefs fcandals than the *Latin* Church, which has given birth to above a hundred arch-heretics, who have rafhly pretended to teach doctrines purer than thofe of their Church. You never heard of a broacher of new doctrines, but was either rich, or, at leaft, had a competency ; for men of this kidney never breed under the difcouragements of poverty ; therefore the *Greek* Church has not produc'd one fince the firft fchifm. Befides, the keeping

---

* A conceit taken from the emblems of *Alciat*, in which a chriftian foul is reprefented under the figure of a young man, who, with one hand, which has wings, points towards heaven, while a great ftone, ty'd to the other hand, drags him downward.

keeping of the clergy in a ftate of abfolute dependence on·the laity for their maintenance, is
attended with thefe two advantages; firft, in
that it obliges them to be always watchful of
their conduct, and to fet good examples to the
laity, for fear of lofing their fubfiftence; fecondly, it excites compaffion in the laity to
ufe their utmoft efforts to relieve the neceffities of the clergy. On the contrary, when
they are not only provided with neceffaries, but
even with fuperfluities, they are quite indifferent what others may think of them, from
whom they have no advantage to hope for,
nor no evil to fear. *Judas*, the caterer and
purfe-bearer of the apoftolical college, is a
glaring inftance of the mifchievous influence
which money may have upon the·foul of an
ecclefiaftic, fince it made an apoftle himfelf
turn traitor. *Jefus Chrift* forefeeing, by his
divinity, what an end *Judas* would come to,
gave him the management of money, either
becaufe nothing worfe could happen to him,
or elfe to keep the fame temptation from falling in, the way of the other difciples, who
were elected. The firft time *Judas* mur-
mured, was when *Mary Magdalen* poured
coftly ointment on the head of *Jefus Chrift*.
He would fain have had it fold, and put the
money in·his pocket; but he conceal'd his
avarice under the fpecious pretence of charity
to the poor. *To what purpofe, fays he, is this
wafte? It might have been fold for three hun-*
dred

dred pence and given to the poor. But the Evangelift adds, *That he faid this; not that he cared for the poor, but becaufe he was a thief, and had the bag, and bare what was put therein.* On the other hand, St. *Matthew* was a *Publican,* that is to fay, an *Ufurer;* but by his renouncing the management of money, he became a pious apoftle, and one of the Evangelifts; whereas *Judas,* who had nothing that he could call his own, by managing the treafure. of *Jefus Chrift,* became fuch an ungodly traitor, that he fold his Lord and Mafter for a fum of money. There's not one of a thoufand, in the whole army of faints, which the Church has produc'd ever fince its infancy, but has found entrance into heaven by the gate of poverty. The very *Pagans* were convinc'd how incompatible riches are with the tranquility of the mind; and *Seneca* laid it down as a maxim, *Si vis vacare animo, aut pauper fis, aut pauperi fimilis.* In fhort, the poffeffion of temporalities is fo far from being of divine right, that 'tis inconfiftent with the very beginning, progrefs, and end of the Church. Every chriftian, and a clergyman more than any other, is oblig'd to regulate his life according to that of *Jefus Chrift,* who never had any provifion of temporalities for his fubfiftence, that we any where read of. On the contrary, we find that *Mary Magdalen,* her fifter, and fome other devout women follow'd him, and miniftred unto him in his neceffities. Indeed his almighty
power

power did not want the affiſtance of human in-
duſtry, for in a cafe of extremity he could
have work'd a miracle ; but we no where
read that he ever did fo for his own fake or fervice. We read, that when he had faſted, and
was an hungred, the devil tempted him to
command the ſtones to be made bread, but he
would not do it. Let it not be fuggeſted, that
he was not liable, by virtue of his divinity, to
the evils of poverty ; for ſin excepted, he was
ſubject, like us, to all the infirmities of human nature. Neither do we read that he ex-
erted his almighty power in creating any thing
out of nothing, that being an attribute which,
it feems,, he was willing. to reſerve to his father, contenting himſelf only with the multiplication of beings, or transforming them :
Thus he multiply'd the loaves and the few
ſmall fiſhes, for feeding the multitude, that
followed him, and turn'd water into wine at
the marriage of *Cana.* In a word, he made
fo little uſe of his almighty power, that his
difciples were fometimes reduc'd to fuch neceſſity; that *they pluck'd the ears of corn, and
did eat, rubbing them in their hands.* And our
Saviour, before he afcended into heaven, commanded them *to eat of every thing that was fet
before them,- without providing for themfelves.*
Certainly, all thefe operations were not the
effect of chance without a myſtery, for *Chriſt*
was not govern'd by chance ; the view of all
his actions being for our inſtruction, and we

ought

ought to ftrive to imitate him, after the example of the apoftles.

Some perhaps may upbraid me with preaching up a doctrine which 1 do not practife my felf, becaufe I wear the habit of an order which is poffefs'd of a great eftate ; I own the truth of the charge in part, but hope, as to my felf, that I fhould be a brother of the order, if my convent had no endowment at all. 'Tis not my bufinefs to deprive my order of its poffeffions; and tho' it were reduc'd even to its ancient poverty, it muft be confefs'd it would fignify very little towards a general reform, fince the many other orders would certainly refufe to come into it. After riches crept into the Church of *Chrift*, they were fo generally valu'd, that the Council of *Trent* pafs'd a decree for excufing all friers from the vow of poverty, without fo much as excepting thofe who had a mind to be excepted ; for, it feems, the monks were not efteem'd by the common people, if they did not appear to live at their eafe, and the Council was not willing that the wealth of fome fhould be tacitly reproach'd by the poverty of others. For the fame reafon the court of *Rome* often complains of *the general coldnefs of charity, and want of refpect among believers;* unhappy difpofitions, which, fay they, cannot be corrected but by deceiving the fenfes, which only judge of what ftrikes them ; from whence they infer, that worldly grandeur is a neceffa-

ry

ry expedient to imprefs men with that refpect and reverence, which, becaufe of their corruption, cannot poffibly arife from the confideration of heavenly treafure. Thus as the Church pioufly makes ufe of images of the deity, to promote the worfhip of God, whom no pencil, nor chizzel, can exprefs, nor no ideas comprehend ; fo, in order to make minifters pafs for great men, 'tis proper to reprefent them to the eyes of the vulgar in the dazzling fplendor of riches. That is the expedient which the *Romanifts* have thought fit to make ufe of. We will not inquire whether it be good, becaufe all expedients being confider'd only as trials of skill, to make a thing fucceed, one does not expect them to be as equitable as a law. Now, fince no expedient, properly fo call'd, amounts to the force of a human law, much lefs does it come up to that of a divine law ; the obfervation whereof is unalterable, and abfolutely neceffary ; not from any law of ftate, but from the equity of the thing in nature. Thus the court of *Rome* carry a mark of that guilt in their foreheads, which they charge upon their enemies, I mean the crime of fubjecting the government of God's Church to maxims that are meerly human ; mean time, can any thing be more contrary and oppofite than God and the world fpirit and flefh ? *My ways are not as your ways. The wifdom of this world is foolifhnefs with God, who taketh the wife in their own craftinefs.* Finally, 'tis certain *that*

L 4 *a man*

a man is known by his converſation. From whence it follows, that if we have recourſe to ſuch human means, we ſhew plainly that the ſpirit of God is not in us; for divine wiſdom ſays, *Truſt in the lord with all thy heart, and lean not unto thy own wiſdom.* He who found-ed the Church has promis'd to preſerve it. *Be-hold I am with you unto the end of the world.* Let us not pretend to find out means which *Chriſt* has not taught, left we be deceiv'd by truſting too much to our ſelves, as men *en-ſnar'd by the words of their own mouths, and ta-ken by their own ſayings.* In fine, if a perſon of acute parts ſhould ſeek for reaſons to prove that the poſſeſſion of temporalities is compa-tible with the prieſthood, I doubt not of his ſucceſs; but he will never be able to prove that poſſeſſion to be neceſſary, much leſs to be injoin'd as neceſſary in the law of God. From hence it follows, that the Church has no title to the poſſeſſion of kingdoms, nor of any ſecu-lar power; for if ſhe may not poſſeſs the eſtates of private perſons, much leſs may ſhe enjoy the patrimony of a prince. Whoever reads the goſ-pel will find, that nothing, next to ſin, was more abhor'd by *Chriſt* than royalty. He there-in expreſly declares, *My kingdom is not of this world; if my kingdom were of this world, then would my ſervants fight, that I ſhould not be deliver'd to the Jews.* And as ſoon as the peo-ple that follow'd him would have made him a king, he fled. Indeed he was ſlander'd by the

Pha-

Pharifees for taking upon him the title of king;
but that was pure calumny; and fo far was
he from owning the legal dignity, that he fubmitted himfelf to be judg'd by the *Roman* Prætor; *They deliver'd him up to an unjuft judge.*
And when *Pilate* ask'd him, *Art thou a king
then? Jefus* anfwer'd, *Thou fayeft that I am a
king.* Again, when they *hailed* him with the
title of *king*, and *Pilate* faid, *Shall I crucify your
king?* and when they fet up the infcription of
KING OF THE JEWS upon the crofs; all
this was done by way of fcorn and derifion.
On the other hand, he was declar'd a *king* by
the prophet many ages before. *Behold thy
king cometh unto thee poor, and riding upon an
afs, and upon a colt, the foal of an afs.* And
the wife men fought him, faying, *Where is he
that is born king of the Jews?* how fhall we reconcile fuch contradictory texts of fcripture?
with this one paffage only, *Be lift up ye everlafting gates, and the king of glory fhall come in.*
This imports that our Lord *Chrift* is *king* indeed, but *king* of an everlafting kingdom;
and in this quality he was acknowledg'd by
the prophets, the wife men, and thofe fouls
that had a triumphant entrance with him into
heaven; and he explains it himfelf in thefe
terms, *My kingdom is not of this world*; by
which he does not deny his being a *king*, but
fays only that he was not *a king of this world.
The prince of this world hath not any thing in
me.*

He

He therefore who pretends to be *Chrifi's* vicegerent upon earth, ought to be like him, in afpiring to the kingdom of glory, and to abhor all temporal fovereignty to that degree, that it may be faid of him as of *Chrift*, he *takes upon him the form of a fervant.* In fhort, they ought to hate it as much as the ancient Popes, whofe title was, *Bifhop, fervant of the fervants of God.* But forafmuch as the mind of man is incapable of raifing itfelf to thofe fublime fpeculations, this feems to me a very fufficient reafon. Our Lord *Chrift* conftituted *Peter* and the apoftles the firft founders of the Church, and furnifh'd them with all gifts neceffary for the building of it. Therefore he would, with very good reafon, be deem'd a heretic, that fhould dare to fay our Lord let them want the neceffary means for advancing and fupporting the Church. Let us fee then what talents, what prerogatives were to be found in the ancient Popes ; for as they were eftablifh'd by the infallible fpirit, they will be a rule to us for diftinguifhing the neceffary characteriftics of true Popes. Now I do not find that they were either rich, or ambitious of principalities or kingdoms ; on the contrary, I obferve they were poor holy men, who mortify'd themfelves by the renouncing of all worldly wealth, and many times facrificed their lives for the faith of our Lord *Chrift.* 'Tis to no purpofe to urge that now the times are chang'd, that the Church is at reft, fince the

martyrs

martyrs have glutted the cruelty of the tyrants, infomuch, that many times the very executioners, tho' in the dark ftate of paganifm, have ftood in admiration at the conftancy of the chriftians, and acknowledg'd this was owing to a power not human, but divine ; and while their hands have been yet reeking with the blood of the martyrs, have fubmitted themfelves to martyrdom, for the confeffion of *Jefus Chrift :* Since thofe times (fome will fay perhaps) when the flower of faith was fufficiently fprinkled by the blood of the martyrs ; fuch apoftolical poverty has ceafed to be neceffary. 'Tis fufficient that every good catholic be perfuaded that the Church's poffeffion of Lands, or acquifition of treafure, dominions, and kingdoms, are not effential to prelates or Popes ; for there has been a Church with prelates and Popes, perhaps more holy than the prefent, who did not enjoy thefe temporal prerogatives. 'Tis pretty remarkable that *Mofes,* tho' God lov'd him fo well that he appointed him the deliverer of his people, and made him the depofitary of his almighty power, to confound *Pharoah,* and to keep the rebellious *Ifraelites* from difobedience, yet he would not have him to be a prieft ; and when there was a neceffity for one, God fingled out his brother *Aaron* for the priefthood ; plainly intimating, that the mitre and the fword, the crofs and the fcepter, were incompatible. Yet he was not a whit the lefs favourable in the
fight

fight of God; for the fcripture fays, *Mofes*
died according to the word of the Lord, and
that when he was alive, God admitted him
to fuch familiarity, that he fpoke with
him face to face. In a word, the Lord made
him a prophet, but not a prieft; for the gift of
prophecy is feparate from the priefthood; and
the priefthood would have as ill become *Mofes*,
as the gift of prophecy would become him
that reprefents the perfon of a fovereign. *Mofes* loved *Aaron* neverthelefs; for one day
their wives being at variance, *Mofes* curs'd his
fifter-in-law; who being thereupon immediately cover'd with a leprofy, *Aaron* had recourfe to *Mofes* to cure her; upon which he
pray'd, and fhe was prefently heal'd. All
thefe privileges he enjoy'd without being a
prieft, for reafons already mention'd. *David*
was fo entirely belov'd by God, that he fays
of him, *I have found a man after my own
heart*; therefore, of a fhepherd, he made him
a king, gave him victory in forty battles, pro-
tected him from the ftrength of the giant, and
the perfecution of *Saul*, gave him the fpirit of
prophecy, fanctify'd him thro' repentance, and
reveal'd fuch divine *Arcana's* to him, that
whatever he wrote was the voice of the holy
fpirit. More than all this, *Jefus Chrift* ftil'd
himfelf the fon of *David*; yet, with all thefe
advantages, *David* was not a prieft, becaufe it
was abfolutely neceffary for the people to have
a good king, and a better could not be found
than

than *David* in any other line ; and I am firmly perfuaded, that if a prieft might have been king at the fame time, no body in the world was more worthy than *David* of both thofe qualities ; but God would not have it fo, either for our inftruction, or not to expofe him to the danger of fuch a ftrong temptation.

We conclude, therefore, that the enjoyment of temporal eftates, dominions, and kingdoms, by a Pope, is foreign to the pontificat, and is like depofiting a ftandard, and fome cannon bullets in a Church, which indeed fhew the devotion of the donor, but have no relation at all to the Church ; and if they are taken from the Church, fhe lofes nothing by the bargain. So, we fay, that the poffeffion of thofe eftates has no manner of relation to the proper interefts of the Church ; fo that every one may difpute her right and title to fuch poffeffion, without violating the leaft punctilio of refpect due to the Pope ; for a man is no more a Pope with the poffeffion of fuch eftates and fovereignties, than he is without any the leaft marks of fovereignty ; which was the cafe of the Popes for a long feries of ages paft. This being fufficient, we proceed to another queftion.

CHAP.

C H A P. IX.

Whether a republic, as well as a free prince, may be depriv'd of their dominions by virtue of excommunication ?

THE decision of this question, in a strict sense, must be own'd to be very unnecessary ; since it was sufficiently prov'd in the 5th Chapter, that a free prince cannot in right be depriv'd of his dominions under pretence of excommunication ; from whence it follows, that such deprivation can, with far less colour of reason, be denounc'd against a republic ; for 'tis a maxim with the court of *Rome* never to excommunicate an entire city, much less several cities and countries, which are generally comprehended in a republic. But in a case of contumacy, the Pope uses to publish an interdict, which is a punishment far less than excommunication, as shall be shewn by and by ; so that since it has been prov'd that 'tis unjust to add the deprivation of estates to another punishment that is more severe, it would certainly be much more unreasonable to add it to a punishment that is not equal to it ; from whence it follows, as a known truth, that when the partisans of the court of *Rome*

are

are agreed, that, according to our firft propofition, a free prince cannot lawfully be depriv'd of his own dominions, they will be oblig'd, with much more reafon, to own the
fame thing with refpect to a free republic; but
'tis in vain to expect they will ever be fo can-
did as to make this fair conceffion ; for, let a.
maxim be never fo reafonable, they will not
yield to the force of it, if it carries the leaft
difadvantage in it to the papal authority; infomuch, that even tho' a truth fhould be demonftrated to them mathematically , they
would, at leaft, raife objections againft it, if
not pretend to confute it. ' For this reafon I
was oblig'd to add this queftion here, for the
abundant confolation of all fincere minds, to
let them fee, as I have already faid, that not
a free prince, and much lefs a republic, can be
legally depriv'd of their dominions, by virtue of
excommunication.

Before we proceed, let us ftate the difference between excommunication and an interdict. Excommunication, as has been already,
faid, is the cutting off, by which an ecclefiaftical judge feparates a chriftian from the whole
body of the Church, by reafon of a pretended
crime : Now, the confequence of this feparation is, that the perfon who is excommunicate is debarr'd from receiving the facraments,
and cannot apply to himfelf the merits of the
head and members of the Church ; fo that he
is look'd upon as a *Pagan* and a *Publican.* In-

deed excommunication does not strip him of
faith, that being an act of the soul, but deprives him of the fruits of faith.   From
hence, therefore, I infer, that excommunication is the worst curse that can be denounc'd
against one who confesses *Christ Jesus*, and that
'tis, in short, the *ne plus ultra* of the Church's
power to punish offenders.

On the other hand, an interdict is no more
than a rod, which the Church makes use of rather to terrify than punish a rebellious sinner,
in order to make him return to himself, and
has, for its view, the correction of such criminals, and not their destruction, either in this
mortal life, or that which is to endure for
ever ; for a christian's being under an interdict,
is no bar to his salvation, since the Church, all
the while, does not deny him baptism, nor
confirmation, nor confession, nor marriage on
certain licensed days, nor the conversation of
the faithful, nor the communion at the hour
of death, nor preaching, nor the recommen-
dation of his soul, nor even the sacrifice of
the mass on certain days of the year.   Indeed
'tis his very great unhappiness to be depriv'd
of the daily mass, of extreme unction, of
christian burial, and of priest's ordination ; because he can have no part in the oblation of
that living sacrifice, which reconciles God the
Father to wretched sinners, nor nourish himself, in this life, with the bread of heaven,
that carries with it all the heavenly graces,
                                                    and

and all the riches of the deity; nor fortify himself with extreme unction, which is the facrament of departing fouls, for his paffage from
the prefent life to eternity. And, finally, 'tis
no fmall grief to him that he is depriv'd of
the confolation of having his bones laid to reft
in the facred cœmetery of chriftians, as in the
bofom of our common mother; but, however, the other facraments, which are free for
him to make ufe of, are, even according to
the opinion of the *Romifh* cafuifts, fufficient
helps to conduct a man to the poffeffion of
everlafting happinefs. To render this difference more vifible, I fhall give this familiar
example : 'Tis the very fame cafe with excommunications and interdicts as it is with the
monks, who abfolutely expel from their convent a fubject who is rebellious and convicted
of any great crime; but only impofe certain
penances on one who is guilty of a fmall fault,
without depriving him of the common privileges of the fraternity. I do not fpeak here of the
facraments of marriage and ordination, which
are forbid to a perfon who is under an interdict; becaufe, tho' both thofe facraments ought
to co-operate to the benefit and falvation of
believers; yet when abus'd, as fometimes
they are, they tend to a perfon's ruin and deftruction; therefore, I do not look upon them
as abfolutely neceffary to falvation. This is
enough to fhew the difference there is between
the two ecclefiaftical punifhments, and that an in-

M   terdict

terdict is a very flight punishment in compari-
son of excommunication. The consequence
therefore is very fair and plain, whether it be
granted, or not, by the *Romanists*, that since
a free prince cannot be depriv'd of his dominions by excommunication, an interdict can
by no means subject him to such deprivation at
the same time; for as the addition of that
clause to all excommunications is irregular, it
would be still worse to tack it to an interdict,
which is a punishment far inferior even to the
minor excommunication. I am apt to think
there is no logician upon earth but will draw
the same consequence, and that enough has
been said to convince scrupulous consciences
how absurd it would be for an ecclesiastical
judge to inflict temporal punishment for a spiritual crime, supposing no other reason for it
than the enormity of such crime, at the
same time that he inflicts a spiritual punishment severe enough for the greatest of crimes.
And from hence it may be clearly infer'd, even
according to the maxims of the See of *Rome*,
that whoever falls under an interdict, has no
reason to fear being depriv'd of his domi-,
nions.

Now we will consider what reason the court
of *Rome* has for not excommunicating a city
or republic, as well as a free prince. How
flagrant soever be the crime and disobedience
of a republic, all the wit of man can only judge
of the fact by appearance, tho' there should

not be the leaft doubt of the real offender. 'Tis
very well known that a republic is a political body, conftituted of many members, which
is not govern'd after the manner of human
bodies, whofe members feem generally different in their particular operations, tho' they act
all upon one and the fame principle and method of operation. Among the aphorifms of
Hippocrates, this is one : " Tis the fame thing
" to draw blood from one vein as from ano-
" ther, becaufe it may be faid of them all,
" *Confenfus unus & confpiratio una.*" The fame
form of government holds in a free ftate, in
which there are various Councils; but they
all receive motion from the will of the fovereign, who, like a heart to the body, diffufes
fpirits, blood, and fuch other alterations as
are fuitable to his own difpofition. But the
model of a republic is different, becaufe every
member, which makes a part of that body,
has its operations independent on the fentiments of the other parts; and every one of
them may be confider'd diftinctly as a micro-
cofm of the whole fphere, of which he is really
ally but a part. Tho' one citizen, or fubject,
may have more power, or parts, than another,
it does not follow that he has a right to com-
pel the other, whether he will or no, to be of
his own opinion. He may indeed do what he
can to perfuade him, but muft ufe no violence ; for if he fhould proceed to extremity,
he would, by fo doing, fubvert the order of

govern-

government, and introduce infupportable tyranny. If any refolutions, pafs'd in a fenate,
are fo far difobedient to the Church as to deferve her cenfures, it will be no eafy matter to
diftinguifh which of the fenators voted for the
affirmative ; and fhall therefore the whole fenate be excommunicated in the lump ? This
would be to involve the innocent with the
guilty, fince it may happen that fome of the
members never voted their way. But to avoid
this extreme, *Chrift* has told us, that it is better to pardon a hundred criminals than to punifh one innocent perfon; and the Church,
which knows how much fhe is oblig'd to imitate that divine mafler, difpenfes with excommunication, which is the extremeft degree of
punifhment, and has recourfe only to an interdict, which, tho' it takes in all republicans,
cannot be reckon'd for a deftructive remedilefs
punifhment, becaufe it carries along with it a
corrective ; for as we have already fhewn, an
interdict does not deprive believers of thofe
helps that are neceffary to their falvation.

It may be objected, perhaps, that when
there is a certainty that fuch refolution of a fenate is pafs'd by the unanimous votes of all the
members, excommunication would, in fuch a
cafe, be denounc'd with juftice againft the
faid fenate, as fuppofing all the members were
delinquent; but I anfwer, this reafon will not
hold with refpect to the reft of the fubjects of
fuch republic, becaufe 'tis impoffible for all

of

of them to be fenators, who, according to the
practice of all the republics in the world, are
only a number of the beft fubjects, chofen out
of the whole. But admitting that a refolution
was form'd by the concurrence of all the fubjects, yet, as they have no fhare in the adminiftration, fo they can have no fhare of the
guilt of it ; and confequently, when a whole
republic is excommunicated, it would be abfolutely impoffible for the innocent to efcape
being punifh'd with the guilty, and the former
might chance alfo to be the greater number.

If the republic happen to be a democracy, 'tis
certain the commonalty cannot be refponfible
for the actions of thofe magiftrates, or fenators, whom they have inftituted, or deputed ;
and it is a mere jeft to fay, that the commonalty, in fuch a cafe, are oblig'd to chufe, or
conftitute other magiftrates, or fenators, better
difpos'd, in order to repair the contumacy, or
other mifconduct of the former, and that if the
commonalty refufe fo to conftitute new ones,
they incur the guilt of their deputy's misbe-
haviour. This pretence, I fay, is not to be allow'd, becaufe the commonalty having deputed, or chofe the fenators, or magiftrates,
with a view, as 'tis fuppos'd, only to the public weal, and the good government of the
ftate ; 'tis not the fault of thofe that deputed
them, if matters do not fucceed accordingly,
and the electors ought ftill to be well thought
of ; fince, by the fame argument, if a doctor

be

be chofe phyfician to an hofpital, and all the patients fhould happen to die under his hands, thofe who deputed him would be to blame for it, tho', when they elected him, they had all the moral certainty, that could be, of his fufficiency. Another reafon ftill, which fecures the commonalty from being refponfible for the faults of their magiftrates, is this : That by appointing a fenate, or magiftrates, and vefting the authority in their hands, they fhut themfelves entirely out of the fecret ; fo that not knowing the caufes which determine the fenate, or magiftrates, to form fuch or fuch refolutions, they have no plea to condemn, or degrade them, and annul their decrees.

From all this it may be concluded, that tho' what I have demonftrated to be true were abfolutely falfe, and that a free prince might be depriv'd of his dominions by virtue of excommunication, yet a republic cannot run that risk, becaufe the fame is never excommunicated *de facto*, nor can it be ever *de jure*, the court of *Rome* themfelves being confcious of their indifpenfible obligation not to confound the innocent with the guilty. Moreover, fince it may fall out there will be fome perfons whofe innocence alone may protect them from ecclefiaftical excommunication, it will be always allowable for every private perfon, in cafe he be excommunicated, to examine ftrictly whether he is innocent or guilty, in order to fee whether his excommunication be juftly founded ;

for

for if it be not, he will, by that means alone, be safe from all the confequences of the excommunication ; which being unjuft, cannot poffibly fubfift, according to one of our maxims, laid down in another part of this difcourfe, and which we fhall more and more confirm hereafter.

Now the confequence of all this is, that 'tis not an article of faith to believe that every excommunication is valid, becaufe it makes a great noife, before it has pafs'd the touchftone of a fevere examination ; fince , as I have faid ·elfewhere, excommunication being only the effect of human judgment, and by confequence fubject to fallacy and delufion, if the judge has actually given into fuch delufion, it would be a wicked thing to fuppofe that God would approve of the miftake of oppreffing one who is guilty only in appearance. Therefore, to prevent fuch delufion, 'tis not only lawful to examine, but alfo an appeal is allowable to make this examination in order, and canonically, as the true touchftone, that can fhew us the truth or falfhood of fuch fentences.

CHAP.

C H A P. X.

Whether a secular-prince has a lawful right to receive the clergy's teaths, and to order what is useful to the state, with respect to the estates and persons of ecclesiastics?

BEfore I proceed to the particular examination of the clergy's tenths, I would have us make some general reflections upon the right that secular princes have to exact the tenths of the estates of their lay-subjects, and to impose on them taxes, gabels, subsidies, tolls, &c. And before we enter into these considerations, we ought to inquire how far a subject is oblig'd in conscience to obey his prince, and whether he sins by disobedience.

The first precept of the second table of the decalogue is to honour our father and mother. Now there is not a catholic expositor upon earth, but, by the words father and mother, understands and includes the spiritual and temporal nobility in such a sense, that a man is oblig'd, by the divine law, to honour his legal father, that is to say, his prince, or his prelate, as much as his carnal father, from whom he derives his birth; unless it should be objected, that the ten commandments are not universal, and that he,

who

who has not a father by blood alive, is only oblig'd to the obfervation of nine. But there is no body who has not either a father, or fu-perior, in fome fenfe or other: In this cafe, every patient is inferior to his phyfician, every layman to his mafter; and even a prince, who has no fuperior *in humanis*, has his fuperior a-mong the ecclefiaftics. In fhort, the Pope, who has no fuperior in dignity, has his fupe-rior in fome fpecial cafes, when, as a finner, he makes confeffion to another, who, during his function, is more a Pope than himfelf. Our Lord *Chrift* alfo, as man, had parents, on whom he depended, who were confequently his fuperiors; and when the virgin *Mary* found him, after tedious fearch, fhe faid unto him, *Son, why haft thou thus dealt with us? behold thy father and I have fought thee forrowing.* She did not fpeak this by way of hyperbole, for fhe very well knew the divinity of her fon, both by the revelation of the angel, and the infpiration of the Holy Ghoft; but fhe fpoke after this manner, becaufe *Jofeph* was his fa-ther by adoption, as God was by nature; moreover, the Evangelift adds, *he was fubject unto them.* Formerly, a father by adoption had fuch authority over his adopted fon, that he had a right to punifh him, when he offended, as much as if he had been his own natural fon. Therefore this neceffity of fubjection, or fub-ordination, from which no perfon whatfoever is exempt, forms a kind of hierarchy, which

leads

leads us to the apprehension and acknowledgment of the necessity of a first principal of all things that are in the world. Thus *Dionysius* the *Areopagite,* before he was enlightned by faith, said as much as it was possible for man, guided by natural reason alone, to say, *Causa causarum miserere mei !* i. e. *O cause of causes have mercy on me !* Afterwards, when he had the good fortune to be instructed by St. *Paul,* with whom he disputed, he profess'd christianity, became the apostle of the *Gauls,* and was esteem'd one of the chief saints of the catholic Church.

It was therefore necessary to make this digression, to shew that every body, from the lowest, even to the highest, has a superior in some sense or other ; a consideration, which, by endless progression, brings us to the pillars of that divine *Hercules,* where is the *non plus ultra* of superiority and grandeur. Now, since every one has superiors, and that he is oblig'd to obey those superiors by the express command of God, it follows, by consequence, that every one ought, by virtue of the same divine command, to pay obedience to his prince. *Fear thou the Lord and the king,* says *Solomon* ; where, tho' he places the king in the second rank, he seems to mean, that the obligation of obedience to God and the king is in some sort equal. This is what I think all are agreed in ; but if I should go about to extend the obligation of *fearing* and *honouring* to
that

that of *contributing*, I apprehend that I should meet with some who would not be so ready to give into my opinion : Yet they are synonymous terms in the law of God. 'Tis said in the *Proverbs, Honour the Lord with thy substance ;* which sort of honour consists in paying tribute or imposts ; for to honour another with one's substance, can mean nothing else than giving him a part thereof.

To pass from the text to the explication of it. We say, that a prince is oblig'd, by divine authority, to defend his dominions, to protect his subjects, to procure them provisions, to guard them against contagions, malefactors, and public enemies, and to do them so many other offices, that a great man, who perfectly knew the heavy weight of government, said, if ever he should happen to find a crown in his way, he would not so much as stoop to take it up from the ground. This being the case, 'tis but reasonable that the prince should be rewarded for all his fatigue, and that for this end, he should have the means in his own hands for obliging his subjects to grant him a supply towards his expences ; which means are taxes, tenths, and various sorts of imposts, which he has the power of raising. 'Tis well known that the treasury resembles the spleen, which is nourish'd with a part of the aliment of the other members, and which, while it is in a certain state of mediocrity, preserves the body in health. Therefore 'tis equally ly criminal in the subjects, to refuse paying the prince moderate imposts, and in the prince, not to take care of the people under his government: Thus, when the night closes the eyelids of mankind to sleep, the heavens open millions of eyes upon them, as it were to watch for their preservation; so that we may say, *astra regunt homines*, with the poet, *& etiam curant*.

This right of sovereigns to levy tenths, and other imposts, on their subjects, both for an acknowledgment of his sovereignty, and defraying the expences of his government, is so lawful and universal, that even infidel princes are not excluded from it; so that christians, who happen to be born in the *Turkish* dominions, are oblig'd in conscience, as long as they live there, to discharge all the duties of their dependence. *Principi populi tui non maledices;* for if we were not oblig'd to this acknowledgment by the bonds of faith, yet those of society demand it; and 'tis, moreover, decided by the canons, that we ought to place an infidel in the rank of our neighbour, because he is capable of being a partaker of the benefits of our Saviour's redemption, if he will obey the gospel. This is what *Jesus Christ* design'd also as a lesson for us, who, when a certain lawyer ask'd him, *Master, what shall I do to inherit eternal life?* the sum of his answer was, *Love God and thy neighbour.* To which the lawyer demanding, *Who is my neighbour? Je-sus fus* told him the ftory of that inhabitant of *Je-rufalem, viz.* one that liv'd after the law of *Mofes*, who falling among thieves, was ftript of his raiment, and fo wounded, that they left him half dead : But by chance there came down a certain prieft of the law that way, and when he faw him, he pafs'd by on the other fide : And likewife a levite, *i. e.* a mi-nifter of the temple, when he was at the place, came and look'd on him, and pafs'd by on the other fide ; but a certain *Samaritan*, one who profefs'd another religion, as he journeyed, came where he was, and when he faw him, he had compaffion on him, and went to him, bound up his wounds, carry'd him to an inn, and paid the hoft for his cure. Now, fays *Jefus Chrift* to the lawyer, *which of thefe three, think-eft thou, was neighbour unto him that fell among the thieves?* why, he did not fcruple to fay the *Samaritan, who fhew'd mercy on him. Jefus Chrift* approv'd of his anfwer, by faying, *go and do thou likewife* : So that a chriftian is oblig'd to look upon him as his neighbour, who fhews him acts of charity. From hence I infer, that if men are oblig'd in confcience to be obe-dient and tributary fubjects to an infidel prince, under whofe government they live, they have much more reafon, furely, to pay fuch obe-dience and tribute to a chriftian prince, their natural fovereign, to whom they are united by the profeffion of the fame faith ; and that who-

-ever

ever tranfgreffes this command, is guilty of
the breach of God's law.

We will now proceed to try how far the
argument will bear with refpect to the clergy.
The queftion then is, whether a fecular prince
has a legal authority· to demand the clergy's
tenths? To this I anfwer readily, that if the
obligation of fubjects to their prince is as general as that of the prince to his fubjects,
(which was demonftrated juft now) the clergy are under an indifpenfible neceffity to plead
fome fpecial privilege that exempts them from
any fuch obligation ; for the fovereign prince's
authority is boundlefs and univerfal, and even
this privilege ought not to be barely human,
but they muft hold it from God himfelf ; for
the authority of the prince is founded on the
divine law, and not on that of man. Some
men, of the beft learning, have been fo fenfible of the force of the argument, that finding
no way to come off, they have given it up entirely, and own'd, that 'tis very true the prince
has a right to exact fuch tribute from all his
fubjects, but that this fecular right terminates
in the laity. A fine crafty anfwer this, but in
the main really frivolous ! for I would fain
know which of thefe two ought, according to
God's law, to be in greateft fubjection to his
prince ? whether a Chriftian to a *Turk,*in whofe
dominions he lives ? or an ecclefiaftic, living
in a chriftian country, to the fecular prince ?
in the one cafe, 'tis my dwelling only that renders

ders me subject to the *Turk,* whose sovereignty over such my dwelling is no less than usurpation and tyranny ; but in the other case, the ecclesiastic dwells in a place where the prince has the legal right of sovereignty, and is moreover united to him by the same faith. I should be glad to know what answer they could possibly make to that objection ; for if they should be so imprudent as to assert, that a christian is more oblig'd to obey a *Turk,*than a clergyman his christian prince ; I would ask them, by what rule have the Popes so often publish'd croisadoes, and invited all christians to fall upon the *Turks,* since such christians, who live under the dominion of the *Turks,* are, if that assertion be true,more oblig'd to obey the *Turk,*than the clergy are oblig'd to own the authority of christian princes? Now, 'tis certain that every clergyman is subject to his lay-prince in all things that are independent on the ecclesiastic ministry. But, in the functions of the priesthood, the ecclesiastic is not subject to the temporal prince, who has in that case no authority over him ; and if he should pretend to usurp it, he would deserve blame and censure, as we have shewn under another head. On the other hand, the payment of tenths is a thing so far from being injurious to the priesthood, that it has no relation to it. For we have elsewhere demonstrated, that the clergy's possession of temporalities is so far from being *jure divino,* that 'tis hardly compatible with the priesthood ;

and

and from hence it neceffarily follows, that by virtue of fuch poffeffions, they are fubject to the prince, and that the fovereign, however he became fuch, has authority to treat them on a level with the other fubjects. Left any fhould accufe me of replying to the fame thing a hundred times, I will reduce all that I have to fay, as to this head, to one fingle point, *viz.* whether 'tis poffible to form an ecclefiaftic fovereignty within one that is fecular? The whole controverfy turns upon this one queftion, which, however, I have divided into fo many chapters, only to render it the more clear and intelligible ; for, tho' I have made twelve feparate articles of it, they have fo near an affinity to each other, that it was impoffible to treat of the one, without breaking in upon the other.

If it be certain that not one good reafon can be produc'd why ecclefiaftics fhould be tolerated in the poffeffion of temporalities, how vainly then do fome people argue, who fay, that the fecular prince is oblig'd to regard them as a thing facred, and, as it were, divine? We will now inquire how tenths came to be firft eftablifh'd. The prieft thinks he is authoriz'd to collect the tenths of the laity's poffeffions by the exprefs command of God ; that confequently, if the eftate, which the prieft poffeffeth, confifts only in the tenths, he fhall be exempt from the impoft of the prince, becaufe it would be unreafonable for him to pay
the

the tenth of a tenth, fince God, by obliging the laity to pay their tenths to the clergy, does not oblige the clergy to pay them to the judge, the governor of the people, or king ; and in things odious (as they fay) there muft be no comment, where the text is filent. But what will they fay, if it be made appear that the poffeffions of the clergy do fo far exceed the tenths, they receive from the laity, that they amount even to one third of all the product of the earth, fea, mountains, rivers, and of all the yearly fruits produc'd by nature? For an inftance, or rather proof of this, I will only mention *France* and *Spain*, where the clergy is the chief and the richeft of the three orders of the ftate. I do not fpeak of *England*, becaufe 'tis known that the greateft and cleareft revenues of the king, at prefent, arife from the fpoils of the regular clergy, or monks of the ifland. To inftance only in the city of *Venice*, the tenth of the laity's poffeffions fcarce · amounts to 200,000 *Ducats*, whereas the tenth of the clergy's eftate comes to more than 500,00, by raifing not the tenth, but only the fifth of the produce of nature, without reckoning the other payments which the laity make, out of their own eftates, to the curates and ecclefiaftic prelates, and which are not included in the above account; becaufe the tenths, which are levy'd upon the clergy, are rais'd only from fuch of their poffeffions as are patrimonial benefices, with an exception to

N

per-

perfons; who, according to the fimplicity of the ancients, remain in poffeffion of *jus quæfi-tum perfonæ,* i. e. *perfonal eftate, and not that which is real.*

But if, for inftance, a fecular prince has no right in himfelf, according to the court of *Rome,* to levy the clergy's tenths, from whence (fay I) muft he raife the fums neceffary for his Expences, and for the defence of his government, cities and fubjects, and even of the clergy? If it be anfwer'd, that he ought to tax the eftates of the laity only ; I reply, that it would be tranfgreffing the precept of mutual juftice and equity, for the clergy to refufe contributing their quota, in proportion to the benefit they reap in common with the public, by their protection : befides, that 'tis uncharitable to lay the whole burden upon the one, and none at all upon the others, or fo much as to lighten their burden, who naturally ought to bear as great a part of it as the others.   Nay, the facrednefs of the ecclefiaftic ftate would tend to the oppreffion of the laity, if the getting into ecclefiaftical orders were fufficient to excufe a man from bearing a fhare of the public taxes.   But to argue more clofely to the point: If it fhould happen, in procefs of time, that all the eftate of the laity, or the greateft part, however, fhould become the property of the clergy, where, I pray, muft the prince raife his revenue? becaufe, according to the fyftem of thofe extraordinary zea-
lots

lots for ecclefiaftical liberty, all fuch eftates
ought to be free from taxation. To fay that
this is fuppofing an impoffibility, is faying nothing to the purpofe ; becaufe, if we may be
allow'd to judge of what may, by what already has come to pafs, and confider the vaft
increafe of church-livings, fince the clergy had
a being, it will appear that their engroffing
the whole to themfelves, is fo far from being
fuch an impoffibility as fome would infinuate,
that 'tis, on the contrary, very eafy, and we
might fay very near their accomplifhment too,
unlefs they meet with rubs ; fuch, for inftance,
as thofe which the wife and vigilant republic
of *Venice* have now laid in their way. It may
be objected, perhaps, that there are fome of
the laity, who, having no eftate, pay nothing
to their prince ; I grant it ; but I take this to
be a cafe wherein the laity are tax-free, becaufe
thofe taxes which a prince lays upon all his
fubjects, are founded on a fuppofition that they
are well able to pay them ; for if a lay-fubject
has no eftate, or at leaft but a fmall one, he
cannot bear a part of the burden, becaufe he
is commonly forc'd to live upon the charity of
the clergy, or elfe to earn his bread by daily
labour, as did *Jofeph's* brethren in *Egypt* ; in
which are manifeft the fad effects of God's
curfe upon mankind, in the perfon of *Adam,*
when he faid to him, *in the fweat of thy face
thou fhalt eat bread.* Now the clergy may as
well pretend to have been created free from

original

original fin, as from this curfe, tho' they are become the executioners of it, by felling a-gain to the laity that bread which they receiv'd from their anceftors, under the title of alms. Upon the whole, therefore, if, while part of the fubjects are exempted from taxes, by rea-fon of poverty, another part plead exemption by fpecial privilege, their fovereign would be much more at a lofs than even the fuperior of a convent, who is oblig'd by his character to govern and maintain his monks, without any income from them. And whoever fhould like to be a prince on thefe terms, I think he would richly deferve to be canoniz'd for a faint, who was poor in fpirit indeed.

'Tis in vain to fay, that when a prince is in thefe unhappy circumftances, the Pope would, by an *indulto,* impower him to lay fuch a tax upon the clergy of his dominions, as might anfwer his demands; for in the firft place it muft be obferv'd, that fuch *indulto* being en-tirely dependent on the Pope's will and plea-fure, might be as well refufed as granted; and, in the fecond place, that 'tis abfurd to fend a prince a begging to another for the ways and means which God himfelf put into his own hands, when he advanced him to the fovereign-ty; for confidering what *Jefus Chrift* faid to *Pi-late,* who was fo far from being a prince, that he was only the minifter of an idolatrous prince; *Thou couldft have no power at all againft me, except it were given thee from above;* it muft
be.

be own'd that princes derive their authority immediately from God, and that by confequence he has given them the means fufficient to fupport that authority, without being beholden for them to the good pleafure of another. This comports likewife with the idea we have of divine juftice : For if a free prince, who is ftil'd prince by *the grace of God,* is only accountable to him for the mifgovernment of his people ; and if fuch mifgovernment is owing purely to the want of the means, he cannot be punifhable, by divine juftice, for what he could not help. An idolater does not commit fin by continuing in his idolatry, if he never had an opportunity to be inftructed in the chriftian faith. 'Tis true, he fins as well as chriftians, if he gives himfelf up to other vices ; but his infidelity, or fin of idolatry, will never be put in the balance with his other crimes, becaufe he is not to be blam'd for not believing what he knows nothing of, either by himfelf, or by tradition. *Who hath believed our report ?* faid the prophet,; and St. *Paul* therefore drew this confequence, *faith cometh by hearing.* To apply what has been juft mention'd to the cafe of a fovereign prince ; if he leaves his fubjects to be invaded, and extirpated by a foreign enemy, or elfe does not defend them againft villains at home, for want of foldiers and ftatefmen, whom he cannot get without money, and a fufficient revenue ; I do affirm, that in this cafe he is not to blame,

any

any more than the mole for not looking up to the fun, or the oftrich for not flying ; becaufe, tho' the one has Eyes, and the other wings, yet they are both too weak for thofe purpofes.

Thofe who ftand up for the maxims of the court of *Rome*, have ftill another objection, and that is this. Then, according to your opinion (fay they) a lay-prince may tax his ecclefiaftical fubjects at difcretion, and fleece them without mercy, much like the king of *England*, who firft took their eftates fiom them, and then turn'd them out of his dominions. But thefe gentlemen, under favour, are too hafty in drawing their conclufions, fince every impartial reafoner will undoubtedly perceive that I have no fuch meaning. For no juft prince will take the liberty to run into that extreme, no not even with refpect to the eftates of his lay-fubjects, and much lefs with refpect to their freeholds; becaufe God gives leave to no body, not even to a mere private perfon, to fquander away his eftate in excefs and debauchery.

St. *Thomas*, in his treatife *de regimine principum*, fays, that 'tis poffible for a prince to be a tyrant two ways; either by feizing an eftate, to which he has no right nor title, or by governing his lawful fubjects in an unjuft manner. The treafure fet apart for the maintenance of thofe whofe profeffion it is continually to offer up praifes to almighty God, ought not to be employ'd in offending and blafpheming him. Eve-

ry

ry time that a temporal prince impofes a tax, he makes himfelf a debtor to God for all the fums he thereby levies, and muft give an account of the ufe he makes of them. Happy therefore are thofe republics, where no exactions what-foever can give umbrage, or uneafinefs, becaufe they who lay on the burden are thofe who bear it, and have not an opportunity to put any of the money into their own pockets.

As the ecclefiaftics can by divine right exact only the tenths from the laity, fo the temporal prince has no authority, as fuch, to exact of the clergy more than an annual tenth ; and if he would have larger fubfidies, he ought to de-fire leave of the Pope, as he is the fovereign prince of the clergy, and the protector of their rights and privileges. I fay, moreover, that every fecular prince, who has not a fovereign and independent power, fuch an one, in fhort, who is merely feudatory, has not a right to ex-act the ordinary tenths of the clergy, becaufe this right is peculiarly attached to fovereign power, and does not fuit with a prince who owns a fuperior, which makes the effential dif-ference betwixt a free prince and another.

At this rate, be a prince ever fo free, yet if he requires extraordinary fubfidies, he muft have recourfe to the Pope, as the good kings of *France* and *Spain* have always done. Indeed there may be an exception as to cafes of ex-treme neceffity ; for, as a private man may apologize for his robbing the altar, and even

for

for committing wilful murder, by pretending, in the one cafe, that he had no other way to get a morfel of bread, for prolonging his miferable life ; and in the other cafe, that he only acted in felf-defence againft a powerful aggreffor, *cum moderamine inculpatæ tutelæ* ; fo a prince, for inftance, who has not time to fend before-hand to *Rome,* may come off very well with the 'Pope, provided he demands, or levies fuch extraordinary fubfidies, with a promife to reftore them, if he has not the holy father's approbation. I remember to have read a brief of *Pius* V. directed to the emperor *Matthias,* which was fill'd both with exhortations and menaces, becaufe that emperor publifh'd an edict in oppofition to the pretended ecclefiaftical liberty, for raifing certain fums above the ufual tenths, in order to fupply fome preffing neceffities of the ftate ; but as foon as ever he made known that indifpenfable neceffity to the Pope, and beg'd an *indulto,* he had it granted, on condition that he would, in the firft place, revoke that odious edict. I have alfo read a letter on this fubject, from Pope *Sixtus* V. to *Philip* II. king of *Spain,* in which he treats him with exceeding tendernefs, as confidering the then circumftances of his majefty's affairs, and thofe of the times. The Pope tells him in that letter, of a great fin that he had committed, by eftablifhing a fort of pragmatic fanction, which included bifhops, archbifhops, and cardinals, and exhorts him to

repent

repent of it before God ; and this affair, like the former, was determin'd by the dispatching of an *indulto*. If therefore we concede to the courtiers of the *Roman* See, that a prince ought to obtain leave of the Pope for raising extraordinary subsidies, they will be so ingenuous as to own that the prince has authority *per se* to exact the ordinary tenths of the clergy.

If they argue, that because the most serene republic, and other sovereigns, raise those tenths by virtue of the . Pope's *indulto's*, they have not such authority in themselves; I answer, that the court of *Rome* has been a long time used to the policy of giving others what they had before, or what they had a right to assume of themselves. And it has happen'd, in process of time, that those who have been in possession of favours of this kind, have sate down contented with such their possession, without troubling their heads whether they held them by a right natural, or deriv'd, or what way soever they came by them. They had their reasons for this conduct, first, to avoid the reproach of ingratitude by disowning the gift ; and secondly, because it seemed to those princes that the said donation was a fresh proof of their acquisition, inasmuch as it oblig'd the donor to support their titles. And indeed, tho' *Paul* IV. had not given the king of *England* the title of king of *Ireland*, I don't see what could have hinder'd him from bearing that, as well as the title of king

king of *Great Britain;* which they have affum'd fince. And when *Pius* V. erected *Tufcany* into a grand dutchy, I think verily that
Cofmus, duke of *Florence,* might as well have
done it himfelf, if he had not lik'd the Pope's
conduct But neither the king, nor the duke,
fhewed the leaft contempt for the Pope's favours of that kind. It was a punctilio which
they did not care to difpute with him, nor to
refufe his good-will for the fake of a ceremo-
nious formality of title, the rather becaufe
every religious prince feeks occafions to fhew
his veneration for the mind of the Pope, who
is their common father in *things fpiritual.*

But, 'as the Pope has granted many fuch *indulto's* of *his own accord,* and as in that which
Clement VI. granted to the moft ferene republic, it was declar'd not only to be of *his own
accord,* but alfo for the good of the Church,
it may juftly be averred, that under pretence
of fuch grants, the Pope flily preys upon that
legal right which every free prince has over his
own dominions; another inftance of which
is this. When a new king of the *Romans* is
chofe, who is then call'd emperor elect; the
election is made by the concurrent votes of
thefe three princes who diffent from the Church
of *Rome, viz.* the elector *Palatin,* and thofe
of *Saxony* and *Brandenburg,* tho', according to
the ecclefiaftical cenfures, they are depriv'd
both of their dominions and rights. What's the
confequence? why the Pope makes no fcruple
never-

nevertheleſs to confirm the election, and declares he does it after much intreaty made to him for redreſſing all the miſtakes in matter of law or fact, which might happen in the ſaid election. But who pray intreats this at his hands? verily, no body at all. For thoſe princes care not one ruſh for his confirmation; and, moreover, think what is called their miſtakes, their ſingular honour. The emperor perhaps does it in order to obtain the confirmation with the more eaſe, yet nevertheleſs no notice is taken of it in any wiſe, either *viva voce*, or in the Pope's bull; and indeed this circumſtance makes ſo little difference in the thing, that 'tis of no ſignification.

We will now examine whether a ſecular prince has a legal right to make any order for the good of the ſtate, with reſpect to the eſtates or perſons of eccleſiaſtics.

This queſtion may be reſolv'd in a very few words; for if it be true that a prince is eſtabliſh'd by God, to defend and well govern the people, it neceſſarily follows that he has a legal power to order, as well with reſpect to his ſubjects perſons, as eſtates, whatever he thinks may contribute towards ſuch good government; and it would be as abſurd to aſſert, that a prince ought to govern where the clergy will not be governed, as to expect that a phyſician can work a cure where the patient refuſes his medicines. The common anſwer to this is, that a ſecular prince has nothing to do
with

188 The Rights of Sovereigns.

with the government of the, clergy, becaufe they are under another mafler, and that all the obligation incumbent on a prince towards the clergy, is to defend them, as well as the laity, from foreign enemies and domeftic villains; and confequently that he is oblig'd to fee that a town be fupply'd with all things neceffary for the ufe of the clergy, as well as of the laity, and to take as much care for the prefervation of the one, as the other. . I would fain know how the clergy would take it, if, in a time of famine, a prince fhould prohibit the felling of bread, or other provifions to them, and pretend that he furnifh'd fuch or fuch a city with provifions, for the ufe only of the laity, who are his fubjects, and not for that of the clergy, who own another governor, another lord, another guardian. I believe that in fuch a cafe the clergy would not only confefs the truth of the axiom I have laid down, *viz.* that the clergy-gentlemen have their particular governor and protector in fpirituals, and in the functions of the priefthood; but also, that as to their own perfons, they are as much fubjects of the prince as the laity. If a river overflows and drowns the lands of the clergy, and the prince takes no care to drain the waters, and turn them into their old channel, on pretence that the ruin of fuch lands is nothing to him, becaufe he has no power over the owners; I doubt not but the clergy would then change their note, and fay, that the fovereign ought

ought to take as much care of their interests,
as those of others : And 'tis as certain, that in
such a case as this, they would not argue for
the absolute necessity of an *indulto* from the
Pope, to raise, above the ordinary tenths, the
sums necessary for draining the waters off of
their drowned lands; because they would say,
while they wait for the consent of the court of
Rome, their corn and plants would rot under
water. This being the real state of the case,
they ought not to stifle the sentiments of their
conscience, but to acknowledge the prince for
their sovereign, when he commands, as well
as when he defends, and not to imitate the
Cutæans, &c. Those *Assyrians*, who being
brought by *Salmanazar* to inhabit *Samaria*, after he had destroy'd the kingdom of *Israel*,
call'd themselves the friends and kindred of
the inhabitants of *Jerusalem*, while they were
happy and gay; but when they were oppress'd,
said, they had nothing to do with them, and
that they were foreigners. To avoid giving
into all these absurdities, there needs no more
than to reflect, that, in order to form the body politic, the prince must constitute the head,
and all the subjects the members. I am not af-
ferting that a temporal prince has an unlimited
power to load the clergy with exorbitant taxes; and it would be unjust in the *Romanists* to
make that inference from what I have said.
It is enough for me, if I can but make appear
how just and equitable it is for a prince to levy

vy the annual tenths, and that on very preffing occafions he may raife extraordinary fubfidies, after leave granted ·him ;· but that if the urgency of his affairs will not admit of a delay, he may, without fuch permiffion· firft obtain'd, force the clergy to contribute their *quota*, for promoting the publick good, of which they are partakers in proportion with the laity. He that foweth his feed in good feafon, gathereth ; but he that foweth out of time, lofeth, inftead of gathering. If one of thofe tenderly confcientious catholics, who thinks it fo highly criminal not to make application, in the firft place, to the Pope, fhould be going a journey, and by misfortune fall and wound his head, I fhould be glad to know whether he would refufe to be heal'd by a man of very good practice ; but being not enter'd as a mafter furgeon, practifes furgery without authority, and without a lawful certificate ; and whether he would chufe to keep his wound open, and in danger of mortifying, till he has fent to the next town for a licenfed mafter-furgeon, who is fo both by profeffion and appointment. The application is very eafy, and the anfwer of the wounded catholic, if it be fincere, will be fufficient to juftify the conduct of fuch lay-fovereign, who exerts his authority over both the perfons and eftates of the clergy. If a brother in a monaftery fhould be afflicted with the plague, I believe that none of the monks would be angry with the lay-fovereign for re-

moving

moving him immediately to an hofpital, but would rather look upon it as a very wife, juft, and charitable precaution of the prince, for the common prefervation of the fraternity. When the *Hugonots* firft introduced their opinions into *France*, the piety of the moft chriftian king, inclin'd him to make very earneft remonftrances to the court of *Rome*, and to defire that a Council might be call'd, as the moft effectual remedy: The Pope was ready enough to fall in with the king's requeft; and I don't deny that a Council is the moft proper remedy that can be thought of, when evils of this kind happen; but the Pope faid it was neceffary that all the chriftian princes fhould give their confent to the calling it. Mean time the error gain'd ground in *France* more and more, fo that 'twas propos'd in the king's cabinet, to call a national Council, for want of a better remedy; but fome remonftrated that this, would, in a manner, break the unity of the catholic Church; when one of the counfellors of ftate wittily reply'd, that he thought it very unaccountable, that while the whole kingdom of *France* was in fuch a flame, they fhould fit ftill, expecting water from the *Tyber* to quench it, when they had fuch large rivers of their own as the *Seine* and *Marne*; plainly intimating thereby, that when danger is afar off, there is time enough to deliberate; but that when deftruction is at hand, 'tis high time to act.

But

But while we plead for this liberty in a temporal prince, let it be obferv'd that we do not
pretend to juftify the excefs of it; fince we
take it for granted that he knows he muft one
day give an exact account of his adminiftration,
efpecially of the laity's eftates, to the divine
juftice. Befides, 'tis his intereft to preferve the
good opinion of the Pope, and other chriftian
princes; becaufe, if a prince be never fo wicked himfelf, he obliges others to do him juftice,
and to fupport his intereft; for 'tis certain, that
with what meafure we meet to others, it fhall
be meafur'd to us again.   Therefore I argue
for nothing irregular, but only for obedience
to the law of neceffity, which is fuperior to
all other human laws.   We will now treat
briefly of the advantages refulting from my
argument.

If the grand feignior had but a fmall glimpfe
of the chriftian faith (for if he had a full view
of it, he would know that he muft renounce
all worldly intereft, when it hinders the profeffion of the faith in *Chrift,* according to thofe
words, *what is a man profited, if he fhall gain
the whole world, and lofe his own foul?*) If, I fay,
he had a glimpfe of it only, and fhould fignify to the Pope, that he is willing to be baptiz'd; on condition that the Pope would confirm him by an authentic bull in the poffeffion
of all his dominions; I would fain know whether the Pope would grant fuch a bull, or refufe it, fince the granting it would be taking

*

away

away the rights of as many chriftian princes as
have been depriv'd of their dominions by the
Turks ? As this cafe indeed has never yet happen'd, the gentlemen of the court of *Rome*
will e'en make what anfwer they lift ; but if
they fhould fay the Pope would refufe it on the
confideration juft mention'd, I frankly own to
them, under favour, that I cannot believe
them ; for, methinks, I already fee a bull of
their own drawing up, in the moft florid
terms, dictated by their own virtue and elo-
quence, fetting forth how advantageous it is
to procure the public good, and to facrifice all
private interefts to it ! how much it promotes
the general good of the Church of God to receive fo potent a prince into her communion,
who, it may be expected, will beftow as many favours and benefits on her, as he has hitherto done her wrongs and injuries ! what a
conqueft it will be over the empire of the devil, to wafh the fouls of fuch a number of infidels in the baptifmal font, and thereby enter
them in the way of falvation ! and, in a word,
how many chriftians condemn'd to death, and
flavery for life, will by this means be preferv'd 1
They would be apt to fay, fome grains of allowance ought to be made for the weaknefs of
human nature, which ought not to be drench'd
all at once with an emetic ; which would be
the cafe, if when a man defires life, he be condemn'd to the bitter portion of reducing himfelf to beggary by embracing the chriftian
O faith.

faith. The prodigal fon, mention'd in the gofpel, had forfeited all further pretenfions to his father's eftate, by fquandering that fortune which he had given him in riotous living; yet, as foon as he return'd, the tender father put the beft robe on him, and a ring on his hand, and made a feaft, at which there was nothing feen but mirth and joy; and all this was done at the expence of the dutiful fon's fortune, it being the common intereft to bring back thofe who are gone aftray. Finally, to thefe reflections, they might add innumerable other curious ones, which do not at prefent occur to my mind. They might fay, that as a *Jew*, when baptiz'd, is permitted to keep an eftate gotten by ufury, as inceftuous marriages are difpens'd with, to avoid the fcandal of whoredom, and the like; fo 'tis but juft to receive a *mahometan* prince into the pale of the Church, and let him continue in the enjoyment of all thofe dominions which the chriftian princes have not only loft to him, but have not the leaft hopes of ever recovering. I doubt not but this conduct would be approv'd; and to fay the truth, there is a great deal of reafon for it. Therefore, fince in fuch cafe it would be thought conducive to the publick good, thus to canonize the ufurpation, or feizure of the eftates of the clergy, as well as the laity: As for inftance, in the ifle of *Rhodes*, which was the patrimony of the knights of St. *John*, as it is now of the knights of *Malta*, the fame rule

rule ought to take place here, and the conduct of a lay-fovereign muft confequently be approv'd, who, for certain urgent reafons of ftate, which he knows better than any body elfe, lays hands upon either the eftates or perfons of the cleigy; for where's the reafon that every one of his fubjects fhould have a fhare in the benefits of his government, and only a part of them bear all the weight of it ? Don't tell me that there's no proportion, comparatively fpeaking, betwixt the impofts, and the advantages fo much boafted of; for I muft needs reply in my turn, that neither are the contributions near fo exorbitant as is pretended. An experimental philofopher will tell us, that by the mere operation of the intellect, he can divide a grain of millet into an infinite number of parts, as eafily as the vaft globe of the univerfe; but, without examining whether thofe parts are alike, all that he pretends to prove is their proportion. 'Tis the very fame cafe with the advantages refulting from that liberty I acknowledge in fovereigns; which, if they are compar'd with the damages or impofts, the latter would appear vaftly lefs than what I have reprefented them. The fea-faring man carries and recarries merchandize fiom one pole to the other, in hopes to enrich himfelf, and is many times oblig'd to throw all his cargo into the fea, when he is come in fight of his port; by which means he lofes, in one moment, what has coft him the fweat and toil of

many

many months, or perhaps years; but life is
fweeter to him than all his treafure : In like
manner, the phyfician cuts off an arm, to hinder the mortification from fpreading to the
heart.   Therefoie, I fay, a prince ought to be
excus'd, tho' his conduct may appear violent
and injurious, when what he propofes is to
procure a greater good, or to prevent a greater evil, *minus malum habet rationem boni.* And
of all thefe things we muft leave God to be
the judge ; who is the fearcher of hearts, and
will render to every man according to his
deeds ; for, on the other hand, to cenfure the
actions of a prince, is to fet up a prince over
his head.

C H A P.   XI.

Whether a temporal prince has a right
per fe, to judge ecclefiaftical cri-
minals ?

S *Amuel,* the prophet and chief prieft, was appointed judge of the children of *Ifrael*
by the exprefs command of God ; but that
capricious nation could not long bear with that
holy judge, much lefs with the rebukes he
faw fit to give them; and nothing would ferve
them but they muft have a king, whom they
earneftly

earneftly demanded of him to grant them. The prophet declar'd to God in the tabernacle, where he us'd to meet him, the humour the people were in, and God commanded him accordingly to indulge their fond defire, and to anoint *Saul* king over all *Ifrael.* The prophet obey'd, and after the ceremony of *Saul's* inftallation was over, the chief prieft took off his mitre, and calling all the people together, declar'd, that if any one had been injur'd during his adminiftration, he fhould bear record of him before the Lord and his anointed; for he was ready to anfwer all accufations, and to undergo the punifhment due to his guilt. God has been pleas'd to leave us this eminent example in the holy fcriptures, as a plain evidence of the obligation that the clergy are under to fubmit to the lawful authority of the fecular prince, when their tranfgreffions come under his cognizance. Neverthelefs, I freely own that this propofition, as general as it appears, is liable to many exceptions, and the facred fcriptures, from whence I fetch all my proofs, favour the opinion of thofe who affert that the clergy are not refponfible to the lay-tribunals for every offence; for thofe which they commit in the functions of the priefthood, are immediately punifh'd by God himfelf, as happen'd to thofe of old, who, for making ufe of ftrange fire, were punifh'd with fudden death; or if God does not punifh them upon the fpot, he referves them for the terrible day

O 3 of

of his vengeance. Therefore, I would be understood in this sense, that the clergy are accountable to the tribunal of their temporal prince, for all the faults they commit, foreign to their priestly functions ; every one knows that the order itself does not make the clergy wiser or better than other men, and that the priest is as much under the dominion of the senses as the layman, and as much subjected to the violence of all the passions ; so that he always appears to be as frail as other men : Would to God their crimes were nothing but the effect of mere human frailty, and that they did not sometimes outstrip the most dissolute debauchees in wickedness! such ecclesiastics are not exempted from the judgment of temporal courts by their character, since this is what they have highly dishonour'd, by striving to blaspheme the law of God ; and if a prince had not authority to pass judgment on such crimes, which are, as we may say, only secular, how would it be possible for the sovereign to keep his subjects in obedience, when notorious, wilful criminals, should plead the privilege of being exempted from the obligation of submitting to punishment ? the only way an ecclesiastic has to keep out of the verge of the secular tribunal, is not to fall into those crimes which it belongs to that tribunal to punish. Then he would have no other punishment to fear than the brotherly correction of the prelate, his superior ; but those who pretend that the sacra-

ment

ment of ordination does fcreen a finner from the punifhment he deferves, which is, in fome fort, to make it no lefs than the fomenter of fin, fhew, that they have not the leaft notion of the doctrine of *Jefus Chrift*, who has no greater enemy than fin, and who hates it more than he does the devil himfelf, whom he hates on no other account but that of his finfulnefs.

The gentlemen of the court of *Rome* will tell me, without queftion, that they are not fo abfurd as to imagine, that an ecclefiaftical criminal ought not to be punifh'd, but that all they difpute about, is the competency of the tribunal; for they hold that fuch a man is cenfurable by none but his bifhop, the metropolitan, or legate, who being conftituted the prime dignitaries in the ecclefiaftical ftate, are the only perfons that can judge canonically of his crime. I always faid, and do ftill fay the fame; but then we muft fuppofe the crime, or offence, of fuch clergyman, to be in a matter merely ecclefiaftical. I have given divers inftances of this in a former chapter; as, when he does not adminifter the facraments rightly, when he changes the form, or matter of confecration; and in a word, when he introduces any the like culpable innovation in the exercife of his miniftry, he ought to be try'd, and punifh'd for it by the prelate, becaufe crimes of this fort are not taken notice of in the civil law. The fecular prince is alfo ig-

O 4   norant

norant of thefe matters, for they are foreign to his adminiftration, and he ought to fay in this refpect with St. *Paul, what have I to do with thefe things?* Nay, I dare go farther than thofe gentlemen, and affirm, that every layman who is guilty of a crime in a matter ecclefiaftical, which has relation either to doctrine or the facraments, ought to be punifh'd by the ecclefiaftical court, becaufe the fovereign cannot be fuppos'd to have an adequate knowledge of the nature of the crime, and therefore knows not fo well how to proportion the punifhment. But let it be remember'd that I fpeak this of fuch crimes only as have fome relation to doctrine or the facraments; for, if a layman commits a robbery in a Church, tho' his crime be no lefs than facrilege, and feems at firft view to be a crime in a matter that is properly ecclefiaftical, yet he is fubject to the temporal prince, and 'tis the province of temporal courts to try the offender, becaufe 'tis poffible for the fovereign to have a fufficient knowledge of the cafe and circumftances of the matter of fact. But, on the other hand, if a layman be accus'd of witchcraft, forafmuch as this crime concerns ecclefiaftical liberty, it does not come within the jurifdiction of the temporal courts. For the fame reafon, if a clergyman be accus'd of adultery, robbery, or the like crimes, which are offences point blank againft the laws of the ftate, 'tis the prince's bufinefs to try and punifh them, becaufe 'tis

he

he who makes the laws, and appoints the punishment due to the transgressors : Tell me not that the criminal might be as well punish'd by the ecclesiastical judge, for, I say, the offender would become the more bold and insolent, if he gets but the least hopes of retarding, tho' not of alleviating the punishment. 'Tis well known, that the shortest term, which the Council has set for the decision of an appeal from the sentences of the ordinaries, is two years. Now, if a temporal prince, who is injur'd by the crime of an ecclesiastic, has not a right to punish him, the latter will appeal from the sentence, and so the sovereign will be oblig'd to go a begging to the ecclesiastical courts for reparation of the injury done him. The clergy ought to shew no examples to encourage the dissoluteness of the laity, yet nothing less can be the consequence, as often as the laity see an ecclesiastical criminal not punish'd in due time and manner, and by the proper court. Besides, it ought to be remember'd that the authority of a secular prince is prior, in point of time, to that of the clergy and bishop's court : 'Tis said, *Touch not my Christs or anointed.* This is true indeed, as far as they are anointed and consecrated, which is the signification of the word *Christos*; but St. *Peter* did not make this exception when he commands obedience to princes, even those call'd *Discoli*, that is to say, such as are unjust, impertinent, and whimsical.

I am

I am fenfible, that notwithftanding what has been urg'd, I fhall be accus'd of broaching a novel opinion, the mere product of arrogance, and founded only on violence; but I leave every reafonable man to judge which opinion feems the neweft, that which I have laid down, or theirs at *Rome*, who deny fovereigns part of their proper jurifdiction. In fhort, what was the end of the old canons, which order'd, that every clergyman, convicted of any enormous crime, fhould be degraded and deliver'd over to the fecular judge? Was it not to fave an ecclefiaftical judge the trouble and vexation of decreeing exceffive and capital punifhment, becaufe it does not become a facred judge to dip his hands in blood, even tho' the enormity of the crime requir'd it? The Council of *Trent* confirm'd this cuftom by an exprefs decree; but confidering that in order to conform this degradation to the manner prefcrib'd by the ancients, they fhould be oblig'd to delay the punifhment of the criminal a long time, becaufe of the many bifhops it would be necef-fary to affemble for that end, they therefore order'd that abbats fhould be fummon'd, in-ftead of bifhops; and for want of thefe, the chief incumbents of cathedrals.

Therefore, I fay, 'tis not facrilege, as is loudly pretended, for a fecular prince to try and condemn ecclefiaftical criminals; becaufe not only the canon laws, but alfo the Council of *Trent*, demand it at their hands. Degradation

dation does not make a prieſt ceaſe to be a
prieſt, for the ſacrament of ordination is one
of thoſe that impreſs an indelible character,
which all the power of man cannot deface.
The whole that degradation does, is the putting a prieſt under a ſtate of interdict, by for-
bidding him the exerciſe of his office. It does
not take away his capacity of performing his
functions ; and if a prieſt, who is degraded,
conſecrate the ſacrifice, it will be valid, tho’
he commit a ſin by doing that which is forbidden him. Moreover, if a degraded prieſt be
condemn’d to die, and a layman happen to fall
ſo ill on a ſudden, that his life is in danger, and
no other prieſt is at hand to confeſs him, then
the prieſt,who is under ſentence of death,might,
and ought to hear his confeſſion, tho’ he is juſt
going to the gallows ; and the dying man, ſo
abſolv’d from his ſins by the ſaid prieſt, will
be truly and properly abſolv’d before God. ’I
ſay, that ſuch prieſt not only *might*, but *ought*
to confeſs the dying man, becauſe the obligation of obedience to the precept of.confeſ-
ſion is greater than the ſuſpenſion pronounc’d
by the biſhops. ’Tis evident, therefore, that, according to the canons themſelves, a ſecular
prince may judge eccleſiaſtics ; and if it happens that he do it without degrading them, ’tis
becauſe every crime is not capital ; but the delinquent, tho’ he does not deſerve death, ought
not to come off without any puniſhment at
all, for the ſake of obſerving that formality ;
besides

befides that fuch impunity would be attended with the inconveniency I have already mention'd, it would promote licentioufnefs among the laity, becaufe fin is always countenanc'd by retarding the punifhment of the criminal, tho' he does not at length wholly pafs unpunifh'd. When a prince happens to punifh a clergyman, without ftaying for his degradation, he fails in his obfervation of the canon that prefcribes it ; and all the fault that the court of *Rome* could pretend to find with fuch procedure, would be only the neglect of a mere piece of formality, in no wife effential in it felf, becaufe degradation does indeed fufpend, but not efface the character of ordination. But to return once more to the ecclefiaftical judges ; are they themfelves fuch ftrict obfervers of thefe canons, that when they find an irregular, fcandalous prieft, in countries fubject to the Church, both in fpirituals and temporals, they degrade him, and then turn him over to the fecular arm ? No verily ; they firft condemn fuch prieft either to the galleys, or the gibbet, according to the nature of his crime, without delivering him over to the fecular power, obferving the diftinction I have already mention'd, *viz.* that they pronounce this fentence not as priefts (becaufe then they would fall into an abfurdity) but as minifters of a temporal prince, or of an ecclefiaftic one, who exercifes a temporal power and authority. By this conduct, they do as good as acknowledge

ledge that 'tis neceffary, for the good government of a temporal ftate, to pafs judgment
without delay, and to condemn the guilty,
whether they are laymen or clergy, without
ftanding for the ceremony of degradation, or
carrying them about from one tribunal to another.   Why then do they fcruple to allow the
fame right to a temporal prince, who is as
much concern'd furely as they are to govern the
fubjects well, and not to fleep when the guilty deferve punifhment ; efpecially thofe who
have committed great crimes ? if they make
no fcruple to break thofe canons which they
ought to obey, I don't think the neglect of
them can be a crime in a temporal prince, who
indeed owns his obligation to obey the divine
law, but does not think he is, nor is he any
way oblig'd to mind the canons in matters relating to his government, fince he has no fuperior to account for it to,   but God alone.

    Thefe are the ufurpations which the court of
Rome would fain fee eftablifh'd all over the
world.   They would have it believ'd that the
ecclefiaftical courts have greater authority, in
thefe modern times, than the ancient prelates
had formerly.   They preach up obedience and
juftice, but leave the practice thereof to others.
If a layman commits a robbery, or murder,
in a Church, and, being profecuted for the
fame at law, flies for protection to another
Church, the canons are againft his enjoying the privileges of the immunity ; becaufe,
                                                             fay

say they, he has already difhonour'd the facred
place by his crime. By parity of reafon, when
a clergyman, who is by his profeffion bound to
lift up his eyes to heaven, and to ufe his hands in
adminiftring the facraments, is the firft man to
fully his facred character by robbery, murder, or
other great enormities, why then fhould he enjoy the privileges of that order which he has thus
defil'd? for ecclefiaftical liberty was eftablifh'd
for our edification, and not for our deftruction.

The Council of *Trent* is full of decrees made
in favour of epifcopal authority, with a view
to render the bifhops more eafy in the government of their diocefes ; which was often molefted and hinder'd by temporal princes granting exemptions, favours, protections, and the
like, to certain places of devotion, military
orders, and royal chaplains ; which exemptions
and privileges, claim'd by offenders, are fo many impediments and obftacles to the right adminiftration of juftice · Therefore the Council
frees the bifhops from fhewing any regard to
conceffions of that kind, and they allow a bifhop the more liberty, in this cafe, to encourage him to conftant refidence in his diocefe,
and to reward him for his pains in it. Why
then fhould not a lawful prince have the fame
free liberty, who holds his authority and government from God himfelf, and the law of
nature? for my own part, I cannot help thinking it intolerable prefumption, to pretend to
make the bifhop's jurifdiction larger than the

† prince's

prince's to whom he is fubject, and in whofe dominions he affumes that authority.

The Council declares in a hundred cafes, that when a bifhop finds himfelf embaraffed, he ought to call for the affiftance of the fecular arm. Is it not the higheft ingratitude then in the ecclefiaftical tribunal, to pretend to difpute the prerogatives of the temporal one, from which it receives protection and fuccour? I know they will tell me, that a prince, fuppofing he be an ecclefiaftic, would enjoy the fame privilege, but that while he is only temporal, he ought not to concern himfelf with perfons that are facred : To this I fhall repeat the fame anfwer I have already given; that tho' the perfon of a delinquent be facred, the action is not fo, and fuch action makes him forfeit his quality and privilege of confecration. 'Tis remarkable that the very canon law excepts twelve moft flagrant cafes, in which the fecular judge is fo far from being bound to regard ecclefiaftical immunities, that he may caufe a criminal attainted of any, or either of thofe crimes, to be arrefted in that very Church to which he flies for protection. Now ecclefiaftical liberties and ecclefiaftical immunities are but one and the fame, and only differ in this, that ecclefiaftical liberty is afcrib'd to perfons, and the other to places that are facred. Since therefore, by the confeffion of the *Romifh* cafuifts, the enormity of the crime juftifies the fecular judge in laying hands upon the
criminal,

criminal, notwithstanding the sacredness of the place, and tho' even the holy sacrament be there, I would fain know why the same enormity, when found in the person of an ecclesiastic, does not authorize the prince to treat him in the same manner. After this, 'tis no wonder if some evil-minded persons take the freedom to say, that all this noise and jealousy of the clergy is not for procuring respect to the dignity, but to the man who is vested with it ; and that a multitude of worldly interests and passions are often cover'd under the cloak of religion. But we shall now conclude this article, on which we have already said more than enough to satisfy those that are impartial, but shall never be able to add what will convince those that are interested in the matter.

C H A P. XII.

Concerning the Pope's infallibility.

WHile I was pondering upon this important subject, I call'd to mind the genealogy which *Aristotle* has left us of natural philosophy. Its great grandfather, says he, was *ignorance*, its grandfather *admiration*, and its mother *doubt*. The sight of those effects, she could not account for, gave birth to *admiration*, for we are apt to admire what we do not know; and in fine, *admiration* excited the unstanding to go in search of the *why* and *wherefore* of these eff.cts, and from hence sprang *doubt*; and the discussion of things doubtful brought forth *knowledge*, *wisdom*, or rather true philosophy. *David* has recorded that *every man is a liar*; and St. *Paul* says, *let him who thinketh he standeth, take heed lest he fall*: And finally, the Council of *Trent* says, *no person can be sure that he has obtain'd the grace of God.* Yet we are told every now and then of a man who has eyes strong enough to look steadily into the sun of truth without being dazled, who can slide upon the slippery ice of human weakness without falling, and who is consequently infallible in all his judgment

At first, a man knows nothing at all of infallibility, then he *admires* it; and in the third place comes to doubt of it; but, at last, with the help of some distinctions, he comprehends it, and solves all his former doubtings. The champions of the court of *Rome* boast that this point has been clearly decided by *Christ* himself in the affirmative. If so, I desire no more; for *Jesus Christ* being the truth itself, one single word of his proves more than all the demonstration which the wit of man can invent; but if the principle, on which their demonstrations are founded, is false, they must be so too; while, on the other hand, the word of our Lord *Christ* is exempt from all manner of falshood.

A cer-

A certain king of *Japan*, having heard it asserted by the missionaries, that if a christian had faith, he was able to remove mountains; he sent to acquaint their superior, that he intended in a few days to see an experiment of the truth of their proposition, and that if they did not succeed, he would punish him and all his countrymen as false prophets. This message was extremely mortifying to the superior, who very much doubted of success; for in all times there have been propositions advanc'd in dispute, which could never be prov'd, when brought to the test. However, an honest cobler apply'd to the missionaries, and desir'd them to tell him sincerely, whether *Jesus Christ* had really declar'd so himself? and they assuring him that he had, he offer'd himself to work the miracle, being thoroughly persuaded, that if *Christ* had said it, he could not fail of success. I think my faith is as strong as the cobler's; and if they can shew me that our saviour has any where promis'd this infallibility, I will instantly believe it, for I know that 'tis *he who hath made us*; and as he has given us frail nature, which is subject to err, he is also able to fortify us, and to set our understandings above the reach of fallacy.

I have prayed for thee, Peter, *that thy faith fail not.* This text is all the proof they bring for infallibility; which, as short as it is, might, however, serve for a proof, if it was not subject to a distinction; for it must be consider'd,

whether

whether this prayer of *Chrift* is confin'd only to faith, or whether it does not rather extend to all the benefits depending thereon, as doctrine, piety, miracles, and eternal falvation. If all thele graces had been promis'd by *Jefus Chrift* to *Peter*, he could never have been without them 'Tis true, he had them all at one time or another; for, after his converfion, he was wholly endow'd with knowledge and the gift of miracles, and was the firft in the apoftolical college, as well as the chief of the faints in *Paradife*, but all thefe advantages were the fruits of his repentance, and he acquir'd thefe great prerogatives as a reward of his faith, for confeffing the name of *Chrift*; fo every one who has been baptiz'd may obtain all thefe rich gifts, as the price of that facrifice which we make of our felves for the name of *Jefus*; for the juftice of God does not deny the labourer his hire, but is rather lavifh in its rewards, than fparing, as God himfelf has given us to underftand in the parable of the vinedreffer.

All the controverfy turns, in fhort, upon thefe two points : Firft, whether it was a privilege attached to the perfon of St. *Peter*, or to his dignity ? thefe gifts were promis'd to *Peter* in confequence of his faith, yet all the apoftles had them as well as he. The fecond, which of the two is perhaps the moft difficult to anfwer, is whether this privilege be perfo-

nal,

212 The Rights of Sovereigns.

nal, or whether it be common to all who fucceed in *Peter's* chair ?

Firſt, let us conſider at what time the pro-
miſe was made. It was when *Jeſus Chriſt* inſtituted the euchariſt at his laſt ſupper with the
apoſtles, when, as it may be ſaid, he impove-
riſh'd himſelf, by diſtributing all that he had
to them; and that they might continue worthy
of the dignity to which he advanc'd them,
he warn'd them of the terrible temptation
which the devil was preparing for them. *Satan,* ſays he, *has deſir'd to have you, that he may
ſift you as wheat ; but I have pray'd for thee,*
Peter, *that thy faith fail not.* Who does not
ſee that hereby *Jeſus Chriſt* manifeſted an extraordinary love for *Peter ?* for the temptation
was prepar'd by the devil for all the apoſtles,
and *Chriſt* warned them all of it ; yet he tells
Peter alone, that he had prayed to the father
for him in a ſpecial manner that his faith fail
not. It may be ſaid that our Lord had for-
ᴄot, or made no great account of the other
diſciples ; but as ſoon as God caſts his eyes
upon human weakneſs, he remembers us, and
makes us ſenſible of his aſſiſtance ; for which
reaſon *Jeſus Chriſt* adds immediately, *and when
thou art converted, ſtrengthen thy brethren.*
Therefore he did not forget his diſciples ; but
it ſeems as if he would give *Peter* the preference of ſuperiority, by his commanding that
their confirmation in the faith ſhould be the
work of that apoſtle, in the ſame ſenſe as *Peter's*

ter's abiding in the faith, was the effect of *Chrift*'s prayer for him, and favourable difpo-fition towards him. An admirable privilege this, without doubt, and a ftrong proof of his dignity ! But obferve what happen'd a few hours after. His divine mafter was no fooner taken into cuftody, but *Peter* is expos'd to the temptation of a filly woman, when that *Peter* who was fo dearly lov'd, that *Peter* who was fo well forewarn'd, that *Peter* for whom *Je-fus Chrift* pray'd in a particular manner, denies him, and fwears that he knows him not ! alas ! how frail is man ! who can ftand, if *Peter* ftag-gers, who had fuch mighty aids ? God forbid that any fhould think our faviour's promife and prayer for him were of no effect. One word of *Chrift* is fufficient ; there cannot be a furer ; and there's no greater proof of it than the thief, who, by virtue of that divine word, afcended directly from the crofs to *Paradife.* But fome will fay, how can we reconcile the promife with the effect ? why, if we duly confider what it was *Jefus Chrift* promis'd, we fhall find that he executed it to a tittle. *I have pray'd for thee,* Peter, *that thy faith fail not.* He does not fay, *that thou fail not ;* which would amount to fuch a confirmation in grace as the angels in heaven had after the fall of lucifer, when they could not fall if pof-fibly they would. *Jefus Chrift* promis'd him that his faith fhould not fail ; for, in fhort, fin does not deftroy faith, till the man apoftatizes.

Tho'

Tho' *Peter* deny'd *Chrift*, it was not becaufe he doubted of his divinity, but the fear of death made him pretend that he knew him not. His crime was not the holding any heretical opinion, as was that of *Judas*, but his being afraid to confefs the name of *Chrift*.

There is a notable difpute among divines concerning what fpecies of crime thofe are guilty of, who are forc'd by the *Turks* to abjure chriftianity. Some fay they fin againft the faith. S^t. *Thomas* is of the contrary opinion, and fays, that be they never fo wicked, they are ftill chriftians in their hearts ; and if they return to their firft profeffion, they ought not to be rebaptiz'd ; but he fays, their fin is a fin againft the confeffion of the faith, which every chriftian is oblig'd to make at the hazard of his life. As for my own part, I fhould be apt to diftinguifh, and fay thus : If they deny *Chrift*, becaufe they do not believe in his divinity, and in his promifes, they fin againft the faith ; for he cannot be call'd a believing chriftian, who does not believe in *Chrift* ; but if they deny him only in appearance, and thro' fear of death, they fin againft the confeffion of the faith, becaufe they prefer this life to the profeffion of the name of *Chrift*. This diftinction will ferve to fhew us of what fort St. *Peter*'s crime was ; he denies his knowledge of *Jefus Chrift*, and backs it even with an oath and blafphemy ; but a moment after, *Jefus* cafting his eye upon him in *Pilate*'s hall of juftice,

juftice, he thought of the guilt he had contracted, repented, and wept bitterly; whereas, if his faith had fail'd him, he would not
have return'd to himfelf with fo many marks
of a fincere penitent. Now this was the effect
of our faviour's prayer, who reftor'd him to
grace after fo enormous a fin, and with that
grace he obtain'd many other gifts; as piety,
doctrine, miracles, and the being chief among
the apoftles.

The canonifts pretend that the privilege of
perfeverance in the faith, from whence infallibility flows, is peculiar to the pontifical dignity. The *Romifh* theologians are alfo agreed
in the fame point, and I my felf have own'd
as much in the beginning of this treatife, where
I have plainly fhewn my readinefs to believe,
that tho' the Popes of our days have not the
fame piety, or the power to work miracles as
Peter, yet they have in all refpects the prerogative of not erring. But what? are we to
fuppofe them fo confirm'd in grace, that they
have no longer need of the facrament of penance? no truly; for St. *Paul* fays, that every
high prieft is encompafs'd with infirmity. To
folve this difficulty, we muft again diftinguifh,
that mannerrs two ways; in opinion, and in
action; and that thefe two kinds of error are
very different. It often happens, that the zeal
of the will eclipfes the judgment; but if this
be folid, and duly regulated, it cannot be im-
pos'd upon by the will. To apply thefe gene-

ral

ral reflections to our prefent fubject, we may argue, that it comports with the juftice of God, at the fame time when he *commands a thing to be done, to furnifh the means for doing it, and that otherwife we might accufe his providence and foreknowledge; fo that *Peter* and his fucceffors being defign'd by God, for the chief directors and minifters of the ecclefiaftical monarchy, he has undoubtedly furnifh'd both the one and the other with the means fufficient for governing the Church; the chief of which means is true doctrine. Some perhaps are fo charm'd with the beauty of holinefs, as to imagine, that the fame is a neceffary qualification for a Pope; but be it fo or not, 'tis certain that doctrine ought to be his chief qualification; for the benefits of piety are peculiar to the perfon alone who has it, whereas the confequences of ignorance muft be fatal to the whole chriftian Church. If he who is fet at the helm of government be endow'd with true knowledge, as much as he edifies by his good example, fo much does he demolifh error by his knowledge. For this reafon, I believe that the Popes hold the doctrine of *Peter* by indefeafible hereditary right, tho' not his piety; but the *Greeks* and *Lutherans* deny the Pope the gift of true doctrine, and acknowledge it only in a Council, according to that paffage, *whorefoever two or three fhall be gathered together in my name, there I will be in the midft of them.* For my part, I agree
with

with·both, but fhall again diftinguifh what knowledge it is the Popes have ; is it univerfal, like that of the angels and the blefs'd fpirits, who upon the fpot, and without examining arguments, comprehend things of themfelves, and are therefore call'd *Intelligen es ?* No, this cannot be it ; for fuch a knowledge does not comport with human underftanding, which is always eclips'd by the mifts of the fenfes. Even *Solomon* had not this knowledge ; and tho' his was the effect of the illumination of his underftanding, yet he had no greater a degree of it, than what demonftrated him to be a man. We will grant then, that the Pope is infallible in his private judgment, with refpect efpecially to the articles of faith ; this fort of knowledge being neceff ry for that dignity to which *Jefus Chrift* has rais'd him ; but I don't believe that becaufe he is a Pope, he pretends to be a learned phyfician, or an able mathematician, which are fciences no more neceffary to the office of a Pope, than the knowledge of all the languages which the apoftles knew, or of all the fciences taught by *Ariftotle*.

I believe that the advocates for the Pope will be fo ingenuous as to own, that tho' the Pope, by virtue o a privilege, which he derives from St. *Peter*, cannot, thro' ignorance, miflead the chriftian flock, yet he may lofe himfelf, and err in his own underftanding, and in other things that are not abfolutely neceffary for faith in Chrift ; and this confeffion may
serve

serve as a foundation of the decision of the present question.

All the Councils, and especially that of *Trent*, distinguish nicely between the divine law, and that which is positive. He who transgresses the divine law, is more guilty than he who breaks the law of man ; tho' such is the lamentable perversion of the times, that some human precepts are more religiously observ'd than the commands of God. Thus men are more careful in abstinence from meats, and keeping solemn feasts, than in guarding against fornication, or taking the name of God in vain. This proceeds from the weakness, or rather ignorance of the vulgar, since the divine commandments ought to be most strictly observ'd. We may therefore conclude, that infallibility is a privilege not to be deny'd the Pope, with respect to articles of faith, that are absolutely necessary to salvation ; but not with respect to the constitutions of positive law, which tend to maintain christianity, but are not absolutely necessary for that end. The Pope's piety would contribute very much to it ; but tho' he does not happen to be pious, he is nevertheless Pope, and the lawful head of the christians as such. It must also be consider'd, that the divine law is unchangeable, because God is not subject to change, whereas the canon laws may be alter'd or annull'd, according to the circumstances of times and persons, which is a proof that infallibility has

no

no fhare in the eftablifhment of fuch laws ; for
if it had, they would not be liable to alteration. But 'tis not fo with faith and its articles. No body can be exempted from believing them, nor can the facraments themfelves
be chang'd, for the Pope cannot difpenfe with
what God explicitly obliges us to. He cannot alter either the matter or form of the facraments,
tho' he has taken the liberty to do it in fome
cafes, nor can he augment or diminifh the
number of them. 'Tis true, the Pope often
decides matters of faith ; but then his decifion
is not arbitrary, and he does not prefcribe fuch
or fuch a duty merely of himfelf, but only declares and interprets the will of God in fuch
a manner as feems to be correfpondent with
the faith. For the maxim in civil law, *illius
eft interpretari cujus eft jura dare*, i e. *the inter-
preter of the law ought to be he who is the law-
giver*, is not admitted in things divine. So
that tho' the Pope has a right to interpret, he
cannot make one fingle article of faith. 'Tis
therefore undeniable that God has endow'd
him with fufficient light for fuch an interpre-
tation, and 'tis in this fenfe that *Jefus Chrift*
promis'd his conftant affiftance to the apoftles,
when he faid, *I am with you until the end of
the world.* God enlightens him with his holy
fpirit, that he may chufe the beft opinion, and
every chriftian, whether prince or fubject, is
oblig'd to receive thofe decifions. This fort
of infallibility is annex'd, and hereditary to
the

the papal dignity, but does not extend to canonical decifions and decrees, that have a regard only to pofitive law. For in this refpect the Pope may err, becaufe conftitutions of this fort are often alter'd and annull'd, and one Pope may undo what was done by his predeceffor, as has happen'd more than once, and as is fet down in the Councils. Indeed the courtiers of *Rome* pretend not to credit it, becaufe they would fain make the people believe, if poffible, that all the actions of the Pope are above cenfure, for that he is infallible ; but men of learning, experience and honefty, are not to be perfuaded into the belief of fuch a notion.

Let no one charge me with endeavouring to retrench a privilege which I own to have been granted to the Popes, becaufe I deny that the faid privilege extends to cafes of pofitive law. The confeffion I make on this account, is not confin'd, and flows from a ftrong and lively faith, becaufe I own the faid privilege has for its object the articles of faith ; the knowledge of which is fo difficult for the wit of man to attain to, and about which 'tis fo eafy to be miftaken. How many are there that have quite loft their fight by poring too curioufly upon this fun of truth, and how many are become like to the beaft in the *Revelations ?* the *Pagans* are highly commendable for their moderation in this refpect, of which they have left us feveral inftances in their fables. Among other

other reprefentations, they prefent us with *Actæon* turn'd into a ftag, and torn to pieces by his own dogs, for endeavouring to fteal a fight of *Diana*'s nakednefs; and when old *Rome* had a being, a foldier was hang'd for his curiofity in inquiring who was the tutelar God of his country. In matters of faith, 'tis better for him, to whom the care thereof is not committed, to be contented with a moderate knowledge, than to endeavour to penetrate thro' them with the eyes of a lynx, for faith and knowledge are as oppofite as the *Antipodes*; and he who pretends to prove the principles of the chriftian faith by human reafon, is not a great way off from an heretic. --

Thefe laft reflections will undoubtedly be very pleafing to the court of *Rome*, who will perhaps retort them upon my felf, as if I pretended to be wifer than is convenient, becaufe I put the learning of the Pope in the balance, to fee what it weighs; but I fincerely declare I have faid nothing but what I verily think in my confcience to be true; and that the fetting truth in its due light has been the fole view of all my inquiries. I don't prefume to undervalue the Pope's abilities, and I fhould be rafh to a degree, if I fhould fo much as queftion one of his decifions in matters of faith; but then, on the other hand, I fhould be a very impertinent fool, to adore him upon this account as a God, and it would be impiety in me to make that an article of faith, which is
not

not fo. In a word, I ought to pafs for the rafh-
eft of mankind, if I fhould prefume to explain
an obfcure article of faith ; but I will never be
oblig'd to regard that as an article of faith,which
has a relation only to political government.

I have read fomewhere, that he who pretends to publifh falfe miracles deferves to be
excommunicated, and I profefs it would be a
great miracle to find out an infallible man, who
has committed many faults. *Solomon*, who acquir'd his great wifdom by contemplating that
deity which was reveal'd to him in a dream,
wrote very pious things, worthy to be recorded, as they are,in the holy fcriptures, for the inftruction of two felect people, thofe under the
law, and thofe under grace; yet how unhappily
did this man fall,infomuch that he turn'd *idolater?*
Therefore 'tis not a neceffary confequence, that
becaufe a man is mafter of one fcience, he un-
derftands all, much lefs that he is infallible in
his actions ; for a general cannot be form'd out
of a particular. The Council has decided, that
the facrifice is always pure and fpotlefs, tho' the
prieft who offers it be unclean and polluted, becaufe God purifies him in the very act of adminiftring, tho' of himfelf he remains in his former
faults, and even in greater, forafmuch as he ap-
proacheth the altar unworthily. I believe likewife that the Pope has a clear and determinate
knowledge as to the doubts in matters of faith,
but that in other parts of knowledge he is fubject to error and miftakes as well as others.

† PART

PART II.

The application of the general pro-
positions in the first part, to the
Quarrels betwixt the court of
Rome *and the republic of* Venice.

IN the twelve foregoing Chapters, I have sufficiently shown how far sovereign princes ought to carry their respect to the Pope, and their submission to his authority, without insisting on the unjust pretensions of the court of *Rome*, for setting up the Pope in place of the old *Roman* emperors, who assum'd a sovereignty over both princes and priests, and for engaging christians in the observation of ancient rites and customs, as is used at that of the adoration of the Pope, whose mouth they will have to be the infallible oracle of all the laws and statutes upon earth,

a thing

a thing which they can prevail with none to believe, but the weak and the stupid, or such students as dare not say their souls are their own. After having establish'd the boundaries to which the one ought to carry his authority, and the other his obedience, it may be necessary to make a brief application of all those general maxims to the particular points in dispute between the court of *Rome* and the most serene republic. Those general maxims, thus proved and demonstrated, shall serve as the *major* proposition of the argument, and the present controversy as the *minor*. I shall leave the judicious reader to make his own inference, and to be the judge whether I have made good my promise in the introduction to this discourse, to shew that, considering the good conduct of the republic in the present case of *Paul* Vth's pretended interdict, all the citizens of *Venice* ought to be very easy, and may enjoy a good conscience. For order sake, and for the ease of the memory, I shall in the first place give a short recapitulation of the contents of the former part of this treatise.

I own'd without reserve, that the Church, the Pope, and other prelates invested with the pontifical dignity, have a right to excommunicate; but at the same time I demonstrated, that in order to excommunicate any one with justice, 'tis necessary that the action for which it is inflicted, be a mortal sin, otherwise the whole structure of excommunication falls to the

† ground;

ground. That when a free fovereign, or other perfon of illuftrious rank, is to be excommunicated, the fentence ought to be pronounc'd by a prelate who has no dependance upon any other, or who is at leaft upon a level with the prince accus'd, upon the foot of his own, and not a deriv'd or precarious authority. I likewife prov'd, that an 'appeal may be made against excommunication, becaufe the fame being only a fentence founded upon the opinion of man, he is liable to be deceiv'd by falfe appearances; confequently, that every one has a natural right to have recourfe to this way of appeal as often as he finds himfelf injur'd by fuch a fentence. I have alfo demonftrated, that fovereign princes cannot be excommunicated with juftice, but when they are found guilty of holding opinions different from the catholic Church, in the articles of faith, or in things repugnant to the true interefts of the Church, or to the propagation of the faith. That in cafe the excommunication is fulminated by the Pope himfelf, the fovereign has a right to appeal from it to a general Council, who in this refpect is fuperior to the Pope. That tho' the grievances complain'd of by the court of *Rome* againft a fovereign be of fuch a nature as manifeftly to deferve excommunication, and to be of the fame clafs with thofe juft now mention'd, *viz.* the hindring the progrefs of the faith, or corrupting the purity of it; yet to fuch excommunication there ought

in no wife to be added the claufe of deprivation of temporal dominions, if they are poffefs'd in their own right, and not by fief; from
whence it follows, that fince this is not practicable with refpect to a prince who is fole and
abfolute fovereign, it would be much lefs tolerable by an independent republic. That the
infringement of ecclefiaftical liberty deferves
cenfure; but care muft be taken to meafure the crime by the true interefts of the
Church, and not by the interefts of the clergy; becaufe there is an effential difference
between the Church and the clergy, not only in the thing confider'd in it felf, but alfo on
a political confideration. That there are many
important arguments to prove, that the Church
does not poffefs temporalities by divine right,
and that the Pope has no greater privileges on
this fcore than other temporal free fovereigns.
That a free fovereign has a legal right in himfelf to raife the ordinary tenths upon the eftates
of the clergy, and to exact from their perfon
and eftates, for the fervice of the public. That,
moreover, if any clergyman be guilty of fecular crimes, that is to fay, fuch as have no relation either to the adminiftring of the facraments, or to the doctrine of faith, the faid offence fhall be cognizable by the lay-tribunal of
the temporal prince. And laftly, I fhew'd
that the Pope's judgment, which the courtiers
of *Rome* cry up fo much for infallible, is only
fo, when he declares the articles of faith, and
adminifters the facraments; but that it does

not extend to pofitive laws, in regard to which his judgment is as liable to the danger of error as other mens, and by confequence fubject to correction and retractation, therefore not infallible, but difputable and revifable.

This is the fubftance of all that I have hitherto proved, without making mention of the moft ferene republic. Therefore 'tis but natural for us now to take a view of the grievances which the court of *Rome* complains of againft her, and fee -whether or- no they are juft, and whether the remedies made ufe of by the republic are not honourable and-neceffary ; and fuppofing they are fo, whether every one that lives in the city of *Venice* may not be eafy, confidering the conduct of the republic, in the cafe of the interdict.

Were we indeed to bring again upon the ftage thofe difputes which have a relation to the prefent grievances, and have been already decided, we fhould never have done, and the controverfy would hold to eternity. Therefore infifting on what we have before determin'd, it will be eafy to fhew that the republic, far from arrogating what does not belong to her, has pafs'd over a multitude of things which fhe had a right to expect, by virtue of her free, abfolute, and independent fovereignty; and which are already eftablifh'd by law. For proof of this; it is eftablifh'd that every free fovereign has a right of himfelf to raife the ordinary tenths upon the eftates of the clergy;

but

but the moſt ſerene republic does not make uſe of her right, and while other princes are commonly forward to plead their independency, by laying hold even on the moſt minute occaſions to extend their rights and power, the republic modeſtly ſtands off at a diſtance, to ſhew her filial obedience to the holy See, and only deſires an *indulto* for raiſing the tenths once in every five or ſeven years. If this be not an evidence of her extraordinary moderation, nothing is; yet the court of *Rome* makes a heavy outcry, and complains of the following grievances.

I. That the republic hinders the giving of lands to Regular Monks and pious places.

II. That they permit the preſcription of the eſtates of eccleſiaſtics in favour of thoſe who only rent them, and thereby improve ſuch rents to a title of property,

III. That the ſecular tribunal concerns itſelf in the trial of all eccleſiaſtic criminals, and meddles with all the civil intereſts of perſons eccleſiaſtical.

IV. That biſhops are hinder'd not only from proſecuting the laity as malefactors, for crimes cognizable by the mixed courts, but even from puniſhing the clergy when convicted of ſcandalous crimes.

V. That biſhops are hinder'd from viſiting frieries, hoſpitals, holy places, mounts of piety, and the like.

VI. That

VI. That the college meddles with the trial of caufes in matters beneficiary ; and when any one has applied to the court of *Rome*, they oblige him to a renunciation *ab impetratis*, *i.e.* of the decrees there obtained.

VII. That they are for fubjecting the clergy to the ordinary taxes, and other impofts laid upon the laity.

VIII. That the regular Clergy are hinder'd from obeying the conftitutions of their order and chapters, by being oblig'd to confer their prelatical dignities upon fuch as are natural born-fubjects of the republic.

IX. That when any difpute happens among the friers themfelves, they are forc'd to put in an appearance in the temporal court, inftead of the tribunal of the apoftolical nuncio.

X. That thofe who have a bifhoprick, or other prelatical dignity, confer'd upon them by the court of *Rome*, are oblig'd to beg and pray to the Council, for the poffeffion of temporalities, and that every bifhop is forced to be precognifed by a *Venetian* cardinal, before he can expect to obtain poffeffion of the vacant See.

XI. That they meddle with what relates to penfions ; and be they ever fo much eftablifh'd and approv'd, the fecular court grants their protection to debtors that refufe to pay them.

XII. That the ordinaries of places are hinder'd from fulminating excommunication, in cafes prefcrib'd by the canons.

XIII. That

XIII. That if any one having a call, takes upon him a religious habit, they either expel him upon the least complaint of his parents, on pretence of his being seduced ; or else let him stay in the monastery, and authorize the parents to keep his estate.

XIV.. That schismatics, heretics, notorious whoremongers and usurers, are suffer'd to live quietly and peaceably at *Venice,* and the prelate is not permitted to excommunicate them, or to punish them in any other way.

XV. And to say all in a word, the ecclesiastical authority is depriv'd of all jurisdiction that legally belongs to it.

To these they add the violences, as they think fit to call them, practised upon those that fail in the gulph, by forcing such as carry provisions, instruments, animals, salt, and the like goods, that pass thro' it into the rivers of *Romagna,* to pay great imposts.

These are the gross of all their complaints. Great cry, but little wool ; and more tare than grain ; so that 'tis necessary to sift it, in order to separate the one from the other, for fear that mistaking the tare for the good corn, it might, instead of giving nourishment, send up vapours and intoxicate the brain, which are its peculiar qualities.

In the first place, let it be observ'd that all disputes of this nature are but of yesterday, and were never so much as heard of in the age

of

of the apoftles. 'Tis true that fome herefies
were broach'd at that time, which were follow'd with difcuffions and decifions, both by
fome of the apoftles in particular, namely,
St. *Peter* and St. *Paul*, and by all in general,
when the whole apoftolical college gave their
opinion in council with others of the faithful.
At that time, difputes turned upon matters of
the laft importance, it being neceffary there
fhould be herefies to follow the truth, as the
fhadow always does the light, for the better
diftinguifhing the true belief from its contrary. *There muft be herefies; and it muft needs be
that offences come*, fays the fcripture. But there
is not the leaft mention in thofe facred writings, of any difputes concerning pofitive law ;
and if there were any in later times, they made
no great noife. St. *Epiphanius* having given holy orders to fome clergymen in the diocefe of
St. *Chryfoftom*, archbifhop of *Conftantinople*,
whofe See was afterwards erected into a patriarchate, it rais'd a difpute among them, which
at length came to no more than this : The archbifhop fays to *Epiphanius*, *O holy man! fince thou
haft done this, I believe thou wilt never get back
alive to thy bifhoprick* ; and *Epiphanius* reply'd, *O
juft man! I don't believe thou wilt die in thine.*
The prophefies of both were verify'd ; for
Epiphanius dy'd in his voyage to *Jerufalem*,
and St. *Chryfoftom* dy'd in exile. Things would
not certainly be fo eafily accommodated in
thefe our days. If the jurifdiction of a prelate

fhould

should be invaded, he would fulminate a terrible excommunication against his brother, and not lay down his arms, till he had receiv'd compleat satisfaction. One might be inclin'd to think that only clergymen would be concern'd in this kind of quarrels; but it will appear, upon due reflection, that a multitude of cases may possibly happen, which princes cannot avoid being concern'd in; as for instance, when the person excommunicated is the subject of another sovereign, and if such person, in obedience to the excommunication, abstains from his pastoral functions, then his diocesans will be without a pastor. Mean time the prelates of our days cannot reproach those of antiquity with a want of zeal for the glory of God, because they were all holy men, and the greatest part of 'em have been crown'd with martyrdom; but our modern prelates are not animated so much by a zeal for God's glory, as for the observation of positive laws. Whoever reads St. *Paul,* will see that he took the liberty to determin articles of faith, as when he enjoin'd the *Galatians* to abstain from circumcision, adding this reproof to his exhortation; O *foolish* Galatians, *who hath bewitched you that you should not obey the truth?* because circumcision was introduc'd among the faithful. He also prescrib'd many other things to the churches of *Greece,* and the provinces of the *Levant.* Mean while he was far from having the primacy, or superiority of St. *Peter,* and

was

was not made an apoftle by *Jefus Chrift*, whom he had never feen in his incarnation, but was *only call'd to be an apoftle,* as himfelf owns. Neverthelefs, all his decifions were affented to by the other apoftles, who had nothing of this fpirit of envy among them about jurifdiction, wherefore St. *Peter* wrote to them after this manner. *Be diligent that ye may be found without fpot,and blamelefs,even as our beloved brother* Paul *alfo, according to the wifdom given unto him, hath written unto you ; as alfo in all his epiftles, fpeaking in them of thefe things, in which are fome things hard to be underftood, which they that are unlearned and unftable wreft, as they do alfo the other fcriptures, unto their own deftruction.*   This was the manner in which St. *Peter* approv'd of St. *Paul*'s decifions, without being angry with him for offering to determin any points of faith.   And the fole aim of thofe times was the eftablifhing of found doctrine, and neceffary ceremonies ; but as for pofitive law, it was either unknown to them, or not at all minded, the natural tendency of it being rather to procure fplendor to the dignities and perfons of the clergy,than to contribute to the falvation of believers.   Thofe who have read St. *Paul*'s writings with the leaft attention, cannot but obferve that he did not care for the large perplexing volumes of the law.All his inftructions perfuaded to mutual love and good manners, and when he fpoke of the law, it was in thefe terms : *I had not known fin but by the law ;*

law ; *for I had not known luft, except the law had faid,* Thou fhalt not covet : *But fin taking occafion by the commandment, wrought in me all manner of concupifcence ; for without the law fin was dead, for I was alive without the law once, but when the commandment came, fin revived, and I died.* I do not pretend to infer fiom thence that there fhould be no fuch thing as pofitive law, but only that the fewer there are in number, the more ufeful they will be, and the better obferv'd.

We don't find that the apoftles made any other decrees befides thofe containing the precepts of faith, tho' methinks it might have been thought neceffary to eftablifh by decrees the authority of prelates, the limits of obedience, jurifdiction, and the like things, which were the more needful then, when this fpiritual dominion was firft introduc'd. Yet nothing of all this was done, becaufe they were perfuaded that the good example of the prelates would incline their flocks to a voluntary obedience. Befides, the multiplicity of laws may be compared to nets ; for the more laws there are, the more muft be the tranfgreffions, and the multiplication of laws is only multiplying the occafions of difobedience. This was a truth known even to the ancient heathens. The *Locrians* permitted none among them to propofe a new law without this formality, *viz.* that he who propos'd it, fhould appear in council with a rope about his neck , and if his

mo-

motion was received, they took the rope off; but if it was rejected, he was ftrangled with it on the fpot, as a favourer of innovations. The inhabitants of the *Baleares Iflands* had only feven laws, under which they lived happily above five hundred years, and one of thofe laws was againft making any new one. The Council of *Trent* made many regulations for putting the old laws in force, but did not abolifh that for prohibiting the marriage of priefts, tho' it was propos'd. Now I fay, this ancient prohibition tends to the faving of the foul, or it does not. If it does, why fhould it be abolifh'd? if it does not, why was it ever eftablifh'd? I know the anfwer will be, that the confideration of human frailty was the motive of the propofal's being debated. But then I infer, that this is a plain confeffion that the faid prohibition did more harm than good. And as in this, fo in other the like cafes, 'tis a conftant obfervation that the great number of laws occafions a great number of errors, which is acting contrary to that chriftian charity which the clergy ought, by their example, to promote in the hearts of the laity; for 'tis not he that has been jealous and watchful of the jurifdiction, and refpect due to him, that will be reckon'd a good clergyman at the day of judgment, but he that has gain'd fouls to heaven. Pope St. *Gregory* has left us a terrible, but very true faying, *Mercenarius eft qui locum quidem paftoris tenet, fed lucra*

236 The Rights of Sovereigns.

cra animarum non quærit, terrenis commodis
inhiat, honore prelationis gaudet, temporalibus
lucris pascitur, impensa sibi ab hominibus reverentia lætatur, i. e. Mercenary is that wretch of
a pastor, who does not seek the gain of souls,
but gapes after the conveniencies of this life, feeds
on worldly lucre, and prides himself in the honour
of prelacy, and in the reverence paid him by his
fellow-creatures. And St. John Chrysostom,
speaking of pastors, adds, Quod abjectum erat
non reducebant, neque quod perierat quærebant,
neque confractum alligabant; quoniam se, non gre-
gem pascebant, i. e. They did not bring back that
which was cast away, nor seek that which was
lost; nor did they bind that which was broken, because they fed not the flock, but themselves. And
St. Paul speaking of all, says, For all seek their
own, not the things that are Jesus Christ's;
and to shew the abhorrence one ought to have
for innovations, he says to the Galatians, But
though we, or an angel from heaven, preach any
other gospel unto you than that which we have
preach'd unto you, let him be accurs'd. Which
signifies that neither himself, nor even an angel,
had authority to alter the written word of
God.

'Tis reported of St. Thomas of Canterbury,
who was persecuted by Henry II. King of England, that one day, while he was officiating
in the Church, a gang of assassins came with a
great rout towards the Church, in order to
murder him. The officers of the Church ran
immediately

immediately of their own accord to keep
them out, and ſhut the gates very faſt;
but the holy prelate order'd them to be
open'd, ſaying, *Eccl·ſia Dei non eſt cuſtodien-
da more caſtrorum*; and he offer'd himſelf to
the aſſiaſſins, chuſing rather to fall by their
cruel hands, than to defend himſelf according
to the cuſtom of perſons now-a-days. O happy and venerable antiquity, when the tongue,
the hands, words, and actions, all join'd together in one accord! I no longer wonder that
St. *Paul* wrote with ſo·much boldneſs to the
*Philippians, Thoſe things which ye have both
learned and received, and heard and ſeen in me,
do; and the God of Peace ſhall be with you.*
For at that time the prelate's innocency was
their natural protection, ſo that they needed
no laws for their guard.

There's not a frier of any order, but hopes
to obtain ſalvation by a regular life; and indeed the more exact they are in this particular,
the more aſſurance have they of being ſaved.
But how many are, 'tis to be fear'd, damn'd
within a monaſtery, who might probably have
been ſav'd *without* one? You ſee by this, I
don't ſpare my own cloth. A monk engages
himſelf voluntarily to an infinite number of
duties, which if he performs, he merits, and
is ſav'd; but if not, he ſins, and is damn'd,
while he may thank himſelf for it, by voluntarily charging himſelf with ſuch a multitude
of

of obligations.   In like manner, the laity may say that many laymen die guilty of the breach of positive laws, who had not been criminal if such laws had not been establish'd ; for as St. *Paul* says, *without the law, sin was dead ;* so that if this had been the case, they had not died disobedient. St. *Ambrose* speaks still more clearly, *Sunt in nobis qui habent timorem Dei, sed non secundum scientiam , statuentes duriora præcepta, quæ non possit humana conditio sustinere : Timor Domini in eis est, quia videntur sibi consulere disciplinæ opus virtutis exigere, sed inscitia in eis est, quia non compatiuntur naturæ, nec existimant possibilitatem,* i. e. *There are those among us who have the fear of God in their hearts, but not according to knowledge, imposing harder precepts than the condition of man can bear : The fear of the Lord indeed is in them, because they think that while discipline is their study, they are only requiring a virtuous act, but then they are grosly ignorant, because they don't consider the frailty of human nature, nor the possibility of the thing injoin'd.*   For my own part, I must say with *David, Set a watch, O Lord, before my mouth, and keep the door of my lips ;* for I am cautious of saying too much, for fear of giving offence ; but the testimony which is due to the truth, obliges me not to be altogether silent   Whoever reads the ancient and modern canons, will find that next to heresy, they treat nothing with more abhorrence than simony ; and there's a great deal of reason for

*

it,

it, becaufe, as *Adam*'s difobedience is fet down
as the firft fin under the old law, fo the wickednefs of *Simon* the forcerer, who would have
purchas'd the gifts of the holy fpirit with money, is reckon'd one of the firft rate crimes under the new teftament difpenfation; and from
his name this crime was call'd fimony.

Now is there any poffibility of concealing
from the whole world that horrid crime of fimony, fo much forbid by the facred canons, and
by all the Councils, efpecially that of *Trent*,
when every body knows the valuation of every
benefice, prelacy and bifhoprick? the good fathers of that Council forefaw that the wit of
men would not be at a lofs to invent fome fpecious titles or other to juftify the raifing of
fums for the compofing and figning of bulls;
and therefore, to prevent all manner of juggle,
they decreed that no more than the eighth part
of a gold denier fhould be given or receiv'd for
a bull or feal, and for the foliciting and difpatch
of briefs. After this, how can we reconcile
the law with its execution, or the command
with the obedience it requires? I am not willing to make ufe of that trite proverb, which
is in every one's mouth, *That there is no greater
evil than evil itfelf*, nor will I fay that fimony is
criminal every where but in the court of
Rome; for fuch an imprudent affertion as this
would difcover the groffeft ignorance of the
mind of God, who makes no diftinction betwixt perfons, and in whofe balance the ple-
beian

beian weighs as much as the nobleman, the
fubject as the fovereign, the layman as the prelate, and the prelate as the fovereign pontiff;
and if there be any difference at all, 'tis this,
that God will weigh him moſt ſtrictly in the
balance, who has the more obligations to difcharge, the higher he is advanc'd in dignity.
Perhaps ſome will ſay, that theſe reflections
are foreign to the matter in hand, and that I
only ſhew my ſpite againſt the court of *Rome*,
by ſaying every ill-natur'd thing that I can invent to their prejudice ; but I take God to wit-
neſs I act upon a quite different principle ; and
it will appear by and by, that theſe reflections
were not malicious, but abſolutely neceſſary.
The court of *Rome* are daily reproaching fovereigns, and the moſt ſerene republic more
than any one befides, with non-obſervance of
the canons, which they argue is not only a ſin,
but a moſt hateful obſtinacy, deferving both
cenfure and excommunication. But I cannot
help ſaying, that I wonder how they dare to
plead the indifpenſable obligation of fubmit-
ting to thoſe canons, while they themſelves
either break them, or elſe with manifeſt contempt evade them. Evil is always the ſame,
and the Pope has not a better road to falvation,
with refpect to his own actions, than every
other chriſtian. *Thy righteouſneſs endureth for
ever, and thy law is truth*, ſays the *Pfalmiſt.*
If therefore, fimony, nay, I may ſay any ſpe-
cies of it, or any of its confequences, is a
crime

crime in a poor prelate, why should it not be
the same crime in the chief of all prelates? To
maintain the contrary, is to do like some
physicians, who, upon the most trifling ail-
ment, prescribe such potions as they never care
to take themselves. *Solomon* says, *Horribly
and speedily shall he come upon you, for a sharp
judgment shall be to them that be in high places.* I
have not made these reflections on simony,
with a view to accuse the court of *Rome*, but
only to diminish the authority of the canons
in point of positive laws, to which canons obedience is challeng'd from those who had no
hand in making them, while 'tis pretended
those who had are exempted from that obedience. *Bede* observes that *Christ* drove those
that sold doves out of the temple, to give us
to understand that such as are partakers of the
holy spirit, of which a dove is the emblem,
ought not to be either buyers or sellers, according to that clause, *quam multi de altari accipi-
unt & moriuntur, & accipiendo moriuntur.* Which
made St. *Jerom* say, *Væ vobis miseris ad quos
pharisæorum vitia transierunt,* i. e. *Wo to you
wretches, who have fallen into the vices of the
pharisees!*

Since therefore, according to the *Romish*
courtiers, the canons may be so explain'd as to
take off the obligation of observing, or obeying them, a prince ought not to be excommunicated for disobeying the canons, when he
finds them prejudicial to his state. The ca-

[PART II.]   R   nons

nons are the handy-work of the clergy, who form them as much as poffible to their own advantage. Now for legiflators to make a law for their own conveniency, and to expect obedience to it, not from their own fubjects, but from free princes, would be the height of infolence on one fide, and blind obedience, or rather ftark blindnefs on the other. I know it will be objected, that when a Council is held, all the princes who receive fuch Council, do thereby approve all its decrees. I grant, they do indeed approve them, but 'tis with a provifo that they do not turn to their prejudice, for 'tis not to be fuppos'd that any one would willingly injure himfelf for another's benefit; but on the other hand, if a prince refufe to receive fuch Council, he is prefently accus'd of obftinacy, difobedience, and contempt of the canon law.

But here I would be glad to know one thing. Why are more indulto's and privileges granted to one prince than to another, by which means the one's difobedience is branded as finful, and the other's not? Does not this making fifh of one, and flefh of another, fignify, that fin, which draws everlafting damnation along with it, depends meerly on the good will and pleafure of the court of *Rome?* But will any one make us believe that God falls in with the paffions of fome, to fave or-damn others, fince we are all alike redeem'd with the infinite price of *Chrift*'s precious Blood.

The

The *Greek* Church never grants Difpenfations. If any one defires his prelate to difcharge him of a burden which he has not
ftrength enough to bear, the prelate fays to
him: " If your weaknefs is real and fincere,
" the righteous God will pardon you, tho' you
" do not fullfil the law ; to what purpofe
" then fhould I grant you a difpenfation, fince,
" in that cafe, fome would be bound by the
" law, and others left free ? But if you are
" under fuch a predicament as the legiflator
" would undoubtedly have excepted, if he
" had forefeen it ; you may act with a fafe
" confcience, for God does not require impof-
" fibility of you : On the contrary, if your
" cafe be fuch, that if it had been forefeen, it
" would not have been excepted, and you de-
" fire the favour, or privilege of fuch excep-
" tion, this would be to defire God to be par-
" tial, who is one and the fame to all man-
" kind." Such then is the behaviour of the
Greek paftors, and whether it be owing to this,
or to their poverty, or to their abhorrence of
whatever favours of temporal dominion , 'tis
certain they have no innovators among them,
and they continue unanimous and unchangeable in their opinions

Before the Popes of *Rome* had any temporal dominion, they expected no more of chriftians than a plain honeft faith, with the ufe
and veneration of the facraments ; but when,
by the generous liberality of fovereigns, they

R 2   became

became· princes as well as they, inftead of
bounding their power, they augmented it as
much as poffible, and not content with defpotic fway, either in their temporal or fpiritual
government, they were fond of extending
their fecular authority into the dominions of
other fovereigns, and fet up to be oracles of
faith for the whole chriftian world.

When a prince, for any reafon of ftate, or
government, declares war againft any other
that is his equal, he would be accountable for
his conduct only to his own confcience, and to
God, *who fearcketh the heart, and trieth 'the
reins, and will render to every man according to
his works,* and is not to be reprov'd for it by
the·Pope, who, as he is the common father of
the Church, feems to have no other authority
in that quality, than to defend the juft, protect
the weak, and oppofe the rafh and litigious
aggreffor.' Yet the Pope is not' bound by
thefe ties, and we don't find that he ever excommunicates a prince for attacking another
unjuftly ; whereas, if a-prince happens to lay
claim to any of the territories of the fovereign
pontiff, which are not yet lawfully devolv'd to
his holinefs, or which he poffeffes by ancient
ufurpation ; and if the prince feeks to do himfelf juftice by force, the Pope immediately proceeds to excommunication, tho' all the prince's
fault is his endeavouring to procure that juftice
by force of arms, which he could not obtain by
good words. - But if, on the other hand, a
prince

prince happens to attack another whose dominions are either totally, or but in part fiefs of
the holy See, the Pope immediately takes the
field with letters monitory, and the thunder
of excommunication, especially if the aggressor
is weak, or has his hands so full of another
war at the same time, that he is not able to
revenge the injury, and to cancel the sentence
with the point of his sword ; in which unhappy case indeed he must be content with the
bare declaration of war. Now I desire to
know the cause of this different conduct, and of
this confounding the spiritual and temporal weapons together. Why should excommunication
be issu'd to hinder injustice, when dominions
are invaded, which do not own the Pope's sovereignty *in temporalibus* ? When a medicine is
known to be good and wholesome, it ought in
charity to be distributed to all that suffer for
want of it ; since to give it to one, and to deny it to another, would imply that those who
have it to bestow, are mighty desirous to prolong the life of the one, and that the preservation of the other is the least of their thoughts.
It must therefore be confess'd, that this variety
of conduct is the fruit of the Pope's temporal
sovereignty, and that if he was still in that primitive state, which was instituted by *Christ,*
and kept up to by the apostles and their successors, for several centuries, he would not trouble himself to guard his temporal dominions
with spiritual weapons, as not thinking he

ought

ought to defend them after the manner of cities.

I would know whether the advocates of the court of *Rome* assent to the truth of that maxim, which is in the mouth of all politicians, *viz.* That when a prince attacks another, after declaration of open war, the prince who is attack'd, may, by right of necessary defence, not only oppose his attempts, and hinder him, sword in hand, from breaking in upon his dominions; but also, if it happens that in the dispute he should make himself master of a part of his enemy's territories, he has a right to keep the said acquisition as the lawful prize of a just war. This is the maxim of all politicians ; and if the gentlemen of the court of *Rome* will assent to it, I ask, if any feudatory duke of the holy See should fall upon a free prince, and thereby give him occasion to fight and overcome him, and to seize some fiefs of the Church, whether the conquering prince would be oblig'd, or no, to restore them ? Mean time, I am fully convinc'd, that if the restitution be not speedy, the thunder of excommunication would soon rattle over the head of such prince, how contrary soever such a proceeding would be to the maxims of christianity. This was the very case of the most serene republic ; which falling into a rupture with the duke of *Ferrara* in 1480, in the time of Pope *Sixtus* IV. the Pope himself improv'd the quarrel ; they fell to blows, and the *Venetians*

tians went and took *Ferrara,* which the republic would have kept as the lawful prize of a juft war; but immediately the Pope had recourfe to an interdict, and the republic thought it moft advifeable to reftore their conqueft.

I fay therefore, that thefe canons, and thefe pofitive laws, are a fort of militia which the Pope keeps up for his own ends, without any charge to himfelf, and which he makes ufe of when it is for his intereft, but disbands when they are not for his purpofe. St. *Anthony,* Archbifhop of *Florence,* in his account of the loffes fuftain'd by the *major* excommunication, fays, that a perfon excommunicated cannot be promoted to any ecclefiaftical dignity, or office, on pain of having it declar'd null and void, and that neither can he be marry'd without fin. This is a rule laid down by him as the conftant effect of excommunication. All herefies whatfoever, and their favourers, are plac'd at the head of the perfons excommunicated by the bull *in cæna domini.* On the other hand, St. *Anthony* refers to an *extravagante* (which is a Pope's decree tack'd to canon law) whereby a perfon is excommunicated for pretending to be lawfully elected a Pope, when he has not two thirds of the voices of the cardinals at the conclave; and he adds, 'that this is the only fault that can be charg'd upon a Pope elect; for if he had the majority of fuffrages, the election would be valid, tho' he were a heretic, provided he be difpos'd to reform; and indeed it

R 4 was

was by virtue of this liberty, that *Æneas Sil-vius,* tho' an heretic, was elected Pope by the name of *Pius* II. but as soon as he was got into St. *Peter*'s chair, he recanted, and retracted every tittle of the heretical propositions which he had written, and which are still to be seen in the catalogue of prohibited books. Now say I, if every heretic is excommunicated by the bull *in cœna domini,* and if every excommunicated person is disabled from being invested with any ecclesiastical dignity, how, according to the strict sense of the canons, can a person be deem'd as a Pope lawfully chosen, who is disqualify'd from being promoted to the dignity of a prelate, or even trusted with the cure of a village? Be the answer what they please to make, for my own part, I cannot compare excommunications, that are fulminated on account of positive law, to any thing better than Gunpowder, which makes a noise indeed, but does no execution

Having now discours'd on these general topics, we proceed to a particular examination of the complaints of the court of *Rome* against the most serene republic.

After the court of *Rome* had drawn up a long list of grievances, they reduc'd all those contumacies (as they were pleas'd to call them) to this single one, *viz.* The keeping the ecclesiastical authority in slavery in all the chief points of its jurisdiction, and cramping it in its rights and prerogatives. If the whole
controversy

controverſy turned upon this ſingle point, and were to be determin'd in a few words, one need only give the ſubſtance of what was deliver'd in the former part of this work, by alledging in ſhort, that all the ſuperiority which can be lawfully challeng'd by the Pope in thoſe territories, which are not in his domain, amounts only to his being the oracle of faith, in the uſe of the ſacraments, in the purity of doctrine, in the propagation of chriſtianity, and the like. In all theſe things, he has a right to command all that have receiv'd the ſeal of baptiſm, and every chriſtian is oblig'd to obey him, and to ſubmit his own ſentiments to thoſe of the Pope; and if any refuſe ſuch ſubjection, they deſerve to be rebuk'd, and ſpiritually chaſtiz'd, even with the thunder of excommunication. But if the grievances run in another channel, and do not concern the Church, but the clergy, 'tis no wonder that a free prince, who owns no ſuperior but God, ſhould have the courage to prevent a ſtate from being ſet up within his own dominions, and to hinder his ſubjects from being cited, by favour of a metaphyſical diſtinction, to a foreign tribunal, which, if it ſhould once come to be eſtabliſh'd, might pretend at length that the prince himſelf was ſubject to it. 'Tis certain, that if a prince ſhould pretend to be offended, becauſe he is not obey'd by thoſe who are not his ſubjects, neither by birth, hire, nor reſidence, his conduct would be thought very

harſh

harſh and diſagreeable. But the court of *Rome* would have it given up as an indiſputable point, that the Pope has of himſelf a lawful authority to command every body in what place, or on what account ſoever, eſpecially where the Church, or even any eccleſiaſtical perſon, is in the leaſt concern'd. And when this principle is eſtabliſh'd, they would have other queſtions diſcuſs'd in their turn: As for inſtance, Whether 'tis lawful, or not, to hinder the eſtates of the laity from paſſing under the dominion of the clergy, and ſo proceed with ſuch grievances to the end of the chapter. If this were, the caſe, their diſpute would ſoon be at an end, for admitting this article of law, all the reſt would be only matters of fact, eaſy to be prov'd; and he muſt be a fool and a madman that ſhould firſt own a power in the Pope to command all the ſtates of chriſtendom, and then ſay it is no crime not to obſerve his canons, and receive his interpretations. But the diſpute muſt be manag'd after another manner; and in the firſt place, let the gentlemen of the court of *Rome* conſider who made the Pope, and undoubtedly they will own it was *Jeſus Chriſt*; then let us inquire what authority he gave him, and we ſhall find by the language and practice of the apoſtles, and the pontiffs of the primitive Church, after what manner they interpreted that authority, and what bounds they gave to it. If in the goſpel, or the conduct of St. *Peter*, and his many pious ſucceſ-

ſors,

fors, there is the least footstep of an authority
exercis'd after the manner of lay-princes, if
there be any promise of temporal domain, such
as the Pope now possesses, or any kind of super-
intendency over the dominions of another, then
they would have reason for managing the dispute as they do, and I will own with that in-
genuity I always profess'd, that the Pope has
more property due to him, under the denomi-
nation of lay-sovereignty, than he has ever
usurp'd of what belong'd to others. But 'tis
certain, as I have shewn in the former part,
that there's no text nor custom that gives the
least authority for such pretension ; and therefore, if they will nevertheless urge the belief of
it, they must look out for such persons as will
take all they say for gospel. On the other hand,
it has been evidently demonstrated that a day
prince derives his free and absolute authority
from God, and this is a truth so notorious that
Christ himself acknowledges it in the person of
Pilate, representing *Cæsar. Thou couldest have
no power at all against me, except it were given
thee from above ;* and St. *Peter* afterwards recommends it in these terms, *Servants be subject
to your masters with all fear, not only to the good
and gentle, but also to the froward ; for so is
the will of God.* St. *Paul,* in his Epistle to the
Romans, says; *Let every soul be subject unto the
higher powers ; for there is no power but of God:
The powers that be, are ordained of God. Whosoever therefore resisteth the power, resisteth the*
ordinance

ordinance of God ; and they that refist shall receive to themselves damnation. For rulers are not a terror to good works, but to the evil: Wilt thou, then, not be afraid of the power? Do that which is good, and thou shalt have praise of the same. For he is the minister of God to thee for good: But if thou do that which is evil, be afraid; for he beareth not the sword in vain: For he is the minister of God, a revenger to execute wrath upon him that doth evil. Wherefore ye must needs be subject; not only for wrath, but also for conscience sake. For, for this cause pay you tribute also; for they are God's ministers, attending continually upon this very thing. Render therefore to all their dues; tribute to whom tribute is due, custom to whom custom, fear to whom fear, honour to whom honour.

Since therefore the gentlemen of the court of *Rome* have heard how fully and distinctly St. *Paul* has explain'd himself in favour of lay-sovereignty, without exempting any one whatsoever from obedience or tribute; let them see to it, how they can pretend to exempt a great number of a prince's subjects from obeying his commands, and paying him the tenths. The free authority of a prince in his own dominions is a general rule, which, whoever opposes, ought to prove his special privilege. 'Tis an unfair way of arguing to say that a lay-prince, who claims jurisdiction over the estates and persons of the clergy, ought to produce an indulto for it from the Pope; for the argument
                                          might

might juftly be retorted upon thofe who ufe it, by faying, that fince a prince is the protector of his own country, the Pope, who pretends to exercife his authority in another's country, is oblig'd to produce a plain text to prove that *Jefus* granted it to him by his almighty power, or at leaft that he muft fhew an authentic teftimony from the apoftles and ancient fathers, otherwife the authority challenged by the Pope in the dominions of another may be more juftly reckon'd ufurpation, than the laws eftablifh'd by princes over the eftates and perfons of the clergy.

That therefore is all the anfwer we have to make to the general charge of keeping the ec-clefiaftic power in bondage ; which, fo long as it does not affect the interefts or circumftantials of the faith, is not, as we have already feen, either flavery, or injuftice, but only the total hindrance of an ufurpation of power, and not the oppofing an authority which is lawful. This anfwer is fufficient to put all the complainants of the court of *Rome* to filence, for till they can fhew a plain text for that jurifdiction which they pretend to in another's houfe, they can have no room to complain of incroachment, or violation of their liberty, efpecially in the dominions of a free prince, forafmuch as no body has a right to complain that his neighbours domeftics do not ferve and obey him. But however, we will give a brief anfwer, over and
above

above 'what has been already faid, to each particular article.

I. The firſt in order is this, *That the acquiſition of lands is debarred from regular monks and places of piety.* This they don't fail to make a mighty noiſe about, and cry out as if the government of *Venice* treats the regular monks as bad as the *Jews*, whom they lay under the ſame reſtriction ; but they don't conſider that this prohibition is laid upon the monks by the lay-tribunal only, becauſe it ſeem'd neceſſary and proper, whereas they ſubject the *Jews* to it, to puniſh them for their obſtinacy in *judaiſm* ; and in a word, 'tis a mark of their captivity.

'Tis plain that the ſecular power was in a manner compell'd to lay the monks under that prohibition, in reprizal for the pretenſions of the court of *Rome:* If the ſaid court would grant that lay-ſovereigns have a legal right in themſelves, not only to levy the ordinary tenths upon the clergy, but alſo in a caſe of neceſſity to impoſe the ſame taxes and ſubſidies upon theirs, as upon the eſtates of the laity, the government of *Venice* would never have thought of debarring the monks from purchaſing eſtates. A prince is only ſuch in reſpect of his ſubjects and revenues. Theſe two things are the parts which conſtitute the whole of a ſovereign, but one without the other only conſtitutes a titular prince without territory ; which is the caſe of many whoſe

dominions

dominions are become a prey to *Turkiſh* invaders; and would to God that the ſame uſurpations had never been introduc'd among chriſtian princes ! In ſuch a ſad caſe, a prince who is robbed of his dominions may ſtill retain his titles; and this is ſo far in his own power, that be the conqueror ever ſo potent, he cannot ſtrip him thereof, unleſs he takes away his life too. Be this as it will, I know not whether a prince's preſerving his titles after the loſs of his dominions, is a greater mark of his dignity, or of his misfortune, and whether it moſt promotes the compaſſion of others, or hinders their contempt ; for I own I look upon ſuch a prince only as a nominal one. And as to a prince who has dominions and ſubjects, but no revenue, I think him more a ſubject than even his own ſubjects ; for beſides his perſonal neceſſities, he is expos'd to others as a prince, and having not wherewith to anſwer them, he would feel the ſame anxiety as if he wanted bread ; for I fancy it muſt be very mortifying to have the title of a prince, and to have miniſters and courtiers always at his ears, dunning him for aids to defray the neceſſities of the ſtate, and not to have the means to anſwer their demands. This is ſuch a crown as I believe the old philoſopher meant, when he ſaid, if he ſhould find it lying on the ground, he ſhould not think it worth ſtooping for. This may be ſufficient to ſhew that in order to conſtitute real ſovereignty, 'tis indiſpenſably neceſſary

ceffary that thefe two conditions fhould be united together, *viz.* fubjects and revenues, otherwife a prince makes but a ridiculous figure.

The fenate of *Venice,* which has verify'd the fable of watchful *Argus* with his hundred eyes, forefaw that the piety of the people on the one hand, and the exemplary lives, or rather the artifices of the regular monks on the other, might go fuch a vaft length in the acquifition of lands, that in a little time the greateft part of their lands might be devoted to pious ufes; therefore they did mighty well to fix a *non plus ultra* to fuch acquifitions. But, thanks to heaven, the doge of *Venice* is not reduc'd to the horrid inconveniency of having fubjects that are not fubject, and territories without revenue, and without profits. If the Pope would by an authentic bull acknowledge the right which all fecular princes and ftates have to tax the eftates of the clergy, as well as others, for fupplying their neceffities, as far as comports with the publick weal, I doubt not but the moft ferene ftate of *Venice* would be ready to acknowledge the courtefy, and would repeal this law, which is fuch an eyefore to the court of *Rome,* of their own accord, and without any other incentive than their natural biafs to acts of piety, efpecially when fuch acts do not interfere with more neceffary reafons of ftate. Nay, I will moreover venture to affirm, that if the court of *Rome,* not willing to part with an old cuftom, refufe to consent confent to fuch an acknowledgment, and thereby to own the characteriftics and prerogatives of all temporal fovereignties ; yet, if they would only determine the cafe by granting a perpetual and irrevocable indulto, as ufual, the moft ferene republic would gladly take fuch a grant as a favour, tho' at the fame time 'tis one of their natural prerogatives, and that in a grateful acknowledgment thereof, they would 1epeal the faid law which gives the court of *Rome* fo much uneafinefs. But fo long as the court of *Rome* continue obftinate in their refolution, and that nothing will ferve their turn but that a petition muft be prefented to them for an indulto to raife the tenths every five years, can it be thought ftrange that the fenate of *Venice* fhould ufe proper precaution, and that inftead of taking the more vigorous refolution of laying extraordinary taxes upon the clergy, of their own authority, as fome kings have done formerly, they fhould take proper methods before-hand for hindering the eftates of their domain from paffing into the hands of thofe who pretend to be privileged and free from taxes ?

This is as neceffary a guard as a helmet and cuirafs againft the point of a fword, and I believe no wife man will find fault with it. The friers in the ftate of *Venice* have engrofs'd fo many eftates into their own hands, as can hardly be parallel'd in any other dominions, confidering the little time they have done it in, and the extent of the country. For he that is not wilfully blind, cannot but fee how many frieries, and the like pious places, are daily founded and erected in *Venice*, fo that if due provifion had not been made againft it, the laity would have had very little left at their own difpofal, in the compafs of an age at moft.   For thefe reafons, the fenate wifely decreed that for the future lands fhall not pafs out of the Hands of the laity, and that as for the time paft, hofpitals, frieries, fchools, and the like places, fhall not be regifter'd as church-lands, forafmuch as their founders and governors never were clergymen.   And I fay it again, that a religious and a wife prince could not do lefs for his own fafety, and that of his fubjects and dominions, at a juncture when the court of *Rome* is fo fevere.

I fhall here add one reflection, for the fake of fuch of my readers as may not happen to be *Venetians*, viz. That the mighty clamour made by the court of *Rome* of this pretended violation of liberty, has no foundation in reafon, but only in appearance.   For all thefe prohibitions do not in any wife reftrain the charity of believers towards the friers, fince no body is hinder'd from leaving their lands to any fraternity whatfoever, by way of inheritance, legacy, or donation; only if the cafe be fo, the heir, or legatee, is oblig'd to fell the faid land at the expiration of two years, and to put the purchafe-money into his own pocket.

pocket. It will be said perhaps, that at this rate the monks will be masters of great sums of ready money, which they may lavish to very ill purposes ; but the republic has provided against this, by ordering that all congregations of friers may either lend out their money at use to private men, or put it in the bank ; so that one way or another, their gain will be more considerable, and more certain, than if they kept their lands, whose crop is liable to be ruin'd by storms of hail, or a season of drought ; whereas, what they would get by annuities, or the bank, is fix'd and certain. Upon the whole then, I advanc'd nothing of a falshood when I said, that all this great outcry of the court of *Rome* has not the least foundation in reason, for the friers hands are not tied from receiving gifts or legacies, or from making the most they can of their money. Therefore the prohibition publish'd by the senate is just, and consistent with christian piety, and prudent policy.

II. They say, *That those who only rented the clergy's estates, are permitted to retain them by prescription, as much as if they were their own lawful property* But this article is more easily answer'd than the first. 'Tis a rule of practice in the secular court at *Venice*, that the term of thirty years prescribes every action which has been in suspence all that while, without any summons, or interrogation of the parties. For instance, if a creditor lets thirty

years

years paſs over his head, without demanding
the repayment of his money from him to whom
he lent it out, he cannot trouble him ſor it
afterwards, and the debtor is only oblig'd to
pay the inteieſt of the annuity ; ſo that the annuity, which was redeemable, becomes perpetual, the law ſuppoſing that the creditor has,
by thirty years continu'd ſilence, voluntarily
forgiven the debt.   In like manner, if he, who
lets out a houſe or land, does not within thirty years renew his rent, or leaſe, with him to
whom he lets it, 'tis preſum'd that he has yielded up all his right of poſſeſſion, reſerving to
himſelf only the rent, which then changes its
name into property.   By this means, he to
whom the houſes, or lands, were let, becomes
the owner of them ; but 'tis on condition of
doing ſome homage, or ſervice, for them,
which becomes ſuch an appendage to thoſe
eſtates, that if the new proprietor ſells them
to another, it muſt be always with this acknowledgment.   It ſeems as if the firſt poſſeſſor did
hereby loſe ſomething of his right, which, however true it may be, is only a puniſhment of
his neglect to renew the leaſe ; but he has this
advantage, *viz.* that the poſſeſſor of thoſe
eſtates is always oblig'd to pay the entire acknowledgment, even tho' the houſes ſhould be
burnt, and the lands laid under water.   This
is the conſtant practice at *Venice* betwixt one
layman and another in the diſpoſal of all manner of eſtates, and the ſenate has order'd that
                                                            this

this kind of prescription shall also take place
with respect to church-lands, but with this
difference in their favour, that the prescription
shall not be till the expiration of forty years;
so that the clergy have the advantage of ten
years more than the laity. Mean time the court
of *Rome* makes a sad outcry; but let us see
with what justice. The layman who rents any
church-lands, perceiving that the lease is not
renew'd, nor alter'd, during the whole term
of thirty years, thinks, that without further
trouble, according to the custom receiv'd a-
mong the laity, he is become the legal proprietor of such lands, and therefore takes care to
meliorate the lands, or to rebuild the house,
being persuaded in his mind that such melio-
rations, or improvements, are his own property, as they are the effect of his own extraordinary pains and expence. Therefore it would
not be reasonable that he should be the dupe
of an establish'd custom, and that after he has
made considerable improvements, a new ab-
bat, or a new prior, should turn him out of
his tenure, and, without any just plea, reap
the benefit of his pains and expence, and that
the poor tenant should, by another's artifice,
be dispossess'd of all his profit. For these reasons the government order'd this prescription,
and gave the advantage of ten years to sacred
places; so that if any one had improv'd his
land, or house, for thirty-nine years, he would
have work'd all the while for the good of the

monastery,

monaſtery, a thing which is not practis'd with
ſo much advantage to the laity.   Therefore, as
to the time paſt, the term of ten years is ſo
far from an injury, that 'tis an advantage to ſacred places; and as to the time to come, the
clergy-may, if they will, prevent any damage,
by renewing the leaſe within the term of thirty-
nine years,ſince by ſo doing they certainly hinder
their eſtates from being liable to preſcription.
Therefore why does the court of *Rome* make
ſuch a ſad complaint ? A ſick man who chops
and changes his phyſicians, becauſe they don't
humour him, becomes at laſt intolerable, Theſe
gentlemen would not only ſwallow up all the
eſtates of the laity, but refuſe alſo to make the
leaſt allowance for all the pains they have been
at in improving them.   Let them but conſider
their own uncharitable temper, and they cannot find fault with the republic for applying to
public charity, to relieve the laity.

III.   That *the lay-tribunal pretends to judge eccleſiaſtical criminals, and the civil affairs of perſons eccleſiaſtical.* As to this complaint, I have
nothing to add to what I ſaid in the eleventh
chapter of the former part, where the reader
will find it ſufficiently anſwer'd, tho' in general terms : And there being, I think, nothing
particular in the cuſtom obſerv'd at *Venice*, the
matter ſeems fully determin'd, and it would
be both ſuperfluous and diſagreeable to repeat
what has been already ſaid.   The fact in ſhort
is this, *viz.* that as an eccleſiaſtic pretends his

perſon

perſon is ſacred all over, and to be reverenc'd, he ought not to degrade himſelf by his actions. *Bonum fac, & habebis laudem,* i. e. *Do that which is good, and thou ſhalt have praiſe there- of.* When a chalice that has been ſet apart, and conſecrated with ſo many ceremonies for receiving the blood of *Chriſt,* is once propha- ned, it goes into the hands of the vulgar, and is ſold to the goldſmith for vile uſes. All the ſacraments, except that of the altar, at which God ought to be worſhip'd at all times and places, are only ſacraments by cuſtom, and contain no grace, but when they are apply'd. Thus the clergy ought to be contented, if they are treated on the ſame footing, and if they are reverenc'd in their ſacred functions, and miniſterial offices.

As to civil affairs, if a clergyman goes to law with a layman for an eſtate, which he claims as due, not to his dignity, but to his perſon, I do not ſee how this can poſſibly be reckon'd the cauſe of the Church; therefore nothing in nature can be more reaſonable, than that a ſecular- prince, who is to maintain his ſubjects rights, ſhould be a judge of thoſe rights, in order to defend the poſſeſſor in his legal property; whereas otherwiſe, if a layman was oblig'd to make his appearance in a ſpiri- tual court, the temporal prince would ſoon find himſelf without ſubjects. The nuncio and the biſhop would be the prince, and the prince would only be the guardian of the city.

'Tis

'Tis enough, then, that according to the eſtabliſh'd cuſtom at *Venice*, when a layman accuſes a regular monk in a civil affair, the cauſe is brought before the tribunal of the nuncio.

IV. That *biſhops are hinder'd not only from trying lay-malefactors for their lives, in caſes depending on the mix'd courts, but alſo from puniſhing the clergy themſelves, tho', convicted of ſcandalous crimes.*

Here we ought to diſtinguiſh ; becauſe this grievance contains two parts, *viz.* the hindring the biſhops from judging the laity, and the not permitting them to puniſh their own ſcandalous clergy. But both theſe complaints proceed from one and the ſame principle, *viz.* the right which the temporal ſovereign claims by law to judge even eccleſiaſtical criminals ; an authority, which if a prince had not, it would follow by conſequence that the prelate would have the liberty of puniſhing criminals of this ſtamp ; and when once he is maſter of this prerogative, nothing would hinder him from proceeding againſt the laity in like manner, for crimes depending on the mix'd courts, and ſubject in ſome ſort to the eccleſiaſtical laws ; ſuch as ſacrilege, adultery, ſtriking clergymen, and the like.

To return to the firſt, *viz.* the complaint that the biſhops are oppos'd in their proceedings againſt the laity, for crimes depending on the mix'd courts; nothing is more eaſy to reſolve

folve to the fatisfaction of the meaneft capa-
cities, for nothing feems more juft than the
conduct of a free prince, who preferves to himfelf the right of permitting the clergy to judge
of crimes depending on fuch mix'd courts. For
if a prince will be a fovereign, he muft maintain his fuperiority and authority over his fubjects, and require their obedience ; and if they
are difobedient, he ought to punifh them. But
if a prince puts the rod of juftice into other
hands, the fubjects will no longer regard him ;
honeft men being obedient out of love to virtue, but the wicked only for fear of punifhment.

Oderunt peccare boni virtutis amore,
Oderunt peccare mali formidine pœnæ.

When a prince gives up his power of punifhing, he immediately becomes the contempt of
his fubjects ; fuch was the happy fimplicity of
the primitive ages, that the fovereigns were
belov'd with an affection that was perfectly voluntary ; but fuch is the corruption of our
times, that they are envy'd on account of their
high ftation, and therefore hated, and confequently 'tis no wonder that they are affronted.
'Tis obfervable that all crimes which come before the fecular tribunal, are tranfgreffions of
the divine law, which confifts in the punctual
obfervation of only thefe two commands, *viz.*
to love God, and to love our neighbour. All
blafphemers,

blaſphemers, perjurers, adulterers, murderers, ſlanderers, and a hundred others, who are triable in the temporal courts, ought to paſs under the cognizance of the mix'd court; becauſe they are tranſgreſſors of the two commands above-mention'd, and has the prelate therefore a right ſtrictly to inquire after, and cite them to his court? If ſo, the ſovereign would indeed have a numerous people to take care of, but he would have few ſubjects at his beck or command. This is ſuch an extravagant abſurdity as I think no man of the leaſt piety can ſo much as comprehend, much leſs approve; and if it were to be ſuffer'd, who is there would not ſooner chuſe to be a biſhop than a prince? becauſe a biſhop would in this caſe have all the advantages of ſovereignty, without the trouble of maintaining it, and providing for the people's neceſſities. But even in the towns of the land of the Church, the biſhops do not enjoy ſo large a liberty, moſt of the ſentences of this kind being iſſuable from the vice-legate, or governor; who, tho' they are eccleſiaſtics, are conſider'd as perſons inveſted with temporal power. Such an authority is therefore far leſs tolerable in the dominions of others. This part has been ſo fully prov'd, that I think I need not ſay more, for I believe there is no diſintereſted perſon, but muſt be ſatisfy'd how much it is the right of ſovereigns, and at the ſame time enrag'd at the pretenſions of the clergy to it; for there are many caſes in which
the

the court of *Rome* would have bishops to be judges of the laity, but not one in which they are willing to allow the secular courts to be judges of the clergy.

As to the hindring bishops from judging ecclesiastical criminals, I refer the reader to the distinction I have already so often made use of, *viz.* that if the crime of a clergyman consists in false doctrine, in an undue administration of the sacraments, and the like, which are crimes merely ecclesiastical, and of which the secular tribunal has naturally no cognizance; then, I say, the cognizance of them ought to be left to an ecclesiastical judge, and the government of *Venice* does not in any wise oppose it; because there is a tribunal of inquisition, which judges of all such causes, and of all crimes merely ecclesiastical, judging not only of ecclesiastical criminals attainted of crimes of this kind, but even those of the laity that are charged with heresy, witchcraft, the abuse of the sacramen s, and the like. But if the crimes in question are such as are merely temporal, *viz.* murders, adultery, fornication, robberies, *&c.* committed by clergymen; then, as I have already said, the clergyman so offending degrades himself, and thereby makes himself answerable to the ordinary tribunal; and the sovereign prince, who is oblig'd by the divine law, and by the many scripture proofs we have already cited, to punish malefactors, may prosecute and punish him. Besides all these reasons,

fons, this is a maxim founded on the laws of juft policy, for the common benefit of honeft men under a good government ; for how could the honour, reputation, lives and fortunes of wives and their children be fecure, if the prince did not reward good actions, and punifh evil ones ? Having, I think, faid enough on this point, I will forbear vain repetition, and only exhort bifhops to take great care of the eftablifhment of the faith, of the diftribution of the facraments, and of the reformation of manners, by their good examples and learning. "If they difcharge thefe great duties, they may with very good reafon boaft that they have not been unprofitable fervants in the lord's vineyard, and that they have duly kept up to the fimplicity of their inftitution.

V. *That the bifhops are hinder'd from vifiting hofpitals, facred places, frieries, and mounts of piety.* The anfwer I have to make to this complaint, is only a brotherly admonition in the terms of the gofpel, *between thee and him alone,* to fhew the court of *Rome* that this accufation againft the republic is rather an effect of the faid court's ufurpations, than difobedience in the temporal prince. The faid court takes it very ill, that all frieries and hofpitals, confider'd as facred places, are not therefore fubject only to ecclefiaftical jurifdiction. That they are places of devotion is not queftion'd, and fo is every private man's houfe, where the people lead moral lives, and do good works; but that

that all places of devotion are sacred, and exempt from the secular jurisdiction, that they
are that *New Jerusalem* which St. *John* saw
coming down from God out of heaven, prepar'd as a bride adorn'd for her husband, and
that this husband is the prelate, this is what
I cannot easily digest : These gentlemen of the
court of *Rome* always found their discourses
and disputations upon the modern times, and
never trace effects to their origin and principal,
whereas the right way to come at the true
knowledge of a thing, is to examine the cause,
scire est rem per causam cognoscere. If we look
back to the origin of hospitals, frieries, mounts
of piety, and the like, we shall certainly find
whether they are ecclesiastical, or secular estates,
and whether they ought to be subject to the bishop, or the temporal prince. Tell me, then,
who were their founders, clergymen, or laymen ? Were those estates given by the priests,
or the laity ? If they say that the donors and
founders were ecclesiastics, I must beg leave to
tell them it is false ; for if those foundations
were of ecclesiastic original, if their revenues
were ever paid by the clergy, the administra-
tors, or governors of them, would likewise
have been clergymen, and without doubt those
of that order would never have suffer'd themselves to be turn'd out, to make way for laymen, without a great deal of clamour and strug-
gle. The clergy, where their interests are
ever so little concern'd, don't use to part with
them

them tamely, but are commonly fo litigious, that 'tis as much as ever a layman can do, to defend himfelf againft their pretenfions, much lefs can he take any thing from them : But if it be acknowledg'd that the inftitution and donation of fuch places was originally fecular, and that fome pious fouls were difpos'd to lay out their money and eftates, and make fuch fettlements, to the end that they fhould be always under the adminiftration of the government, what foundation have the clergy for that fuperiority they pretend to have over them ? The mafter of the vineyard in the gofpel faid, *Is it not lawful for me to do what I will with my own ? Is thine eye evil, becaufe mine is good ?* If the founder of fuch hofpital, or place of devotion, would have had the fame govern'd by clergymen, he would have declar'd it exprefly in the very deed of fettlement, or endowment, and either himfelf, or his next heir, would have inducted them into the poffeffion of fuch adminiftration ; but if there be not one word of this in the deed, and on the contrary, the donor there declares his intention, that the fuperiors, priors, or directors, fhall be laymen ; and if they were put into poffeffion of the adminiftration, from the very firft, what reafon can the clergy have for pretending to fuch a fuperiority ? It feems the private men, who own'd fuch eftates, had not the grace to bequeath them as a legacy to fome prelate, but difpos'd of them in another manner ; yet for

all

all this, does the prelate leave one ſtone un-
turn'd to get the whole into his clutches? At
this rate, may not a mount of piety, which is
only a place for lending to the poor upon
pledges, become by degrees an ecclefiaftical
fief? I know they will pretend that a prelate
does not aim at this fuperiority for the fake of
managing the revenue, or putting any of it
into his own pocket, but only to fupervife the
adminiftration thereof, that every thing may
be manag'd with order and juftice, as if the
lay-fovereign's infpection were not fufficient;
but let me tell 'em, I will take who I pleafe
for my phyfician, and not the man that brags
he knows more than him I have chofen: Such
conduct as this, brings to my mind the faying
in the gofpel, *Friend, let me pull the mote out
of thine eye.* This would be a circumftance
more facred, *viz.* if a dying man fhould, by
his laft will, recommend a certain number of
maffes to be faid for his foul, and the fuperior
of the convent, on whom they are injoin'd,
fhould examine whether the heir has fulfill'd
the will of the dead, I don't believe that the
biſhop would meddle in the affair, or pretend
to call him to account for it. To what purpofe then does the biſhop claim fuch fuperiority over works that are indeed pious, but
not totally fpiritual, fuch as the care of the
fick, and the lending of money to the poor?
Wifely therefore has the fenate declar'd, that
places of this fort, tho' devoted to pious ufes,
are

are not number'd in the register of ecclesiastical places, and that the bishop has nothing to do with them.

VI. That *the college pretends to be a judge in matters relating to benefices, and that when any one enters an action in the court of* Rome, *he is oblig'd to a renunciation* ab impetratis, *i. e. to renounce the decrees he has there obtain'd.*

This is another branch deriv'd from the same root. In answer to which complaint, we lay down this as a fundamental principle, that every temporal free sovereign has a right to judge in all matters but such as relate to faith, to the sacraments, the institution of sacred ceremonies, and the like; which cannot be regulated, or executed, but by the priests. These things only excepted, the prince is establish'd by God himself over such or such a people, to do justice, and to keep all his subjects in their duty, either by rewards or punishments, so that he is not only the representative and depository of the public authority, but the vicegerent of God. This St. *Peter* and St. *Paul* have deliver'd as their own opinion in such terms as are express, and clear enough to satisfy those who have ears to hear, and which we have already quoted more than once; and as the submission we owe to an apostolical precept, renders it a point not to be disputed, so 'tis equally establish'd and confirm'd by the law of nature; for as all the members of the body receive motion from the heart, the whole body from its soul, every
individual

individual from one fpiritual intelligence only, all light itfelf from the fun, and all difcourfe from reafon alone; fo every government depends on its fovereign, and all hierarchy on one fingle principle; and as in our contemplation of nature's machine, the world, we afcend upwards to God, the caufe of all caufes; fo in human and civil judgments, we ought never to go beyond the only fovereign; for to imagine that a ftate can be well govern'd, which depends on two different princes, is quite as abfurd as to conceive a body with two fouls. There is but one way to eftablifh an union betwixt men, whofe genius, fortunes, and tempers, are fo widely different, and that is, to let one only be their head and mafter; for tho' a republick may confift of a thoufand members, yet they have but one fovereign; for all and every one of thofe members acknowledge the fovereignty to be either in the whole collective body of the ftate, or elfe in a leffer body of deputies, or delegates from the whole.

In the times of pagan *Rome*, we read of a chief prieft who prohibited the building of one temple both to honour and to virtue, tho' according to the notion that.then prevail'd, there was a certain affinity betwixt thofe two idols; the reafon of which prohibition was, that one temple ought to ferve only one deity. In fine, then, we may well fay that the republick of *Venice*, taught both by reafon and experience, is more concern'd than any other republick, constantly to maintain the same unity of sovereignty, as judging that it would be as great a heresy in politics, to suffer, in their dominions, the least division of sovereignty in things *human,* as it would be impiety in things *divine,* not to believe the unity of the godhead. This being the case, the court of *Rome* ought not to wonder that in *Venice* there's no one altar set up against another, either for causes relating to benefices, or for other controversies of the people. Causes relating to benefices concern the clergy only, and not the Church, the dispute being not for the depriving, or instating of any minister, but only to decree who is the legal minister; and when the college, or council, assumes cognizance of the cause, 'tis not to usurp the right of nomination to benefices, but to put an end to the dispute betwixt those who lay claim to such benefices. As to the collation thereof, 'tis left entirely to the discretion of the court of *Rome,* and every body is at full liberty to apply to the said court, when a vacancy happens The republick therefore interferes only to obviate and compose disputes between their subjects, when more than one pretends a right to the same benefice, which is the more necessary; because the *Venetians* are not us'd to obey any sentence which is not pass'd in their own dominions.

As to the obligation upon such as sue in the court of *Rome,* to renounce *ab impetratis,* 'tis a necessary consequence of the maxim just now establish'd ;

eftablifh'd ; and the due reward of fuch rafh litigious people, who, tho' they know they have a tribunal of their own to apply to, have recourfe at every turn to a foreign one, on pur-pofe to perplex the caufe by querks, and fhifts, becaufe they have not one good plea to produce in their own favour.

VII. That *the* Venetian *clergy are requir'd to pay the ordinary-taxes, and other impofts, as well as the laity.*

A certain prince, who was well read in uni-verfal hiftory, faid, tho' he was not within the pale of the Church, that he wonder'd all the chriftians did not go to *Rome* to make their for-tunes, by attaining to fome great ecclefiaftical dignity, which no one need defpair of getting. For my own part, I verily believe, that if all the canons propos'd to us by the gentlemen of the court of *Rome*, were to be obferv'd at *Ve-nice*, every layman would be glad to take or-ders, and all the clergymen in other countries would be mad to come and fettle at *Venice* ; fo that we fhould be forc'd to build houfes in our very lakes to entertain the new colony. It would be a fine world indeed, if the clergy were to be exempt from obeying their tempo-ral fovereign, if they could be as wicked as they lift in fpite of his teeth, and if they were to pay no taxes, impofts, nor fubfidies ! Were the clergy at *Rome* once poffefs'd of thefe fine privileges, they might well boaft of reviving the golden age, when the fields brought forth

T 2 their

their fruits without any toil, and the lands were fallow without plowing or fowing; mean time I often hear complaints of the poverty at *Rome,* while at *Venice,* where the very bread is excis'd, they live in a happy abundance, and with lefs expence. A fovereign prince may fitly be refembled to a river, which derives its mafs of water, be it more or lefs in breadth, or depth, from a vaft number of rivulets that flow to it, as tributes from the neighbouring plains; and, according to the opinion of *Empedocles,* who eftablifh'd atoms as the principle of all things, the greateft bodies are form'd by the union of an infinite number of fmall ones. Now where's the rhetorician that can, with all the tropes and figures he is mafter of, perfuade to the belief of this impoffibility, that a perfon can expend money unlefs he has it to lay out, or live by the air alone, without any other nourifhment? *Ariftotle* one day hearing a conceited fophift prating that there was no fuch thing in nature as *motion;* and endeavouring to fupport what he faid by falfe reafonings, he gave him no other anfwer, than by *walking* about the room, it being but trifling to produce arguments from reafon for a thing which is demonftrable by experience. Indeed, if the court of *Rome* will teach the officers of the *Venetian* mint that fecret in alchymy of tranfmuting iron into gold, I doubt not but they will foon be made eafy in their demand, and that the clergy fhall be exempted from all the

burdens

burdens of the ftate ; but till'then, they muft be filent, and permit the fovereign to provide for the neceffities of the ftate in the ordinary way, which is always abundantly better than the extraordinary methods of filling the pub-lick treafure ; which when ambition drains, wickednefs commonly replenifhes. *Si thefau-rum ambitione exbauferimus, per fcelera fupplen-dum fit.*

The clergy cannot expect to enjoy the light of the fun, without being at the pains to open their eyes, any more than the laity. In like manner, if they expect protection and mainte-nance from the fovereign, 'tis neceffary they fhould contribute all they can on their part, towards furnifhing him with the means ; for there's no creature upon earth can do any thing without the help of means, that being a pre-rogative peculiar to God alone. If the facred character of clergymen gave them the privi-lege of living without confuming any provi-fions, then it would be but juft to excufe them from paying excife. On the other hand, it would be unjuft to defire that the character of clergymen fhould be fuch a charge to the lai-ty ; for their enjoying thefe exemptions would not be reckon'd as favours of their prince, but a robbery on his other fubjects, which is con-trary to the precepts of *Jefus Chrift*, wherein all partiality, and refpect of perfons, is exprefly forbidden.

T 3 VIII. That

VIII. That *the regular monks are hinder'd from obeying the constitutions of their order and chapters, by being oblig'd to confer prelatical dignities upon such friers as are natural born subjects of the republick.*

If it always hold true that a physician, who has been afflicted with many distempers himself, knows better than another how to cúre them in his patients; it muft be granted that *Venetian* friers cannot be better govern'd than by a *Venetian* fuperior; who knowing the cuftoms of the country, together with the tempers and blind fides of his countrymen, better than any other, knows beft what are the moft proper meafures to be taken. The canon which commands parifhioners to confefs to their parochial paftor, gives this as the only reafon for it, that fuch paftor being more thoroughly acquainted with the moft common fins committed before his face, is better qualify'd to examine the penitent, and to remedy irregularities with the more dexterity and fuccefs. Therefore *Chrift* faid, according to St. *John, He that entreth not by the door into the fheepfold, but climbeth up fome other way, the fame is a thief and a robber. But he that entreth in by the door, is the fhepherd of the fheep; to him the portér openeth, and the fheep hear his voice, and he calleth his own fheep by name, and leadeth them out.*

Has

Has the court of *Rome* then reafon to complain of the fenate of *Venice*, for their obedience to the gofpel, in enjoining the regular monks to admit of no fuperiors but what are natives of the ftate ? And is it not ridiculous to accufe the lay-fovereign of being a gainer by the execution of this decree, when his fole motive was a charitable zeal for the good of the friers ? In fhort, can any thing be more productive of mutual charity among them, than to be united all by one rule, at the fame time that they are more endear'd to one another by the natural genius of the country ? For a ftranger is like the water of a brook, that flides away as foon as it comes, whereas a native of the country is like the fand that ftays at the bottom. Were we to add to this any reafon from law, it would appear unjuft, that the lands of *Venice* fhould pafs into the hands of thofe who have no affinity with the *Venetians*, and who, after their adminiftration is expir'd, would not care one brafs farthing whether they left a good, or a bad name behind them, in the management of revenues and lands they are never to enjoy, and which perhaps they fhall never fee any more.

This may be farther illuftrated by the following inftance, which comes as near to the prefent cafe as any that can be thought of. A poor man that was troubled with the palfy, had moreover, to aggravate his affliction, running fores in one of his legs, which, for that

T 4 reafon,

reafon, was fo plagu'd with flies, that he was not able to keep them off. An honeft man paf-fing by, and taking pity on him, offer'd his fer-vice to blow them off; but the patient pray'd him not to do it by any means, thinking it bet-ter to bear with thofe that had already glutted themfelves in his fores, than by driving them off, to make way for new guefts, that might come to his leg half ftarv'd, and fall on with-out mercy. To this I fhall add, that methinks a prince ought at leaft to have as much liberty as a private perfon; now, where is that mafter of a family who does not appoint what ftew-ard he pleafes? for by fo doing, his fervants are better treated, as being govern'd accord-ing to their mafter's good pleafure; and from hence it follows, that the mafter is better ferv'd. This decree is not in the leaft prejudicial to the friers, but they are not willing to entertain a good thought of it. The court of *Rome* it felf has no reafon to complain of it, and 'tis to be wifh'd, that other princes would imitate the *Venetians* by publifhing the like decree.

I fhall conclude with this reflection, *viz.* that the leffer fpheres are regulated in their mo-tion by that of the *primum mobile:* And there-fore, as fince the time of *Adrian* VI. who fill'd the chair in 1522, there has not been one Pope who was not an *Italian*; fo I find no difference betwixt the law now publifh'd at *Venice*, and the conduct of the court of *Rome.*

IX. That

IX. That *when any dispute happens among the friers themselves, they are forc'd to prosecute in the temporal court, instead of the tribunal of the apostolical nuncio.*

'Tis for private men, rather than the state, to answer this complaint; for the *Venetian* government concerns itself in affairs of this kind only, when any persons, aggrieved by their superiors, or their superiors disobey'd by their inferiors, have recourse to the secular arm, and demand the interposition of public authority, which voluntarily lends its' hands to reduce those to their duty, who depart from it. What I pray can the government do in such a case as this, but protect the honest, and relieve the oppressed? what can the gentlemen of the court of *Rome* say to this? O! I hear some saying they would have the secular tribunal, after they have receiv'd the first motion, or notice of the cause, be silent of their own accord, and refer the affair 'to that of the nuncio. What a strange piece of work would this be! would not the *Venetians* hereby madly strip themselves of their proper authority, to cloath a foreign court with it? and would it not be uncharitable to the subject, when he most of all wants and desires assistance? *Define regnare nisi vis audire,* was the saying of a certain woman to one of the *Cæsars.* Therefore 'tis not on the account of any public advantage, that the friers are hinder'd from referring their controversies to the nuncio, to receive from him

the

the explanation of their rules, and to be fpiri-
tually punifh'd if they are difobedient.

The government leaves them at full liberty
upon this account; but when one of the parties, out of a guilty confcience, and for fear
not of fpiritual, but of corporal punifhment,
has recourfe to the fecular tribunal, in expectation of a more fpeedy trial, then the fenate
does not refufe affiftance to the party who has
right on his fide. Therefore 'tis at the friers
own difcretion, whether or no they will have
recourfe to this jurifdiction of the lay-tribunal, who, they may depend on't, will not fail
to do them juftice, in cafe they apply to them
for it; for where their judgment is not defir'd
by fome word, act, or fign, given for that end,
it is never granted. They fay, I know, that
tho' the motion be admitted in the temporal
court, they may chufe whether they will try
it; but I believe every man of fenfe fees the
extravagant abfurdity of this plea, and
that if they acted thus, it would look as if they
own'd they wanted authority, or that they
knew not how to exercife it. I dare affirm,
that if it was put to the gentlemen of the
court of *Rome*, they would not be fo complaifant to yield up their rights; and if this be
true, 'tis a terrible breach of charity to expect
from others what we would not grant them if
they ask'd it of us. But fuch is the pofition of
our eyes, and the rays of fight are fo difpos'd,
that we quickly fpy the leaft mote in our brother's

ther's eye, but can hardly fee the beam in our own ; which made *Diogenes* examine all his actions by a looking-glafs.

X. That *thofe who have a bifhoprick, or other prelatical dignity, conferr'd upon them by the court of* Rome, *are oblig'd to have recourfe to the Council for the poffeffion of temporalities, and that every bifhop precogniz'd by any but a* Venetian *cardinal, fhall not obtain poffeffion, and the See fhall remain vacant.*

This complaint contains two parts. 1. The obligation laid upon all perfons to obtain the poffeffion of their temporalities from the fenate. 2. The refufal of fuch poffeffion to bifhops that are precogniz'd by any but a *Venetian* cardinal.

The firft of thefe is not particular to the republick alone, but the general cuftom of all fecular princes. The fecond, indeed, is the prerogative of crown'd heads only. As to the firft, 'tis evidently a rule of civil law, univerfally receiv'd, that 'tis not enough to acquire an eftate by title of purchafe, exchange, donation, inheritance, or the like ; but that to be truly proprietor of a real eftate, 'tis abfolutely neceffary that a perfon be put in actual poffeffion of what was not his originally, but becomes his property by virtue of this new title. A man who comes into an eftate this way, has fuch an advantage, that if he be difabled to prove his acquifition, either by the lofs of papers, or by reafon of fire, or becaufe of his minority,

nority, 'tis enough for him if he comes at the possession honestly ; and whoever goes to dispute it with him, must be oblig'd to prove a better title by Papers and other documents, without obliging the possessor to shew his ; and if the claimant does not produce a better title, he would be cut off by the law, *uti possidetis ut possideatis.* This is a law not only favourable to the possessor, but also serves as a rampart against another's usurpation, because it does not leave every rash man at liberty to intrude by forcible means, and by his own authority, into an estate that does not belong to him, for the law never grants possession without a good title.

Now, what's the consequence of this? Why truly the court of *Rome* complains of a thing which is advantageous to the patron, or collator of a benefice, because the secular tribunal never grants possession, without first seeing whether the bull of collation be dispatch'd in due form. If the secular tribunal did not take this precaution , I do but think how many would creep into some abby, or other church-preferment , and the court of *Rome* know nothing of the matter, nor when they did, be able to help it ; and how many others would have the impudence to get into church livings, without any bull at all. Perhaps it will be pretended there's no danger of this, because those who usurp ecclesiastical benefices in this manner, are excommunicated *ipso facto.*
Good

Good God! Is it poffible that the fear of excommunication can be any check to men's defires! Alas! 'tis not now as it was heretofore, when excommunication was fuch a terrible bugbear, that it frightned *Attila*, even a *Barbarian*, to the abandoning *Rome* and his conquefts. Indeed the weapon is the fame as formerly, but has loft its' edge; and being got into other hands, what with the too common ufe of it, and the paffion with which it is denounc'd, 'tis become vile and contemptible. I believe the court of *Rome* will readily excufe me the trouble of fetching inftances to prove this, fince their own experience has fhewn it them too often in very many cafes. Therefore I think I have reafon to fay, that if the temporal fovereign did not intimidate the wicked by threats and punifhments, all the Pope's thunder and *anathema*'s would not keep ecclefiaftical benefices from being enjoy'd by the firft poffeffor. But undoubtedly the holy father knows that he is a hundred times better obey'd in countries where he has united the fceptre and the mitre, the fpiritual and the temporal fwords, than in foreign domains that are purely fecular, tho' at the fame time as much at the Pope's devotion and obedience as any.

To this the court of *Rome* will, it may be, reply, if the *Venetian* government piopofes by this to do any fervice to thofe that have benefices, let them do it only when they are defir'd, and not trouble their heads with thofe

that

that think the obtaining a bull of inveftiture, the moft honourable way of entring into pof-feffion, and look upon every thing to be inju-rious that is faid only in defence of the rights of the patron. This, I fay, would perhaps be their anfwer; but to be ingenuous, which is what I always profefs'd, perhaps too, that was not the fole motive of the *Venetian* law ; but if any ftate motives concurr'd, it muft be own'd that the *Venetian* politics never deviate from ftrict juftice, and that if the court of *Rome* does not approve them, 'tis only becaufe they are wont to prefer their own politics be-fore receiv'd cuftoms, and the law of nations. All the political views of the fenate are con-ftantly directed by equity; for what is more equitable than to require that benefices fhould be conferr'd only on their own country-men, men of unfpotted characters towards God and their natural fovereign? for otherwife they would be as rotten, corrupt members, unwor-thy to be nourifh'd by the heat of the body to which they belong. And in a word, what is more equitable than to hinder the inveftiture of one from being the ruin of another, who has a better right ? All thefe confiderations are fo juft, that any one of them is fufficient to juftify the whole conduct of the fenate in this refpect.

As to the precognizing of bifhops, let it be only remark'd, that 'tis a cuftom conftantly ob-ferv'd in this cafe in the court of *Rome* ; and if it be admitted there, that 'tis a privilege of crown'd heads for bifhops to be precogniz'd by the cardinal protector of their own nation, why all this complaint and admiration, that the moft ferene republick, which ftands in the fame rank with crown'd heads, is jealous of its rights in this circumftance, left any pre-judice be flily done to the prerogatives annex'd to its juft title of royalty? It is impoffible to be too much upon the guard againft that court, who fight with a two-edg'd fword, that cuts all ways, *ubi bene, nemo melius.*

To this it may be added, that according to the canons every new bifhop ought to pafs ex-amination at *Rome.* Now who can give bet-ter information concerning the talents of pre-lates elect, than their countrymen? This feems to be a reafon of fome weight, unlefs what is then done be mere ceremony and grimace; as happens in abundance of other cafes, where every thing is decided, not fo much according to the fpirit of the law, as according to the will and pleafure of the holy father.

But in all this complaint of the court of *Rome,* I don't fee where they are really hurt. The Pope admits to examination whom he pleafes; the examination is commonly made in his prefence, and the precognition is afterwards made in a full confiftory. Does not the whole grievance then only turn upon the cuftom of the republick, becaufe in this ceremony they act, like crown'd heads, by the cardinal protector

tector of their own nation ? If the court of *Rome* thinks fit to alter this cuftom, of which the republick is in poffeffion, there is no reafon for one fovereign's going to plead in the dominions of another, confequently he is in the right to defend his prerogatives in the beft manner he can ; which may be done by-publifhing his decrees with fuch authority,. that they may be executed in his own dominions, inftead of going to defire the concurrence of another prince's fuffrage. In good truth, whoever examines the matter ftrictly, and without paffion, will find that the court of *Rome* pores too clofe upon the conduct of the republick, which they ought rather to view thro' a perfpective.

XI. That *the* Venetians *intermeddle in the affair of penfions, which, tho' already eftablifh'd and approv'd, the fecular tribunal grants their protection to debtors who refufe to pay them.*

It cannot be deny'd that this is an article which touches the favorites of the court of *Rome* in the moft fenfible manner ; but it does not follow that their complaints are juft. Thofe bleffed penfions are the *ne plus ultra* of all their defires. They are, as we may fay, the fource of a large deep river, whofe mighty waters form the great fea of ecclefiaftical riches. There are befides many rivulets ; as collations, difpenfations, annates, indulto's, indulgences, privileges, and feveral others that have no name, which alfo fend their waters thither ;

but

but of which, fome are only tranfient in one
fenfe, tho' in the main they are always running.
The penfions are as the chief corner ftone of
the vifible ftructure of that monarchy, which,
tho' in its own nature altogether fpiritual and
metaphyfical, affects to make the fenfes witneffes of its grandeur, and always prefers a
real mathematical demonftration to one which·
is dialectic, and exifts only in the imagination.
No wonder therefore thofe gentlemen cry out
fo, when they are touch'd in the moft tender
part. Their complaint is divided into two
heads. 1. Againft the intermeddling in the
eftablifhment of penfions. And 2. Againft
the protecting of debtors that refufe to pay
thofe that are already approv'd.

The republic of *Venice* meddles in the eftablifhment of penfions no farther than to oblige the perfons, in whofe favour they are granted, to demand being put in poffeffion of their
temporal right, acquir'd by an indulto of the
court of *Rome*, to the eftates of any benefice,
or prelacy ; for the Pope has not the fame prerogative as a lay fovereign, to put the beneficed perfon into the poffeffion of the temporal
part of his benefice. Now the privilege of
putting a penfioner in poffeffion of his penfion,
amounts to the very fame thing ; otherwife,
if the one was practifed, and the other not,
'tis certain that the court of *Rome*, who never
lofes any advantages for want of feeing them,
would foon fwallow up nine tenths of the re-

venue of benefices, by giving the titles thereof
to some obscure persons, and leaving them under an obligation to lay princes for their possession of the temporalities, whilst the Pope
would not fail to assign exorbitant pensions to
persons of greater note, and his holiness's chief
favourites, who by that means would possess
such great revenues, without the least dependance for it on the sovereign, out of whose
dominions they arise.   This alone is enough to
confirm the sovereign in his resolution, besides that such pensions would be assign'd to
foreigners as well as natives, and perhaps more
to the former than to the latter; so that by
this wise piece of courtesy they would easily
triumph over the simplicity of the laity.   For
this reason, and to avoid inconveniencies that
may happen by any one's enjoying estates in
the republic, without owning their dependence
on *Venice*, the senate has prudently oblig'd all
that have revenues, or titles to any benefices,
to own their legal and natural authority.   As
to the pretence of protecting debtors that refuse to pay the pensions already settled upon
the temporalities, of which they are put in possession; it deserves a more particular consideration, and 'tis necessary that we pause a while,
to inquire into the nature of those pensions,
together with the time when, and the end for
which they were establish'd.

Pensions are, or ought to be, in their nature,
an effect of christian charity, not much different

rent from the precept of giving alms; for if every believer is oblig'd by the gospel to relieve his necessitous neighbour with part of his superfluity, how much more is a beneficed clergyman bound to obey our lord's command, by relieving, with part of his revenues, others of the clergy, who want necessaries, since he came *gratis* to the possession of the same, without its being either his acquisition, or his patrimony? Now, as all countries are not alike fruitful, nor all men equally rich, so all the prelates have not the same revenue. But the obligations of christianity are the same in all places, and require all mankind universally to discharge the duties of fathers and pastors towards all believers, and towards their neighbours; as they would avoid the reproach of the prophet, who said, *The little ones begged bread, and none broke unto them*; and moreover, *Jesus Christ* has taught, that *he that serveth at the altar, shall live by the altar.* From hence it follows, that the richest prelates ought to relieve the most indigent; which is doing two good things at once, *viz.* taking away the superfluity of one, and relieving the necessity of the other; both which will be meritorious of salvation to those who fight under the banner of *Christ.*

At first, there was no bull for settling the pensions; charity alone provided for the necessities of the poor clergy, and every rich prelate, of his own accord, inform'd himself what poor prelates were in his neighbourhood, and

imme-

immediately relieved them as far as in confcience he thought convenient. But time, that
deftroys all things fubject to its revolutions, by
degrees caft fuch a damp upon thofe good and
charitable difpofitions, that in order to animate
the cool zeal of fome on the one hand, and to
prevent confufion on the other, left one perfon
fhould have all the charity, and others be left
to ftarve, it was found abfolutely neceffary to
pafs that into a law and obligation, which was
at firft but a cuftom, and depended purely on
good will. The eftablifhment of penfions was
certainly very good, if it had not in fome meafure had the fate of Lucifer, who, at his crea-
tion, poffefs'd all the beauties, all the perfec-
tions, of which a creature is capable; but
for his abufing them, became the type of all
faults, and of deformity itfelf; and this, becaufe he tranfgrefs'd the end for which he was
created and endow'd with thofe great qualities. The fame vice is common in all things,
for the end is the caufe of natural caufes, and
the agent moves only with a view to its end;
from whence it follows, that 'tis the end which
diftinguifhes actions, and makes them either
good or bad. For example, a furgeon and a
ruffian ufe the fame means, *viz.* wound-
ing, and effufion of blood; but their actions
are quite different, and even contrary on two
accounts, the manner, and the end; the one
keeps a meafure in letting out the blood, and
has for its end the prefervation, or rather the
reftoration

reftoration of health; the other is ftinted by
no meafure, and has for its end-nothing but
deftruction and death : Therefore the one is
good, the other dangerous ; the one laudable, the other abominable. If our penfions
now-a-days were as well laid out, as formerly,
in the relief of ftarving paftors ; and if care
was taken, at the fame time, to over-rate no
man's benefice beyond reafon and equity, penfions would undoubtedly have all the merit
and beauty ftill which they had at their original inftitution ; nor would they be branded as
fcandalous, and held in abomination, as they
are now, but commended and applauded

    In the facred canons, nothing is more talk'd
of, next to the purity of faith, than the frailty of prelates, who ought to be examples to
us ; and it muft be confefs'd that experience
tells us, they have a very ftrong byafs towards
riches. If thofe riches indeed are annex'd to
their prelacy 'tis well enough; for 'tis expedient
that fome prelates fhould be rich, for the honour of the order, and for the advantage of
religion on fome accounts ; but if, with all
their riches, they imitate the leech, which
gluts itfelf with the blood of others, till 'tis
ready to burft, there is no bearing with fuch
conduct ; but as opportunity offers, there will
be an abfolute neceffity to prevent the corruption from growing to a head. 'Tis an obfervation of phyficians, that a human body of the
moft healthy complexion, which is in perfect

                            good

good order, and free from any malignant humour, is in much danger, from a too great
fulness of blood. Some women with child,
if they would go out their time, ought to be
blooded; whereas, if others were to do so,
they would certainly miscarry; for what would
be dangerous to some, would be safe for o-
thers, in whom nature has form'd too much
blood. Remember that saying of the wise
Pittacus, nequid nimis.

If indeed a prelate be not able to bear the
weight of the pensions with which his revenues are charg'd, either because the harvest is
bad, or because of any unforeseen losses, or
extraordinary expences, and the creditor in the
mean time proceeds to a sequestration of all
his revenues, what shall the prelate do to supply his cure, unless the prince assists him by
taking off the sequestration till he is in better
circumstances? *Venter non patitur dilationem.*

Every heir has by law a year's time allow'd
to pay legacies; but where a legacy is design'd
to keep the legatee from starving, the heir is
oblig'd to make immediate payment of it, because the withholding necessary subsistence, due
to him that wants it, is the same thing in effect as putting him to death. How is it possible for a poor prelate, that must serve the
Church with a decorum suitable to his Dignity, to pay certain stated pensions regularly out
of his revenues, when his said revenues are so
uncertain at best, and liable, in case of any of
the

the aforefaid accidents, to a total annihilation?
To oblige a prelate, in fuch a cafe as this, to
pay penfions of this kind, before he lays by for
his own fubfiftence, is the fame thing as to
force a wretch that is e'en famifh'd, to hold
bread in his hand, and not to eat it. *Mofes*
faid in the law, *Thou fhalt not muzzle the
mouth of the ox that treadeth out the corn.* If a
prelate, in fuch a predicament, has recourfe to
his native fovereign, who muft be fuppos'd to
know better than a ftranger the nature of the
accidents alledg'd, and whether they are una-
voidable and real, fhall not the fovereign
grant him an abatement of the penfion, or
longer time to pay it? I imagine that the
gentlemen of the court of *Rome* will have two
anfwers to make; one relating to order, the
other to merit: As to order, they will be apt
to fay, the cognizance of affairs of this fort is
in the breaft of the Pope, that *illius eft interpretari cujus eft condere,* i. e. *he who makes the law
ought to explain it;* that no body fhould prefume to interpret the Pope's bulls, and that if
the accidents alledg'd are real, the Pope, after
knowledge of the caufe, will not fail to relieve the petitioner. But to this I return the
fame anfwer I have often given already, *viz.*
That if the prelate who is thus aggriev'd, ap-
plies to the Pope for an abatement, the fenate
of *Venice* will never oppofe him; but if the
prelate implores relief from the fenate, it cannot be expected of them that they fhould de-

ny

ny it him. The senate know better what belongs to the rights of sovereignty than to commit such an error, and they are punctual to a nicety in discharging the most indispensable obligations of government. The complaint is of more consequence to the prelate who appeals; than to the sovereign to whom he makes it; but if I may be allow'd to speak my mind, I must own in conscience that I think such prelate has very good reason to decline his appeal to *Rome*; for he would be grosly mistaken, if he thought that whatever right he had, considering the unexpected misfortunes fallen upon him, he would find any relief from the court of *Rome*, who are persuaded 'tis their interest not to authorize, by any example, the opinion of those who alledge that pensions are capable of alteration. Mean time the court of *Rome* reckon this an obligation so indispensable, that whoever does not perform it, must never hope for preferment, tho' he has all the talents for an illustrious prelate; insomuch, that if, when a person passes his examination for the dignity of a cardinal, any one charges him, or any of his associates, with disobedience in this respect, 'tis enough to exclude him for ever from the purple. I don't wonder therefore at any one's refusing to plead before a court, which is both judge and party at the same time. Let it not be urg'd that the Pope is judge, and not the courtiers; for 'tis very well known that the Pope scarce .

ever

ever judges in this matter, but delegates commiffioners, and that if, in cafes of very great
importance, he happens to give judgment himfelf, he always depends upon the report of his
courtiers in the commiffion ; and when they
cannot fucceed otherwife, they fpin out fo
much time in trying new projects, or expedients, as eats up more than the profit of the
revenue, and very often the party dies before
he obtains a verdict.

The other objection I am aware of from
that quarter is, that all the pretences for not
paying penfions are feign'd, becaufe penfions
are never granted but upon fuch overplus of
the revenues of a bifhoprick, or other prelacy,
as is more than fufficient to maintain the prelate; and that a penfion is never afcertain'd,
without due regard had to contingencies, that
may happen either by bad feafons, or otherwife ; from whence it is evident, that avarice,
and not neceffity, furnifhes the debtor with
pretences to refufe payment of the penfions.
This is what they fay, and if true, the pretence of penfions would fall to the ground ;
the conditions indeed would be obferv'd, and
nothing would be wanting, but to rectify the
end of them, by granting them only to neceffitous prelates, inftead of rich ones, and
fometimes even to the laity. But 'tis one
thing to affert, and another to prove. For
this reafon, fay I, the Council of *Trent* made
an order that penfions fhould not be rais'd upon

on bifhops that had not above a thoufand ducats revenue, or curates that had but five
hundred ; a remedy which needed not to have
been prefcrib'd, if the evil it was propos'd to
cure had not been poffible *in rerum natura.* But
from hence it follows, that a penfion of a thoufand nine hundred crowns may be rais'd upon
a bifhop, who has a revenue of twenty thoufand. Were the government of *Venice* to be
the ftandard, if the bifhop of *Padua* had not
above a thoufand ducats for his maintenance,
the rank of this fee would indeed give him the
preference to the bifhop of *Caorle* ; but the latter would be counted the more wealthy man,
tho' his revenue be but fix hundred ducats ;
the reafon is this, becaufe the expence ought
to be proportion'd to the city, clergy, and people. Therefore I think it muft appear very
unjuft that the bifhop of *Padua* fhould be
ftript, by this means, of the 20th part of
his revenues, while I frankly own it, as my
opinion, that the revenue of the bifhop of *Caorle* ought to be augmented with three or four
hundred crowns. But without pretending to
aftrology, I can divine that the firft cafe will
come to pafs fooner than the fecond. If therefore the firft, or what comes up near to it,
fhould happen to be the cafe, and the prelate
fhould invoke the fovereign for relief, I verily
believe that the prince, befides the common
obligation on him to do juftice, would be
fway'd by the motive of felf-intereft not to
fuffer

suffer the ruin of his moſt eminent prelacies,
and to let his biſhops be reduc'd to want for
the ſake of inriching another that was wealthy
before, and of making two biſhops over one
biſhoprick ; the one to receive the revenues,
and the other to ſupport the charge of it.

If one were to conſider the invincible byaſs
of the preſent age to penſions, it muſt be
own'd that in ancient days people were much
more frugal and moderate, which proceeds indeed from a canon of the Council of *Trent*,
but without any fault of the law-makers. The
good fathers of that Council , among their
many decrees, made one of the beſt concerted,
and moſt juſt that could be in poſitive law,
which was a prohibition that no body ſhould
poſſeſs more than one biſhoprick, or benefice,
with cure of ſouls, at one and the ſame time.
In the days of old, it was a very ill cuſtom
for a prelate to be ſet over ſeveral Churches,
and a biſhop over ſeveral Dioceſes, a thing altogether as abſurd, as for a man, who pretends
to be a chriſtian, to have more wives than one
at a time. This irregularity gave cauſe for
that laudable precaution contain'd in the canon, which has contributed ſo much to the advantage of the Church and people, and been
obſerv'd ſo much more inviolably than all the
others ; for no bull has yet been diſpatch'd
contrary to it with the clauſe *non obſtantibus*.
But ſee now to what ſhifts ſome men have recourſe for evading this law, either in whole,
or

or in part ! As to the prohibition of poffeffing feveral Sees at once, they make up for it, or rather evade it, by having only one in poffeffion, but by enjoying the revenues of feveral added to it by way of penfion. And from hence it comes to pafs that there are few prelacies with handfome revenues, that can efcape being, as it were, moth-eaten by penfions, unlefs fuch prelacy be in the hands of fome perfon of credit. This therefore is another juft motive for the *Venetian* Government to oppofe art with art, in cafes that require their affiftance, and is a farther juftification of their granting protection to thofe that implore it.

XII. *That the ordinaries of places are hinder'd from fulminating excommunication, in cafes prefcrib'd by the Canons.* And,

XIV. *That fchifmatics, heretics, whore-mongers, and ufurers, are fuffer'd to live quietly and peaceably at* Venice, *while the prelate is not permitted to excommunicate them, or to punifh them in any other way.*

The near affinity betwixt thefe two complaints, and our averfion to trouble the reader with vain repetition, have engag'd us to make but one article of both ; the rather, becaufe there's no treating of the one without touching on the other. We cannot well inquire into the reafons why the ordinary is hinder'd from fulminating excommunication againft the laity, till we have examin'd the crimes for which thofe excommunications are iffu'd. And

in

in the firſt place we will lay down this for the principle of our anſwer to theſe complaints. That at *Venice* the ſecular tribunal has always been conſider'd as the only one, appointed by God himſelf in this ſtate, to do juſtice, and to diſtribute rewards and puniſhments. The *Venetians* don't admit of the diſtinction made by the Court of *Rome,* that a man who is born the ſubject of one ſovereign prince, can, upon any conſideration, become the ſubject of another ; for at this rate, a ſubject is made the ſubject of another ſubject, whenever his biſhop happens to be in the liſt of the ſubjects born within the ſame dominions. Whoever looks into the goſpel, will find that the apoſtles gave the name of flock to the company of the faithful, and that of ſhepherd to the eccleſiaſtic ſuperior. St. *Peter,* when he puts ſubjects in mind of obedience to their temporal ſovereign, addreſſes himſelf both to laity and clergy. *Servants, be obedient to your maſters with fear and trembling.* All that obey another, are not his ſubjects in a ſtrict and proper ſenſe ; and tho' a degree, which has another ſuperior to it, may ſeem to imply a ſort of ſubjection, 'tis *analogice,* and not *univoce.* Thus in the cœleſtial hierarchy, the archangel carries the commands of God to an inferior angel ; but this does not imply, that an angel of the loweſt choir is ſubject to any of the higheſt. In a monaſtery a prior commands his monks, whom he calls his ſubjects, but very improperly ; for they are not
his

his fubjects, but his brethren in the fame obligations of monaftical difcipline, only with this
difference, that 'tis the bufinefs of the prior
alone to fee the rules thereof obferv'd. 'Tis
the cuftom now-adays for bifhops and prelates of any orders, to give their diocefans, or
monks, the title of fubjects. Perhaps it arofe
at the fame time when the Popes firft affum'd
the title of Sovereign Pontiffs, forgetting the
old appellative of a bifhop, *Servant of the Servants of God.* It may be the gentlemen of the
court of *Rome* will here be apt to think that I
feek, by favour of this axiom, to retract what
I have fo often own'd in this treatife, *viz.* that
there are very many cafes in which laymen are
fubject to ecclefiaftic jurifdiction; but if they
fhould think fo of me, they will be quite
miftaken, and I know that a difputant can do
nothing worfe than to expofe himfelf to the
lafh of his own arguments. I do not deny
what I have confefs'd, but am for examining
into the true notion we ought to have of a
fubject. I know very well that the laity may be
guilty of crimes which are cognizable by the
ecclefiaftical tribunal, but I will not own that
they thereby become its fubjects. Let it not
be faid that this is a difpute about words, for
'tis a neceffary diftinction, to which, it muft
be remember'd, I have already faid, recourfe
ought certainly to be had in thefe cafes, otherwife; if this point were to be given up, it
would be needlefs to difpute the reft with
them :

them : Therefore I repeat it ; if it be true, that all who are in fome refpects under a prelate's jurifdiction, are effentially his fubjects, it would follow unavoidably that he might legally proceed againft them for all manner of crimes, and it would be a crying injuftice, if the fovereign fhould go about to violate that liberty. Let us now pafs to the examination of the particular offences mention'd in, the complaint :

As to the moft heinous and enormous in the whole catalogue, *viz.* herefy, I agree that it comes within the verge of the ecclefiaftical court. The government of *Venice* never took cognizance of a crime of this kind, which is quite out of the laity's ken; and the fecular tribunal neither ought, nor can penetrate into the feveral degrees of herefy ; becaufe, to make this difcovery, 'tis neceffary to compare the doctrine of faith with the external marks of herefy given by the perfon accus'd. This is an examination by no means fit for a layman to make ; befides, in order to be a judge of this crime, 'tis neceffary for the judge to have good attestations from fome public academy, that he is an able divine. This knowledge may fall to the fhare of fome private perfon, but a temporal prince would be never the better for it. Therefore I have reafon to perfift in my opinion, that crimes of this kind come before the fpiritual court *de jure & de facto* ; and it was for this in particular that the Pope eftablifh'd

the

the tribunal of the inquifition, which, as oc-cafion requires, not only condemns the guilty to fpiritual penance, but even to corporal punifhment. Indeed it does not inflict excommunication, becaufe recourfe ought not to be had to it for a crime already confummated, unlefs the criminal be obftinate and contumacious. But if, on the other hand, a man who has been convicted of herefy, either in his difcourfe, belief, or actions, repents of his crime, I grant that he may be punifh'd corporally, but not driven from the unity of the Church by excommunication; fo far from it, that if he be already excommunicated, he fhould be reftor'd to the Church, which ought to imitate the example of God, who punifhes the greateft finners by the death of the body, and not by the deftruction of the foul. And as foon as a finner repents of his herefy, the complaints ought to ceafe, that which was the caufe thereof being remov'd.

As to fchifmatics, the complaint on their account can only concern the *Greeks,* who have that name given them by the court of *Rome.* I fhall only bring one argument to refolve the whole difpute. If the lay tribunal of *Venice* fhould fuffer the prelates to inflict corporal punifhment on thofe they call fchifmatics, would not they thereby help to ruin and deftroy their own fubjects? for the *Greek* religion being receiv'd in a great part of the dominions of the republic, thofe of that Church would be oblig'd

lig'd always to fhun the face of their natural
fovereign, if they could not come to *Venice*
without the danger of imprifonment, or ba-
nifhment, for their different opinions. Now,
as the difcuffion of this difference does not lie
before a temporal fovereign, fo he ought not
to tyrannize over the confciences of his fubjects, and thereby provoke them to go and
live under the *Turk*, for the fake of enjoying
liberty of confcience. Therefore we muft
pray to God to remedy this diforder, who, as
he has founded and built his Church, both can
and will repair and reftore it to its primitive
luftre, in the time appointed by his eternal
decrees.

As to that part which relates to whoremongers and ufurers, it requires a more particular
confideration. Thefe two crimes are fome of
thofe which ought to be refer'd to God's tribunal at the day of judgment. Indeed there are
few or no crimes deem'd as fuch by the judges
of the earth, which will not be criminal in
like manner before God's tribunal, becaufe civil laws are founded in the main upon the law
of nature and the decalogue ; but it does not
thence follow that every action, which is fin before God, is punifhable by a humane tribunal,
unlefs in cafe of immediate injury done to one's
neighbour, to which muft be added crimes
that directly attack the divinity ; as blafphemy,
which contains an infult upon God, and fcandal to our neighbour, and confequently calls

for twofold punifhment ; one in this life, on the part of human juftice ; and after death, eternal damnation by the judge of heaven.

We return to examine what is meant by whoredom and ufury. Ufury offends one's neighbour, becaufe by wicked arts it feizes on the eftates of others with rapacity and avarice. 'Tis a crime altogether fubject to the temporal court, whofe judge will be qualify'd to know as much of it, as is neceffary, by the law and his own ftudy ; and to pretend that 'tis a crime cognizable by the ecclefiaftic court, becaufe it offends the juftice of God, and does injury to one's neighbour ; this is fo general a reafon, that it would fubject the cognizance of all crimes, how fecular foever, to the fpiritual tribunal. Confequently, were it to be admitted, there would be nothing more to do than to acknowledge the fpiritual tribunal for fovereign in *Venice,* as well as at *Rome* ; but the *Venetians* are not yet fo dim-fighted as not to fee the confequence. They have a magiftrate on purpofe to take cognizance of all contracts of ufury, and to do juftice to the fufferers ; for if they fhould punifh any as public ufurers, without better proofs than appearance and common fame, they might eafily be deceiv'd, becaufe none but God can judge without the help of witneffes and proof.

As to whoredom, 'tis a crime that offends one's neighbour only by ill example, juft as fimony, at which every one is moft certainly

ſcan-

scandaliz'd, who sees it in a prelate. If every crime a man commits against his conscience, whereby he shews an ill example, were to be punish'd with corporal punishment, there would be a necessity for establishing a perpetual tribunal, which would have business more than enough; for every evil action carries an ill example along with it, and every sin is an evil action; from whence it will follow, that the whole world would be the prison of such tribunal, and the judge of it himself would not be free from censure; for a man scarce holds his integrity more than seven years. But this would be a severity not to be parallel'd, either in the law of *Moses*, or that of *Jesus Christ*. As soon as *Adam* sinn'd, he was only threatned with death; which, if we understand of the body, was deferr'd 930 years; and if of death eternal, he triumphed over it by his repentance. Frailty is one thing, malice another; and tho' there is no frailty where there is not some small tincture of malice, yet malice, properly speaking, is that which directly attacks the almighty power of God with an impenitent heart. We at *Venice* admit of a doctrine which the court of *Rome* cannot comprehend, tho' it be confirm'd by numberless experiences, *viz.* that brotherly correction is more effectual, than the sword of justice, to bring back those that have gone astray, and that good examples reform more than all punishments; *magis movent exempla quam verba.*

St. *Au-*

St. *Auguſtin*, while he was a monk, reſolv'd one day to go and preach thro' the city ; accordingly he took his hood, and having only walk'd about with his companion till night, he then return'd to his convent. Upon this his companion took the freedom to ask him why he did not preach. I did preach ſufficiently, ſays he ; and this was really true ; for the life of that holy man did as much good as his preaching, becauſe he ſhew'd forth temperance and good manners, by his example, to that degree, that the people were more edify'd and convinc'd by ſuch his ſilent way of preaching, than if they had been ſtated auditors of labour'd, poliſh'd harangues.

Experience ſufficiently demonſtrates, that this mild treatment at *Venice* brings a greater number of ſtragglers into the pale of the Church, and to the exact obſervation of diſcipline, than the ſeverity us'd in other governments, which proceed to excommunication and impriſonment againſt the diſobedient ; beſides, that this ſeverity gives ground for hypocriſy ; for when the impenitent find themſelves in danger of excommunication, they will do all they can to avoid ſuch a brand of infamy, and render themſelves ſtill more guilty before God, by approaching his altar without preparation , and for another end than merely to ſave their ſouls. Medicine, if taken in time, is wholeſome , otherwiſe 'tis poiſon. Every one of our ſaviour's actions ought to be
a leſſon

a leffon to us. He fet a fifherman at the head of his Church, and not a huntfman ; becaufe the one ufes thofe murdering inftruments the gun and fpear, the other the net. The difciples having toiled a fifhing one whole night, and taken none, *Chrift* bade them caft their net on the right fide of the fhip, and immediately they had a great draught. Both thefe inftances teach us, that a finner muft be taken, but not put to death ; and that he muft be catch'd with art, and not with violence : At *Venice* therefore a prelate never proceeds to excommunicate thofe who refufe to come to the holy table of the paffover, left one, who is already a fornicator, fhould become guilty of facrilege ; for if an article of faith, decided by the council of *Trent*, is true, *viz.* That the ungodly cannot be juftify'd without preventing grace, this grace is not in all the power of man to beftow, whether by rewards or punifhments.

XIII. *That if any one, having a call from the fpirit, takes upon him the religious habit, they prefume to expel him upon the leaft complaint of his parents, on pretence of his being feduc'd ; and when any one is left in a monaftery, the parents are authoriz'd to keep his eftate*

When the apoftle St. *Bartholomew* preach'd the gofpel to the *Indians*, the king fent for him to cure his daughter, who was poffefs'd with a devil. The Bracmans had try'd their skill a long time in vain; but the

X 3   holy

holy apoftle only commanded the evil fpirit, in the name of *Jefus*, to depart out of her, and accordingly he left her. This was very pleafing to the king's officers, and was not only a comfort to the king, but fill'd him with admiration of the deity, which was newly preach'd to him ; neverthelefs, he was not converted : However, to fhew his gratitude to St. *Bartholomew*, he gave him a great deal of gold ; but the divine apoftle convinc'd him that he did not defire riches, but that he expected a much greater reward, *viz.* that he would make a prefent of his foul to *Jefus Crift*, who would take great care of it in this life, and commit it at laft in glory to eternity. The king, charm'd with his noble fpirit, believ'd, and was baptiz'd ; and tho' born in a country where there was an annual harveft of gold, he thought the contempt of worldly goods was a more certain proof of the truth of the new doctrine, than even the working of miracles, and cafting out devils. During the *Babylonifh* captivity, *Daniel* the prophet obferving the blindnefs of thofe people, in trufting in their falfe gods, often endeavour'd to convince them of their folly. Thofe ignorant wretches, to prove the divinity of their pretended deities, told him that their king fent every day into the temple forty fheep, feven oxen, a great quantity of bread and wine, and that tho' the gate was then fhut, and fealed

with

with the king's feal, yet next day in the morning to be fure all was confum'd. *Daniel* could not help fmiling at fuch a proof of a godhead as this was, and faid, that was rather an attribute of a wolf, and not of a true God, who has no paunch to fill, nor no occafion to feed. They are your priefts, fays he, who live upon thofe victims, who, being as arrant cheats as the idols they worfhip, knavifhly rob the altars of the facrifice. Therefore, having fcatter'd afhes privately upon the pavement of the temple, they difcover'd the footfteps that led to the den, thro' which the priefts enter'd privately in the night, and ftole away the offerings, with which they plentifully maintain'd their families.

St. *Ignatius*, the moft pious founder of the fociety of *Jefus*, gave an inftruction to the Jefuit *Cofimus Torres*, travelling to *Japan*, which might ferve as a gofpel and rule to all clergymen, efpecially the regular friers. The fubftance of which inftruction was, to fubdue their paffions, to throw off all felf-intereft, and efpecially never to touch the alms of believers to the poor; becaufe, faid he, 'tis almoft impoffible to touch pitch, and not be defil'd therewith. This holy man us'd to fay, that if he had but four companions entirely difengag'd from felfifh views, he would not defpair of converting the whole world; for he faw that this virtue had every body's good word, but that very few practis'd it.

The

The *Florentines* were fo edify'd by the good example of their countryman *Philip de Nery,* that one of his kinfmen, who was very rich, offer'd to make him his heir ; but he, good man ! tho' ty'd to no order, nor no monaftic vow, thanked his generous kinfman, refufed the offer, and advis'd him to find out an heir of another temper, who would, no doubt, very gladly accept it. All thefe remarks muft fatisfy the wife reader, that religion and riches are by nature quite incompatible, tho', for certain reafons, they are fometimes permitted to go together. I myfelf, who affirm this fo pofitively, cannot fay I am altogether free from cenfure in this refpect. I was form'd of the fame clay as the reft of mankind, which, tho' never fo much feafon'd in the fire of charity, comes out as brittle ware as the other veffels of the age. *Ifaiah* faid, *all our righteoufneffes are as filthy rags.* But as on the one hand, I make this confeffion in juftice to the truth ; fo on the other, I cannot help praifing that fovereign, who, when he difcovers that any perfon is feduc'd to take the habit on him, makes ufe of his abfolute authority againft fuch facrilege, by fetting the perfon feduc'd at liberty ; for even fuppofing the vocation to be really from the fpirit, this interruption can never deftroy it, but it will rather come out finer, like gold out of the furnace. How many rubs did St. *Thomas* of *Aquinas* meet with, both from his father and kindred, who were loth he
fhould

fhould embrace the monaftic life ? But what end did they ferve, only to fhew that his was not the perfuafion of his mind, but the call of grace ? *The wind bloweth where it lifteth, and thou knoweft not whence it cometh, nor whither it goeth.* This conduct is fo far from being injurious to religion, that 'tis ftrictly conformable to the canons, which prefcribe a great many cautions to be us'd in the examination of thofe who come to make their vows, thereby to difcover whether they are fincerely difpos'd to make an entire furrender of their will to God's. Let not the fenate therefore be accus'd of too readily lending an ear to parents complaining of fuch feduction. For, I fay, that when a diforder is to be prevented, too much credulity is a lefs crime than to tolerate the inconveniency, out of a fcruple to oppofe fuch or fuch friers. Religion is never a gainer by perfons that are merely feduc'd into it; becaufe, as 'tis obferv'd in nature, *that nothing violent is lafting* , repentance comes upon the neck of fuch rafh refolutions, and drives a great number of fouls into utter defpair. Religion lofes no more by not admitting fuch friers, than a captain does by not inrolling a faint-hearted, cowardly foldier. Now, on the other hand, if the accufation be falfe, the perfon is at his liberty either to enter into the fame order in another country, or into another order in the fame town, and is welcome to make profeffion thereof accordingly ; for *in my father's*

ther's houfe are many manfions. Every monaftery is a ftrait road to heaven, if the monks
that belong to it don't reel out of the way.

But the other part of the grievance is, that
if a novice ftays in the cloifter, the parents are
authoriz'd to appropriate his eftate. The only
way to prevent a gangreen, is to lay the plaifter
right upon the wound. 'Tis amazing, I think,
that we hear no complaint of any one's being
forc'd to quit the habit of an order of friers,
who don't allow of poffeffion of lands, but
live, as we fay of oifters, upon the dew of
heaven. The *Partifans* of the court of *Rome*
will tell me that parents, inftead of afflicting
themfelves, are commonly very eafy when any
of their family puts on the habit of that order,
becaufe then their eftates remain to them without any trouble; and therefore, if their children, &c. were feduc'd, they would have no
need to complain. But there's nothing in all
this objection ; for feduction, as to thefe orders, is a perfect chimæra, and can exift no
where but in a difturb'd brain ; and therefore no
wonder they don't complain of what is not in
being. *Omne agens agit propter finem,* i. e. *every agent acts for some end,* faid a certain philofopher ; and *David,* in his addreffes to God,
fays, *I have inclin'd my heart to perform thy fta-
tutes alway, for the recompence of reward.* What
would a capuchin be the better for perfuading
any one to put on his habit, fince the new
frier would be incapable of doing him any
good,

good, either in public or private? on the contrary, the more there are in commons, the lefs muft be every one's allowance. I will not here mention by whom, and when fuch complaints have been made e'er now. I will only fay, that St. *Ignatius* made good laws, which, obferv'd with that zeal that commonly attends novelty, have contributed very much to the edification of the mind, but little or nothing to the edification of the convents of his order. St. *Paul* lays down the rule of an apoftle's life in two words, as *having nothing, and poffeffing all things.* 'Tis often faid, I know that miracles are ceas'd, and that therefore 'tis a duty, where 'tis poffible, to give the preference to the laft claufe, and to avoid the firft. But I declare this is a mere carnal reafoning: 'Tis fo, they will anfwer; but fuch conduct is now permitted. I don't deny it; but then 'tis by way of difpenfation, not to procure a great good, but to prevent a greater evil. The *Pharifees*, hearing *Jefus Chrift* preach that matrimony made two bodies one flefh, objected to him, that *Mofes* allow'd writings of divorcement in his law. But what faid *Jefus Chrift?* he faid to them, *it was not fo from the beginning;* and *Mofes* fuffer'd you to put away your wives, *becaufe of the hardnefs of your hearts.*

To return to our argument. Tho' the moft ferene republic is very careful to prevent perfons from being feduc'd into a cloifter, they don't deny any one that's free to enter; and if
any

any one, whether great, fmall, or rich, has a mind to put on the habit of any order, and gives proofs that 'tis the effect of matuie deliberation, in a proper time and manner, he need fear no oppofition from the fenate ; and if he has a mind, he is free to leave all his eftate to the monaftery. But St. *Auftin* fays, *Qui vult ecclfiam inftituere, & filios exhæredare, alium quærat confultorem quam Auguftinum,* i. e. *He that would difinherit his children, and make the church his heir, muft not come to me for counfel.* Let it only be a caution, that a refolution of fuch importance to the age, to the parents, and to the perfon himfelf who makes his vows, be natural, and not counterfeit. How many of the moft ferene doges, furfeited with human grandeur, have put on the habit of St. *Benedict,* without the leaft oppofition? But all our concein is for thofe raw ftriplings, who, young as they are, **yet** boaft they fhall always hold out againft the motions of nature, which is fo prone to evil. To fum up all in a word, youth are interrogated and examin'd ; but as for adult perfons, who 'tis fuppos'd are wife enough to refift feducers, they are not fubject to fuch fcrutiny.

The laft grievance of all is the *violences, as they think fit to call them, practifed by the fenate upon thofe that fail in the gulph, by forcing fuch as carry provifions, merchandife, inftruments animals, falt, and all other goods that pafs thro' it into the rivers of* Romagna, *to pay certain impofts.* After

After so long a discourse, we are now fallen, as we may say, into an ocean of complaints, since we are come to those grievances which relate to the gulph. These complaints, in order to be just, ought to have at least one of these two motives, *viz.* either that the duties demanded are exorbitant, and unreasonable; or if they are moderate, that they are demanded by violence, and without any legal title. When the sovereign, by exacting any tribute, offends in either of these two respects, he justly incurs the reproach of committing an injury, and an unjust action. To answer in two words the complaint against the exorbitancy of the duties demanded, I will only say, that the duties and excise, which the most serene republic demands of those who transport effects thro' the gulph to the markets in the Pope's dominions, are neither more nor less in weight, and measure, than what the government demands of merchants that import the same wares into *Venice*. I don't know that 'tis any where commanded us to love our neighbour better than our selves, this being a peculiar attribute of *Jesus Christ*, who loved human nature better than his own humanity.

When sailors are caught endeavouring to run goods into *Romagna*, without first paying the duties, they are condemn'd to the confiscation of more than those duties would amount to. This is the common method of punishment in *Venice*, and every where else,

for

for thofe who are taken defrauding their fovereign of his rights. All impartial perfons look upon it, too as an act of juftice; for if, when fuch fraud is committed, he who is guilty of it runs, no greater risk than paying the bare duties, there's no body hardly but would venture being a knave on fuch terms, becaufe he might chance to find his account in it; and if he fhould happen, not to fucceed, he runs no risk, becaufe, if he is difcover'd, he can but pay the duty; and if not, he gains all the value thereof clear to himfelf.

This, I fay, is the weight and meafure dealt to the fubjects of the republic, according to the common ftandard. Therefore there's no reafon for complaint on this head, and thofe who make it, muft be fuch as love to complain, whether they have reafon or no.

I will add further; if the goods that pafs thro' the gulph fhould be extraordinary dear, or wanted in *Venice* for the fupport of the inhabitants, then they would be ftopt by force and authority from going to *Romagna*, and not fo much as fuffer'd to be carry'd out of *Venice*. Mean time it could not be reckon'd a piece of injuftice; but rather a cafe of neceffity, and authoriz'd by the cuftom of other princes, who in the like cafes of extream neceffity, which is fuperior to all laws, have not only caufed provifions, but even ready money, to be ftopt, when they have wanted the fame to anfwer public occafions. There are many
inftances

inftances of this, but the moft ferene republic never us'd this method with refpect to money. Princes are juftify'd in acting thus, becaufe every thing within their dominions ought to be fubject to their commands, when their views are honeft, and when they take care to afcertain a juft equivalent. But enough of this already.

Now, if the court of *Rome* complains not againft the violence of exacting thofe impofts, but queftions the authority and title of the republic to raife them; I fay, that both their authority and title are indifputably legal, fo long as the republic is own'd to be the fovereign of the gulph; for 'tis by virtue of the fame title that every fovereign has a right of demanding the impofts, or duties of importation, from all merchants that trade in their dominions; and 'tis by virtue of this fame title that the Pope himfelf raifes the gabels in St. *Peter*'s patrimony. Therefore the whole objection muft vanifh upon the proof of the republic's legal fovereignty over the gulph; which being an affair of the greateft concern, not only to the Pope, but alfo to other fovereign princes, it would require a difcourfe of equal length to the importance of the fubject, becaufe in matters of this nature nothing lefs than the fulleft proof will avail: But, as a formal treatife on this head would be ungrateful to the reader, we fhall only give the fubftance of what might be urg'd, with all poffible

fible brevity ; and, after having faid juft enough
to prove our thefis, fhall referve to our felves
the liberty of faying more, to fatisfy the curiofity of the public,* at another time and
place.

It was a good obfervation of a fkillful lawyer,
that whoever went about to prove a title of
poffeffion, founded upon law, in favour of a
private man, could not poffibly fucceed, unlefs
it concern'd the *Jews* with refpect to the promis'd land, which God gave to that nation, or
unlefs it concern'd any other perfon in our own
times, who fhould purchafe of the lawful fovereign the *Flafhes* of any river. The producing the fucceffive titles of the third, fourth,
and fifth poffeffors, is no full proof that there
was not fome ufurpation formerly, during the
invafion of the *Barbarians* upon *Italy*, and efpecially in the time of *Attila*, when our fore-fa-
thers left their towns, and agreed to bury all
the gold they had at the bottom of wells,
which they could never find out again, becaufe fire, defolation, and death, had deftroy'd
all the marks of their former habitations. Their
defcendants remember'd very well that there
were treafures hidden ; but not knowing
where, they were fo wife for many ages, that
when they fold one another a houfe, or land,
they took care to infert in the deed of fale

*   thefe

---

* Father *Paul* afterwards compos'd three treatifes upon this fubject, which
make a part of the fixth Tome of his works.

these words, *salvo jure putei*, i. e. *saving what's in the well*; by which the seller reserved to himself all his right to all the great treasure that might, by good luck, be found out one time or other in such house or field. This has been the custom for so many hundred years, that if such treasure were to be found now, it would be impossible to know the true owner of it, because every seller had the precaution to stipulate the same saving clause for himself; so that it would be necessary to go back to the time of *Attila*, which would be impracticable, on account of the variety of accidents that have happen'd since. Therefore it was at last agreed that the reservation should be in favour of him who was in actual possession, at the time such treasure might be found, of such field, or house where it was conceal'd; because, in things which depend on time very far back, there cannot be a better title in nature than a long and continu'd possession. Now to apply these reflections to the case in hand.

The republic is in possession of the sovereignty of the *Adriatic* sea, which all modern cosmographers, forgetting the ancient name, call the gulph of *Venice*. Whoever shall offer to dispute that sovereignty, must of necessity shew that some body had the legal domain thereof before the republic, and what right any one had to it; it must also be prov'd that such possessor never forfeited those rights, or suffer'd them to be lost. If the Pope should dispute this sovereignty with the republic, on pretence that the rivers, which run west into the gulph, come out of his dominions, the republic might justly urge the very same plea, because the rivers that fall into the gulph, from their dominions, on the eastern coast, are more, in number than those that come from the dominions of his holiness. The same pretence might also serve the king of *Spain*, because *Abruzzo* and *Apulia* lie upon the coasts of the said gulph; but his rights are confounded with those of the Pope, because those provinces are a part of the kingdom of *Naples*, which the kings of *Spain* hold as fiefs of the holy See; and certainly their rights cannot be greater than those of the direct lord of the said fiefs; consequently the pretensions of those monarchs must be inferior to those of the republic. The *Grand Turk* might as well claim the same right, upon account of *Albania* and *Epirus*; but I don't believe the Pope would join issue with that potentate, because there is such a mortal enmity betwixt them, that they study each other's destruction. Thus it has been fairly prov'd that the Pope, who makes such a sad outcry about usurpation, can produce no reason, no law, that is fit to be put in the balance with the rights of the republic. Perhaps the Pope, finding he cannot be sole lord and master of the gulph himself, would be glad

to

to fee the fovereignty of it fhared: But this is what the republic will never confent to ; for befides other reafons, that are common alfo to the holy See, they have the right of poffeffion almoft time out of mind ; and moreover, if the difemboguing of rivers into the gulph gave any right to the fovereignty of it, the *Turk* muft alfo come in for his fhare. This poffeffion, in its own nature, added to many other very important circumftances, extreamly fortifies the republic's right of fovereignty over the gulph.

When the republic firft took the advantage, of this fovereignty, 'tis hardly to be fuppos'd that fo many princes, as are concern'd in that See, would have put up with it fo filently, if at that very time they had not been convinc'd of the *Venetians* right to that poffeffion. For then it had been liable to be call'd in queftion as new, and no doubt it had been protefted againft, becaufe it was eafy to forefee that time would have corroborated their pretenfion. But 'tis certain that all the princes concern'd to fpeak were filent, as being convinc'd they had nothing to fay againft it.

Wherefoever the conftitutions of *Juftinian* are receiv'd, this maxim of law is conftantly obferv'd, *Quæ in nullius bonis funt, fiunt occupantis,* i. e. *Thofe things which belong to no body in particular, become the property of the poffeffor.* Now, I fay, there are two ways by which a thing may be faid to be-

long

long to no body; the firft, when it never had an owner; as the beafts in the woods, the fifh in the fea, and the birds in the air; which whoever takes in a public place, becomes the legal poffeffor of; the fecond, not becaufe it never had an owner, but when its owner has long neglected it, and not defended it as he ought, nor reclaim'd it after its falling into other hands. This defertion confider'd after fuch a term of time, longer, or fhorter, according to the importance of the thing, gives reafon to think that the mafter has voluntarily given up his property therein. I will give an inftance of this from the Scriptures. *Ruth* gather'd up the ears of corn, which the reapers had left in the field: Their mafter *Booz* faw, and permitted her, which made her the legal proprietor of all the fheaves fhe had glean'd, tho' they were before the property of *Booz*, in whofe fields they were fown and grew, but efcap'd the reaper's fickle.

Upon this principle I fhall now propofe a dilemma, taken both from the divine law, and thofe of the empire. Either the gulph had never an owner, and in this cafe the republic might juftly take it into their poffeffion, or elfe it depended on fome one or other who abandon'd it; and in this cafe too the republic was in the right to take it to themfelves; becaufe the former proprietor, whoever he was, did, by virtue of fuch abandoning it, lofe, or give up his right. Now let us fee which, of
all

all the chriftian princes of our time, might
have been anciently lord of this gulph, and by
that means we fhall know whether he has actually abandon'd it.   If the Pope pretends to the
ancient fovereignty of it, by reafon of his territories lying upon it, I have already obferv'd
that the republic has more land contiguous to
it than he; befides, that the being lord of the
fhore, does not neceffarily imply being lord of
the fea too ; for how many private men are
there who have lands which form the banks of
rivers, and yet have nothing to do with the
ftream ? the fame objection will hold alfo a-
gainft *Spain*, not only on account of the vici-
nity of its territories to the gulph; but becaufe it holds thofe territories as fiefs, and not
by the title of direct fovereignty. If we were
alfo to mention the *Turk*, which is really needlefs, the beft we could fay, would make for
the advantage of the republic; for the *Turk*,
tho' barbarity and rapine are his profeffion, has
no view to the gulph, being convinc'd that
the republic has the beft right to it.   We infer therefore upon the whole, that the Pope
can plead no right to the gulph, upon account of the rivers in his dominions that have
their mouths in it.   This being demonftrated,
what will the court of *Rome* fay next ? why
undoubtedly they will have recourfe to the
donations of the emperor *Conftantine*, and the
countefs *Mathilda*, or *Maud* (of *Tufcany*.)
But let them fay, for argument-fake, that thefe

dona-

donations transferred all the rights, which the emperor had over the gulph, to the holy See, and that as at that time there was no such thing in nature as the republic of *Venice*, the Pope was left sole lord and master of the gulph. I answer, that donations resemble indulgences, which, in the opinion even of the court of *Rome, tantum valent quantum sonant.* If either of these celebrated donations makes express mention of the gulph, it follows of consequence that the Pope would have been in possession of it at that time ; but if they do not mention it, 'tis as plain a consequence that he has no pretence to it ; we find, every day almost, that one man gives another the crop of his land, when 'tis not to be suppos'd he means to give him his land into the bargain, but only the power of gathering in the product of it. Neither is there any more reason for claiming things on the score of being appendages, when those same appendages are of little less importance than the principal, if not altogether equal to it. A person who has a house given him, or bequeath'd to him by will, would make himself very ridiculous to lay claim to the goods also therein contain'd; because, if the donor, or testator, had so intended it, he would not have fail'd to express that condition, especially since it often happens that the furniture is worth more than the house itself. A stout *Corsair* desir'd leave of the governor of a maritime place to enter his port, and stay there

till

till next day. The governor confented ; but when he was got in, he pretended he'd tarry there for good and all, and that the port was, by that piece of complaifance, yielded to him. What we have faid, is only to fhew that donation cannot have this effect ; but fuppofing, for once, that it did, the Pope would ftill have loft his right exactly in the fame manner as the emperor of the eaft has loft his ; for as to the emperor of the weft, he never pretended to it. Now the emperor of the eaft loft his, either by voluntary defertion of the gulph, or by his inability, or neglect to defend or keep it ; from whence it follows, that the republic has poffeffion on this account, by the legal right of the firft poffeffor. It was about the year of our redemption 300, that *Conftantine* was baptiz'd ; and foon after he tranflated the feat of the empire to *Byzantium*, to which term is referred the grant he made to the Pope of the provinces, which form'd the terreftrial dominions of the Church. From the 3d century, to the end of the 8th, the Popes receiv'd from *Conftantine's* fucceffors, one while favours and privileges, another while outrages and imprifonment ; and as the authority and credit of the emperors in *Italy* declin'd every day more and more, that country was fometimes tyranniz'd over by the *Lombards*, and at other times ranfack'd by the *Goths* ; during which, the *Adriatic*-fea was always infefted by the *Corfairs*. The emperor abandoning the defence

Y 4

fence

fence of thofe countries, partly by his own inclination, and partly for want of ability to protect them, the Pope was often oblig'd to have recourfe to the *French*; fo that at length *Stephen* III. going to *France* in perfon, did there obtain fuccour againft the *Lombards*. From that time, the maritime forces of the *Venetian* republic began to be formidable; for 'tis recorded in the annals of *Venice*, that in 728, at the intreaty of the emperor *Juſtin*, and Pope *Gregory*, the *Venetians* forc'd the nephew of the king of the *Lombards* to retire with his garrifon from *Ravenna*, and reſtor'd that city, *bona fide*, to the jurifdiction of the *Exarch*. This event proves that then the emperor had but few fhips in the gulph, if he had any at all; that the Pope had none neither, and that both the one and the other were oblig'd to implore the naval affiftance of the *Venetians*.

Another inftance of their power is as follows: *Charles* I. king of *France*, who was afterwards call'd *Charlemagne*, or *Charles the Great*, having a mind to befiege *Pavia*, the republic, in 773, fent him a good fquadron of armed barks, which pafs'd thro' *Teſino* to the *Milaneze*. This great king was fuch a hearty friend to the interefts of the Popes, that as he deferv'd, fo he receiv'd the greateft favour that ever was conferred by the holy See, *viz.* the privilege granted by *Adrian*, and confirm'd in a Council of 153 bifhops, whom the faid Pope affembled at *Rome* for that very purpofe, by

which

which grant the kings of *France* were put in
poffeffion of a right to elect all future Popes ;
a privilege fo glorious, that it dazzled the eyes
of *Lewis, Charlemain's* fon, to that degree,
that he renounc'd it in the reign of Pope *Paf-
chal,* reftoring the election to its ancient channel, on condition, that when the Pope elect
was confecrated, or rather crown'd, he fhould
fend embaffadors to *France* to confirm the
peace.

At length, in the year 800, Pope *Leo* confidering the daily declenfion of the eaftern empire, and how much injury the papacy fuffer'd
by it, becaufe *Italy* was in a manner abandon'd ; he had the courage to crown his trufty
fiiend *Charles the Great,* with the title of *Roman* Emperor, in St. *Peter's* Church at *Rome,*
exclufive of the then *Greek* emperor *Conftantine,* Son of *Ireneus* ; who was forc'd to bear
the injury with patience, becaufe he was not
in a capacity to refent it ; which is a further
proof that at that time the *Adriatic*-fea, or
gulph, was at the mercy of the *Corfairs,* and
become the eafy prey of the ftrongeft power,
in which number the republic of *Venice* had
fhewn, by paft experience, it might juftly be
reckon'd. Not long after, *Conftantine* fell a
facrifice to the fedition of his fubjects, and
Niceforus fucceeding him, occafion'd that famous divifion of the empire into eaftern and
weftern, in the year 802 ; to which three fovereigns confented, all from different motives.
The

The Pope, to give a fanction in fome meafure to his right of crowning the emperors, which he had affum'd in the perfon of *Charlemain,* without any authority ; *Charlemain,* to give a fanction to his new poffeffion, which he had juft acquir'd, without any right ; and *Niceforus,* to diminifh the number of his enemies ; for he found, that having not 'the power in his own hands, he could not revenge the affronts he had receiv'd, and was but too fenfible that his own advancement was merely owing to violence. A peace was therefore patch'd up between thefe, two emperors, by the mediation of the Pope, after having divided the whole chriftian world, and affign'd each of them his fhare thereof, leaving only three dutchies exempt from fuch fubjection, *viz.* thofe of *Rome, Benevento,* and *Venice ;* and moreover, the embaffadors of thofe two emperors declar'd, that the *Venetians* fhould enjoy entire liberty under their own Laws. To the eaftern emperor, *Niceforus,* were affign'd in *Italy, Apulia, Calabria, Sicily,* and the dutchy of *Naples,* as far as *Gaeta ;* and all the reft of *Italy* was *Charlemain's* portion, as emperor of the weft.

Thus I have perform'd the promife I made, to prove that *Conftantine's* donation gave the Pope no manner of right over the gulph, and that, if it had, the then Pope yielded it up, by confenting to the divifion of the empire, and by approving the fettled limits thereof, as already

already mention'd; for the emperor of the eaſt
could never have made himſelf maſter of *Apulia* by force of arms, if the gulph, thro' which
he muſt paſs directly from *Conſtantinople* to *Apulia,* had belong'd to the Pope. I ſay nothing
of *Sicily, Calabria,* and the dutchy of *Naples,*
tho' they are territories that lie not far from
Apulia, becauſe they are ſituate upon the
lower, commonly call'd the *Tyrrhenian,* or *Me-
diterranean* ſea. Add to this, that the then
Pope *Leo* would not have been ſilent, and ſuffer'd thoſe limits to be aſſign'd thus, without
diſputing it, if he had but ſo much as thought
that the ſame was any prejudice to his property; ſo far from this, he was the very man that
negociated the whole affair; for *Niceforus* had
his hands too full at home, by reaſon of violent inteſtine quarrels, to think of carrying his
arms into *Italy.* We may well conclude therefore from this Pope's ſilence, that he was per-
ſuaded he had no reaſon to complain of harm
done him, for, in ſhort, he never had any naval force in the *Adriatic* ſea.

Admit therefore, according to the remarks
already made, that there's not the leaſt mention of the gulph in *Conſtantine*'s donation, it
will follow very clearly that the Pope has no
right to it, eſpecially ſince, as we have already
ſhewn, his poſſeſſion of rivers that run into
it, ſignify nothing to the purpoſe.

After

After *Conſtantine's* time, the forces of the republic increaſed every day, ſo that in the year 805, they were ſtrong enough to ruin the army of *Pepin,* who was ſo officiouſly obſequious to the ſolicitation of *Fortunatus,* biſhop of *Grado,* that he dar'd to ſurprize *Chiozza,* and even to attack the city of *Venice* from its lakes, where he was routed ; which ſoon produc'd a treaty of peace with the republic, whoſe bravery, on that occaſion, gained them a great deal of glory.

In 828, the republic gave farther proofs of their valour by ſea. The *Moors* of *Africa,* after having landed in *Tuſcany,* and made an inroad as far as to *Rome,* where they plunder'd the Church of St. *Peter* and *Paul,* without the walls, went on board again, and fell upon *Sicily,* which was a dependency of the *Greek* empire. But the *Venetians* diſpatch'd a fleet into thoſe ſeas, which made the affrighted *Africans* retire ; and thus they preſerv'd that iſland to their friend and ally the emperor of the eaſt. I do not mention theſe things to celebrate the glory of the moſt ſerene republic, this being neither a proper time nor place for it ; but only to convince the reader, that both the *Greeks* and *Italians* were then quite deſtitute of naval forces, while thoſe of the republic were, on many accounts, formidable. It follows therefore from thence, that the gulph, being abandon'd by the *Greeks,* was defended only by the arms of the *Venetians,*
who

who by confequence were very properly mafters of it, as has been prov'd by demonftration as clear as any in the mathematics.

About the year of our Saviour 1000, the
people of *Iftria* being quite weary of obeying
a Prince who could not, nor would not defend them, and being alfo expos'd to the continual incurfions and piracies of thofe of *Na-
ranto*, fent embaffadors to *Venice* to offer their
fubmiffion to the republic ; accordingly they
were receiv'd as good fubjects, and the then
doge, *Peter Urceolus*, pafs'd into *Iftria*, at the
head of an army, to take poffeffion of their
country, threatning the *Narantines* with utter
deftruction if they continu'd their incurfions.
Upon this they comply'd, and begged peace,
which was granted them ; and thereupon, of
their own accord, they yielded up all their
pretenfions to the gulph   The republic had
not held their new dominions long before they
were difturbed ; for in 1059 *Zara* revolted at
the inftigation of the king of *Hungary*, fo that
there was a neceffity of applying to force, for
the recovery of what was firft obtain'd by a
voluntary furrender ; and this the doge, *Dominicus Contarini*, effected accordingly, fword
in hand.

Twenty years after, that is to fay, in 1079,
Robert de Guife, being affifted by the *Normans*,
attempted to drive the *Greeks* out of *Tarentum*,
having already taken *Otranto* ; but the *Venetians* confederating with another *Niceforus*
(*Botaniates*)

(*Botaniates*) gave him battle, and defeated him, so that he got nothing at all by his invasion. If the *Greek* emperors had thought the republic's pretensions to the sovereignty of the gulph an injury to them, they would not have call'd upon the *Venetians* so often for their assistance, as their good friends and allies. But as *Tacitus* well observ'd, that a new servant is commonly mark'd out for the sport of the rest of the domestics, the same thing is true of princes, the newest of whom is sure to be the butt of the others jealousy, or hatred. The king of *Hungary* could not bear the *Venetians*, his new neighbours in *Dalmatia*; therefore he push'd on the *Zarians* to a second revolt, which provok'd the republic to take arms again, and under the conduct of the doge, *Ordelafo Faliero*, in 1117, they were reduc'd to their good behaviour.

In the year 1123, the republic being as zealous, as any christian prince whatsoever for the propagation of the faith, and to give testimonies of their piety, sent towards the conquest of the holy land a strong fleet of three hundred ships, commanded by the doge *Dominicus Michael*, who caus'd the siege of *Jaffa* to be rais'd, and conquer'd *Tyre*; of which city the other christian princes, their allies, yielded them one third of the domain, as an acknowledgment of their service. The doge being at that juncture in want of money, because he was so long absent, had recourse to

an

an expedient to coin money of leather, which every one took readily upon his credit ; and he was no fooner return'd home but he call'd it all in, paying the full value in gold and fil-ver ; and to this day, the defcendants of that illuftrious general bear the faid leather coin in their arms, in memory of the faid event.

This expedition lafting above two years, the king of *Hungary* gave a plain proof of his ill intentions towards the republic, by enga-ging the *Greek* emperor to forgoe the many obligations he had to the *Venetians*, and to join with him in invading their dominions in *Dalmatia*. Accordingly they made a fudden incurfion, and prefently took in *Zara*, *Spalato*, and *Trau*. Upon this the doge *Michael* was re-call'd with all fpeed from *Syria*, and he came time enough to give fuch a check to the empe-ror, that he was able neither to purfue his con-quefts, nor to hinder the doge from making juft reprifals for the lofs which the republic had fuffer'd, and from recovering all that the ene-my had taken. The doge return'd from this expedition crown'd with laurels, and every one was then convinc'd that the moft ferene repub-lic was in a condition much rather to be fear'd by their enemies than defpis'd. Tho' the reci-tal of thefe events may feem foreign to the fubject in hand, yet they ferve to prove, that as the republic was in poffeffion of the fovereign-ty of the gulph fo long ago, fo they have fince
been

been in a condition to maintain that sovereignty, and to confirm it more and more.

When the empire of the east changed hands, the confequence of it was no more than what we fee happens every day. *Manuel Comnenus* was as great a friend to the republic as his predeceffors were enemies ; and the former hatred betwixt the two dominions was fucceeded by a ftrict alliance, with a view to oppofe the invafion of *Roger* II. who not only took *Sicily* from the *Greeks*, but furpriz'd *Corfu, Corinth, Thebes,* and *Negropont.* The doge, *Peter Polani,* join'd the forces of the republic to thofe of the *Greeks* in 1149, and gave fuch a blow to *Roger's* fleet, that after the lofs of twenty of his gallies, he had no way to get off but by flight ; and in the heat of the victory the doge reconquered for the emperor all the country which his enemy had taken from him in the *Levant.*

But a little time made it fully appear that nothing is more flippery, or lefs to be depended on, than the friendfhip of princes. Tho' the emperors of the weft certainly ow'd the origin of their dignity to the Popes alone, yet in procefs of time, and by the change of interefts and fentiments, they became the Popes fharpeft perfecutors. The great fchifm began during the pontificate of *Alexander* III. who was the true Pope, having been canonically elected, and invefted in the holy fee by a greater majority of the cardinals than was neceffary ;

ceſſary; for only three of the conclave-voted
for *Victor*; who, tho' he had no right to the
popedom, for want of friends and ſuffrages;
yet preſum'd to take the name of Pope, and
had recourſe to the emperor *Frederic Barba-
roſſa*; whom he made the judge of his title:
Alexander made no ſcruple to reject the authority of the ſaid tribunal; and *Frederic*, without hearing him, paſs'd a decree in the Anti-
pope's favour, contrary both to order and the
merits of the cauſe; contrary to order, in that
Frederic made himſelf a judge in a cauſe which
was not within the cognizance of the ſecular
power; contrary to right, for that he gave the
cauſe in favour of an apoſtate. *Alexander*
therefore, juſtly provok'd at this outrage, fulminated the *major* excommunication againſt
both. *Frederic* was as hot as the other, and
declar'd himſelf openly the enemy, and perſe-
cutor of Pope *Alexander*, being fully reſolv'd
to take that ſurprizing vengeance, which was
the ſource of all the grievances, with which chriſtendom was afterwards oppreſs'd: *Alexander*
being frightned with the emperor's blunt menace, ſtole privately out of *Rome*, and retir'd
to *Venice*; where he was for ſome time *incog.*
But the divine providence making him known,
he was accoſted with the honours due to him;
and not only ſo, but aſſur'd that he ſhould enjoy all the privileges of a ſanctuary; and command what ſuccours he pleas'd from the republic. Accordingly the doge *Ziani* ſoon after

[PART II.] Z pre

put to fea with a fleet of thirty galleys, in queft of that of the emperor ; and the Pope having accompany'd him to his fhip, blefs'd him, and with his own hands gave him the general's battoon, not after the manner of the cuftomary prefents which the Popes are us'd to make to princes that deferve well of the holy See, nor as a prefage of his future victory, but as a teftimony and token of the *Venetians* fovereignty over the gulph. He fail'd, found out his enemy, fought, and routed him in the fea of *Iftria,* near *Albona,* where the people obferve the anniverfary of the victory, even to this day. The imperial army was quite ruin'd, and *Otho,* the rebel emperor's fon, taken prifoner. Thus the illuftrious doge revenged two injuries at one and the fame time, *viz.* the perfecution rais'd againft the Pope, and the difturbing of the *Venetians* navigation in the gulph ; and at his return to *Venice,* the Pope receiv'd him with all imaginable refpect, and greeting him with a world of joy, made ufe of thefe expreffions *Salve, dominator maris, & accipe annulum aureum, & fingulis annis, in die afcenfionis domini, defponfabis mare, ficuti vir mulierem.* i. e. *Hail, lord of the fea, and take a gold ring, with which every year, upon the day of our lord and faviour's afcenfion, thou fhalt marry the fea as a man doth a woman.*

Some would infer from thefe words, that the republic holds the fovereignty of the gulph only from an indulto of the Pope; but they are

are quite miftaken; firft, becaufe the Pope could not grant what he had not to give, or difpofe of any thing to which he never pretended any title. Secondly, thefe words, confider'd with refpect to fovereignty, are only fpoke in a fenfe declaratory, and not conftituent, juft as when a perfon, faluting a prince, gives him the title of lord or king, whereby he owns, but does not inveft him with that dignity. In fhort, if thofe terms of fpeaking had included a grant, the Pope muft neceffarily have exprefs'd the particular fea of which he gave him the fovereignty, for otherwife the general expreffion of *dominator maris* would fignify the dominion of all the feas upon the face of the globe; which would be perfectly ridiculous, and as much as to fay that the Pope thought himfelf qualify'd to difpofe of the fovereignty of the whole ocean. But confidering the holy father's expreffion, as we explain it, in a declaratory fenfe, he was not under a neceffity to explain himfelf more particularly, when he faluted the doge with the title of *lord of the fea*, becaufe this naturally referred to a thing known of itfelf, *viz.* to that fea of which every body had before own'd the doge for lord and fovereign. The forms of expreffion which the court of *Rome* make ufe of in their indulto's are clear and ftrong, *damus, concedimus, indulgemus*, and carry no fuch fuppofition in them as is couched under the Pope's compliment to the doge. Therefore all that looks

like

like conceſſion in this whole affair, is the ceremony of marrying the ſea, and the gift of the ring; in which he diſplays his authority, to prevent this *Venetian* ceremony from being treated ever after as ſuperſtition, or an abuſe of the ſacrament; for which reaſon the Pope, in this reſpect, uſes a term conſtituent, and not declaratory, *deſponſabis mare ſicuti vir mulierem,* i. e. *thou ſhalt marry;* but he does not ſay, *dominaberis mari,* i. e. *thou ſhalt govern the ſea.* Abſolute authority, or dominion, does not follow from that marriage; for other kings do not marry their dominions, yet they poſſeſs them. The doge does not marry *Venice,* yet he is maſter of it; and the Pope marries neither *Rome,* nor the papal ſee, yet he is the lawful lord of both; ſo that we muſt keep to the allegory the Pope made uſe of, *deſponſabis mare ſicuti vir mulierem.* The Pope with all his might cannot marry two parties that are averſe to matrimony; he may, 'tis true, celebrate the ſacrament of marriage, but 'tis abſolutely neceſſary that the conſent of the parties be firſt had, otherwiſe the marriage, tho' ſolemniz'd by the Pope himſelf, cannot ſtand good. Thus in the preſent caſe the Pope has declar'd that the republic of *Venice* may challenge the ſame authority over the gulph, as the husband may over his own wife; but the ſovereignty ſubſiſted before this declaration of it, in the very ſame manner as conſent ought to precede the tying of the marriage-knot.

To

To return to our fubject. This rout cool'd the haughty emperor's courage; but I know not whether he was vanquifh'd more by the *Venetians* frank carriage to him, or by the fortune of their arms. However it was, he yielded to the perfuafions of his fon, who was fent home upon his parole, accompany'd with twelve *Venetian* noblemen, confented to a treaty, and went to *Venice* to make his peace with the Pope, who, after he had profefs'd his hearty repentance of his crime, and kifs'd the holy father's feet, gave him his bleffing; fo that he was reftor'd at the fame time both to the good graces of the common father of the faithful, and to his imperial prerogatives, which he had forfeited by his offence.

After a fhort ftay at *Venice*, during which, thofe great perfonages had frefh teftimonies of the republic's liberality, becaufe they were treated with all the ftate due to their high rank, thofe three princes, the Pope, the emperor, and the doge, emulating each other in courtefy, refolv'd at length to go to *Ancona* on board the *Venetian* fleet, in order to reconduct the holy father to his See, and to give reciprocal proofs of a perfect reconciliation. The people, his faithful fubjects, came to receive them on the fhore with a thoufand bleffings, and brought drums, banners, chairs, canopies, and flambeaus; all which the grateful Pope made a prefent of to the doge, as a teftimony of his obligation to the republic; and the

doges,

doges, his succeffors, ufe them to this day on the moft folemn occafions. This ftory confirms the proofs I have already brought of the power and prerogatives of the republic over the gulph, becaufe in the year 1159 they were in a condition to reftore a Pope to his See, to vanquifh an emperor, and to take revenge for an infult made upon them in the poffeffion of the faid fea.

Thus we are come down to the year 1200, about which time the chriftian princes made a formidable crufado, for the conqueft of the holy fepulchre. The republic very readily contributed not only their quota, according to treaty, but much more ; fo that the *French, Flemifh,* and *Italian* princes, who were the chief parties in that holy war, agreed to begin firft with the reduction of *Zara,* thereby to compenfate the republic for their efforts and credit in the alliance. This was done with all the eafe in the world, and the doge *Dandalo,* who commanded the *Venetian* forces in perfon, recover'd poffeffion of that rebellious town. While thefe great armies were in *Dalmatia,* the princes of the holy league comply'd with the earneft folicitations of young *Alexis,* then emperor of *Conftantinople,* who, after a conference with his old friend the doge, was admitted into an alliance with thofe generous princes, who lent him their forces to re-eftablifh him on the throne, from which his rebellious fubjects had unjuft'y depos'd him , and, as an acknowledge-
ment

ment of this favour, he propos'd several advantageous conditions to them ; the chief of
which was, that as soon as he was restor'd, he
should gain the consent of the *Greek* Church
to own the superiority of the *Latin*. This
proposal seem'd of such importance to all those
princes, that they agreed among themselves to
suspend their voyage to *Palæstina*, and bend
their whole force towards the re-establishment
of *Alexis*. Therefore they immediately tack'd
about to *Constantinople*, and so happily succeed-
ed by their arms and councils, that the rebels
were driven out, and their friend *Alexis* restor'd to the empire ; but they no sooner quit-
ted the *Bosphorus*, than the traitor *Marsufus* as-
sassinated his lawful prince, and arrogantly
seiz'd the imperial throne. This infamous outrage was the reason that the princes of the holy league generously put off their voyage to
another time, being resolv'd to take the most
notable revenge ; the rather, because they
esteem'd it as an insult partly upon themselves; considering the friendship they had contracted with the unhappy *Alexis*, of which
they had given signal proofs, by restoring him
to his dignity They conquer'd the rebels a
second time, and punish'd their obstinacy by
putting the villain *Marsufus* to death. The next
thing to be done, then, was to look out for
a new emperor ; they consider'd that the families of the ancient emperors were quite ex-
tinct, and that on the other hand there was no

trusting

trusting to any one of the *Greeks*, notwithstanding that in gratitude for their enthroning
him, he might enter into an advantageous alliance with them : Therefore they resolv'd at
last to chuse one of their own number, to the
end that they might be always sure of a constant friend to requite them for the assistance
of their arms, and for the dangers to which
they expos'd themselves. 'In order to make
this election, they deputed fifteen persons, partly clergymen, partly laymen ; some of whom
were princes, others private persons, but all
qualify'd by some eminent talents or other for
the employment they were put upon. Of this
number were the doge *Dandalo,* and five
Venetian nobles. Here now the moderation
of the *Venetians* is exceedingly remarkable, because, if they had been pleas'd to give themselves any trouble in the election, they might
have got the imperial dignity into their own
clutches ; having, besides a strong army at hand,
six voices that they were sure of to a man,
while the other candidates, being disunited by
different interests, countries, and genius's, were
not in a condition to oppose their party : But
their prudence prevail'd over all other considerations ; for those illustrious personages wisely
consider'd how much it would change the ari-
stocratical constitution of the republic, if one
of their subjects should be rais'd to the imperial dignity, which was the first both in rank
and time. This consideration made them sa-

crifice

crifice all their private interests to the public
welfare, and to concur readily in the election
of *Baldwin,* count of *Flanders,* who, having
also the suffrages of the other electors, was,
without any difficulty, plac'd on the throne;
but the republic had the honour to name the
patriarch of *Greece,* who was *Thomas Moro-
sini.* They were possess'd at that time of no
less than three eighths of the empire of *Roma-
nia* ; and therefore to reward several *Venetians,* who had contributed with their swords
and purses to this expedition, they gave them
several islands in fief. Among these feuda-
tories of the doge of *Venice,* was *Rabano Dalle
Careeri,* a *Veronese,* who had the isle of *Negropont* granted to him, as a reward for the vast
assistance he gave to the republic. Now, who
can dispute the republic's just acquisition of
the sovereignty of the gulph, founded on so
many titles, considering that, long before this,
they were masters of three eighths of the
eastern empire, had as much jurisdiction in the
city of *Constantinople* itself, as the *French* and
the new *Flemish* emperor, and had so many
countries at their disposal, that they thought
fit to ease their hands of part of them by erect-
ing them into fiefs? Thus were we to trace
the sovereignty of the gulph back to re-
motest antiquity, we shall find that at the very
beginning it did not belong to the Pope, because
the Popes had no temporal domain for a mark
of their dignity, but what some generous lay-
princes

princes were pleas'd in courtefy to give them ; the firft of whom, for dignity, power, and antiquity, was *Conftantine the Great.* From *Julius Cæfar* to *Nicephorus,* there was but this one emperor of the univerfe ; and he, not being in a condition to manage and defend that empire by himfelf, confented to divide it. And if the *Turk* had not feiz'd fo great a part of chriftendom, the emperor of *Conftantinople* would have been mafter at this day of the greateft part of our hemifphere, *Italy* efpecially. Therefore none but that emperor would have a right in fuch quality to quarrel with the republic, on pretence of their ufurpation of the gulph. And fuppofing that the divifion of the empire ftill fubfifted, then the emperor of the eaft would be the only perfon concern'd to queftion their right and title to the gulph, becaufe it would be included in his fhare, as has already been fhewn. If, on the other hand, the poffeffion of any countries remains annex'd to the feat of the empire, this controverfy will concern the *Ottoman Port,* as fovereign of the imperial city, and of the far greateft part of that empire. But fuppofe the *Turk* were to improve his rights not by violence, but by law, it would then be eafy to convince him that he has no right, by proving to him how many times the ancient emperors loft it by abandoning it, and how long the republic has been in quiet poffeffion of it. Moreover, we may alledge the acquifition which the republic made of

three

three eighths of the empire, and of part of the imperial city; therefore 'tis not to be imagin'd but the *Venetians* were already absolute sovereigns of that sea which washes the city of *Venice*; because, if they had not, they would surely have taken that opportunity to have plac'd the said sovereignty to account in that part which was to be assign'd to them.

When *Alexander the Great* conquer'd *Darius*, he soon made himself master of the best part of his dominions; and *Darius* being deprefs'd by the valour and fortune of so great a man, sent his ambassadors to him to sue for peace, offering him, on that condition, all the countries he had conquer'd to that day. *Alexander* smil'd at the offer, and said, that if *Darius* expected a peace, he must yield him up great part of his own dominions; because whatever he (*Alexander*) was master of before, ought not now to be plac'd to his account as conqueror. Therefore I conclude, that as formerly the gulph made a part of the empire, consider'd either before or after its division, it was always under the jurisdiction of *Constantinople*; now the republic having acquir'd the half of that city, and little less than half of the dominions depending on it, can it be imagin'd that the gulph, which bounds on those dominions, was not included in that part of the empire which they then acquir'd?

The

The titles upon which the republic found their right of fovereignty over the gulph are fo many, and fo lawful, that if the fame were to be try'd, like the titles of private men, before a fcrupulous judge, they would infallibly carry their caufe, tho' the Pope fhould be on the other fide of the queftion, for this reafon only that I am now going to mention, which I look upon as *argumentum ad hominem,* and conformable to the ecclefiaftical axioms. The Council of *Trent, Seff.* 25. *cap.* 9. ordains, that if any perfons be fo rafh as to appropriate to themfelves the dependency of ecclefiaftical benefices, by pretending to the right of patronage over them,* " the juftification of fuch
" right fhall be taken from foundation or do-
" nation, or prov'd by fome authentic act, or
" by a great number of prefentations made at
" all times; mean while, this muft be under-
" ftood of private perfons; for as to commu-
" nities, or univerfities, which may be more
" eafily fufpected to have ufurp'd this right,
" there muft be more exact proof ftill; for
" that of time immemorial will not avail, if
" it be not verify'd by prefentations, repeated
" without interruption, for the fpace of, at
" leaft, fifty years." Thefe are the words of
the Council, upon which I argue thus : If the
canon will juftify a title ufurp'd by a commu-
nity,

---

* M. *Amelot's* Tranflation of the Council of *Trent* is that which is here follow ed.

nity, who of themfelves are very liable to be
fufpected of ufurpation, when the ufurper has
maintain'd his ufurpation for fifty years together over eftates, and benefices purely ecclefiaftical, who is the filly wretch that will dare
be fo infolent as to queftion the right of the republic, who have been in poffeffion not of an
ecclefiaftic, but of a fecular eftate, I will not
fay for fifty, but for five hundred, nay, twice
five hundred years ? Let them anfwer this if
they can. The fame Council in the fame Seffion, *cap.* 19. decrees, * that if a regular monk
would fain be excus'd from his vows, on pretence that he took the habit on him, and made
the ufual profeffion by force, or alledges any
other defect, his complaints fhall not be heard
after the expiration of this † term. Now what
I infer from it is, that if, in the validity of a
vow, on the obfervance, or non-obfervance of
which depends eternal falvation, or damnation,
a fpace of time fhall make a thing which is invalid deteftable and facrilegious, fuch as the
violence in the act of embracing a monaftic
life, not only to become a canonical obligation,
but alfo to have the force of binding us to God
(as the canons exprefs it) why fhould not time
alfo

* Tho' there's a palpable fault here in the *Italian* copy, yet it was not
thought fit to vary from it, that the editor might not be charg'd with having
introduc'd corrections of his own head ; but whoever examins the hiftory of the
Council, will find that 'tis the 19th article of the fift chapter of the 25th
Seffion, which is call'd, *The Decree of the Reformation*
† By this 'tis plain that the whole period has been ill tranfcrib'd, for the decree of the Council fays, *The term of five years after his profeffion.*

alfo be capable of confirming the gulph's fubjection to the republic, efpecially fince there
have been no valid objections againft it for a
thoufand years paft ?

I fhould here fet bounds to this difcourfe;
but perhaps fome man of wit will tell me, that
I am very much in the wrong to prove the republic's poffeffion of the *Adriatic* fea by force
of arguments and reafons, fince they have
prov'd the faid right more than once by the
thunder of their canon.   I own that's the common ftyle of princes; but to the glory of the
republic it muft be acknowledg'd, that they give
free liberty for difputing even thofe prerogatives of which they are moft tender, which is
one very good fign of the juftice of their
rights.

If I were call'd upon to name any prince, I
believe I might venture to fay there's not one
upon earth that can produce legal proofs of his
dominion, and that the only title of all fovereigns is immemorial poffeffion ; for ancient
poffeffion is a proof that there have been fufficient forces to maintain that poffeffion, and
forces are the beft arguments that a fovereign
can give of the validity of his rights.   'Tis
poffible there may be fome princes in the world
that enjoy their eftates *bona fide*, which indeed
is the cafe of all the chriftian princes of our
days, who poffefs theirs by right of fief, by donation, or by inheritance ; neverthelefs, if
their eftates were to be traced back to their
origin,

origin, they would appear to have been gotten by ufurpation.

A learned genealogift offer'd his fervice to a certain king to draw a genealogical tree of his family. He demonftrated that the firft king of his royal family was the fon of a duke, he the fon of a prince, the prince the fon of a marquifs, the marquifs the fon of a count; and fo on; but the king tore his draught in pieces, and forbad him to raife his tree any higher, faying, he feared that if he went on, he would come at laft to a peafant. Every man by nature is born free, and would be fo always, if the civil law did not put him under a reftraint; for the divine law had never fet a king over a people, if they themfelves had not defir'd him. If one were nicely to fcrutinize into the Pope's temporal fovereignty, one would oblige him in the firft place to fhew the authentic inftrument of *Conftantine*'s donation. Undoubtedly 'tis either quite decay'd by time, or loft by fome other accident; but fuppofe it could be produc'd, one fhould then examine the contents of it, and fee whether the donor was legally poffefs'd of what he gave; and if fo, whether the thing granted was capable of being alienated; for all the dominions which a king is mafter of are not alienable at his will and pleafure. But all this would not avail to vindicate the Pope from ufurpation. *Conftantine* held his dominions by no other right than as fucceffor to *Julius Cæfar*, and the latter poffeffed

feffed

ſeſſed them only as the repreſentative of the *Roman* republic, his country, of which he aſpired to be the ſovereign, and not the ſubject. In fine, the *Roman* republic was nothing at the beginning but the ſpoils of *Latium*, and afterwards of the reſt of the world. But it being in vain to trace royal power ſo far back as to its primary ſource, I ſhall conclude with the words of *Eccleſiaſtes*: *I, the preacher, was king over* Iſrael *in* Jeruſalem, *and I gave my heart to ſeek and ſearch out by wiſdom concerning all things that are done under the heaven. (This ſore travel hath* God *given to the ſons of men, to be exerciſed therewith.) I have ſeen all the works that are done under the ſun, and behold all is vanity and vexation of ſpirit.*

When *Philip* II. among many pretenders to the crown of *Portugal*, after the death of cardinal *Henry*, the laſt king, cauſed a juridical deduction of his rights to that crown to be drawn up, the *Spaniſh* civilian, who was employ'd in it, cloſed his learned diſſertation with this *nota bene*, that king *Philip*'s title would certainly have been deem'd valid, provided it had been back'd by thirty thouſand Foot, and ſix thouſand horſe.

The *Salic* law in *France*, and the national law in *England*, are look'd upon as ſacred; nevertheleſs, what are they founded on but cuſtom, and the power of their ſovereigns?

When

When a new Pope is chosen, a week hardly passes over his head but a dozen or two of prophecies are apply'd to him, which are all on a sudden found verify'd in him. Before the election, no body dreamt of 'em; but after the election, every body concludes positively from those predictions that it was so predetermined in the decrees of providence, and that they were bereaved of their senses in not discerning it before-hand. *Plato*'s opinion that man's knowledge wholly consists in his memory, is very applicable to the present case. If any one seizes the dominions of another by force, be his title ever so frivolous, yet when he has once got possession, he will find a multitude of pleas and events to justify it. Thus time, which destroys all dominions, serves as the grand basis of the rights of sovereigns. And whoever should in these days call in question the rights of the Pope, the emperor and other kings, because they cannot prove them *ab origine*, would be guilty of equal folly and impertinence. Every one knows, for instance, that the *Swissers* were formerly subjects of the house of *Burgundy*, from whom they revolted; yet, for all this, I can't think that any one would presume to dispute their liberty, because they have enjoy'd it so long with the consent of the whole world. And shall not the republic found their right of possession of the gulph on such long duration of time with equal reason?

[PART II.]   A a   When

When the prefident *Jeannin* was fent by *Henry* IV. to the *Dutch*, to perfuade them to a truce with *Philip* II. king of *Spain*, the ftates were very backward to come into it, becaufe it feem'd to them that the terms which the *Spaniards* made ufe of in the treaty did not import a fufficient acknowledgment of their being a free people ; and they concluded that, upon the very next rupture, the *Spaniards* would not fail to treat them again as rebels. The prefident reply'd, with a franknefs more than what is common to courtiers, that where the matter in debate is a houfe or land, it ought to be left to the pleading of lawyers ; but that ftates and dominions are to be difputed *vi & armis*, at the point of the fword ; and that if in time to come the *Spaniards* fhould think fit to renew the quarrel, they would not try their caufe at the bar, but in the field.

Roger, king of *Sicily*, who, by his valour and good fortune, conquer'd feveral dominions, caufed this hexameter to be engrav'd upon the plate of his fword,

Apulus & Calaber, ficulus mihi fervit & Afer;

for he thought his fword was a better proof of his rights than all the codes in chriftendom.

The fenate fent *Marius* to *Mithridates*, king of *Pontus*, to perfuade him to withdraw his troops from the lands of thofe who were allies to the *Romans*. *Marius* therefore addrefs'd
himfelf

himſelf to the king in a conciſe, but pithy oration, to this purpoſe : " *Mithridates,* ſays " he to him, if you think to do what you " liſt, you muſt firſt be ſure that the *Romans* " are not a match for you ; but till then, make " no difficulty to obey their orders."

Perhaps the champions of the court of *Rome* will accuſe me of relating theſe ſeveral paſſages of hiſtory with a view only to juſtify violence and uſurpation ; but the charge would be very unjuſt, for I have had no other Aim than to ſtate the candor and civility of our conduct in its full light, and have only done what every private man would do in his own caſe, name-ly, demonſtrated the rights of the republic by proofs and reaſons, whereas to have gone after the manner of princes, in the paths already trodden by others, might have been the ſhort-eſt and moſt effectual way. If this affair ever comes again upon the ſtage, whatever I have deliver'd cannot diminiſh the merits of the cauſe, for the caſe is in truth ſuch as I have de-monſtrated it to be.

The reader is here presented with that very bull of excommunication and interdict against the Venetians *, which is so often referred to in the foregoing treatise, and which Father* Paul *has, in both parts of it, so fully demonstrated to be both unjust and invalid.*

PAULUS PAPA V.

‘ VEnerabilibus fratribus patriarchis, archie-
‘ piscopis, & episcopis, per universum do-
‘ minium reipublicæ Venetorum constitutis, &
dilectis filiis, eorum vicariis in spiritualibus ge-
‘ neralibus,necnon universis abbatibus,prioribus,
‘ primiceriis, præpositis, archidiaconis, archipres-
‘ byteris, decanis, plebanis, & parochialium ec-
‘ clesiarum rectoribus, aliisque personis in dig-
‘ nitate ecclesiastica constitutis, in eodem domi-
‘ nio existentibus, tam secularibus quam quo-
‘ rumvis ordinum & institutorum regularibus,
‘ salutem & apostolicam benedictionem.

‘ Superioribus mensibus ad nostram, & apo-
‘ stolicæ sedis audientiam pervenit, Ducem &
‘ Senatum reipublicæ Venetorum, annis elapsis,
‘ in eorum consiliis plura ac diversa decreta,
‘ tum

' tum fedis apoftolicæ auctoritati & ecclefiafticæ
' libertati, ac immunitati contraria, tum gene-
' ralibus conciliis & facris canonibus, necnon
' Romanorum pontificum conftitutionibus re-
' pugnantia ftatuiffe.

' Et, inter cætera, fub die vigefima tertia
' menfis Maii, anni M.DCII. fumpta occâ-
' fione ex quadam lite, feu controverfia inter
' doctorem Francifcum Zabarellam ex una, &
' monachos monafterii de Praglia nuncupatos
' ordinis Sancti Benedicti, congregationis Caffi-
' nenfis, alias Sanctæ Juftinæ de Padua in dioe-
' cefi Paduana ex altera partibus vertente, in
' eorum confilio ftatuiffe, non folum ut dicti
' monachi tunc, aut deinceps ullo unquam
' tempore, actionem, per quam fub quovis ti-
' tulo, aut colore, in bonis ecclefiafticis emphi-
' teoticis, a laicis poffeffis, præferrentur, præ-
' tendere, ac etiam jure prælationis, feu confo-
' lidationis directi cum utili dominio, aut ex-
' tinctionis lineæ in prima inveftitura compre-
' henfæ, aut alia quavis caufa bonorum præ-
' dictorum proprietatem fibi vendicare minime
' poffent; fed tantummodo jus directi domi-
' nii illis præfervatum effet, verum etiam, ut
' idipfum, quoad cæteras omnes perfonas eccle-
' fiafticas, feculares & regulares, monafteria
' monialium, hofpitalia, & alia loca pia, in eo-
' rum temporali dominio exiftentia, declara-
' tum, & firmiter deliberatum cenferetur. '

' Et fub die decima Januarii M.DCIII. ad
_ fuperiora quædam confilia, ab eorum majori-

' bus, ut etiam afferebant, habita refpicientes,
' quibus cavebatur, ne quifquam, five fæcula-
' ris, five ecclefiafticus, in urbe Venetiarum,
' ecclefias, monafteria, hofpitalia, atque alias
' religiofas domos & pia loca, fine eorum fpe-
' ciali licentia, fundaret & erigeret, in confilio
' rogatorum congregatos, iterum decreviffe, ut
' id eandem in omnibus jurifdictionis eorum lo-
' cis vim obtineret, & præterea exilii, ac per-
' petui carceris, & publicationis-fundi, vendi-
' tionifque edificii contra fecus facientes, pœ-
' nam edixiffe.

'Ulterius, eofdem Ducem & Senatum, die
' vigefima fexta menfis Martii, anni, M.DCV.
' inhærentes alteri decreto, anno M.DXXXVI.
' ab eodem Senatu facto, in quo, ut afferebant,
' erat expreffe prohibitum, ne quis, fub certis
' in illo contentis pœnis, in urbe Venetiarum,
' ejufque ducatu, bona immobilia, ad pias cau-
' fas, teftamento, feu donatione inter vivos, re-
' linqueret, aut alio quovis titulo alienaret,
' five, ad earum favorem, ultra certum tunc
' expreffum tempus obligaret, (quod in illum
' ufque diem, ut ibi etiam dicebatur, ufu re-
' ceptum & obfervatum non fuerat:) non mo-
' do iterum id vetuiffe, fed expreffe etiam pro-
' hibuiffe, ne bonorum ejufmodi immobilium
' alienationes in favorem perfonarum ecclefi-
' afticarum, fine Senatus prædicti licentia fie-
' rent; ac infuper decretum ipfum, & pœnas
' in eo contentas, per univerfum eorum domi-
' nium extendiffe, & per rectores, & poteftates
' civitatum,

' civitatum, & locorum fui dominii, promul-
' gari fecifle; atque bona immobilia omnia,
' quæ contra præmifforum formam vendi, aut
' quovis modo alienari contingeret, ultra nul-
' litatis pœnam, publicari & vendi, eorumque
' pretium-inter rempublicam ipfam, magiftra-
' tum exequentem, & ejus miniftros, ipfum-
' que denunciatorem dividi mandafle, & alias,'
' prout in decretis, & mandatis Ducis, & Se-
' natus prædictorum latius dicitur contineri.

' Ac præterea, eofdem Ducem & Senatum,
' Scipionem Saracenum canonicum Vicentinum,
' & Brandolinum Valdemarinum Forojulienfem,
' abbatem monafterii, feu abbatiæ de Nervefa,
' Tarvifinæ diœcefis, perfonam in dignitate ec-
' clefiaftica conftitutam, ob quædam prætenfa
' crimina, in civitate Vicentina, & alibi, per il-'
' los, ut dicebatur, conimifla, carceri manci-
' pafle, & mancipatos detinuifle, fub prætextu
' quod eis hæc facere, liceret, inter alia, ob
' quædam, ipfis Duci &, reipublicæ, a quibuf-
' dam Romanis pontificibus, prædeceftoribus
' noftris, conceffa, ut afferebant, privilegia.

' Cumque præmiffa in aliquibus ecclefiarum
' jura, etiam ex contractibus initis, ipfis ecclefiis competentia auferant, ac præterea, in il-
' lis & aliis, fedis apoftolicæ & noftræ auctori-
' tati, & ecclefiarum juribus, & perfonarum
' ecclefiafticarum privilegiis, præjudicium, in-
' ferant, ipfamque libertatem, ac immunita-
' tem ecclefiafticam tollant: ac ea omnia, in
                    A a 4   ' ipforum

' ipforum Ducis & Senatus animarum perni-
' ciem, & fcandalum plurimorum tendant.

   ' Et cum ii, qui fupradicta, & fimilia edere,
' & promulgare, illifque uti aufi funt, in cen-
' furas ecclefiafticas, a facris canonibùs, gene-
' ralium conciliorum decretis, & Romanoium
' pontjfcum conftitutionibus inflictas, necnon
' etiam privationis feudorum, & bonorum, fi
' quæ ab ecclefiis obtinent, pœnam, eó ipfo
' incurrerint, a quibus cenfuris & pœnis, non
' nifi a nobis, aut Romano pontifice pro tem-
' pore exiftente, abfolvi & liberari poffint, ac
' præterea inhabiles & incapaces fint, qui ab-
' folutionis & liberationis beneficium =confe-
   quantur, donec editas leges, novis edictis,
' atque decretis fuftulerint, omniáque inde fe-
' quuta reipfa in priftinum ftatum reintegra-
' verint.

   ' Cumque etiam Dux & Senatus prædicti,
' poft plures paternas nóftras monitiones, a
' multis menfibus citra eis factas, adhuc decre-
' ta, & edicta præfata non revocaverint, ac
' eofdem canonicum Saracenum, & abbatem
' Brandolinum carceratos detineant, & illos ve-
   nerabili fratri Horatio epifcopo Hieracenfi,
' nóftro & apoftolicæ fedis apud eos nurcio, ut
' debebant, non confignaverint : Nos, qui nullo
' pacto ferre debemus, ut ecclefiaftica libertas,
' & immunitas, noftràque & fedis apoftolicæ
' auctoritas violetur & contemnatur ; inhæren-
' tes plurium generalium conciliorum decretis
' ac veftigiis reverendæ memoriæ Innocentis III.
                                             ' Hono-

' Honorii III. Gregorii.IX. Alexandri IV. Cle-
' mentis IV. Martini IV. Bonifacii VIII. Bo-
' nifacii IX. Martini V. & Nicolai V. & alio-
' rum Romanorum pontificum prædecefforum
' noftrorum, · quorum aliqui fimilia ftatuta,
' alias contra libertatem ecclefiafticam edita,
' tanquam ipfo jure nulla, invalida & irrita re-
' vocarunt, ac nulla, invalida & irrita effe de-
' creverunt & declararunt ;' & · aliqui contra
' fimilium edictorum ftatutàrios, & alios ad
' excommunicationis promulgationem, necnon
' ad alia infra fcripta, feu eorum' aliqua deve-
' nerunt.

' Habita cum venerabilibus fratribus noftris,
' fanctæ Romanæ ecclefiæ cardinalibus matura
' confultatione, de ipforum confilio & affenfu,
' licet fupradicta decreta, · edicta & · mandata,
' ipfo jure nulla, invalida & · irrita fint, ea ni-
' hilominus ipfo jure adhuc de novo nulla, in-
' valida & irrita, nulliufque 'roboris, & mo-
' menti fuiffe, & effe, & neminem ad illorum
' obfervantiam teneri, per præfentes decerni-
' mus, · & declaramus.

' Et infuper, autoritate omnipotentis Dei,
' ac beatorum Petri & Pauli apoftolorum ejus
' ac noftra, nifi Dux & Senatus prædicti, intra
' viginti quatuor dies, a die publicationis præ-
' fentium in hac alma urbe faciendæ, compu-
' tandos, quorum primos octo pro primo, octo
' pro 'fecundo, & reliquos octo pro tertio &
' ultimo, ac peremptorio termino, & pro mo-
' nitione canonica, illis affignamus, prædicta de-
' creta

' crȩta omnia, & in illis contenta, & inde fe-
' quuta quæcunque, omni prȩrfus exceptione
' & exculatione ceſſante, publice revocaverint,
' & ex eorum archiviis, feu capitularibus locis,
' aut libris, in quibus decreta ejufmodi annota
' ta reperiuntur, deleri, & caſſari, & in locis
  ejufdem dominii, ubi promulgata fuerunt, re-
  vocata, deleta, & caſſa eſſe, neminemque ad
' illorum obfervantiam teneri, publice nunci-
' ari, ac omnia inde fequuta in priftinum fta-
' tum reſtitui fecerint, & ulterius niſi a ſimili-
' bus decretis contra libertatem, immunitatem,
' & jurifdictionem ecclefiaſticam, ac noſtram,
' & fedis apoſtolicæ auctoritatem, ut præfertur,
' facientibus edendis, & refpective faciendis in
' poſterum cavere & pœnitus abſtinere promi-
' ferint, ac nos de revocatione, deletione, caf-
' fatione, nunciatione, reſtitutione, ac promif-
' fione, prædictis certiores reddiderint, & niſi
' etiam prædictos Scipionem canonicum, &
' Brandolinum abbatem, prædicto Horatio
' epifcopo & nuncio cum effectu confignaverint,
' feu confignari fecerint, ipfos tunc, & pro
' tempore exiſtentem Ducem & Senatum rei-
' publicæ Venetorum, ſtatutarios, & eorum
' fautores, confultores, & adhærentes, & eo-
' rum quemlibet, etiamſi non ſint fpecialiter
' nominati, quoɪum tamen ſingulorum nomi-
' na & cognomina, præfentibus pro expreſſis,
' haberi volumus, ex nunc prout ex tunc, & e
' contra excommunicamus, & excommunica-
' tos nunciamus, & declaramus : a qua excom-
                              ' muni-

' municationis sententia, præterquam in mortis
' articulo constituti, ab alio, quam a nobis,
' & Romano pontifice pro tempore existente,
' etiam prætextu cujuscunque facultatis, eis,
' & cuilibet illorum, tam in genere quam in
' specie, pro tempore desuper concessæ, seu
' concedendæ, nequeant absolutionis benefi-
' cium obtinere : & si quempiam eorum, tan-
' quam in tali periculo constitutum, ab ejus-
' modi excommunicationis sententia absolvi
' contigerit, qui postmodum convaluerit, is in
' eandem sententiam reincidat eo ipso, nisi man-
' datis nostris, quantum in se erit, paruerit :
' & nihilominus, si obierit, post obtentam hu-
' jusmodi absolutionem, ecclesiastica careat se-
' pultura ; donec mandatis nostris paritum
' fuerit.

   ' Et si dicti Dux & Senatus per tres dies, post
' lapsum dictorum viginti-quatuor dierum,
' excommunicationis sententiam, animo, quod,
' absit, sustinuerint indurato, sententiam ipsam
' aggravantes, ex nunc pariter prout ex tunc,
' civitatem Venetiarum, & alias civitates, ter-
' ras, oppida, castra, & loca quæcunque, ac
' universum temporale dominium dictæ rei-
' publicæ, ecclesiastico interdicto supponimus,
' illamque & illud supposita esse nunciamus, &
' declaramus, quo durante, in dicta civitate
' Venetiarum & aliis quibuscunque dicti domi-
' nii civitatibus, terris, oppidis, castris & locis,
' illorumque ecclesiis, ac locis piis, & orato-
' riis, etiam privatis, & domesticis capellis, nec
                                                   ' publice,

' publice, nec privatim, miffæ tam folemnes,
' quam non fólemnes, aliaque divina officia
' celebrari poffint, præterquam in cafibus a
' jure permiffis, & tunc in ecclefiis tantum &
' non alibi, & in illis etiam januis claufis, non
' pulfatis campanis, ac excommunicatis &
interdictis prorfus exclufis : neque aliter quæcunque indulta, & privileg a apoftolica, quoad hoc quibufcunque, tam fecularibus quam
regularibus ecclefiis, etiam quantumcunque
exemptis, & apoftolicæ fedi immediate fub-
jectis, etiamfi de ipforum Ducis & Senatus
' jure patronatus, etiam ex fundatione, & do-
' tatione, aut etiam ex privilegio apoftolico
' exiftant, ac etiam fi tales fint quæ fub gene-
' rali difpofitioné non comprehendantur, fed de
' illis fpecialis, & individua mentio habenda
' fit. Monafteriis, ordinibus, etiam mendi-
cantium, aut inftitutis regularibus, eorumque
' primiceriis, prælatis, fuperioribus, & aliis
quibufcunque etiam particularibus perfónis,
aut piis locis, & oratoriis etiam domefticis,
' ac capellis privatis, ut præfertur, in genere
' vel in fpecie, fub quibufcunque tenoribus, &
' formis hactenus conceffa, & in pofterum con-
' cedenda, ullatenus fuffragentur.
  ' Ac ulterius, eofdem Ducem & Senatum, &
' quemlibet eorum non folum reipublicæ, fed
' etiam privato nómine, fi aliqua bona eccle-
' fiaftica in feudum, feu alias, quovis modo a
' Romana, aut veftris, feu aliis ecclefiis conceffa, obtineant, illis feudis & bonis, necnon
' etiam omnibus, & quibufcunque privilegiis, &
                                  ' indultis

' indultis, in genere vel in fpecie, in quibuf-
' dam videlicet cafibus & delictis contra cleri-
' cos procedendi, illorumque caufas, certa for-
' ma præfcripta, cognofcendi, a Romanis pon-
' tificibus prædecefforibus noftris forfan quo-
' modolibet conceffis, ex nunc fimiliter, pro-
' ut ex tunc, & e contra privamus, ac priva-
' tos fore, & effe nunciamus & decernimus.

 ' Et nihilominus, fi ipfi Dux, & Senatus in eo-
' rum contumacia diutius perftiterint indurati,
' cenfuras & pœnas ecclefiafticas contra illos,
' eifque adhærentes, & in præmiffis, quovis
' modo faventes, aut auxilium, confilium &
' favorem præftantes, etiam iteratis vicibus
' aggravandi, & reaggravandi, aliafque etiam
' pœnas contra ipfos Ducem & Senatum decla-
' randi, & ad alia opportuna remedia, juxta
' facrorum canonum difpofitionem, contra eos
' procedendi facultatem nobis, & Romanis
' pontificibus fucefforibus noftris, nominatim
' & in fpecie refervamus. Nonobftantibus
' quibufvis conftitutionibus, & ordinationibus
' apoftolicis, necnon privilegiis, indultis, &
' literis apoftolicis eidem Duci & Senatui, aut
' quibufvis aliis perfonis, in genere vel in fpe-
' cie, præfertim quod interdici, fufpendi, vel
' excommunicari non poffint, per literas apo-
' ftolicas, non facientes plenam & expreffam,
' ac de verbo ad verbum, de indulto hujuf-
' modi mentionem, ac, alias fub quibufcunque
' tenoribus, & formis, & cum quibufvis etiam
' derogatoriarum derogatoriis, aliifque effica-
          ' cioribus,

' cioribus, & infolitis claufulis, ac irritantibus,
' & aliis decretis, ac in fpecie cum facultati-
' bus abfolvendi in cafibus, nobis, & apofto-
' licæ fedi refervatis, illis quovis modo, per
' quofcunque Romanos pontifices, ac nos & fe-
' dem apoftolicam, in contrarium præmiffo-
' rum conceffis, confirmatis & approbatis :
' quibus omnibus & fingulis, & aliis fupra ex-
' preffis, eorum tenores præfentibus pro ex-
' preffis habentes, hac vice dumtaxat fpecia-
' liter, & expreffe derogamus, cæterifque con-
' trariis quibufcunque.

' Ut autem præfentes noftræ literæ ad om-
' nium majorem notitiam deducantur, vobis,
' & cuilibet veftrum, per eafdem præfentes com-
' mittimus, & in virtute fanctæ obedientiæ, &
' fub divini interminatione judicii, necnon fub
' interdicti ingreffus ecclefiæ, ac fufpenfionis a
' pontificalium exercitio, ac fructuum menfa-
' rum patriarchalium, archiepifcopalium &
' epifcopalium perceptione, quoad vos fratres
' patriarchæ, archiepifcopi, & epifcopi, ac e-
' tiam privationis dignitatum, beneficiorum,
' & officiorum ecclefiafticorum quorumcun-
' que, quæ obtinueritis, ac etiam vocis activæ
' & paffivæ, ac inhabilitatis ad illa, & alia in
' pofterum obtinenda ; quoad vos filii vicarii,
' & alii fupradicti, eo ipfo incurrendis, aliifque
' arbitrio noftro infligendis pœnis diftricte præ-
' cipiendo mandamus, ut per vos, vel alium,
' feu alios, præfentes literas, poftquam eas re-
' ceperitis, feu earum notitiam habueritis, in
' veftris

' veſtris quiſque eccleſiis, dum major in eis
' populi multitudo ad divina convenerint, ad
' majorem cautelam, ſolemniter publicetis, &
' ad Chriſti fidelium notitiam deducatis, necnon ad earundem eccleſiarum veſtrarum val-
' vas affigi, & affixas dimitti faciatis. Et
' ulterius volumus, ut præſentium tranſumptis,
' etiam impreſſis, manu alicujus notarii pub-
' lici ſubſcriptis, & ſigillo perſonæ in digni-
' tate eccleſiaſtica conſtitutæ, munitis, eadem
' prorſus fides ubique habeatur, quæ ipſis præ-
' ſentibus haberetur, ſi forent exhibitæ, vel
' oſtenſæ, quodque eædem præſentes, ſive illa-
' rum exempla, etiam ut præfertur impreſſa,
' ad eccleſiæ Lateranenſis, & Baſilicæ prin-
' cipis apoſtolorum, & Cancellariæ noſtræ
' apoſtolicæ valvas & in acie campi Floræ,
' ut moris eſt, affixæ, & publicatæ, eoſdem
' Ducem & Senatum, ac alios quoſcunque
' prædictos, voſque etiam univerſos, & ſin-
' gulos, reſpective perinde afficiant, ac ſi
' eorum ac veſtrum cuilibet perſonaliter di-
' rectæ, intimatæ, & præſentatæ fuiſſent. Da-
' tum Romæ, apud Sanctum Petrum, ſub
' annulo piſcatoris, die decima ſeptima Apri-
' lis anni milleſimi ſexcenteſimi ſexti, Pon-
' tificatus noſtri anno primo.

M. Veſtrius Barbianus.

' Anno a nativitate domini noſtri Jeſu
' Chriſti, 1606. Indictione quarta, die vero
' decima ſeptima menſis Aprilis, pontificatus

' ſanctiſſimi

' fanctiffimi in Chrifto patris, & domini no-
' ftri, domini Pauli, divina providéntia Pa-
' pæ V. anno ejus primo, fupradictæ literæ,
' earumque exempla impreffa, affixa, & pub-
' licata fuerunt ad valvas ecclefiæ Lateranenfis,
' ac Bafilicæ principis apoftolorum, & Cancel-
' lariæ apoftolicæ, necnon acie campi Floræ, ut
' moris eft, per nos Chriftophorum Fundatum,
' & Joannem Dominicum de pace, apoftolicos
' curfores.

Petrus Aloyfius Peregrinus,
Curforum Magifter.

APPENDIX.

I N the collection of Father *Paul's Letters* (which was printed near thirty years ago for Mr. *Chiſwell*) there's one directed to M. *Gillot*, a worthy proteſtant, and one of the *French* King's council in the Parliament of *Paris*; in which the Father gives his opinion of ecclefiaſtic and civil government, of the uſe of the word [Power] in the Church, and of the ſo much controverted text, *My kingdom is not of this world.* And becauſe this letter in general bears an affinity to the ſubject of the foregoing treatiſe, and may be of uſe for explaining the ſaid text, it is thought fit to inſert an extract of it, as follows. *N. B.* The letter is dated from *Venice, December* 1, 1609.

" I have carefully read over the *Confiderations* of
" your famous divine M. *Richier*, who has learned-
" ly and ſolidly manag'd the whole Argument, by
" *one only diſtinction*. He ſays there are two ſeveral
" powers in one and the ſame chriſtian common-
" wealth, the ecclefiaſtic and the kingly or civil
" power, neither of which is ſubject to the other;
" but both of them are ſubject to God. I am afraid
" this is to make the Commonwealth have two

* A a
" heads

" heads; for now I muſt, as Logicians do, bring
" the matter to a ſufficient diviſion. Either one
" of theſe is ſubject to the other; or if not, both
" of them are ſubject to one, or elſe they both re-
" main ſupreme, and neither by turns, nor any other
" way, are ſubject to one another. · He that will
" aſſert this laſt will make a monſter of govern-
" ment, that will not continue; and I believe that
" for this very reaſon *England* and *Germany* were not
" able to keep in their former ſtate. But he that
" will go about to make both ſubject to one, if it
" be to any humane Power, 'tis well, and I will not
" diſpute it, but ſhall be ſatisfied in it; but if it
" be to a divine power, he will never avoid the
" monſter I was ſpeaking of. But if either be ſub-
" ject to the other, 'tis well.

" Our *Romaniſts* will have the royal power to be
" ſubject to the papal, and to make one chriſtian
" commonwealth, and the Pope to be head of it.
" Whoever allows this, muſt make Kings no more
" than clients and beneficiaries; nay farther do, by
" their opinion, make them precarious tenants, that
" hold of the Pope of *Rome.* For they think that
" Kings may not only be deprived for their faults,
" but for any other reaſon of the Church's profit
" and good; wherein, as the Pope is made judge,
" he only is the Prince, according to theſe prin-
" ciples, that has majeſty and ſovereignty belong-
" ing to him. And why ought I not to infer and argue
" thus, when Pope *Clement* V did decree, that an
" oath of fidelity to him ſhould be taken by 'the
" Emperor? And you muſt not ſay that this is a
" ſingular caſe concerning the Emperor, and that
" other Kings ſwear no ſuch thing to the Pope; for
" then you will have to do with *Bellarmine*, who,
" diſputing at this time with his majeſty of *Great*
" *Britain*, would have us think that there is I know
" not

" ,not what *fecret* oath made to the Pope in the
" báptifm of Kings; but he will find an *exprefs*
" oath taken by them at their inauguration, when
" they fwear to the people; and from hence there
" will arife another fort of conclufion.

" I have feen the Duke of *Nivers*'s oration for
" the King, printed at *Rome*, where the word obe-
" dience is never named but in great letters. But
" muft it be fo then, that the ecclefiaftic power is
" to be fubject to the kingly? I am contented with
" it; for then the Church will fare juft as it did in
" *Juftinian*'s time. No man can better learn what
" the government of the Church was, than by reading
" the novel conftitutions of his making, only *that*
" is to be explained after what manner it may be
" that the chriftian religion may not be a worldly
" thing, when it is made fubject to worldly and po-
" litic power. Concerning power ecclefiaftical I
" have diftinguifh'd thus; that one part of it be-
" longs to the kingdom of Heaven, the other con-
" cerns the external government and difcipline of it.

" I do not fpeak of powers abftractedly, or as to
" the effence of them, but after the *Italian* way of
" fpeech, as we call him that is chief in a city the
" *Podefta*. And that I may explain my fenfe of it
" further, it muft needs be, unlefs we will have a
" Kingdom to be a monfter in point of government,
" that either the King muft be fubject to the Pri-
" mate, or the Primate fubject to him; and fo I
" avoid all abftractednefs by thofe words. M.
" *Richier* did ingenioufly decline the abfurdity,
" when he fays, that they are both of 'em fo affec-
" ted and co-ordinated, that they mutually help
" each other; and that God has feen it fitting
" that they fhould both be link'd together by mu-
" tual helps as fo many bonds; and that the Pri-
" mate has power over the King in cenfures, and
*A a 2 " the

" the King power over him in punishments ; and
" that this is the sense of the canon *Duo sunt*, dist.
" 96. But the difficulty which I had at first does
" not seem to be removed by what has been said,
" but grows stronger. For what if the King and
" Primate should both take the same matter to
" themselves, and the Primate make use of his
" censures against the King, and the King on the
" other side make use of his punishments upon the
" Primate? Would not the commonwealth be dis-
" turb'd at this? Let us suppose for instance the *Ve-*
" *netian* controversy. The King says that church-
" men have too much lands already, and that it is
" not for the good of the commonwealth that they
" get any more. The Primate by his censures will
" have the King to revoke this edict. What now if
" the King should take from the Primate his life and
" estate? And now you see the monstrous form of
" such a commonwealth. I should willingly tell
" M. *Richier* that they cannot be link'd together by
" any way, bonds, or ties, unless one of the two
" be wholly, and in all things, subject to the other:
" For divide the offices of the commonwealth into
" a thousand parts, and give the King nine hundred
" of them, and yet make the King inferior to the
" Primate in the odd hundred that remains, and
" with that last tenth part he will be able to trample
" upon the King, and get into his hands all the
" other nine. We find this by experience; where a
" magistrate has a casting vote, and is unaccount-
" able, he presently makes the administration of
" the commonwealth his own ; for when any thing
" happens which he has a mind to take cognisance
" of, he declares that to be in his power, and to
" be so without further appeal. That the Bishop
" should mutually assist the Governor, and the Go-
" vernor him, is good and profitable, if both be
" under

" under the King: A middle way of ferving or
" commanding the King I fee none. I once faid
" there are fome things which mutually help each
" other, as a Commander of foldiers in fhips, and
" a fea Captain; the fea Captain is under him
" when they come to fight; the Commander under
" him as to matter of failing and working his
" fhip. But then I faid again, this is not amifs, if
" both are under the King. But here you may fay
" that the King himfelf commands the foldiers at
" fea; and he even in matters of navigation is not
" under the Captain or Admiral; and you will tell
" me, will not the King obey him, when he has
" given him his place in the fhip for his own fafe-
" ty? Shall not the Admiral or Captain here com-
" mand the King? Yes he muft; but the reafon is,
" becaufe the King in this cafe brings himfelf un-
" der command; and he that commands him muft
" be commanded by him, becaufe his right of com-
" mand depends upon the King; and if the Admi-
" ral commands the King by any other power but
" his own, the King is turned out of his power,
" and the Admiral turned rebel.

" In a word, majefty admits no mutuality; but
" all power muft depend on him, and be under
" him. Nothing muft be greater than the King;
" nothing muft be equal with him; if you are ex-
" empted from him, if he ftands in need of preca-
" rious help, he has no kingdom. Here I meddle
" not with perfons; for *Lucius* and *Marcus* were on-
" ly one *Roman* emperor, and the *Venetian* nobility
" makes but one prince. And M. *Richier*'s example
" taken from the goldfmith and the coiner is not
" current; but as both of them are under the
" prince or people, who fet the price on the metals
" they work upon, make them but fubject to none,
" and

" and prefently they will be at a lofs about the
" value of the bullion.

" As to *the kingdom of Heaven*, Chrift is a Prieft
" and King without doubt : *He hath made us all,*
" fays St. *Peter, Priefts and Kings* ; that is, he hath
" made his Church a royal Priefthood, by making
" his minifters partakers of the royal and prieftly
" power. Admit this, he hath made his ftewards
" and Minifters Viceroys in his abfence, this is
" certain. *As my father fent me,* fays he, *fo fend I you;*
" but *that power is not of this world*; it belongs to
" the kingdom of Heaven ; it neither receives nor
" gives any thing of mutual help from or to an
" earthly King. And there is no wonder in all this,
" for they do not walk together, they cannot meet
" together. Chrift's minifter and vicar has his
" converfation in Heaven, from whence we look
" for Chrift the faviour, *Philipp.* 3. The King of
" *France* has no diminution of power, becaufe his
" dominion does not reach up to the feven ftars.
" The kingdom of Heaven is further off from the
" *French* nation than thofe ftars are. *The kingdom of*
" *Heaven is within you,* fays Chrift, St. *Luke* 17. But
" whether an earthly prince does any thing towards
" the kingdom of Heaven, he will be beft able to
" fay, who learns by hiftory how much more it
" thrived under *Dioclefian* than under *Conftantine.*
" No body comes after Chrift but one that takes
" up his crofs.

" The kingdom of Heaven begun by the crofs,
" 'tis augmented and perfected by the crofs ; not
" but that the Church may flourifh under peace;
" but becaufe God doth fometimes plant it by the
" favours of princes, and fometimes plant and in-
" creafe it by perfecutions, *thro' honour and difhonour,*
" *by evil report and good report,* 2 Cor. 6. *all things*
" *work together for good to thofe that love God:* I have
                                                    " not

" not took the word of the *Kingdom of Heaven* as
" meant of the Church [here below,] and fo I con-
" ceive the fcriptures teach me to underftand it.

" They are Chrift's minifters who have the keys
" of the kingdom committed to them: No body
" can fay properly, that he who keeps the keys of
" the houfe is the houfe itfelf: And thofe words in
" St. *John's Revelations, Thou haft made us unto our*
" *God Kings and Priefts, and we fhall reign on the earth,*
" are not only fpoken of his minifters, but of all elfe
" of every tribe, language, people, and nation, that
" are cleanfed and redeemed by the blood of Chrift.
" But I never difpute willingly about names. Let
" it be fo, that as when we fpeak of the kingdom
" of *France,* we do not only mean the people, but
" fuperior order of men, and the King himfelf; fo
" let it be underftood of the Church, that upon
" that reafon it may not only be *all of it* call'd the
" kingdom of Heaven, but let thofe who govern it
" enjoy that title too. Yet for all this it would be
" but ill for the kingdom of *France,* if the fecond
" fignification being not laid afide, and retained no
" further than the name or word goes, all others
" fhould have no manner of right or property left
" them in the kingdom; for what there is appoin-
" ted in the canon * *Bene quidem, Dift.* 96. is very
" manifeft of itfelf.

" When the title of Vice-God was firft given to
" the Pope by the *Vatican* courtiers, the flattery
" began to look fo grofs, that it was three months
" under the confiderations of the cardinals, who
" were prefidents of the inquifition, who debated a
" little about reproving and difcountenancing that
" blafphemous new complement. But here the Pope
" clapt

---

* Which forbids all lay-men to difpofe of any ecclefiaftic
matte.

" clapt in with his wifdom above theirs, made
" them know that he liked the title, and would have
" no man deny'd liberty of confcience that had a
" mind to beftow it on him.

" The thing that you are debating with yourfelf,
" whether the name of *Power* in the Church be ad-
" mittable or no, is really worthy of your thoughts.
" No body fhould much need to regard words and
" names, but that evil and perverfe men do by abu-
" fing them, abufe things alfo ; as when once they
" engrofled the name of *Church* to themfelves, they
" prefently feized upon thofe goods and eftates
" which belong'd to the whole Church, and were
" only in the difpenfation of the minifters of it, as
" their own proper inheritance, and fhut out every
" body elfe from any right of meddling with them.

" Though I am a man that exceedingly hate the
" abufe of the word *Power*, yet I think it may be
" fafely ufed; becaufe the apoftle, 2 *Cor.* doth
" twice ufe the word ἐξουσία; and in the firft epiftle
" ufes a verb, made of that noun, in a fenfe of com-
" manding and governing ; tho' before I knew fo
" much as I do now, I ufed to fpeak more freely
" as to the ecclefiaftic miniftry : But thofe of *Rome*
" have made me to be drawn in *effigy* in hell, be-
" caufe I did not allow them a coercive power over
" Sovereign Princes, nor over *any body elfe*, but by
" fome *grant* of thofe Princes. —— For fome men
" are fo prepoffefled with darling opinions, fuch
" δοξαλάτροι, or worfhipers of their own imagina-
" tions, that they are prefently offended, if a man
" do not fpeak very foftly againft them, who never-
" thelefs are not worth offending ; becaufe, whether
" they are deceived by others, or do deceive them-
" felves, there is no getting them out of the fetters
" of thofe opinions.

CONTENTS.

CONTENTS.

HE author's introductory difcourfe upon the alarm of the *Venetians* by the Pope's interdict ; upon the diffe-rent ways of thinking between great genius's and mean fpirits ; and upon the common people's being kept e-qually in ignorance of the maxims of

In

The

The

374 CONTENTS.

That

CONTENTS 375

B b 4   Important

376 CONTENTS.

Inſtances

That

Instances

380 CONTENTS.

                                   That

CONTENTS. 381

That

ters of faith, they are as fallible in other parts of knowledge as other men   Page 222

PART II.   223

The

The

388 CONTENTS.

                                                    A re-

                                That

When

Remarks

FINIS.

Lightning Source UK Ltd.
Milton Keynes UK
UKOW06f1845170815

257087UK00013B/433/P

9 781330 587201